For Mohm

SPIRIT OF SURVIVAL

GAIL SHEEHY

Spirit of Survival

WILLIAM MORROW AND COMPANY, INC.
NEW YORK

Printed in the United States of America

Foreword

S*pirit of Survival* is inspired by an extraordinary young Cambodian girl who lived through the genocidal regime of Pol Pot. Her entire family, with the possible exception of a brother, was wiped out. She arrived in America as a refugee at the age of twelve and became my daughter.

But Mohm is more than an exotic survivor. Although her tribulations were staggering, her story offers lessons that we all can apply to everyday misfortunes. The human spirit has resources to prevail over tremendous adversity, to heal itself, and to emerge strengthened. By reminding us of that power to prevail, Mohm is more than a survivor. She is hope.

Most Americans have been spared direct experience with war or the violent political upheavals common in two thirds of the rest of the world. Yet we may see ourselves as survivors of more common life accidents: an absent or alcoholic parent, a bitter divorce, a child gone haywire, crushing debt, a career crash, serious illness, or paralysis by drugs. These occurrences, too, can pitch a person into a dark tunnel from which there appears to be no escape. More and more, the stratagems used by ordinary people to survive such a period of personal upheaval resemble the techniques resorted to by the classic survivor.

The classic survivor is forced to endure a prolonged state of pain, privation, uncertainty, or fear. Time loses all its comforting boundaries, and there is no concrete reason to hope for deliverance, yet the person endures. This book is meant to saturate the reader in that *survivor condition*. What I hope the reader may absorb from Mohm's experiences, as she lived them and as I later relived them with her, meditating on them as an examined life, is the texture of personality and tenacity of action that together forge a gallant stand against seemingly insuperable odds.

A line from Sara Teasdale, "One who makes the most of all that comes and the least of all that goes," describes in a phrase the victorious personality, a developmental ideal I have tried to define in this book. My work adds to the research confirming that many people faced with great pain or trauma develop a self-healing capacity. Rather than being scarred for life, they are actually immunized against many of the adverse effects of future life accidents and may be better able to "tough it out" than those who are overprotected or cushioned by privilege or chance.

*

As the shattered story line of Mohm's past was pieced together over several years, the work of healing and the writing of this book became indistinguishable. For the first year our talks took place irregularly, accidentally, sometimes reluctantly on Mohm's part. A seemingly innocuous event in Mohm's new life would kick up a shard from the smashed vessel containing her past. That past was like a richly decorated jar, painted in the Oriental fashion, showing sweet memories of her family life before disaster wantonly destroyed all that mattered, but it also depicted fantastic elements from what she recalled as her past life in the ancient temple kingdom of Angkor. Mingled with the remembered squeals of delight left on the wind as she rode behind her father on his motorcycle through the streets of Phnom Penh, there were dreams of emerald roofs on which peacocks danced and cries of cranes from the lotus pool of some resplendent king in whose garden, hundreds of years ago, she believed she once had resided.

We examined each of these fragments together, but with the gloved objectivity of the scientist. Mohm could recognize them and, out of her grab bag of new English, classify them; yet when it came to the recent past she resisted claiming the experiences as her own. I did not push her. She wanted more than to forget her recent past; she wanted to slough it off and at times to bury it entirely.

Gradually, I gathered that her reluctance to fit the pieces together stemmed from a fear that they would reveal a pattern, one that might bind her inextricably to the past. Cambodians are legendary for their smiles, but although they normally conceal darker emotions beneath a placid exterior, sudden eruptions of savage fury are a common theme in their national history. For all Mohm knew, an etching had been left on the soul of her people that would sooner or later erupt again in a frenzy of absolute evil.

But it is not only Mohm's jar of life that carries this flaw. The stunned suffering in the faces of refugees from Cambodia, more than in any others since the end of World War II, has come to symbolize the apparently unceasing capacity of human beings to behave brutishly to their own kind. Given our two million years of history as animals, compared with the scant ten or twelve thousand years of culture, we are operating from a still superficial discipline and set of local habits laid over our creature instincts. Civilization is very fragile. It takes only a few destructive events to transform a highly evolved civilization into a group of mere survivors, struggling to stay alive.

The present historical period (at least in American society) is also marked by the knowledge that a fresh start is possible for the individual at any age—although there is that small percentage of people who, by innate temperament, are extremely susceptible to ill effects from any change or trauma. Except for them, people who struggle and find their way into more benign circumstances are quite likely to profit by deprivations of the past.

The lessons of survivorship might have been conveyed by means of an encyclopedic book about many different people who endured under disparate conditions. But given the gift of Mohm in my life, I chose to search for universal truths in the particular. Following this one victorious child step by step, I began to see that her path is the same spiral traveled by survivors from the Old Testament and the *The Odyssey* to *Moby Dick*. That mythic narrative seems to have four turnings. First is the uprooting from "home" (family, security, or good health). Next, one is cast off into wilderness (external and internal) where a confrontation with danger, uncertainty, or evil batters previous beliefs. At the end of one's wanderings there awaits the reconciliation with a new and larger reality, and with one's own renewed self ("And the end of all our exploring/ Will be to arrive where we started,/ and know the place for the first time").[1] Finally, triumphantly, there is the return to home—but return with a difference.

*

People naturally want to know how Mohm felt about the writing of this book. For her first six months in America, knowing no English,

Mohm had to depend on me to be her voice. Our initial year together established a provisional trust. By the second year, our conversations had become compelling. Two creatures from contrasting cultures and of different religious traditions, we talked about everything: death and God, trust and love, politics and sex, the nature of evil, the rebuilding of faith, the merits of forgiveness versus revenge, the wonders and abuses of personal liberty. Naturally, we also pondered the tribal rites of American teenagers. And how to get Mohm's hair to curl and how seriously to take boys, and health food ("Is your friend still a vegetation, Mom?"). No matter how harrowing the subject, we never spoke for long without laughing. That was only one of many secrets of renewal I learned from Mohm, delivered in her simple statement "There's always something to laugh." If we all could absorb even that principle, our resilience in times of trouble would be increased a hundredfold.

I remember the day in November 1983 when I mentioned to Mohm an idea that had just occurred to me. "What would you think if I wrote a book about the people who came out of Cambodia and used your experiences to show what a survivor is?"

"I can help you with that, I think," Mohm said.

"I think you can." Smiling at her understatement, I asked if she knew the meaning of the word *survivor*. When she hesitated, I explained it.

"Oh, that's an easy one."

A month later, Mohm asked me, "Did you write that book yet?"

"It's not such an easy one for me," I told her. "Have you thought about it?"

She said she had. "I think people can take something from that book. If what I go through can give them a different idea, maybe it's not for nothing. So, I think it's good."

The survivor wears many faces. Day by day over the next two years, through daydreams and nightmares, defiance and prayer, confession and play, Mohm relived the acts committed or omitted under subhuman conditions. Taking courage from each other, we worked at discovering the person Mohm truly was beneath all the masks. "You're a mirror for me," Mohm said at one point. "I can see myself in you, whole parts I want to change. Also, I can see that I am giving."

As I became the sounding board for Mohm to reconcile her past, she became the catalyst of my own renewal. My world was made startlingly unfamiliar by seeing it through her clear child's eyes. Just in time, I appreciated the struggle of my teenage daughter, Maura, who did not want to lose me to gain herself. And I saw clearly for the first time how to meet in harmony the man I loved.

The trust of two strangers grew into the bond of mother and daughter, and the power of the unconscious led us to levels of mutual understanding I had enjoyed only with Maura. The voice of Mohm became a song inside my head, sweet, hypnotic; I could not get it out of my mind.

For Mohm to give to the book was, of course, a much larger and more painful project than she had any way of knowing. Later, she expressed some doubts. "It's hard to reveal the truth even to yourself, after so many years of hiding it, but it's scary to think of strangers who read the book knowing everything about me." After receiving some fan mail in response to an article I wrote about her, Mohm said, "The last thing I want is for people to think of me as a hero. Other people survived, too. And more could have survived if they had a dream, a belief, even a fantasy to keep them going."

As I wrote, it occurred to me that some people might think the book exploitive. I have no unimpeachable answer for that. I believe that our work together on the book was a work of healing. Unlike adults, children do not often speak out about their fears and anxieties. They need a catalyst, like drawing pictures or storytelling. For Mohm, the catalyst was the many hundreds of hours we spent together—reading about Cambodia's history and mythology, playing its music and considering its religious mysteries and magic, but mostly just talking heart to heart. We also read about and visited other survivors. I learned to take my tape recorder along even if we were just doing an errand in the car, and often, after our spontaneous discussions, I would stay up late writing notes. Revelations about Mohm's own life came forth in a random, associative manner, not chronologically as they appear in this book. In that way, she was able to approach indirectly the wells of doubt and guilt and shame and the surprising deposits of dignity and wit that she might not have uncovered until much later, if ever. For me, it was a labor of love.

Mohm came to consider work on the book as a moral assignment. Most Cambodians, I discovered, feel strongly about bearing witness to the lessons of history. And having outlasted a regime that made any form of free expression an act of suicide, they appreciate that writing truly matters. The many Cambodians who reopened their private hells in order to help me did so because they wanted to see recorded one of the great moral outrages, committed in their people's name, and also because they felt that if they could contribute to others' salvation in the future, it might compensate in some measure for all that had been taken from them.

The reader will notice that Mohm's voice in the early sections of the book is primitive. This is a deliberate attempt to be faithful to her groping English of that period. It became clear very early, however, that Mohm had an innate storytelling ability. As she took the power of words into her own hands, her writing became the symbolic theater where painful things could be expressed with some disguise. It was through writing that she at last dared, demanded of herself, to see the truth.

*

When I was able to get inside Cambodia, to walk the streets of Phnom Penh and see some of the countryside with my own eyes, I tried to link things up. I melted before the Khmer smile and the gentleness and zest of the people. I saw the magnificent stone temples of Angkor with their marvels of sculpture, so immense and at the same time serene that they rival the wonders of Egypt, Greece, and Rome. I pondered the philosophy of Buddhist kings who preached nonviolence but who could be ferocious warriors. I was enchanted by elephant terraces and leper kings and magic grasses that shivered and shut at a human touch, and I puzzled over the heavenly *apsaras* depicted in the bas reliefs, their bodies carved as succulently as mangoes but their expressions sexless. I stared at the mounds of skulls piled up in cribs over the clawed land.

The images did not link up.

It took another year and a half to read and study every book I could find, then to contact the handful of Cambodian scholars who had escaped to the West, and finally to travel with Mohm to pockets of Cambodian survivors around the United States and compare notes.

As I began to write, I thought of Cambodia as a human landscape over which I was flying, a landscape of unlinked lakes and magic diagrams, perhaps decipherable only by their gods, certainly unyielding to foreigners. Mohm's own vision of Cambodia, I later discovered, was of a world that is flat and square, like a series of rice fields surrounded by mythical oceans—Cambodia as its own planet.

But what happened in Cambodia did not draw inspiration from a separate planet, nor from a unique state of mind. It is a condition of dehumanization that a small group in power can force on its people; it has happened before in the advanced West, and it could happen again virtually anywhere in the world.

This book is my attempt to connect those unlinked lakes and magic diagrams, which I cannot know firsthand, from out of reportage, memory, dream, and nightmare—to build a bridge of words.

Acknowledgments

I want to acknowledge with deepest thanks the gifts of memory and observation and the details of feeling provided me by the people named in this book. My family—Mohm, Maura, and Clay—have given by living it, editing it, and offering it with me at considerable risk to their privacy. My fellow journalists have contributed context. My friends committed to helping Cambodian refugees have opened many doors. My friends in academia have explored enthusiastically with me the views put forward on child and adult development, and added the invaluable depth of their own lifetimes of work. And Ella Council has stuck by me, as always, lending quiet wisdom and comfort.

Contents

PART I

Parting Rips

That the hands
of the sisters
Death and Night
incessantly softly wash again,
and ever again, this soil'd world.
—WALT WHITMAN
"Reconciliation"

Cambodia . . .
April 1975

I keep trying to think of the reason my mother and father die.

Before Pol Pot come, I wake up in my bed in Phnom Penh and the mosquito netting is a soft white cloud over me. I dream I hear the sound of my father's motorcycle stop outside. But it's not my father. It's the bomb sound. One night rockets fall down all around the city and I think the stars are coming loose from the sky. Next day fire everywhere. It lick up the street the way wild dogs do.

Everybody leaving. Everybody run in the streets, this way, that way, say terrible things going to happen. Really important people, really rich people, run away. My father is a soldier, he go away to fight. So many months he does not come back. Now, even the government run away. Why my father not run away, too?

Cannot leave the city. Cannot hear stories on the radio at night anymore. Cannot visit my grandma. It's time for Cambodian New Year, but nobody go to visit their families this time. No New Year. Just sit in the house, feeling scared.

One day my mother say, "We must kill the chickens."

That night I don't sleep at all. You can see our neighbors carrying all their things and leaving home. It looks like a fairy tale to me. I think it's exciting.

Next morning I wake up and it's very quiet. Empty sound. It's a city but you don't hear cars, nobody going to work, can't even hear a baby cry. Everybody leave. We have to wait here for our father. We don't know if he is alive or not. We don't know if he can come back for us. Maybe we are the last family in the city.

*

My father comes home in a truck with a white flag. He throws me up and I'm so happy. But have to hurry up. His men come in and they all change to simple clothes. My father buries his uniform. My mother takes the chickens and cooking pots. She says I can take one thing. I carry my teapot bank in both my hands. It is full of paper money. I save that money for my whole life, for six years.

Pretty soon our family is in the street, on the way with the people left. We can't look back at our house. Pretend we live in the street too. My father put my little brother on the back of his motorcycle, because he is sick. The soldiers stop us. They children, too, big children, boys in all black, girls too. They hug on to their guns very tight, look a little nervous. They ask my father our family name.

"Phat," he say.

I start to laugh. My father playing a trick on those boys! Phat is the pet name for my father, it's not real. I look at my mother. She is not smiling. They tell my father to turn off his motorcycle.

"Must walk," they say. They are not respectful. Their speech is impolite.

I hear a man with a loudspeak shout to people, "Must leave immediately. Americans come bomb city. Take no suitcase, you come back, three days. We clean up first." They play a trick on everybody.

I see a woman stand in her door with a tiny baby. She won't move. She shout back at the soldier. "You'll never get me out!"

The soldier lift up his gun and hold out his arms stiff, shoot up and down the house and shoot holes right through that woman. Her baby roll down in the street, soft head mush like a mango. I turn my back to the soldier. This is the first time I see that Pol Pot soldiers can stand there, by cold blood, and mean to kill people. I walk away from the soldiers, really shaking. I feel in my back, are they going to shoot me?

I put it out of my mind.

*

Sick people and old people lie beside the road on their hospital beds. I say to myself, "That's okay, they just having a rest." But the wheels on their beds so weak, like little buttons pop off. I know their families get too tired to push. At night, my family has to cook outside and sleep under a tree. It is stink, like dead animals smell, but next day keep walking. Day after, keep walking. The soldiers stop us and ask for our names again.

"Phat," my father says again.

Don't laugh.

They tell my father he can go to any new zone to work. We want to go to Kompote, where my grandma has our family house.

One of those boys in the black pants come over and grab my father's motorcycle. "We take care of it for you," he say. He mean he take it for himself, I know. Why my father say nothing?

After five days, I hear people say, "They send us away to the forest. Everybody must work in the fields."

I think it's exciting, what they do. I won't have to go to school! My father won't have to go away anymore. Maybe our whole family go to stay with my grandmother in the countryside. I can plant a vegetable garden and ride the cows. It going to be fun!

*

Sun so hot and nothing to drink. I ask my mother if we can stop for sugarcane on a stick. She say we cannot stop just now. All around the faces of the people are sick and scared and sorrow. My little brother is crying. My little sister is so hungry.

I going to find a sugarcane man and buy a sweet for her. I ask, "Can I break my bank now?" My mother does not look at me.

"Money is not useful anymore," my father say.

"What? How can people buy things if there is no money?" I ask my father.

He does not answer.

I look at my teapot bank, my one thing I brought with me, it's no good. This new way is not what I dream. Not a game. Nothing fun at all. This is a nightmare.

I throw my bank down on the street. It smash. All the money I save for my whole life blow away. We keep walking.

*

They give us land to clear. My father and mother make a hut. One day I take a nap on the bamboo floor. It's rough, not like my real bed in

Phnom Penh. Just fall asleep and a black cloud swallow up the moon and fall on me. I feel really heavy, really in danger. I wake up and it take all my strength to push that cloud off of me.

My mother and father come back with my older brother from the meeting and they say we must leave that place. Cannot tell who we are really. Must be tricky. My father kiss his Buddha figure. He always teach us Buddha's way, the way of truth. I tell myself, "It was just a dumb little dream."

But I remember my grandmother, when she look at the full moon not long before. She see a dark ring around it. If the dark ring swallows up the moon, she say, Cambodia going to be taken over by crows. Black crows going to fill the sky, she say, and turn everything into a long cruel night.

Long Island . . .
August 1982

My only daughter and I are moving on, at least she is. She is about to shove off from that shoal of time called childhood. We have passed each other over the last year like half-noted presences in darkened rooms. She is still here in a physical sense, but each time the storms break between us, she wrenches her heart from the mooring a little more violently and I, well, I seem to be stiffening like some salt-dried knot, as if she had already gone and I had no more give. In the mornings I awake from a dream of something precious, ripped.

Today, for example. It is one of those flawless days of late summer and we are in the country and there is less than a week before she goes off to college, and yet, the bond is not holding.

Now look, we are going to make this a beautiful day.

"Rise and shine!" I call outside her door.

No answer.

I breeze in and part the eyelet curtains and sequins of sun fall on her face. Maura half opens her eyes and groans. Her skin is as fragile as week-old cherry blossoms, her eyes the shivering deep blue of Scottish lochs. She is tan repellent and exercise resistant and presumably considers her mother, standing here in jogging shorts and a New York Marathon T-shirt, further evidence of the decline of the Platonic ideal into an obsession with thin thighs.

"Perfect day for Gardiners Bay," I say brightly.

"No way, José," she croaks. "Sore throat."

Lifting her chin in the practiced fork of my hands, my eyes click down to f-stop 16. Pure fraud. Ignore it; we are going to have a beautiful day.

"The bluefish are jumping. Said so on the radio. New boat, clear skies—what more could we ask for?"

"You want to take that dumb little boat out into Gardiners Bay?" She will fight me all the way. I am the parent she has lived with all along, still lives with, so of course she cannot look into me and know what makes her as she is.

"Momzo," she goes on, "you haven't taken that thing out more than twice. What if the motor konks out? What if we get tangled up in lobster pots?"

"What if, what if? What if we run into crazed marijuana smugglers —it's an adventure."

"I'll get more adventure from reading Spenser." She rolls over and sticks her nose into the vastness of *The Faerie Queene*, a work of metaphysical poetry on analyzing which my literary daughter has spent two years. I turn to go. In seconds, the soft place where it hurts becomes a bitter compound, and I turn back with an imperious announcement.

"Ella wants to get in and strip your bed. Before she leaves."

"Jesus, why didn't you say so? If I'd only known I could have slept on the floor. Or outside on the air mattress. Better yet, you could have shipped me out with the footlocker before—"

"Go ahead. Ruin one of our last days together."

"I just wish everyone would stop making such a big deal over 'the last time we'll see you.'" She burrows deeper under sheets worn soft by summers and summers. "Think about what it's like for me. Think about leaving home for the first time in your life when all you've ever known is home."

My rational daylight self keeps reminding me that I must hide my own needs and give her a gentle push, but instead I keep feeling her departure as an abandonment. She is the one who will have to pull away.

Later, she comes into the kitchen with an old navigational chart of Gardiners Bay. "Look. Tide rips. Where you want to go is some of the trickiest water around Long Island."

"What's a tide rip?"

"See?"

"C'mon," I try once more. "Taking the boat out for a few hours to get some sun and exercise doesn't disqualify you from being a woman of letters."

"Exercise is your thing."

I kick off my jogging shoes. "You're right. Just another jogged-out branhead teetering on the edge of decline."

I walk into the bathroom and close the door and look in the mirror at my sinking face. It looks much younger without the makeup I am about to apply because I am too insecure about my looks not to, especially now, at this stage—call it the parking lot at the end of youth. It's where one pauses as long as one can before traveling on to middle age.

"Momzo, are you in there? I have a terrible feeling you're in there putting on nail polish or giving yourself a permanent or something."

I do not answer.

"If we have to go out on this dumb boat, let's go."

The phone rings. It is my accountant. A dispute flares up over the instrument I have tried to create to pay for my daughter's higher education. "Doesn't anyone ever listen to me?" I hear myself saying. "What am I—just some tuition machine!"

By the time I go outside to find Maura, she is curled, protectively, under a tree. "I feel you changing," she says quietly. She looks up at me with her beautiful grave face as if she is studying a foreign country. "You've made your life what you want it to be, so you can afford accountants and lawyers and all that stuff to help you with the maintenance work. But you get caught up. You let them tie you up. Mother, what's happening to you? Wouldn't you rather be writing?"

She is right. I am changing, but this is not the form I will take; this is some wildebeest's head I am wearing midway through the metamorphosis. A new phase of my life is being shaped, not by me, I am not in control here. Everything around me seems to be drying up or losing color or breaking down. It still looks green, but overnight I imagine it being transformed into an exhausted cornfield after harvest when the bare bleached stalks are too much trouble to pull up. I look at this lovely child and I feel a part of me dying.

"I'm trying as hard as I can to set it all up right." The words punch out of me as if from some autonomic system, while I walk around the garden pinching off dead marigold blooms.

"Don't try so hard to control everything," she says gently. "I mean, can't you let yourself be wrong sometimes?"

I look off into the woods to where the wildflowers did not come up for the wedding that did not take place last spring. "I guess I just didn't expect to be standing here, at this point in the journey, alone."

Neither one of us mentions my attempt to sponsor a Cambodian refugee, an orphan of twelve, who expressed a desire to resettle in the United States with me. It has been eight months with no good news.

Maura is quiet for a while. "Did you ever have something to say that you know about a person," she begins, "and you know that after you say it, it will make everything different, or else it won't have any effect at all?"

Images flood into my mind of many long-dead hours of happiness with Maura: curled up on a couch reading poetry to each other, or watching *Saturday Night Live* and being silly; being marooned with Maura in the desolate beauty of the Aran Islands off the Irish coast, during a big blow, reduced to the ferocity of nature and the few books we had brought with us, dreaming ourselves, as writers, into the souls of ancient Celtic queens and warriors, or murderers or monks—we had always been soul mates. Close, probably too close. One night earlier this summer, when thunder had torn her out of sleep and seemed certain to split the earth for kindling, she had crept up to my bed. I had slipped my arm over her shoulders and rolled her in, a gesture performed how many thousands of times in the past, and I felt her shudder as if she'd found a cave where she could rest as long as she liked without having to do anything or be anyone. "It's all right, sweetheart," I remembered whispering, "I'll always be here for you."

"Your arm is so soft," she had said. "It's almost too soft."

*

"Mom," she is saying now, "some dangers you just can't predict or control. Don't try to control that you're going to be alone. You'll come through. But when you do, you'll be on different ground. Just—let go."

"How do you know all this?"

"I don't know. But I know."

It is too uncomfortable to put weight on this moment. "Well, if you're going fishing with me, honey," I say, "you'll need a hat."

"I hate hats."

"To keep the sun off."

"I never tan anyway."

"That's why you need a hat."

*

The clothes disputes were not so severe in the summer because one did not have to deal with the bum's coat. Whenever I took her to the theater, she insisted upon wearing the big black bum's overcoat that she had bought with her allowance for ten dollars and that hung, buttonless, threadbare, almost to the tips of the clogs she wore with bare feet. For me, the sound of cheap clogs smacking against the grout of tenement floors as I climbed four flights with a baby strapped to my back was not a distant enough memory to transform such footwear into an emblem of solidarity with the oppressed peoples of the world.

Here is how it was for us, you see. I wanted secretly to be a writer. And a wife and mother, of course, and a giving person and an eternal size six and liked by everyone. I was Gail Henion then. And in that epoch, for a woman to speak openly of having her own career dream was seditious. So I'd disguised it as social good. Marrying a penniless medical student had seemed, beyond the poetry of our romance, to make perfect sense. While he turned progressively greener and scalier, ultimately attaining the full badge of pallor common to interns, while he slaved in the wards every other night for what worked out to be a weekly emolument of eighty-nine cents an hour, his golden future was subsidized by my toil in the bush leagues of journalism. On the in-between nights, clogs kicked off, we would bed down at ten, only to pop up again at midnight; he would have a moonlighting call from the county medical society to pronounce dead some wretched derelict in a Bowery flophouse, and I would make tea for him. And in that ritual, having served the nobler cause of public health however marginally, I felt justified sneaking in a few hours with my typewriter until he came home.

We worked our way up to a fourth-floor walkup in the East Village and had a beautiful baby girl and then he fell in love with somebody else and we were divorced.

I still wore clogs for several years thereafter. Still woke up at midnight to make tea. Still sneaked in to work on my typewriter, only now there was no one to come home, so I stayed at the writing until the landlord's son yelled. The landlord's son liked to watch television with a loaded gun in his lap until about four in the morning, whereupon he would raise the window just beneath me and howl: "Fuckin' potheads! Get offa my street!" You've probably heard the old saw "It ain't over till the fat lady sings." I told myself about the writing in those days, "It ain't over till the landlord's son yells." That left time for a two-hour nap before Maura awoke. Then I'd be on the stairs, in the clogs, curling my toes to keep from waking up the whole house, clomping down four flights to the Ukrainian grocery for fresh eggs.

I had thought that was what a writer's life would always sound like: cheap clogs, climbing walkups.

But a writer's life is feast and famine, I discovered. When my fifth book hit the best-seller list, I came into real money for the first time, and a new apartment was in the cards. Alas, Manhattan real estate took off and accommodated smartly to my new financial status. So we exchanged a big moldering barge on the West Side for a much smaller apartment, a tiny rental on the East Side that seduced me with its windows over the park. It was a view with a room.

It bothered Maura that there was no place to escape from My Mother's Work. It bothered me somewhat less that she and her high school friends never went "out," in the sense of to a party or a movie or on that ancient tribal custom called a date. They preferred to sit on the steps of the Metropolitan Museum in 30-degree weather and beat the sleeves of their bum's coats. Or to hang around home, in packs. Adolescents are like cockroaches: They come out the minute you leave town, crawl the walls, feed indiscriminately, reproduce alarmingly unless drugged, and will certainly outlast you.

*

When I follow her now into her room to look for a hat, I notice an official-looking form stuck under her journal.

"What's this?" A small alarm goes off. "It looks like the forms for your meal contract at college."

"Mmm, yeah." She starts humming.

"You haven't sent in your contract yet?"

Here it comes. She knows it.

"Where is your head, Maura? Why can't you ever follow through?"

"Thank you," not allowing a nick to show in her expression. "Now would you mind leaving me alone?"

Please let it go; let this be a beautiful day; let me not overkill.

"Never mind," I say. "Let's just go."

"You're on dangerous ground now, Mother. I'll be living in a dorm in a few more days. You won't have me at your mercy in that dumb little apartment where I can't get away from you."

"I kill myself working to put you through the best schools and move us from walkups and railroad flats finally to a place with a view, and you tell me our apartment isn't good enough for you!" And I'm off, hurtling around as if in some asteroid field of collected rejections, throwing insults I will regret—unreachable.

"I didn't mean—" she stammers. "I mean what kills me is New York, how you have to live in those concrete boxes—"

"You'd like it better in the Jersey flats?"

My daughter tries to fend me off. "It's not you, it's all those phones ringing and your working at home—"

"—my working at home! If only you'd had a mother who was a bank teller—"

"—and being in a city where you can't breathe, and you have to spend money for everything, and wherever you go there are always people."

"—poor deprived child, having to come home every day after school and find your mother *there*." At the peak of fury, I feel something collapse inside. Perhaps it is the narrative line—the fiction we harbor about ourselves and the effect of our major life decisions. Quietly, defeated, I say, "I did the best I could."

She watches her mother turn and walk out of the room. "Goddamit, Mother, don't you understand?" she screams. "I have to get away. From you!"

Had she seen my eyes at that moment, the terrifying vacancy that opened up in them, she might have gone back over the conversation, softened it. But she saw me as always the stronger one. How could her mother have self-doubts; she was thin and flush and her book was published in sixteen languages, even backward in Japanese. How could her mother ever be afraid of not knowing the next thing to do?

A half hour later I come back into her room and say, "You know, honey, we don't have to go. I'd just thought it might be fun if we picked up a six-pack and bopped around the bay together."

"I'd like to go, Momzo."

*

How do I make that scene convey the curious mixture of sweetness and savage defiance ruling a young person at the precipice of adulthood? How to account for the cutting, bruising, bloodletting behavior by both of us, to which we would not subject our worst enemies?

Maura, Maura deep, I see you as a timeless sea-floor creature; calm and self-contained, opalescent like an angel fish, but one of a kind. With your instincts close to the undercurrents, you can sense when one of those shifts occurs after which nothing will be the same: a rearrange-ment, or derangement, of natural forces. You must know about the storms that stir up vast sleeping currents on the ocean floor. You know that surface currents give little clue to such erratic changes below. How often have you been swept up in my storms, unsuspecting? You have learned to defend yourself by disappearing into opacity. But having dug yourself out from the sediment set whirling by the last storm, you leave yourself unprotected. Now that is changing, and that is good. Painful, but good.

I can see your first year of college ahead of us. You are preparing to come home. You anticipate the sweetness and the terror. I give you a last-minute phone call. Our conversation is warm and fizzy. Then a slip is made, an inconsequential slight, and my voice tightens. You picture the sudden stoniness of my face. All at once you do not want to come home, but you dare not say so. The migraine begins churning in your head. It stirs up a blizzard of sediment. A thousand and one disheveled feelings for your mother are set whirling and chief among these is the sadness. Right now, your mother is too dangerous to love.

We are caught in the snarl of will be and was. And neither one of us can quite let go.

Bangkok, 1981

Meeting Mohm was serendipity—unless it was destiny.

The Christmas before Maura's last summer at home, the man of my life had urged me to join him in Southeast Asia. I had just completed a cross-country book tour. A virgin trip to the Far East seemed a sure cure for the paralysis of will that seems to settle on book writers after they deliver to the public the imperfect incubus they have lived with for several years, which was how I happened to be on the tarmac of Singapore Airport on Christmas Eve. In transit. The pilot had said we would be taking off at the latest by eleven. When my watch showed midnight and Christmas Eve passed unmentioned, we were still confined in the airless plane with my companion slack in sleep in the next seat and my daughter half a world away. It had been eighteen years since her conception; I remember thinking that as I felt the clot drop: the blood apple of something like the three hundred and sixtieth ovum, falling, waste. A wind of emptiness seemed to blow through me. I began crying softly for what it was too late to have.

At three-thirty in the morning, Clay and I were welcomed into the Oriental Hotel in Bangkok with a respectful "Merry Christmas" from the Buddhist bellhop. Red satin bows had been tied around the giant teak bells with gilt gongs that hung from the soaring lobby. We walked outside and down to a veranda over the *klong*, the wide canal, letting the humid air enter us with the high sweet rot of jasmine and floating waste, and we watched water hyacinths drift through the lacquered water. He held my hand tightly. It felt good to be somewhere again.

Beyond the pool we discovered the original hotel, now called the Authors' Wing, a genteel, shuttered, bone-white structure, like an exquisitely carved ivory box, its suites named to call up the fateful attraction of the East to Western writers . . . Maugham, Conrad, Michener. Suddenly the old lust for adventure pierced my Christmasy bathos. We were leaving for home the day after tomorrow—too soon.

We retired to a pleasantly pastel room, and a floor boy brought wild orchids and mangoes and a split of champagne. I took off my jumpsuit and sandals and lay down in the languorous air with an orchid in my navel.

"This is the Colette room, in case you didn't know."

He laughed. "Just let me take off my banana republic suit."

I shut my eyes and we were the same as we had been ten years before, he the volatile editor of *New York* magazine and I a footloose free-lance writer. He was excitement, danger, the mentor one can never satisfy, the story one never finishes.

Being by now past the season of marriage, we too were in transit. But to what new state, or stasis? I had never felt it necessary to be remarried, yet I was always afraid of being left. Maybe that was the real reason I had gone away on a trip over my daughter's last Christmas at home; I would leave before I could be left. And so, after a phone call to Maura at her father's home, Clay and I floated off to sleep. We awoke in a blaze of sun several hours later: Christmas Day, Bangkok. We lay on our backs running musky and translucent with our sweat. *What now?*

And then we were on the veranda ordering breakfast, mesmerized by the great hippos of rice barges nuzzling through the *klong*, up to their noses with cargo, when he pointed out a story in the *Bangkok Post.*

"Honey, this will interest you." He passed me the paper.

Thousands of children, most of them under twelve, orphaned by the genocide in Cambodia, have been existing in holding centers inside Thailand for over two years. Many suffer from persistent malnourishment and other medical problems. Little help can get to them. They have scant hope of being adopted or resettled in third countries.

Suddenly intense, I stammered, "Maybe we could do something, I mean, personally . . ."

"You can't expose a child to the lack of acceptance he or she would find in the States," he said, knowing exactly my mind; indeed, as usual, having seeded the inspiration, set the saga in motion, he then got cold feet.

"But what is our country about, if not acceptance?"

"It's not a good future for a child."

"Compared to rotting away in a refugee camp?"

The waiter brought papaya and a basket of croissants. I picked up the paper again. "Listen to this. If these kids try to cross the border to get back into Cambodia, they'll be caught between two armies—the Vietnamese and Pol Pot's Khmer Rouge rebels." I plunged the lime toothpick into my papaya and pushed it away. I was thinking about the Cambodia Crisis Committee I had been asked to join by Rosalynn Carter, and the blind naïveté we had brought to our work. "Beautiful. We raise millions to bring starving Cambodians to the border, and then what? We leave them to rot or run back into the arms of the monsters who murdered their parents? I mean, I was on the damn committee that raised the money."

"Don't beat yourself up, honey. Cambodia is ancient history to American TV viewers. They're on to Lebanon now. Christians against Jews is always good for ratings."

"I don't believe you're as cynical as you sound."

"I showed you the story, didn't I?"

We agreed to find out about the situation the next morning at the American Embassy. I felt restless and excited.

As we walked down the Soi Raum Rudi to a Christmas service, the silent-footed procession of a Thai family passed us, precariously balancing towers of gladiolus and baskets of food wrapped in red cellophane to be taken for blessing to a temple. They picked their way down a plank over the *klong* and turned to help the ancient grandfather. The children folded him up and passed him to the grown-ups who lifted him into the water taxi. In seconds the diesel engine, probably stripped from a Toyota, had them flying across the canal on a high-tech magic carpet. The children squealed with delight. Family ritual. A childhood without family would be a mouth open for the sweet apple and fed only the core.

"Clay?"

"Hmm?"

"We've got to visit those camps."

"On our last day?"

"At least we have another day."

He looped an arm over the back of my hips. "And I planned not to let you out of the room."

The lure of a last day devoted to your standard decadent Western pleasures held a strong appeal for me, but even as we walked arm in arm across the Oriental's luxurious lobby toward the cool elevators, I broke away.

"Where are you going?" he said.

"To hire a driver."

*

We stayed an extra day to get permissions from the Foreign Ministry, the Supreme Command, and the First Army. The Thais were jumpy about letting journalists into these holding centers, as the government wishfully called them, fearing that news stories would swell the already indigestible lump of human refuse from ten years of war in Southeast Asia. The first wave of fleeing Vietnamese had been flushed efficiently enough through the pipeline to the West, followed by Laotians and Hmong hill people; most of the ethnic Chinese were already running noodle shops in Orange County. But when it came to the Cambodians, luck and compassion had run out. The soft touch refugees found in Jimmy Carter had turned into the tight fist of Ronald Reagan. Resettlement offers from other countries had been drying up.

The Thai government, which had agreed reluctantly to provide first asylum for Cambodians, feared it was going to be left holding the bag, so to speak. Vietnam, whose troops now occupied Cambodia, had no intention of repatriating any of those who had fled. So the Thai government had officially closed the border between Cambodia and Thailand to prevent more from entering. Our informants at the embassy hinted that the Thais had forced people back to Cambodia, at gunpoint, over a precipice pocked with mines. Still, right now, there were three hundred thousand Cambodians and other Indochinese in camps inside Thailand—not to be confused with refugees. They were officially labeled "displaced, pending clarification."

We met our driver in the early dark. To hear Mike tell it, Henry Kamm, Sydney Schanberg, and all the star war correspondents had bounced five hours to the border in the seat behind his tiny mechanical window fan. That may have explained why he giggled at most of our questions. We were Americans, we came and went, filled with self-importance, and in the end we were irrelevant. The Vietnamese army controlled events at the border now.

We studied the monotonous countryside scarved in early mist, the way its watery skin brought tiny fish to the surface of roadside canals, the way its belief system brought out monks to beg. By afternoon, we could see the dull blue cyclops of TV deep inside nearly every stilt house.

"Is this it?"

Khao-I-Dang camp was not the swarming pool of stick bodies we expected. First impressions were of neatness and order. International relief agencies had provided food, birth-control injections, electrification for rock bands, you name it, plus a hospital with exquisitely trained volunteers from Europe and the States and enough high-tech equipment to put one in mind of Mass General Hospital as laid out by Club Med.

This was obviously the show camp. The intricately plaited bamboo marquetry of the administration buildings all but exuded sighs of tedium. Restless hands had fashioned tight little rugs of private vegetables in front of each of the hundreds of thatched dwellings, and now people were spilling down the sides of an irrigation ditch to plant rice. They had enough food; what they didn't have was enough to do to kill acres of time.

The U.N. director was occupied, but permission was granted us to take a brief tour of the camp. Immediately, children scampered around us, giggling. Ragged clothes hung over their bodies, but their eyes looked clear, and their smiles were delightful. Older brothers and sisters appeared and beckoned us to follow. They led us to a large makeshift structure covered with a lattice of bamboo. Inside, hangings of gold paper and tinsel gave off reflections on the dirt floor. A large hand-painted mural of Angkor Wat rose across the back: It was their Buddhist temple.

As the children spread mats for us, several adults appeared and pressed mugs of hot tea into our hands. The young men, although most were small in stature, had muscular chests and legs and moved gracefully. Some of the adolescent boys cradled babies in their arms. The women, with their high breasts and beautifully modeled heads, seemed made with a sculptor's eye.

Each encounter began with a shy smile and the traditional Khmer* greeting. Pressing their palms and fingertips together, the Cambodians would create a lotus blossom of their hands. Delicately then, they would dip their chins to the tips of their fingers.

"What does it mean?" I whispered to Clay.

---

* Khmer is the word for the racial or ethnic group known as Cambodians. The Cambodian language is also referred to as Khmer.

"I think it's a sign of respect," he said.

The gentle majesty of the gesture struck me even then, although it was much later that I learned about the rich layers of symbolism contained by the lotus and expressed in the greeting. The lotus flower is pure white; its openings and closings mark day and night; its petals cup to create a secret sanctuary. When rain falls on those waxy petals, the drops roll around like pearls and only enhance the flower's beauty. But the more extraordinary power is this: The lotus always floats—above the mud from which it grows, above a rising tide; when the waters beneath are in tumult, the lotus simply undulates over the surface until the storm has passed. For Buddhists the lotus is one perfect, complete symbol—purity out of mud.

"A third Christmas here, but not much has changed for these people." It was the unaccusing voice of a Cambodian camp administrator who had caught up with us to deliver a message: The U.N. field director was ready to see us.

The U.N. director, a reedy Finn named Erkki Heinonen, didn't like it that we had been talking to people. "It could put ideas into their heads."

"Ideas?"

"These are simple people," he said, offering us tea. "They may have learned how to build a bamboo house or do paramedical work, but what good would this do them if they went to the United States? Anyway," he sounded bored, "none of these people wants to resettle in the West."

"All eighty-five thousand of the Cambodians in this camp are just waiting to go back?" I asked incredulously.

"Well, some have already gone." He dodged a direct answer.

"What about the orphans? Can I see some of them?"

"We call these people unaccompanied minors," the director said, as if proud to possess "these people" utterly. "And we don't have any here."

He stood up impatiently. I stalled long enough to ask about the three giant plastic bags I could see stuffed under a table.

"Oh, those"—the director brushed it off—"resettlement fever. It happens whenever we have a movement. A few people went to France the other day."

The director excused himself. When we were alone in the office, I bent down to those cloudy plastic bags. The dust on them looked weeks thick, maybe more. Crammed inside were thousands of letters. The ones I looked at were addressed to embassies, mostly to the U.S. Embassy, pleas smothered before they had been heard.

On the flight home to New York, Clay and I fell to musing about the excesses of world leaders: What transformed them from visionaries into tyrants? Think of Mao; think of Stalin. Pol Pot, having directed the autogenocide of two million of his people, was still alive and smiling his double Yamaha-keyboard smile and commanding a rebel army on the Cambodian border.

"You saw the sweet, ordinary people in that camp," Clay said. "All they want to do is take care of their families, and they're at the mercy of these mad leaders."

"But leaders can't always be madmen, can they? And the people who carry out their tortures can't *all* be coerced."

"Well, that's right. What about all the Red Guards that Mao whipped up to do the killing for him?"

"And they were kids, teenage kids."

"Convinced they were guardians of the social good."

"Does it happen only in Asia?"

"Remember Hitler Youth?"

More disturbing questions surfaced. What did the orphans of Cambodia have to do in order to survive? Could the scars of the past ever be erased? Was it merely my post-Freudian prejudice to believe that the better angel could be brought out in any child? We had no answers. We had seen too little. And it was so easy for us, Americans in our airborne playpen, simply to lie back and suck soft drinks and plug a dumb movie directly into our brains.

Barely hitting the ground at Kennedy Airport, I went for a phone and called an editor at *The New York Times Magazine*. How about a story on the refugees America had forgotten?

"Where? Oh." Pause. "We already have a story in the works on the Vietnamese boat people. . . ."

A few bags of unsent letters was hardly a newspaper scoop, after all. Not in those days, with the hostages in Iran and the war in Afghanistan and the price of gasoline soaring. But it hadn't been a total brushoff. So at home I made dozens of calls, and each one referred me to a man they said knew more about Cambodian refugees than anyone in the world: Peter Pond, a minister without a church. He lived in New Hampshire with an extraordinary family of five adolescent survivors of the Cambodian genocide. Officially, Pond worked for the Lutheran Refugee Service; unofficially, he was a humanitarian hustler. He found me first.

"I thought we should join forces," he said on the phone.

"I don't know much yet," I said. "Only that the pipeline for resettlement seems to be shut down."

"Even for the unaccompanied minors?"

"They wouldn't say, but that's my hunch."

"Grim," Peter Pond said. "There hasn't been any movement out of the camps since last June, when the U.S. government allowed a quota of thirty thousand for fiscal year 1981." His voice raced. "The unaccompanied minors haven't been subject to a freeze before. But it's been everybody's silent policy that these kids oughta go back and fight with the Khmer Rouge against the Vietnamese, never mind coming to the United States."

"But that's ghoulish!" For a second I lost my journalistic cool. "They're still children, aren't they?"

"That's a good question. Mostly teenagers now. But these children were held hostage by the Khmer Rouge for three or four years. About a hundred thousand of them were separated from their parents and trained as the future of the country. Not intellectual training, school was the rice field. Some were forced to carry guns at the age of ten or eleven—"

"Against whom?"

"When the Vietnamese invaded."

"How many of them survived?"

"At least half of them died, and most are still in Cambodia. But about three thousand managed to sneak across to Thailand. They've been in the camps ever since."

"Are they safe in the camps at least?"

"We believe that as many as a thousand of them were abducted by the Khmer Rouge and taken to the border to fight."

A week later I was back in Thailand to write a newspaper story about child survivors of Cambodian genocide—the pawns of war.

*

Dark. Airless. Cocoon of white overhead, a screech splitting the air—
where was I?

Laid out on the wood floor of a Thai house, under a mosquito net,
next to a nun from Providence, Rhode Island. Of course. It must be
just before dawn; weren't those roosters screeching?

"Is it time yet?" Sister Angela Daniel asked. She was a good skate
with a sense of humor; a collection had been taken up by the Cambodian refugees in her diocese to investigate why their family members
could not join them.

"I don't know, Sister." I groped for a flashlight to see my watch.
"It's only three-thirty. Can't they tell time?" I went to the window.
The yard was full of cocks, and now they began strutting in full chorus.

"Sister? Would you give your blessing to a cock sacrifice?"

"You've got it."

But the roosters quieted down. Before six we could hear a stew of
voices from the camp, a concentrated sound, gradually boiling up into
what sounded like light screams.

A panic was on Sakeo camp, officials had warned. The first movement to a third country in a full year had taken place two days before,
and the rumor was around that it would be the last.

The last road sign read CAMBODIA—20 KM before the blacktop
dropped off into dust. In the camp, thousands of bamboo huts on stilts
were fenced into a few square miles. Guard towers rose above the alleys
between huts, dust alleys that bore hand-painted street signs with
names like Phnom Penh, Battambang . . . cities of a lost civilization.

As soon as our car pulled in behind a truck carrying Thai soldiers, our
pale faces and my red hair attracted hundreds of camp inmates.

"I would like to ask you"—a man with a smile of gentle desperation
came to the car window—"the people here, do they have a chance to
go to United States?"

Hundreds of people were suddenly swarming around us, then more
came, pressing letters for the embassy into our arms. Neither of us
could move. We tossed our heads, trying to throw the oniony sweat out
of our eyes. We were trapped. Suddenly a pair of high young shoulders
appeared above the swarm of shorter people, then a face, a smile.

"Guide for you, okay?"

He introduced himself as Nhep Sarouen and he opened the crowd
like a gate. Sarouen was a muscular sixteen with a hunger to talk English. He held out his battered English copybook, surprising me. I had
just learned that camp authorities had outlawed the study of English as

part of the campaign to quash hopes for resettlement. "This my best friend, I sleep with, I play with," Sarouen said. In it he had copied out an entire English dictionary.

"You America?" he asked.

"Yes, Americans."

"America means freedom," he said, "something no one can smash out of our minds."

"Do people have serious hopes of going to America?" I asked him.

"All the people here very afraid they send back to Cambodia, Vietnamese kill them."

"Why?"

"Because people who escape from Cambodia, the Viets think betrayers of the country. They execute."

"Is there real danger of being sent back?"

Sarouen looked over his shoulder at the Thai guards and sucked in his breath. "Take people, at night, in a truck, no one know who."

Sarouen led us to the Thai commander's office. The camps were under joint control of the United Nations High Commissioner for Refugees and that frontier branch of the Thai army known as Task Force 80, a mélange made up mostly of ex-convicts, sociopaths, and homosexuals. The Thai official in charge of the camp that day received us scowling. "No camera. Not stay long. We do not consider these people refugees. They are illegal immigrants." As we sat, he was served a glass of hot water by a young Thai guard wearing orange lipstick.

I asked the commander if Cambodians were still fleeing across the border and entering the camp.

"Camp closed," he barked. "Border closed. Must put in your story!"

I was negotiating to keep my camera when a young boy was rushed past on a litter, his leg a bloody stump.

Chasing the litter, I caught up with a volunteer medic. "The only way into this place is through a jungle," he explained, curt, British. "Twenty minutes in and their legs blow off in a mine. Unless they're fortunate enough to reach the border, where they can be shot in the foot by a Thai guard."

Despair hung over the camp like the dust of dry season. The place originally had been plastic sheets thrown over bamboo poles and set down on a marsh at the end of the rainy season. Doctors spent nights moving patients out from under torrents of water. One of the main causes of death in those early days was drowning. When the dry season came, the dust throttled people's windpipes and few could sleep at night for the coughing.

Looking for interviewees, I stopped to talk to a random collection of Cambodians. "It doesn't matter anymore if I die," a widow told me. A farmer shrugged. "I am hopeless of going to a third country, so I go to the border when they take me, to put myself in the cycle of chance again."

This time, when the children surrounded me, I knew enough to press my palms into a Khmer greeting. They smiled as if in appreciation. I reached out to pat their heads. Only the most minute tremor of the children's bodies signaled to me that something was amiss—another reminder that I was ignorant of the simplest cues to enter this culture.

We passed a raised stage set in a city block's worth of playing area. Huge speakers blared out a curious mixture of bootlegged American rock beat and melancholy Cambodian lyrics. A group of young girls was mouthing to the record. I noticed one in particular, a slender girl who wore a flowered sarong.

"Can I talk to her?"

Nhep Sarouen did not respond.

"Where does she live?" I persisted.

"No mudder, no fadder, like me," he said.

"But where does she live in the camp?"

He shrugged, pretending, I thought, not to understand.

We walked on, passing a flashily dressed young girl with the dimpled beauty of a billboard model. In order to escape a forced marriage to a Pol Pot soldier, Sarouen explained, the girl had pulled out her teeth and chopped off her hair and acted "crazy." The accommodation she had made with camp life was to be a "taxi girl"—one who went outside whenever a Task Force 80 guard wanted her.

A counselor joined us. Dropping his head in embarrassment, he explained to me, "Camp is not safe for girls. Guards sneak into huts at night—I don't know in English—use them like wife? If say no, guard punish them, send back to border. If say yes, shame so great, family reject. The girls turn gray, and not from sickness."

Walking on, I thought I caught another glimpse of the girl with the flowered sarong. The starfish of young people fanning out around me made it impossible to see clearly.

Sarouen led me to a sequestered and peculiarly quiet area of the camp known as the Children's Center. It was administered by the

International Rescue Committee, a private American agency that had been helping Cambodian refugees in Thailand since 1976. A young American volunteer was in charge, Margie de Monchy, and she was prepared to use the full deck of her bureaucratic powers to keep me from interviewing the unaccompanied minors.

"But why?"

She laid her cards on the table. "Look, there've been visitors who tried to steal children. For rackets. We have to be very protective. Emotionally protective, too. These children see a *barang* and go a little crazy. They write more letters. Then you get back in your plane and forget."

"What's a *barang?*"

"A foreigner. Us. French, American, we all look the same to them."

I persuaded, I charmed, I carried on about the larger social good. A writer will say almost anything to get access.

"Don't you want publicity, to help get them out?"

Margie looked at me wearily. "We've had a tracing program for their parents going on inside Cambodia for over a year now. Almost no hits. Some kids have had a tentative contact from a relative, but reunification was impossible because of the political situation inside Cambodia. I think now the tracing has gone on too long—it makes the kids ineligible for resettlement."

I said it would be important to interview children of different ages from a variety of backgrounds. It was late, and I was wearing Margie down. She asked me to write out a specific request. I specified a sixteen-year-old boy of peasant upbringing, a twelve-year-old girl of urban background, one of the nearly eighteen-year-olds who soon would ripen out of the special status of "minor" and presumably be left to rot. Further, I asked to talk both to those who were psychologically depressed or withdrawn and to those who seemed to be coping exceptionally well, to those who were mourning their lost parents and to those who refused to acknowledge relatives in the camp whose claim on them could dash hopes of resettlement. At last Margie agreed.

*

The next morning, four boys and girls are lined up waiting for me outside the Children's Center. On the way, I pass bamboo dorms arranged around vegetable gardens tended with the meticulous attention of children living in stopped time. Again I glimpse the girl I had seen yesterday, her hungry, wary eyes. Are they following me, like a deer through the forest? Then she is gone, the girl in the flowered sarong.

A translator is assigned to me, Darvy Um Heder, a pretty wisp of a woman with sad eyes. She had married an American scholar and escaped the Pol Pot regime only to be dumped in Ithaca, New York, and divorced. We sit behind a table on a raised platform, Darvy on one side, Margie de Monchy on the other, myself in a khaki jumpsuit; I remember thinking we must look like some sort of war-crimes tribunal. The first boy lurches up the steps of the information center with a crude crutch under his arm. He has half a leg.

"He does not know how to start his story," the translator says.

"Can he remember back to a good time?"

The face of Rin, a sixteen-year-old, peels back in incredulity upon hearing this translated. He has soft raisin eyes, but his face looks skinned of the sweetness of childhood. The past for him, for all of them, is divided into two distinct nightmares: "during Pol Pot time" and "after the Vietnamese."

From the nearly four years between April 1975 and January 1979, when Pol Pot and his Khmer Rouge soldiers practiced their barbaric experiment in textbook Marxism on the Cambodian people, Rin remembers three things. Work. Hunger. Death. He rose at four in the morning and carried rocks until night. He always fulfilled his quota because if he did not, he would get no rice or be taken away. When the soldiers took people away, there was only one punishment. It was the same as the punishment for wearing eyeglasses or using the polite form of speech or forgetting to throw your fishbones on the ground—any giveaway that one had been educated. "What is infected must be cut out" went the slogan.

One day in January 1979, North Vietnamese communist soldiers swarmed through Rin's district, and the sky grew heavy with helicopters and gunfire and greasy smoke. When the sky cleared, the Pol Pot soldiers had fled.

"All the people run behind the Vietnamese, for protection," Rin remembers. His first thought was to search for food. Someone told him that the Vietnamese had come to rescue the Cambodian people. He was happy that day, he says. And then, again there was nothing to eat, and the fighting did not stop.

Rin walked six days without food to get to the border. A soldier on the Thailand side watched him step on the mine. The translator adds that Rin felt lucky, because so many were shot dead when they came across the border.

I ask what he hopes for his future.

Rin swings his head from side to side, a battered, head-against-the-wall movement. Margie de Monchy leans over to whisper that Rin is desperate to go to another country but so nearly without hope that he cannot speak the words. "The one thing the children can't talk about," she says, "is the future."

I ask Rin if he would ever consider going back to Cambodia.

"If he dies right away, all right," conveys the translator, "but he says he has no more strength for suffer."

Rin pushes himself to a standing position and sways there, without his crutch. He had refused to accept an artificial limb. All the legs in the last shipment were right legs, and all white-skinned, but I doubted those petty humiliations were the reason he refused. The boy had given up his leg for what the *barang* called a "future," and no other prosthesis could make him whole.

At the end of three more interviews like that one, I am pretty wrung out. But I haven't yet seen a child from an urban background. There is a delay; something is wrong. The child scheduled for that interview is not available.

And then, the girl with the hungry eyes appears. In the midst of the dust and chaos, she is perfectly groomed. Her black hair is combed and draped behind one ear and runs down her back like a river. Her startlingly long nails are clean and well shaped. She has presence.

But it is her face that compels attention: The features are modeled so delicately across the broad, amber-colored smoothness of her skin, they shift in the fraction of an instant between animation and an expressionless mask. We look at each other for a long time, as if enchanted. Never once during the interview does she take her eyes off my face.

Darvy, the translator, explains that this girl must substitute for the one scheduled, who cannot be found.

"Do you remember a good time?" I ask the child.

She looks at me through the translator's words and her face brightens to the innocence of a child—almost.

"Yes, she has happy memories," says the translator. "She was always with her family, her brothers and sister. She had picnics by the river with them, she went to see movies with them. They had a stone house, quite a fancy house. She was in school, just beginning. . . ."

From the description of her quarter of Phnom Penh and her grand-parents' gold-working shop, it sounds as though she came from the Sino-Khmer merchant class, a prosperous and politically influential group centered in Phnom Penh, where intermarriage had mixed Khmer blood with Chinese. That would explain her light amber skin.

"How old are you?"

The child says she was born in the Year of the Dog, which last occurred in 1970, making her twelve—exactly what I had requested.

"Were your parents both Khmer, or was one Chinese?"

The translator appears uncomfortable with this question, why I don't know, and hastens to assure me that her parents were full Khmer.

"What happened to your family?"

The child speaks in a quick soft monotone, without inflection, digging the nails of one hand under the nails of the other, then flicking them apart with a high, clicking sound.

"Her father was a soldier," conveys the translator.

"In the Lon Nol army?"

"Yes, on the side of the United States. He went away to fight. And then Pol Pot came. She was hiding in the trench with her mother, and the father came back with his soldiers with a white flag to . . ."

"Surrender?"

"Yes, surrender."

As the account of the family's forced march into the countryside and its systematic deterioration continues, I am struck by two things. For one, the apparently casual tone with which each facet of disaster is described, and then there is the language of her hands: extraordinary hands. The long tapering fingers, seemingly boneless, bend back as effortlessly as a lily opens.

"Her mother was the first that Pol Pot's soldiers took," reports the translator.

"Why?"

She clicks her nails.

"She doesn't know why."

"What happened to her mother?"

"*Slap*," says the child. I am accustomed to the sound by now; it is the most frequently spoken Khmer word in all my interviews; it means dead.

"The father, too, the same. They took him three days later."

"*Slap?*"

"*Slap.*"

Did she have brothers or sisters?

Click click.

"Small brother and sister, very sick, they were eating only roots."

"Dysentery?"

"Yes. Then they came and took her away from the family. Sent her to work somewhere else, to a wilderness. Sent her older brother away to a different place."

"Did she see her small brother and sister again?"

"She lied to the soldiers to see her sister. But when she came home, the sister died three days before."

"And her little brother?"

"He starve."

"Did she see that?"

Click click.

"She saw."

"*Slap*," says the child.

When I ask why they took her mother and father and what they did to them, the child places the heels of her hands together, and now the fingers curve back unimaginably far, five petals in either direction, fully open, a lily of flesh.

"She heard that when they took away the people, they killed them," offers the translator.

Finally, impatiently, through the translator, the child replies: "Communist never say. Just tell you what to do. You do, or you die."

"Did she"—this is not a question I want to ask—"did she see anybody beaten or killed, with her own eyes?"

"She saw a woman and a man, for love."

"For love?"

The translator has some difficulty relating the grisly story. A woman forced to marry a Pol Pot soldier was discovered with her former beloved. The authorities announced the crime to everyone in the settlement at a political meeting.

"Then they bring the couple to the big meeting to punish them in public. Beat them with a stick."

Horror flicks in the child's eyes as she hears the story recounted, even in English.

"Beat them, to death?"

"Yes. To death."

"And she saw this, too?"

"She saw."

"Oh, God, what did she think?"

"She think of her parents, maybe they die like this."

Tears glitter in the now expressionless eyes, but they do not spill over. She puts her arm in front of her face and drops her head to the table, soundless, a trembling in her tiny back barely visible. The sadness swamps over me, and I hear the sound of muffled sobs, but not from the child; the child is not crying. Margie de Monchy is in tears, and so is the translator.

"I never see her like this before," whispers Darvy.

"She's never told her story before," Margie adds. "We don't have the time to ask, just names and dates—I feel terrible."

I massage the child's back and wait for her to compose herself, and then the Thai guard with the orange lipstick comes by and demands to know when I am leaving.

Five minutes pass, more.

The girl lifts her head. Her face is as bland as a Buddha.

I ask for permission to take her picture. We walk outside and she stands beside the children's vegetable garden. Her tiny body is straight up. The language of it says—I am special—and borders almost on arrogance. As I raise the camera, she sways a little and her body falls into a natural curve, a waxing moon. Her eyes are luminous and she lifts her lips into a shy smile. Through the lens of my camera she looks like the celestial nymphs that dance in stone around Cambodia's ancient temples. She is not of this time and place, I remember thinking. She is an angel floating between worlds, a soul waiting to transcend, a flower without a stem.

I begin to mumble endearments to the child; I ask the director if I can send her barrettes. The unspoken ground between us has changed utterly since the start of the interview.

"She thanks you from her heart, and she—" The translator breaks off in midsentence.

"What else did she say?"

Click click. The child works her nails.

"It's nothing. She's confused."

"Please, what is it?"

Margie de Monchy speaks now with the weariness of defeat. "She thinks you will take her to a free country. All she wants is to get away."

"Oh, my God—can you explain, I mean, this is just for the newspaper. . . ."

The child immediately entreats the translator to put things right. "She is very sorry if she make a mistake."

Stammering, furious at my own insensitivity, I try lamely to smooth it over. "Please," to the translator, "tell her that her story, I mean, sharing the pain of it will help, it'll help people in other countries to remember the plight of Cambodians—" I am making myself sick.

The child backs away. The spell is broken.

It seemed as if all at once, incontrovertibly, her soul had clicked shut. She stood there straight and dry-eyed, the sores shut up again behind the chicken-bone body. She would not succumb to the apathy of refugee: She would be her own refuge. The child bowed her head to me. Her hands, sweetly forming the Khmer good-bye, remained at the same time waxen and closed.

And then I was outside and immediately besieged by a new crowd of letter bearers. "This my mother." A woman held up a picture of her mother and father at the Chicago zoo, smiling in their cutoff jeans and carrying cameras. "Why U.S. take my mother and reject me and my children?"

A soft cry came from nearby. I tried to move through the press of people toward it. A few more paces and I could see Sister Angela pinned against the car with its backseat already awash with letters. "Help me . . ." The tiny nun's arms were splayed out on the roof like a suspect in a drug bust, to show that she could take no more.

I could not reach her. Suddenly I caught the eye of the translator. "What's her name?" I shouted over the heads.

"Who?"

"The last one."

The translator shook her head; she didn't understand.

"The girl who couldn't cry."

Three letters came floating over the heads. M-o-m. That was all.

My eyes closed, people pressed in, overwhelming me. Only an airborne observer—one of those crisp U.N. officials in an antiseptic helicopter—might have seen in perspective the figure of a pale-skinned woman: turning, turning, her arms bursting with letters, in this tiny doomed de-evolutionary pool of a people who had survived genocide only to be confined to a dust heap.

*

An hour in the shower and the dirt was not yet out of my ears. Hair still damp, I was seated at a highly polished table as a guest of the number-two man at the American Embassy in Bangkok, Stapleton Roy. He was an expert on China, but he had never been to the camps.

"The Cambodians won't be taken, because you see"—his tone hushed down to that of inside authority—"they really don't want to go to the United States badly enough."

I was not hearing correctly, must be the dust in my ears.

"They're not motivated, like the Vietnamese boat people," he added.

Servants brought sweet lotus seeds for dessert.

"Does that mean," I said, forcing the fury down the back of my throat, "that Cambodians who flee by land have to get themselves raped by Thai pirates before the U.S. will take their pleas seriously?"

"Between you and me," the American said, "anybody with guts would probably go back to the border."

*

The border was no-man's-land. Since 1979 when the Vietnamese had driven the Khmer Rouge out of Cambodia, they and the two noncommunist rebel groups had retreated to the Thai-Cambodian border and holed up in a string of makeshift camps. An estimated three hundred thousand displaced Cambodians were perched along this strip, able to trade but unable to get into Cambodia or out to the West. At least half were civilians. It was a marginal existence, under plastic sheeting and bamboo poles, with crude open "platforms" as medical aid stations and weekly distributions of rice from the U.N. Food Program.[1] They were hemmed in on one side by Thai soldiers with orders to shoot illegal entrants, and sitting ducks for attack on the other side by the Vietnamese.

I had visited two of the anti-Vietnamese resistance camps, one operated by Prince Sihanouk and one by his former prime minister, Son Sann, Cambodia's neutralist leaders before Pol Pot. Recruits training with wooden weapons and civilians working out with punching bags gave these places the air of YMCA camps. The people in them may have had guts to begin with, but they had languished for several years on international welfare in these pathetically earnest Potemkin villages.

Pol Pot's forces, said to number thirty to forty thousand, were the

only ones with a direct source of military aid. The money was channeled by Deng Xiao Ping from Beijng to Bangkok, where it purchased
weapons that were shipped to the border past deliberately averted Thai
eyes. At that time the ultimate aim of the Chinese was to form a
united front with Sihanouk and push the Vietnamese into a coalition
with, in Deng's words, "the eventual appointment of Sihanouk as Head
of State and Comrade Pol Pot as Prime Minister in charge of national
defence and Commander-in-Chief of the armed forces."[2] As if that
prospect weren't chilling enough, Pol Pot's legitimacy as the rightful
leader of Cambodia was also being supported by the United States
government at the United Nations.

Before leaving Thailand, I felt compelled to try to see one of Pol
Pot's camps. On December 31, armed with passes from Thai authorities, I got as far as Aranyaprathet, a black-market boomtown spawned
by the border war. But to take me on the two-hour drive through
parched and lacerating scrub and up into the Cardomom Mountains to
find Ta Prik, Pol Pot's major camp in the south, I had to coddle a local
cab driver all the way; none had been there before, and no one wanted
to go.

We managed to talk our way past three Thai military checkpoints,
but at a fourth we were stopped cold. Two Thai soldiers peered out
from a sandbagged bunker and waved and shouted somewhat frantically. One didn't need a degree in Thai to know they meant "Scram." I
stepped out to talk with them, but they seemed too agitated to leave
their bunker. So I shrugged, smiled dumbly, and insisted the cabbie
drive on. He thought I was daft, and he turned out to be right.

The final ten kilometers took us onto dirt road. We kept passing
buses crammed with people: Cambodians from the look of them; certainly not tourists. Where were they coming from? Where were they
going? Why?

We crossed a stream and all at once, uneventfully, we were in
Cambodia. The driver was not happy. We started climbing. Up
through the dust-pewtered trees I could see the Cardomom Mountains,
but not Ta Prik camp. It was supposedly hidden in the declivities of
those rolling mountains, under canopies of jungle.

A lone Thai soldier was patrolling the entrance road to Ta Prik when
we stopped. "No go!" he shouted. Suddenly, six more Thai soldiers
jumped out of the scrub. They looked astonished. They also looked
scared.

"Please tell the camp leader *The New York Times* is here."

The first Thai soldier suddenly stiffened, turned, pointed his rifle, waited, then turned back. He was obviously jumpy about something. He ordered, then urged, then finally pleaded with me to turn back.

"No, no, tell leader *New York Times* here; he see me, very good for him."

"Please, please, you go now," the distraught Thai guard was begging. "Please, save your life!"

I turned back. The next morning, after the five-hour drive to Bangkok, I read in the newspaper that the camp had been under attack by the Vietnamese army. This year's dry season offensive had begun.

In my bloody-minded determination to see those butchers face to face, I had overlooked one simple, unrelenting fact about that part of the world. Cambodia had been engulfed in war since 1970. This was New Year's Day, 1982, and everything had changed but nothing had changed. Cambodia was still at war.

Stopped Time

Back home in New York, I was unable to forget the little girl who could not cry. I never did find out her full name. Taking a wild chance, I sent a letter to the camp in Thailand addressed simply to "Mom." I tucked in twenty dollars and a pair of barrettes. Some weeks later I received a reply from "Phat Mom."* She wanted me to sponsor her to come to America. Clay was ambivalent; Maura thought it might be worse for the child than staying where she was. I said nothing more, but I did apply to sponsor her.

For the next eight months, I wrote one article after another about the thousands of Cambodians languishing in Thailand or on that border. But in all the activist journalism, I never stopped thinking about Mohm. The process of "calling out" a particular refugee was untested, however, and my efforts kept falling through holes. By the end of summer the answer seemed to be unequivocally "no." I must have kept nurturing a secret hope, because when I came across a poem by Shuntaro Tanikawa, it moved me to think of Mohm with tenderness:

> A child is still one more angel
> however much we don't believe in god
> A child is still our reason
> reason for living
> reason for risking death.[1]

And so it was, having anticipated all the previous year that Maura's departure might leave me inconsolable, I had tried to do something

---

* *Mom* was the original spelling of Mohm's name, but led to mispronunciation: *Mom* as in "Mom's" apple pie, instead of *Mohm* as in "home." It is customary among Cambodians to put the family name first.

about it, and I had failed. Now the moment was here, I had to face it:
an ending.

*

The day that spreads before us when we finally do agree to go boating is
a beautiful day. The roadside fences of late summer are still roped in
roses and the sun brightens the dingy tassels on full-grown potato fields.
Turning off the woods road, we can hear the halyards on the sailboats
brushing against their metal masts, the high sweet steel band of a
marina.

"That you, Miz Sheehy?" Jesse, the elderly boat handler, squints
through his soft yellowish eyes. "Dint recognize you, got your girl walking with you. Thought you two was sisters."

Jesse drives a forklift under the flat wide belly of our little boat and
gently lowers it into the water. Its seventy-horse outboard is all gassed
up. All we have to do is turn a key. This is not boating, it's Sunday
driving on water. Never mind, it will be a beautiful day.

"How long does it take to get to Plum Gut?" I ask the boat handler.

"Not long." He casts us off. We barely catch the words of his after-
thought, something about a tide rip.

"What's a tide rip?"

"Where ocean and still water, they meet."

"Are you expecting bad weather?" I call.

"Don't 'spect so."

The breeze is fresh in our faces and the boat sits plumply on the soft
swells. "Okay, navigator, plot us a course to Portugal!" I call to Maura.
She hangs the beer over the side.

Beyond Sammy's Beach I open up the engine. As I look back over
our braided wake, the blithe spirit comes up in me—the child I was,
exploring in my rowboat abandoned houseboats and islands inhabited
by feral dogs—yes, this is how it felt.

"What are all those buoys for?" Maura asks, pointing to the head of
Gardiners Island.

"Probably to scare people off from going ashore to swim." I continue
on course toward Gardiners Island, intending for us to go ashore and
swim.

"Look, Momzo, the buoys make a line all around the point."

"So what?"

"So they must mean something."

I am in my element; she is not. She registers danger and hates being made dependent again. She gets out the chart and studies it.

"It says 'Danger Area.' "

"Where?"

"Right ahead of us." She reads from the chart triumphantly. " 'U.S. Government property prohibited to the public. Area is dangerous due to live undetonated explosives. . . .' "

"You couldn't have made that up." I laugh and she laughs. "Okay. Shall we set course for Plum Gut?"

"It's pretty far out," she says.

"But look at this day." As I see it, the gentle wind is partnering wave after wave in uniform arabesques. Gulls carve graceful arcs in the blue sky. My daughter sees it all differently. "It's going to get worse," she says.

We turn our craft 30 degrees east and make our way toward that mile-wide slot between bay and open sound they call Plum Gut. The tip broken off it is Plum Island, and it appears uninhabited. The few buildings have barred windows. The only sound is of barking dogs, a hollow, penned-in, wolfish sound.

I throw over the anchor. We will fish awhile, have a picnic lunch, take a swim, take a nap, have a real nice day.

From dozing in the sun on my stomach I am awakened by a sudden disequilibrium, as if the water had belched just under the boat.

"What's that, a whale?" I say.

"It's the waves," she says, "they're changing."

I sit up and look out at the water. The swells have sharpened into seraphs and along the edge of the seraphs is an eyeleting of white foam. "Pretty, aren't they?"

"Pretty high."

"C'mon, don't be so negative." I notice all over again how deep and guileless are her eyes, how pure the feelings that play over her face. "We're a team here, don't you feel part of this adventure?"

"Sure I do, Mom." A beat, and then: "I guess I don't feel part of anything."

My face must have flinched.

"But it doesn't bother me anymore," she goes on. "I used to think of myself as a divided thing, going back and forth between my two families, that sometimes fit it in, and sometimes didn't. But that's not how it is anymore. Now *I'm* the whole. I refuse to be two half-people anymore. I have to become a whole person." She rubs her strawberry-bright nose. "The only thing real to me right now is myself, in the moment."

The waves grow a little cockier. She has never trusted the ocean. Moments later the ruffled foam is thick and the ocean deepens in color to a stony gray-blue. Maura shudders.

"I think we should go in," she says.

"You're right. Should we have a swim first?" I start climbing over the side. "Race you to Plum Island?"

"Don't go near there!" It pops out of her with premonitory force. She cannot explain why. "Can't we start back?" she says.

"Okay." I start up the engine and move from a fast idle to running hard. Smack and plunge. Suddenly we are in a different sea. Waves are churning up like a tantrum out of the southeast. The broad-bottomed box we are in slaps at the swollen waves like a fat lady at flies on a beach, its loud and indiscriminate percussions belying any affinity for the natural surroundings. I decrease the speed and try to nudge into the waves at an angle and cut off the tips.

Maura looks at me. "Shouldn't we try the C.B.?"

"I can handle it."

She goes below and tries to call on the Coast Guard channel. "Line's tied up with Hispanic truckers," she reports.

"Don't worry about it."

Without warning or noticeable provocation, a full squall is coming up. Irrational danger is being introduced into our benign situation. Now and then a three-foot wave makes a rocking horse of the little craft, teasing it, flipping up its bow and then smacking it flat against the trough. The wind must be up to 25 or 30 knots. If the boat doesn't bury itself bow first like an arrow in a barrel, it might just be flipped onto its back like a tortoise.

Maura prevails on me to stop fighting it and drop anchor while she tries the Coast Guard again.

"*Basta! Basta!*" she shouts into the microphone. "We need this band for a distress call." After repeated tries, she makes contact with a voice that says it can't do anything and suggests we put in to the nearest land. "Plum Island?" she asks incredulously. "Guess so," says the voice.

We look back at the mysterious island. A large man has appeared at the edge of its beach. He looks as though he's imprisoned there.

"We can't go there, Mother," Maura announces emphatically.

"Okay, why don't you use the radio to try to reach Lester," I suggest. Lester is the solicitous owner of our marina.

She goes back to the C.B. and works at it with a patience I would not have. In a while she reaches the town police who say they will try to contact our boatyard. "Call Lester," she repeats. Meanwhile, elegantly pluming waves throw back spray in our faces. In an hour, it will start to get dark. Is there nothing to do but sit and rock in this dumb little boat?

"You never listen to me, Momzo."

"Don't I? I should. It's almost as if you have a third eye. You can see far things close up, and connect them."

"That's why I prefer not to look ahead."

I sigh. "You're always so negative."

*

I am reminded of how dismayed I was when we sat together beside a salmon-fishing stream in Scotland two summers before, and Maura began rambling about the future.

"The future is cold to me," she had said. She was all of sixteen. "I have no reason to expect it will get better or even be as good as it's been for you. I don't have the conviction that the world we know will be around five or ten years from now. The only place I find reason for living is in the past." She delivered this statement not petulantly but in a curiously neutral tone, like a newscaster on an atoll after the bomb.

"Sometimes," she continued softly, "traveling through unfamiliar cities, I feel like a creature from Mars. 'Did the Normans come through here?' I wonder. 'Did the Crusaders carve crosses on the trees?' I just don't feel the continuity."

"You'll find the reason for living in your writing," I tried to tell her. "Just don't cut yourself off."

She withdrew her hands, plump, childlike hands.

"Talk to me, sweetheart," I remember saying.

"I'm afraid to talk to you again." She folded her hands over her stomach. "I never know when you're going to fly up into the red zone and attack. The things you say, the way you say them . . ."

I felt the rims of my eyes swell.

"I guess I feel shucked." There, I had said it. "Everything you do lately feels like a shucking off of me."

And last summer, seated across from each other in an after-theater café, an even more startling revelation had spilled out.

"Oh, God, Mother, if you only knew how much I did love you. I would have been totally helpless in your power." Her tears seemed to ooze through her cheeks, her nose, her eyes, a back-up drain of sadness. "It's only in the last year that I've grown a protective layer, so you can't cut me down."

I had threaded the hair back from her wetted cheeks, but of course that only embarrassed her.

"I'd come to the point of believing we might never make it," she said solemnly. "As mother and daughter, I mean. We might never accept each other. It made me so sad. . . ."

She tried to hold back the tears, then stopped trying and let them fall hard. "I wanted more than anything to be enough for you, but I wasn't. I was hanging on to a relationship that shredded my self-confidence. I had to break it off before it broke me."

Inside, I had felt a trembling. I had no idea it was that close to rupture. Over the previous year my intellect kept telling me that I must give her a gentle push, hide my own fears, but instead I kept feeling her departure as an abandonment, another one.

＊

Now, she lifts her head. I look into her eyes, our eyes, the mirror of our mutual discontent.

"This time together has given me hope again," she says.

"Dearest, sweet Maura," I hold her very tight. "We'll find each other again. We will."

I shudder with love for the child I almost lost.

All at once we look up and face a wall of water. It tumbles into a gravel of white just off the bow. The boat has drifted to where the ocean meets still water—exactly where we should not be. The anchor is not holding.

"Hang on!" I shout.

The spillover digs up the bow and holds us at a crazy angle for what seems like an eternity. Then the earsplitting smack as the wave lets us down. Our knees snap. I see Maura grab for the back of the fishing chair. Another wall of water rises up. "I'm scared, Mom."

"I'll try to swim to the island and get help," I call to her.

"Don't go near that island!"

I work my way over to her and we hold on to the chair and hang on to each other. In our closeness, knees rising and sinking now in rhythm with the rocking and tossing of the waves, we surrender ourselves to nature. After a while, we hear the hum of an engine.

"It's Lester!" Maura shouts. "He got my call."

Lester jumps in from an escort boat and cautiously tests our craft against the waves. They buck him, too, but it was not for nothing that Lester was a mate on the great schooner *America*. He goes at the sea like a roping cowboy and never admits the danger until, an hour and a half later, we have cleared the mouth of the harbor.

"Guess I should have put in at Plum Island," I say sheepishly.

"Good thing you didn't," Lester draws out the suspense. "That's where they test incurable diseases and Agent Orange. They'd probably have put you in quarantine for weeks."

She had seen the hidden danger, my daughter. She saved the day. My daughter, her self.

I look at Maura full of hope. She will survive this sea change between us; I am confident of it now. For myself, the way is not yet clear. I seem to be in a state of suspension. I cannot go back to a past life. But neither can I make myself move on to a future without angels.

Rainy Season, 1975

It's not so bad in the beginning.

The way that Pol Pot keep the people, divide them into two kinds. The people that live with Pol Pot for a long time or villagers who hide his soldiers, they call them the Old People. People like us they call the New People.* Nobody know where to go. We pass through towns, nobody in it. Houses empty, rice throw all around, cars look like somebody pull out their eyes. We want to walk all the way to Kompote [a province south of Phnom Penh] where my grandmother has the family house. But no more food, so we cannot go that far.

Where we stop, they give us land to clear. About a hundred families. Everyone have to share exactly the same. My father and mother make a hut. Huts all in a row, same size. My parents dig in the soil with stones, that's all they give us. The children help. I think it's fun, all building a new little house together. Just a little hut on stilts, leaves for the roof, the floor bumpy made of bamboo. We sleep on the floor, the whole family, no more mattress like our house in Phnom Penh. But we in the country, all together, my grandmother too.

I say, "Boy, I wish I have another month and then we can go back home."

I don't know it's going to turn out that way. I don't know what communist means. In the beginning I cannot imagine how cruel they going to be to people.

*

I'll try to give the story in your language. It's hard to express the way I feel in it, but I don't feel the pain so much when I talk about it in your

* Those educated and urban Cambodians who were teachers, students, merchants, or members of the civil and military service.

language. My own words carry too much weight. But I always worry when I finish a part, did I say enough? Did I really connect by those words? You see, your language is set for your way of thinking. It's like a different current. The situation I want to explain is set for another current, and that current carries the strong feelings from a different way of thinking. So it's like plugging a lamp into the wrong current. The energy I put into it takes more than it gives out. And a lot of the time, I don't want to tell the details. How would people look at me?

*

After a while everyone go to work in the rice fields, except little children like me.

When I meet my mother with her work group, I start to give a bow and greet her the respect way, *"Chumriap sua, nay madai."*[1]

No, no, my mother say with her eyes.

Pol Pot children never say hello, they just walk by. In Pol Pot time children talk to adults as if they are equal. I try to remember not to greet my parents the respect way.

One day I take a nap. Something comes to kill me. Just a face, an arm, arm floating down on me with a knife and I cannot move, cannot! Cannot see who it is, but I know. Every time I open my eye, I see my head come off my body. It's real, it's reality, something terrible is going to happen!

I wake up shaking. I think, "They must kill my mother and father." I run out to see.

But my parents come back from the meeting and they don't say a word. My father bow before his Buddha figure. He has it on a shelf with a bright red scarf under it. Sometimes, late at night, we burn a candle and a beautiful light comes out from Buddha's face and touches my heart so softly. My father always teach us Buddha's way, the way of truth.

In that time my grandmother's family and my family still live together, all move on to the same new town. Now I think it's exciting again, the way they do. Oooh, yes! Children can go with their friends, play, do what they like.

My grandmother always tell me the old stories, about ghosts and spirits. She read and read to me, she always have a point. She tell me about one of those spirits, *pramat prumong,* a big monster, it's very evil and it can fly. It has magic, too. It likes to catch children and split them open from their throat to their legs and lay them down over the river for a bridge. That's why little children cannot go anywhere but straight home after school. Cannot even go to another town, because who know what might happen? My grandma read and read to me, she always have a point. She have fifteen children, something like that, my mother's the second oldest. I'm very close with my grandma.

I tell my mother about that dream I have. She say it must be a spirit trying to capture me back to my past life. I tell the girl I play with all about it. She ask about my past life. I tell her about living inside the temple mountain, I tell her my father must be a king. In the moonlight long ago we sit on a terrace over a silver lake. It sparkles with lotus flowers like stars drop into the water. We watch the dancing girls, all diamond and gold around their arms and legs, so beautiful to watch. In the black forest behind I hear the elephants dancing too.

When my mother hear me tell that story, she get so angry. She say, "Forget! Don't talk about it! Do you want to get us killed?" They don't allow any religion or king or god anymore, everybody have to be equal. But I don't know that in the beginning. In the beginning I just talk the way I used to when I'm a little child.

*

Pol Pot leaders come around and call to the young students. Say they should go to a special college. They tell them, "You're going to learn all these new bright ideas and you can help to run the country." A lot of people ready for anything after all those years of war. But only thing is —I laugh when I hear it—they say don't take any books. How can they teach with no books?

My uncle hear about this and he want to go. He is the oldest one in my grandma's house not married, a student. He used to play boys' games with me and my brother. Most Cambodian girls cannot play boys' games, but I like it. He's supposed to go to France to study politic. But after Pol Pot take over, he's in the hospital. He hear the loudspeak, calling up all the students. All of them are boys and they get into the truck, excited to go. They call his name off too.

My grandpa say, "Can't go, the boy is sick, in the hospital." He try to hide him.

But my uncle run out of the hospital shouting, "See, I'm here! I'm not sick!" He want to go with them.

My grandpa shout at his son, "You stupid one!"

Why is my grandpa so angry? Maybe he's just too old to change. I wish I'm bigger so I could go away and learn all new things.

We never hear of my uncle again. He the first one lost in our family.

*

My older brother, he always has to be right. It's just one of the boy ways of dealing with things, I guess, but I never can understand it. One time I go to catch crabs for our family; what they give us is not enough to eat and it make me sick in the stomach. My older brother come to see me.

"Why you take so long!" he say to me.

"It's hard to catch them when the water come up so high," I say. My feet all wrinkly and white from stand in that water.

"Half a day!" he shout.

"So, never mind then." I turn over the basket and let all the crabs run away.

I'm stubborn when I little.

My father is so mad, that's what I remember, frighten of him. He say food is too hard to find. My mother talk to me very fair. She say if we fight with each other we going to lose. "You don't just hurt yourself, you hurt your whole family," she say. "Family is everything. Maybe it doesn't seem so now," she say, "but if you don't love and care for your family, you going to feel sorry."

That night I vomit up all my food.

One night my mother brushing my hair. She let me try on her hair clip. In that time they chop off her long hair because everybody have to be the same, but she hide her clip to remember. She is beautiful, my mother. Even when they say everybody must dye sarongs black, she hide some of our pretty color sarongs. Funny thing she say to me, she say, "If I'm not here to take care of you, do not ever forget who you are and who your family is. Don't be rude to other people, don't be like street children." She say, "You must love your brothers and sister and help one another all the time. You be the mother."

Why does she say all these things? I don't pay much attention, then.

*

I keep trying to think of the reason my mother and father die.

It's just a normal morning. Wake up at six, have to run and meet my group, go to work in the rice field. So happy, I laugh till I have a stomachache.

The other children ask me, "Mom, why are you so happy today?"
I don't know why.

Leader of our group gives me an ugly look. "You are happy without reason," she say. "You laugh at nothing."

People say to me, "When you are happy without reason, sometime it turn out to be sad."

Heat of the day buzz in your ears, the sky is blank. Shoots of new rice plants shine like ribbons, like gold. You pull them out by hand and shake the mud off against your foot, then other people plant them again so they grow strong and tall. Everybody in my group is playing around, kick mud in the face. It's one of the most fun days I have since Pol Pot time.

Laugh so much I cannot walk straight. Why? Maybe trying to forget my dream. I begin to scare myself.

Midday break. Clouds crack open. Rainy season, I love it. Rain fill up the rice fields and make little square lakes as far as you can see. There's a bump of soil to run along between the watery fields. I play a silly joke on one of the girls from Phnom Penh, same kind of people as I am. Push my foot under her legs, shout. "Watch out! Monster fish going to eat you!" She fall over into the water headfirst. I laugh so hard. Other girls push me off the bump too. Feels cool in the water.

Water throws up a fish. Dead fish. Its eyes jump on me. Cambodian people say a dead fish in your path is bad luck. Maybe it's the spirit of a person who die but no one bless him with a burial ceremony. He lie there eyes open, staring up like a dead fish. It means he cannot leave this life, just a miserable spirit flying around without rest.

Quick quick I pull the fish out and say, "My God, I got to take this home, then it bring good luck."

Run right to the hut and wait for my parents. Feel a little shaky. Everything seem dark and danger. My sister is outside the hut playing in the dirt with a cup. After a while my brother come back from work. I try to forget about that fish, those dead eyes.

Already dark. I wait. Only my father come home.

My father doesn't throw me up. My father always throw me up to make me laugh. He bend down and dig up my baby sister in both his hands. She so little, only one or two. Then he pick up my little brother. Give them both a little bath, very tender to them. He never do those things before.

My father, of course, he doesn't say. But his expression, you can guess from it. I remember that most of all. He's pale, he moves like something floating in air, like he's not really there.

Wait until he finishes giving my sister a bath. Then I ask him, "Where is our mother?"

He doesn't answer. He just lay my baby sister down and put a cover over her. Maybe my mother could be just sick. My older brother run out of the hut and ask somebody who work with her.

Nobody can tell. Nobody, even really good friends cannot tell. I ask my brother does he know. He tell me to be quiet, I'm just a little girl. But next day my brother blow up with anger, he can't stand it either that nobody tell.

After two days, I go to ask the lady who work with my mother. Bother her and bother her. My voice shakes. "What happen to my mother?"

"Do you swear to me that you don't tell?" she say. I say yes. She tell me, "They take your mother away with hands tie behind her back." She say the reason is, my mother fighting with another woman.

My mother never fight. That's just a make-up story. Somebody else say maybe they take the wrong person. But that's not true either.

I try to remember how long since they send us to the rice field. I don't know day from week anymore. Maybe it's the seventh month of the Year of the Rabbit. But my mother work so hard, my father act like a simple farmer—nobody can know about us. Nothing is going on. People always being taken away, sent to some other work, a different village. It's impossible to think my mother will not come back.

The girl I play with try to be my really good friend. Maybe she talk nice and then go back to tell Pol Pot what I say. Children spy on you. You never know where they are, up a tree, sit on a buffalo, squat under the bamboo floor at night listen to your family talk—children so small no one see, even children six or seven, like me. I don't know that before they take my mother away. Maybe that's why they know about our family.

A sound boil up inside of me. It twist in my throat and push out, but it's not a cry, not a laugh. It's a broken sound. Wild and high. Who is making that sound?

I am trying to think of the reason my mother and father die. Cannot ask. Cannot talk. I never talk anything about it at all.

People say the night of Pol Pot time is like a pineapple, it has a thousand eyes. The eyes are the children.

*

Three days after they take my mother, I pass the platform where they give political meetings. It's pile up with people's clothes and private things. In the pile of colored sarongs a piece of cloth jump out at me—a bright red scarf. It's the sacred cloth my father put underneath his Buddha! Suddenly all the strange things my mother say, the gray faces on everyone, the silence, they fit. I feel the silence move into me like a ghost.

My father is gone. They take my father, too.

Back in the hut I look for my father's Buddha. I look for my mother's hair clip. I wish I have something from my parents, to remember them. Nothing left, no memories. Maybe my childhood is over.

New York City . . . April 1975

What was I up to that spring when Mohm's world was turned upside down and emptied out into the paddies? Going through my old journals, I was able to pin down the preposterous fact that on April 11, 1975, the day before the last American "presence" left Phnom Penh to the rabid roaming child-rebels of Pol Pot, I had a meeting with my editor to discuss midlife crisis. Crisis, that's rich.

Manhattan was preoccupied with the coming of spring. Tassels drifted off the city's transparent yellow trees and pale violet twilights poured into its soft nights, and I was in love and not yet old. Unlike Mohm, my own preoccupation with crisis was an intellectual one.

It wasn't crisis in the catastrophic sense of wars or revolutions or starvation that concerned me. And I had only passing interest in *au courant* spiritual crises, such as were being brought to a peak in Madison Square Garden by Reverend Sun Myung Moon, whose shrill and unintelligible solfeggio was being lapped up, milk for kittens, by young fugitives from free will. Physical crises, the sort where one's body is neatly excavated by the surgeon for the routine removal of polyps and found to have crouching three or four toads of cancer, those I neatly set off to one side in my book with the phrase "life accidents."

What I was after were predictable changes in the inner realm: crises of change in our perception about ourselves and others as we move from one stage to another throughout adulthood. Elective crises, I might call them now. Luxury crises. At the time I thought of them as universal.

*

April 11, 1975, and I followed the maître d'hôtel to a table reserved for my editor. A quirky April sun slanted through cottagey print curtains. I inhaled the fragrance of lobster heads bubbling for bouillabaisse in their bath of saffron and garlic and felt giddy. I was not one of the ladies who lunched. But every six weeks or so my editor would invite me out to discuss the work, worlds away from bank overdrafts and overdue deadlines, where it was unimaginable to munch tuna dripping oil on the typewriter keys. These were my civility breaks.

He was for once late. I passed the time comparing the polite publishing crowd, sipping their Kir and decaf, with the serious business crowd, gouging their steaks and holding tight to their tumblers of Dewar's on the rocks. And then my editor appeared, breathing hard. He unloaded the Army-Navy knapsack he used for a bookbag, as if called back in the midst of bivouacking through Barnes & Noble. He was uniformed in a cashmere turtleneck under a twiggy Scottish sports jacket.

"So sorry, really sorry. Have you ordered yet?"

"No, I've been savoring the once-in-a-lifetime experience of being early."

"You must try the Kir Royale. They make it with lingonberries."

He took out my manuscript and flipped through some pages. I tried to appear cool while kibitzing. My Kir Royale arrived. I stared at the pale green berries trembling in the plume of reddened champagne. It was the most beautiful drink I had ever seen. My editor ordered a Tab for himself.

"The only real problem is tone," he said. "A little too magazine-y."

"I know."

There it was, you see. I did not have permission to write this book. Every morning I woke up to the demon standing over me who jeered, "You're just a journalist." I had three books in print and one already out of print, but this was the first book all over again, which is to say, panic.

A magazine article is like a swimming meet under pressure; the lanes are marked and the finish line is clearly visible. But this, this was like standing on the tip of Florida and plotting a swim to Greenland. Or did Labrador come first? Anybody see Cape Cod in the overcast? I had set out to describe the stages of adult life and the turning points, or crises, or whateveryoucallit, between them. I had been swimming for two years and three months.

"Have you decided on the title yet?"

All at once it popped into my mind and was out of my mouth.

"How about *Passages*?"

He sipped his Tab. "People will think it means excerpts."

"It might grow on them."

Long silence. We went back to titles with the word *crisis* in them.

Crisis. One of my suburban interviewees had given another meaning to the word. "Oh, God, drove around your block would you believe, *twen*tee times, and no parking space. They'd better do something about the parking crisis in this town."

"The problem with crisis," I said, "is that it's been cheapened—it's now almost anything that doesn't meet the Howard Johnson motel standard that Americans consider the minimum for survival."

"What about *Changes*?" he suggested.

"What about putting *crisis* in a subtitle," I countered.

"Let's think about it some more."

He slung on his Army-Navy bag. I wrapped up the limp blue-veined chapters in a newspaper like dead fish.

"See you a few chapters from now," he said brightly. "Just keep on writing."

Keep on swimmin'. It's a long way to Labrador.

*

I dashed uptown to pick up my daughter. Maura was eleven then and ravenous for my attention. It was the day for her first grown-up haircut, and I remember how she sat in the Madison Avenue salon with its showy mirrored ceiling, sat swimming in the barber's cape on two telephone books, unsmiling, and how her clear blue eyes, even then, worked into a furrow that gave a cast of solemnity to her face. She did not take easily to change.

Outside, the day was turning fine. From the gray trunks, suddenly browned branches were supporting tiny leaves graduated in size like a choir. People were shedding jackets, even street people, rolling down into doughnuts their multilayered leg coverings to head for a sunbath in the park. I persuaded Maura to try on a pair of platform sandals we saw in a shop window.

"They're silly," she said. "I only like clogs."

"But clogs are so clumsy." An old and futile argument.

"Clogs are all I need." Discussion closed.

Maura and I walked thirty blocks to the park and wolfed down hot dogs and stretched out in the sun to read. Rowboats drifted by on the boating lake, as many of them carrying a mother and daughter as carried lovers. I was struck by the parallel. The cigarette I was fishing for surreptitiously, having promised at the beginning of every book or article that I would stop smoking when I was finished, had been mangled under the fish-roll of manuscript. I came up with a stub only the truly desperate would smoke.

"Damn."

"Mom, when are you going to be finished?" Maura asked, gravely.

A writer is never finished.

My regimen for the winter had been: Rise at 5 A.M., write until three, then exercise, read the newspaper, return calls, try to do my bit for God and country as well as the laundry. It didn't leave much leeway for attacks of lust or flu.

Maura had thrown herself into the spirit of the thing; she looked up words for me in the dictionary and ran off copies of the chapters as they were completed. She was the sun in my days. I'm sure, looking back through the retrospectoscope, I abused the privilege of her unconditional love. When the fevers of self-doubt overtook me, it was she who absorbed my emotional tempests, and because of her steadiness I knew the ship would never go down.

It was Friday night and I flipped on the *CBS Evening News*. Walter Cronkite looked unusually somber.

Good evening. Cambodia, as an anti-Communist nation, may be in its last hours. Most of the American Embassy people have gone and American correspondents have been told to stand by for imminent evacuation. Khmer Rouge . . .

The doorbell rang—Clay. We had a dinner party to go to and I wasn't finished dressing. Standing in the doorway, he smiled shyly and said, "Hi, I'm glad to see you."

"C'mon in, honey, gotta watch the news."

Sternly: "We're due at seven-thirty."

. . . not enough to shut down the American airlift of rice and ammunition . . .

"I know, but this is important."

. . . the Khmer Rouge are moving closer and closer to the airport. . . . Ancient T-28s have been bombing almost continu-
ously.

The film showed plumes of smoke rising above feathered sugarcane
trees. The blam-blam of rocket rounds alternated with the whine of
ambulance sirens. Fantastic shapes of metal lay scattered on the ground
—American planes, they said, blown apart during the airlift.

"C'mon, Gail, we're going to be late."

Oh, how I didn't want to go to that dinner party. How I didn't want
to debate the dying of somebody else's country over demitasse with
other hors d'oeuvres doves. It was a good bet I would flare out in self-
righteous indignation and insult somebody. I had too long and too
argumentatively been against American military involvement in a war
we had no clear business being in and no certain way to win.

This report from Richard Threlkeld reads like the last chapter in
the five-year-old war that has ravaged Cambodia.

"Last chapter for us," I said sarcastically, "a blank new page for
them."

Most of the foreigners have gone now, but the Cambodians are
still here, thousands more of them every day, a whole nation of
refugees jamming itself into a city with no place to put
them. . . .

Tuberous-limbed men in shorts stirred huge vats of rice soup in
street kitchens for the TV cameras. Flies buzzed around the eyes of a
mother and child lying on a hospital litter, but the life was sinking out
of them and they did not even brush the flies away for the TV cameras.

"Mom, do we have to watch that gory stuff?"

"Shhh, Maura."

I hated dinner-party debates in those days, where no one had been to
the front. Especially because I'd wanted so badly to go to Vietnam.

"Mom, can you get that math thingy for me?"

"Ummhum. Tomorrow."

"Gail, we *have* to go. Please, get dressed."

"I really *need* it tomorrow, Mom."

"I *am* dressed."

"You're wearing *that?*"

He dropped me off after the dinner party. "I'm coming down with something." He didn't stay.

I found Maura's note on the coffee table.

Dear Mom,

Don't be angry with me and if you are never mind but when you come home please wake me up or else bring me in your bed. I cried and cried when you left because I really miss Daddy and I really want you to like Dad. After you left I wanted you to talk to and hold me but I couldn't because you weren't here and I was afraid to ask you to come over for a minute before you left because I thought you might get mad at me. PLEASE DON'T BE MAD WITH ME.

I love you. Maura

I kicked off my shoes beside her double-decker. She awoke and we whispered, I don't remember about what, and then it was three A.M. I must have dozed off. How many hundreds of times had I fallen asleep this way?

As I lay there, crabbed up in my clothes, wondering if the book would ever be done, pressed into an envelope of soapy sheets where nothing was more important than being sealed with a kiss, she whispered, "Don't go yet."

*

The next evening, a Saturday, I forgot to get up from the typewriter in time for the evening news. I caught only the tail end of Richard Threlkeld's report from Phnom Penh, the tail end of "that little war."

So America's Cambodia policy ends after five years on the deck of an American warship in the Gulf of Thailand. Perhaps now there may be some agonizing reappraisals, perhaps some recriminations, but all of that seems a little pointless now, because for better or worse the Cambodian crisis is now just that, purely Cambodian.

Back to Uncle Walter.

In Saigon today . . .

Click.

That was the signal; we could turn off the Cambodian crisis now and get back to the sort of crises that are purely American: When he moves out. When she still can't get pregnant. When he's passed over for Number One. When the last child out wants to move back home after her first divorce. When gas goes to a dollar a gallon.

The cause that had consumed fifty-eight thousand American lives and chewed up the bones and flesh and nerves of countless others simply evaporated into the ozone of unpleasant memories; the little yellow people suddenly vanished; thousands of hours of videotape came unspooled. The plug had been pulled on America's living-room war.

Before the Fall

Imagine what it was like before the war being a member of the middle class in the lovely languorous city of Phnom Penh. At six in the evening, a sky of pinkish gold and the street tringing with cyclo bells, the prickle of ginger and chili peppers beginning to float over the broad boulevards, the powdery gold buildings four or five stories high—see up there, the women stir-frying just inside lacy balconies; and over there, coming back from the market in the center of town, youngsters in flip-flops, bearing giggling brothers and sisters on their hips. And the girls, always the beauty of Cambodian girls, modest in their high-buttoned blouses, gold jewelry gleaming against their coffee-colored skin, moving sinuously under their sarongs as they pedaled their bicycles home.

Metal grilles banged shut across the fish and vegetable shops around six, and people moved into the living quarters behind them. But the night had a vibrant life of its own. Then the streets filled with the Mercedes of the elite and middle-class families climbed into cyclos pedaled by old men from the provinces, their braided leg muscles knotting and unknotting to push their passengers through the crowds to a film or show, perhaps to see a comedian appeal to the Cambodians' highly developed sense of the ridiculous: They especially loved to see royalty fall on its face.[1]

Most of Phnom Penh had electricity during the peaceful Sihanouk years, but late in the evening the city would conserve power by shutting off the lights. Flickers of kerosene gold could be seen through a window, a doorway, eventually dressing the city in tiny cones of light. As night clamped down, the cones moved deeper inside to where the children were bedded down under clouds of mosquito netting. At last, time for the adults to sit on their balconies with a cup of tea or a special dessert, gossiping about their neighbors.

*

Off Monivong Boulevard in Phnom Penh before 1975 one could shop in glass-fronted French boutiques. But most of the commerce was in the hands of Chinese who had intermarried with ethnic Cambodians. Except for some rubber factories encouraged by the French, industry was virtually nonexistent.[2] Foreign exchange was earned almost exclusively from exports of rice, rubber, and corn. When in the early 1970s the elite of the capital developed a taste for hard-currency bank accounts, and frequent trips abroad, imported cars, luxury housing, Western-style restaurants, and the bolder musical beat and brasher fashions of Paris and New York, the Sino-Khmer stayed closer to their Chinese connections. Mohm's older brother, for instance, had spent a year in China living with his maternal relatives. And her father had welcomed a holiday in Hong Kong as an official reward. Although Cambodians exposed to urban culture knew something about the attractions of Western life, most seemed content with the simple pleasures and drowsy grace of a preindustrial society. Their *joie de vivre* was a delight to foreign visitors.

The daughter of an army officer, Mohm lived in Tuol Kuok, a suburb to the west where the stone villas were occupied by government ministers and diplomats and high-ranking military officers. It was an upper-class district, by all accounts, although there was also a middle-class section with apartment houses occupied by teachers and younger military families—the coming elite—and it was here that Mohm's family probably lived. What she recalled of her house was a two-story white stucco building, either a small villa or an apartment house, surrounded by a tall fence covered with crimson bougainvillaea. Behind it ran a wide, deep body of water.

In the early 1970s officers came back from the front every day for dinner. Mohm remembered listening for her father's motorcycle, her mother running to open the gate, the nightly ritual. She cherished a memory of holding tight to her father from the back of his motorcycle and feeling the wind fly through her hair—they'd be off to the central market, Phsa Thmei. Under its yellow-ribbed dome, one's senses would swim in a riot of smells: hot soups being stirred, *satays* sizzling on grills, puffs of Chinese dumplings, and hundreds of colorful desserts. Mohm's favorite treat was to pick out a sugarcane sweet on a stick.

The highest status symbol among that stratum of society was a motorcycle. TVs, stereos, and cars were imported luxuries generally out of range even for the urban middle class. Mohm's family was in the vanguard, with their cassette player and radio combination; half the neighborhood might come over to hear a new tape of love songs by the popular singer Sisamuth or to sit around enchanted by a sentimental soap opera, the Khmer equivalent of *Dynasty*.

On Sundays after going to the temple and taking food to the *bonzes* (monks), families flocked to Mouk Vang, the lovely park beside the joining of the Mekong with the Tonle Sap River. After picnicking there, they might promenade through the formal gardens in front of the old royal palace. To grandmothers fell the duty of seeing that girls gave no encouragement to the young men racing their shiny new Hondas up and down the riverfront. As early as 1971, artillery attacks on the countryside were visible just across the river. They lit up the sky like fireworks. The *bonzes* floated by beneath parasols, indifferent as birds over disaster.

*

Mohm's grandmother and grandfather lived near the central market and ran a prosperous gold-working shop. They adorned her with gold earrings before she was two years old. One of her aunts was married to a private-school administrator, which lent high rank. Among urban Cambodians, education was the chief mark of status. The higher one's diploma, the more people one could command. Children of the upper-middle and upper class generally received a private high-school education at a traditional French lycée and for university degrees went to Paris.

Of the scant details that survive in Mohm's memory of her father, she recalls that he studied in France at a military college. He married her mother when he was in his early twenties; she was fifteen. Women of Mohm's mother's generation and class customarily were married anytime after the age of fourteen and almost always to men selected for them. But Mohm's mother was reluctant. Half-Chinese and exceptionally pretty, she was imbued with the traditional Chinese veneration for education and wanted to finish secondary school. Besides, a military officer was absent so often. But like virtually all Khmer daughters, in the end she obeyed her mother.

Despite her reluctance, their home was harmonious. Parents did not quarrel in front of the children. As in most Asian societies, the family —not the individual—was the fundamental social unit. Divorce was rare.

Sojourns in the country with her grandmother and any number of aunts and cousins were among the highlights of Mohm's early childhood. A spacious house and cultivated land in the province of Kompote had been passed down through her mother's side of the family to the favorite daughter upon her marriage; it then belonged to Mohm's mother. Set on tall stilts, the wooden house soared to twin-peaked tile roofs. A polished teak veranda curved all around, and Mohm was allowed to sleep there at night. That private, satiny place, playing games under the cool of the house, running out under the rain for a shower— these were the things she cherished about the country. And the stories her grandmother gave her to dream on.

*

Under normal conditions as a child of her class, Mohm would have been trained to be polite, placid, and to wear the screen of a smile over her true sentiments in front of strangers or guests. As a girl, she would be expected never to accept the attentions of a boy unless he was intended to be her husband. Although historians of Cambodia's glorious past wrote of women astronomers and mathematicians and a female militia that protected the king, having proved themselves by saving him in battle, the primary attributes cultivated in contemporary young women were shyness and physical modesty. To be sure, some shopgirls wore miniskirts and high heels by the early 1970s, but most girls still mimicked the demure manner of their mothers and the doll-like, high-throated soprano of love-song singers.

Nevertheless, the position of women was becoming somewhat freer. If things had remained normal, Mohm probably could have expected to go to college. It was common for children of the officer class to be sent to Paris to study; even, by the 1970s, to send exceptional daughters.

But from the year of Mohm's birth in 1970 until the fall of Cambodia in 1975, less and less was normal. Conditions in her country went from hope to chaos.

*

The North Vietnamese have always wanted to dominate Indochina. First they had to force an end to French colonialization, which occurred in the mid-fifties. Simultaneously, they made their move on South Vietnam and at the same time sponsored a small group of young Cambodians who would become the core of the Khmer Rouge (or Red Cambodian movement) intended to ripen Cambodia like a cherry and pick it off for them. For nearly twenty years, the nascent Khmer Rouge cadre studied revolution in Hanoi and then hid out in the jungle with child recruits, waiting for their opportunity to strike. But for those two decades, the Chinese, suspecting North Vietnam's territorial ambitions, were determined to foil them, even if that meant ultimately stabbing in the back their brothers in the anticolonialist struggle. From these basic motives flow all the rest.

*

Norodom Sihanouk was crowned king in 1941, an eighteen-year-old perfumed, epicurean playboy in the opinion of some, a "fascist novice" in the eyes of Vietnamese communists.[3] He had been selected by the French governor general during the Nazi occupation of France. In 1954, after he successfully secured independence for Cambodia following the bitter French defeat in Indochina, Sihanouk vowed to mend his profligate ways; in 1955 he abdicated the throne to stand for election. Despite his abdication, Sihanouk continued to enjoy veneration as a god-king; his people called him by the Sanskrit term *Samdech*, Father.

Like the ancient Egyptians, Cambodians believed their king was superhuman. Cambodian thought, as well as society, had for centuries been structured around rigid hierarchies, and people naturally fell into place behind a leader. Indeed, people in power were believed to be born with *barami*—greater merit owing to past lives of service or privilege.

As Sihanouk used to say frequently, "There are three countries that run the risk of becoming extinct—Israel, Poland, and Cambodia." Surrounded on both sides by militant and antagonistic neighbors—Vietnam and Thailand—Cambodia had been forced throughout history to

protect itself either by committing to the patronage of one or the other
or by appealing to an outside power for protection. Many Cambodians,
particularly the educated, feared national extinction.[4]

A visitor to the prince's Phnom Penh in the sixties would land at an
airport built by the French, drive down a road paved by the Japanese,
pass a hospital erected by the Chinese, and on and on. Sihanouk accepted patronage from everybody. The bigger the international um-
brella he could open over Cambodia, he believed, the more it legiti-
mized his country. He maintained one of the largest diplomatic corps;
he published a magazine and made movies distributed in the West.
Later, President Nixon would call him "vain and flighty . . . totally
unrealistic,"[5] but there was a method in Sihanouk's mad activity. If he
kept Cambodia on the map in the minds of foreign powers, her preda-
tory historical enemies might not swallow her up.

In 1965 the United States bombed North Vietnam and invaded
South Vietnam. Cambodia severed diplomatic relations with the
United States. Wanting above all to protect his country from the war
reaching across its border from Vietnam, Sihanouk hotly maintained
his country's neutrality. Also realizing that the dominant Chinese did
not want to see the Vietnamese take over all of Indochina, he looked
primarily to China for protection.

As America's war with the Vietcong grew hotter, Sihanouk tried to
appease Hanoi by permitting supplies to pass along the Ho Chi Minh
Trail inside Cambodia to revolutionary bases in South Vietnam. Despite his cooperation, North Vietnam began stirring up Cambodia's
tiny communist movement. Some of the "Hanoi Khmer"—Cambodians who as youngsters fifteen years before had gone to North Vietnam
to become indoctrinated in Ho Chi Minh's movement and then been
returned to Cambodia—began appearing along the trail. The Vietnamese were always patient. They had waited for the right moment to use
what came to be the original cadre of the Khmer Rouge.

Sihanouk became convinced that the Americans were on the brink
of invading Cambodia. Indeed, the American press was openly weigh-
ing the pros and cons of such an invasion, intended to "clean out the
Vietcong sanctuaries" just inside Cambodia's borders. Sihanouk
warned the United States that if American troops moved into
Cambodia, he would look to China for help. He appealed for a diplomatic mission.

In November 1967, Jacqueline Kennedy visited Cambodia with England's Lord Harlech. Under intense press speculation that America's

celebrated widow was having a romance with her companion, formerly the British ambassador in Washington, their actual agenda was not reported. Sihanouk spotted it. As Stanley Karnow, veteran American correspondent for *The Washington Post,* gathered from talks with Sihanouk, "They wanted Jackie to be able to reestablish diplomatic relations between Cambodia and the United States without the United States having to fulfill the conditions set by Cambodia." Sihanouk met Mrs. Kennedy and acknowledged that Cambodians were always sensitive to "the beauty of Venus." But the resumption of U.S.-Cambodian relations, he declared, was "out of the question."[6]

Yet all through the formally anti-U.S. years, Sihanouk never repudiated his desire for an American protective shield against the communist Vietnamese. At the end of 1967, selecting Karnow as his conduit, Sihanouk indirectly granted the United States the "right of hot pursuit" into Cambodia along Vietcong trails. Ambassador Chester Bowles was dispatched to Phnom Penh to assure the prince that the United States had no aggressive intentions. Sihanouk affirmed that he was ready to restore relations with Washington if—and on that "if" probably hung his eventual loss of Richard Nixon's support—if the Americans would respect the inviolability of Cambodia's borders and limit their hot pursuit to uninhabited areas.[7] This condition was not respected. Sihanouk felt betrayed. And when on January 30, 1968, American forces were taken by surprise with the Tet offensive, Sihanouk became convinced that all of Southeast Asia eventually would go communist.

*

A surprise coup engineered by his ministers in 1970, while Sihanouk was in Paris for a diet cure, suddenly overthrew the *Samdech.* He was replaced by General Lon Nol, who received immediate recognition by the United States. As Sihanouk's minister of defense, Lon Nol had been the most sanctimonious hard-liner against the Vietnamese communists, even as he enjoyed the profits of a covert business trucking their arms through Phnom Penh to the border. Nixon rode roughshod over the doubts of his State Department; Lon Nol was his man. Having General Lon Nol in control in Phnom Penh almost certainly meant an invitation to U.S. forces to extend their war into Cambodia. But inside Cambodia, where support for Sihanouk had eroded, particularly among his coterie in Phnom Penh, high hopes for the new government quickly turned sour. Lon Nol was naïve and uninformed. And now the Americans, unrestrained by this weak leader, dealt with Cambodia purely militarily. Six weeks after the coup, in early March, without the consent of Congress or the knowledge of Secretary of State Rogers or the American people, Richard Nixon ordered the secret invasion of Cambodia.

The television speech delivered by President Nixon on April 30, 1970, conjured up a nightmarish vision of the world. "We live in an age of anarchy," Nixon said, wiping sweat from his upper lip. He lashed out in paranoid frustration: America was seen by the world as "a pitiful, helpless giant." And he insisted, "This is not an invasion of Cambodia."

*

The covert, indiscriminate American bombing of Cambodia from 1970 through 1973 was not the cause of the country's destruction, but it was a catalyst. It set off a conflagration among the Cambodian, Vietnamese, and Chinese communists that otherwise might have remained only a brush fire.

With the abrupt overthrow of their traditional leader in 1970, Cambodian society experienced a vacuum—a profoundly unsettling, and for many perhaps psychologically intolerable, condition. That fact, together with the spillover of America's war in Vietnam, provided the conditions for which the small insurgent Khmer Rouge movement within Cambodia had been waiting.

The Khmer Rouge in 1970 was a ragtag bunch of no more than three or four thousand men, with no prospect of success.[8] But immediately after the coup, Sihanouk had flown to Beijing where he was persuaded to throw in his fortunes with the Pol Pot clique of the Khmer Rouge. Although they scarcely had a military unit yet, the Pol Pot group was able to exploit Sihanouk's name to sell a nationalist movement to villagers who still venerated him as the *Samdech*.

The ground was not particularly ripe for this sale. Cambodian peasants were neither stereotypically impoverished nor temperamentally disposed to strong communalism. But the Khmer Rouge rebels were able to exploit the support of Sihanouk and the inexplicable destruction dealt by secret American B-52 bombings to win over many peasants to their tiny rebel forces. Shrewdly placing a soldier on the roof of a school or hospital, the Khmer Rouge would use the man as a decoy to attract American spotter planes that would summon a B-52 to the target, then blame the Americans for the slaughter of innocent civilians. Cambodian peasants only knew "Americans" from fifty thousand feet up.

After the coup and the American invasion, everything began falling apart. That same spring of 1970, the North Vietnamese swept through the Cambodian resistance to the gates of Phnom Penh, but passed the city by to wage war in the countryside. Cambodian government troops were expanded so rapidly that most were untrained and poorly armed, many were barefoot, pitifully old or very young. Volunteer student recruits were quickly cut down by the Vietcong. Desertions became staggering. By June, when Prime Minister Ky arrived in Phnom Penh to offer South Vietnam's help in repulsing the Vietcong, Lon Nol could not get all his fingers together in a credible salute.[9]

Seven months later, Lon Nol suffered a massive stroke. He left the hospital with slurred speech and an even feebler grasp on reality than before; he would remain in "power" for four years after his stroke. The U.S. government pressed on; its zeal for blasting away the Vietnamese sanctuaries surpassed only by enthusiasm for the futile goal of finding and capturing COSVN—the mythical enemy headquarters. In 1971 alone, according to Nixon's secretary of defense, a single B-52 unit dropped on Cambodia half the tonnage of bombs dropped by all U.S. air forces in the Pacific theater during World War II.[10] The estimated death toll of Cambodians during the war years is half a million.

Meanwhile, in the cities, massive American aid invited the elite to new excesses of corruption. Between 1970 and 1975, Lon Nol's republic received from the United States almost a million dollars a day.[11] The middle class of Phnom Penh became increasingly disaffected, helped along by Khmer Rouge radio broadcasts from Beijing into Cambodia's cities in 1973 calling upon listeners to "purify" themselves by renouncing "corrupt" Western ways. Western clothing, music, and literature, listeners were told, were being used by Lon Nol's American-backed regime to enslave Cambodia.

Very gradually through the early seventies, as *Time* correspondent Robert Sam Anson described the capital, "more sandbagged bunkers were appearing, more concertina wire was being unrolled. Slowly, Phnom Penh, the most beautiful capital in Indochina, is taking on the appearances of Saigon, the most ugly."

Mysteriously, implacably, the Khmer Rouge was gaining more

strongholds in the countryside. By 1974, Cambodia was engulfed in war with its own communist rebels, and losing. Inflation had skyrocketed to the point that even government soldiers and loyal bureaucrats could not afford to feed their families. Many people were driven to activities—bribery, blackmail, chicanery—that violated basic Buddhist precepts and perverted the core values of Khmer society. Even officers of the Lon Nol army were not being regularly paid. Civilians were resorting to private payments to induce government soldiers to fly over an area under attack and protect them. With the war tearing up the countryside, wave after wave of inhabitants abandoned their towns and hamlets to congregate in the nation's capital. This blissful place, abounding with food and with no more than 600,000 residents before the war, had swollen, by late 1974, to two million—more than a quarter of the whole population.[12] Sick and wounded broke out like boils in downtown streets.

By that time, Mohm's father had not been home from the front for months. The tension kicked up a heart condition in her mother. And although Mohm had started school that September, schools were discontinued a few weeks later. Travel was too dangerous. Food became scarce. Highway travel was banned. There were no more trips to the family house in the country. And finally, as moving across the city became too hazardous, there were no more visits to Grandmother either. The scream of the government's antiquated planes was answered almost daily with artillery fire from Khmer Rouge units just across the river. Shells landed in the streets and fires leapt wantonly. On April 1, the last town held by government forces fell, and the same day Lon Nol fled the country. Grown-ups talked in whispers while children like Mohm pretended to be asleep, knowing not what, but that something, was very wrong.

*

Phnom Penh, the Nixon administration concluded in March 1975, was undefendable. Believed to the end by city dwellers to be miracle workers, American Embassy personnel disappeared by April 12. The only international relief had been the American airlift of rice and ammunition, and now that dried up as well. A hush of waiting settled on the capital, waiting for destruction by the mystery guerrillas—or for deliverance. So mysterious were the Khmer Rouge that none knew for certain what to expect.

The end came the day after Khmer New Year, on April 17, 1975. An army of bewildered-looking country boys, most barely eligible for beards but laden with sophisticated Chinese weapons, moved through Phnom Penh. Trained to despise the "parasites of the city," most had never actually seen a city before, nor cars, nor motorcycles, cameras or watches. Ironically, a government photograph shows children and adults alike in front of the Honda sign on a main street of Phnom Penh, waving white flags and applauding the young troops.[13] "People were so tired of the inflation, corruption, and rockets," explained Chan Dara Lot, a survivor, "they just wanted peace, so many of them welcomed the Khmer Rouge."[14] Relief and jubilation quickly turned to dread.

By the time Mohm's father returned home, the center of town was virtually deserted. Tuol Kauk evacuated on the eighteenth. Soldiers with loudspeakers warned the people to leave immediately. They were told to take nothing with them because they would return in a few days; the ruse was that the Americans were going to bomb Phnom Penh. The city was emptied within forty-eight hours.

Scattered in every direction on brutal marches, two million people were driven into the war-wrecked countryside and wilderness. Twenty thousand of these city people perished along the roads over the next month or so.[15] Mohm's family was pushed toward the southwest and probably settled initially in a new zone in Kompote Province. That region had been the center of communist activity during the 1960s and early 1970s and would become the breeding ground of the most brutal Khmer Rouge leaders.

*

All across the country the uprooted population was divided into two groups. The "New People"—those educated and urban Cambodians who were teachers, students, merchants, or members of the civil and military service—would now labor in the rice paddies. The "Old People" or "base people"—mostly illiterate peasants who had acquiesced to the Khmer Rouge drive through the countryside before 1975—were elevated to be unarmed overseers of the work groups and enforcers of arbitrary orders.

The entire society was turned upside down and literally brought under the yoke of Pol Pot's Khmer Rouge. Money was abolished, private property repudiated, schools shuttered, and Buddhist temples smashed. Every aspect of life was controlled by *Angka*, Khmer for "organization," which became the new deity, an anonymous and invisible Big Brother supposedly the incarnation of the people's will. Parents were stripped of authority and children venerated as the unspoiled vessels of *Angka*.

Overnight, Mohm's family tried to shed its identity and fade into the obscurity of the street.

Cambodia . . . Sometime Between 1975 and 1976

I do not know where I am, what province, what direction, what it is called. They change all the names, put up different signs on the roads. It is a new world. Everything I see is for the first time.

They move my grandmother away. I stay on in the hut with my bigger brother. Try to take care of my little sister and my little brother, they so small. But I'm not good like my mother, just a child myself. I think our mother and father coming back for us any day.

This the first time I live away from my family. I try to remember again why they take my mother. She not a soldier.

My father tell me before they take him away, never tease or hit the Pol Pot children; they'll report us to their parents. I think he knows at some point they're going to finish him off. I think what he worry the most was, I have a tiny sister and I'm not really grown up myself yet. And of course me and my older brother, you know how children are, we fight a lot.

Then everything become harder and harder. They take away our pots and plates. You cannot have private things, private feelings, anything private. You cannot cook with your family either. Have to go for food to a big eating place. You supposed to give all your clothes and gold and ring and watch and everything to them. Everybody supposed to have just the same. Men, women, children, everyone gets one black shirt and one black trousers. That's all. Your house is not yours anymore. Later on, even your son is not yours anymore. Like we would say he is the son of God, they say he is the son of *Angka*.

Now Pol Pot have a new idea—no time to waste, all children must work too. We march to work two by two, no smiling, no talking, like a

line of black beetles follow dumb along the jungle floor. They make us
chant a song: *To eat, must work.*

After they do all these things, then they begin to kill.

*

I remember how mad my father get before when I don't eat the soup
they give us. Agghh, it make me sick to my stomach just to smell it.
Doesn't taste so bad. But it hangs on you, that smell. I'm the same as I
always was, spoiled about food. I can't eat.

*

In the beginning they let some New People work for Pol Pot. Not
leaders, just do little jobs. They are pretty easy on us at first. If someone
stays away from work sick, they maybe can still come to have a meal.
Some people sneak away to hunt or fish for extra food, bring back to
share with the group. Some people use their gold to make a little trade.
These are the important things now.

The woman who work with my mother, the one who tell me the
story about why they take my mother away, she is one of these New
People. I don't know her real name. Her face so sweet and kind when
she comes inside to see us. She brings us something shiny to eat. Bite it.
Hard to chew.

"Leeches," my brother says.

Oh, no! I throw up everything. He knows I hate worms and snakes
and anything crawly under the ground, so why doesn't he tell me?

The woman who work with my mother before, she sees me that
night in the eating place. Not eating. Laughing and crying at the same
time. Her face suddenly change. She looks around to see who's watching. She comes over to my table and points at me.

"Must not cry for your mother! She is not loyal to *Angka*. She's a
criminal. Must be punished. You cannot have any feeling for her."

"You're right." I have to pretend to accept what she says.

I put my head down on the table. Don't want her to see. A string of
green comes out of my mouth. Nothing in my stomach but still I vomit
up.

*

I don't cry very often after that. Sometimes, though, when I bend over in the fields, water drops down from my eyes. Keeps dropping, won't stop, like a spring coming out between rocks.

I try to remember why I laugh so much the day they take my mother away. Did Pol Pot take my mind?

*

Few more days, the woman who work with my mother before, they take her away too. Why? Nobody can have one fake face and one real face, I guess. Imagine if you were her, you know deep down that *Angka* is wrong, killing innocent people without feeling. Are you the same evil thing? At some point she must slip. You can get killed like that.

Our village have hardly any families left. They start with about a hundred families; so many killed, maybe only six families left. So they have to put our village together with another new village. It's a mix-up time, until they tell you what to do for work with your group. So I just run away. My brothers and sister and I run to another village, not too close and not too far. You don't really count, all the little children like us. If they let you live, you can go to stay anywhere.

The committee here says yes, we can stay. My work group takes care of a vegetable garden. So pretty here. Water vegetables grow wild and bloom bright yellow and blue. I like to fall asleep under a big banyan tree. Wake up early. So quiet. No soldiers. Wind blowing on the vege-table blooms, they sway like the temple dancers in my past life, I forget where I am . . . the ground is dancing like a big flowered sarong.

"Wait a minute," my bigger brother say one day. "Isn't this the village where they move our grandmother?"

We run to our grandmother's hut. She look normal, healthy, plump not skin; she so glad to see us. I love to spend time with her, maybe even more than my mother; I love to listen to her tell ghost stories and legends. She the greatest grandmother you could have. We sit together. She still have five children live with her. I tell her all about what happened to my parents.

We talk about an hour but we haven't finished it yet and a young man come in to call my grandmother. He say the leader of the town need to see her. So my grandmother leave. I'm not really paying attention. Wait inside the house. Don't go out. I don't want to show anybody that I'm her family.

Half an hour goes by. She doesn't come back. Time I have to go to work again in the vegetables garden with all the children same as I am.

Why they say the leader need to see my grandmother?

The water vegetables come up high. There are bushes around the garden and a road just outside the bushes. Very sudden the Pol Pot girl leader shouts, "Nobody look! Lie down!"

Lie down, but I put my head up. I see about twenty people in a line with hands tie back behind them. I see my grandmother in that line. Five soldiers pointing their guns. Nobody talking, nobody smiling. People tie to people like cows. Two soldiers in front of the line lead them down that road to the forest.

My heart beating really fast. I don't believe it. I think, if I don't go to her, maybe she will not get killed. My mother is her daughter; nobody know that before I go to see her. I just can't believe that all this is happen. I stand halfway up and look.

My grandmother, a minute ago she was with me!

Tell myself don't look, bend down, don't cry. Don't let the other children know it's part of my family.

I know right away they going to kill her.

*

They put us in a house with eleven other children. All of them have their parents taken away by Pol Pot. It's one room divided, pretend divided, just a straw mat for a place to sleep. My older brother still live with me, and my little sister and little brother.

Nobody say, "Where's my mother?" No one ask, "Is my father coming back?" Nobody ever talk about their parents.

Children like us have to get up earlier and go far away to work. Even little children like me, take them seven or eight years old. Not allowed to speak. Not allowed to sing.

We have so little food. They don't give it. Just throw it away or keep for themselves or send to China. But they won't give to the people. All food must be shared, cannot hunt or fish for yourself or even catch a crab.

I think about my father, why he doesn't tell us all that's going to happen?

I am trying to think why they take my grandmother. It wasn't me. They must already know before that. Maybe they just look at her skin, light, not black; they know the way you talk, they can tell. It wasn't me. Was it?

*

The house is hard mud, like rock; I don't know, maybe a farmer use it to store rice in old times. A road lead to it through trees. No one go on that road now, only the children with nobody to take care.

I find a papaya tree beside that empty road—two, no three, no five papaya tree! I scramble up and pull off a fruit—bright green spotted yellow, peel off the skin, feel that sweet orange fruit filling up my mouth, oh, it taste good. Peel off another. It crunches when I bite. Not ripe. I run to another tree, try another one. If they catch me, I be punished for selfish. Rule says cannot pick fruit, cannot pick anything even it grow wild, not for your own self. Only can pick if share with everybody else. I feel a little scared, eat quickly, start to run back to the house. Before I can stop it, all that fruit come up.

A pool of orange lay in the sun. All the sweetness gone out of me.

After that, I wait and watch those trees. Every day the fruit turns yellower, a little reddish, pretty soon so bright and shiny I think I can smell it. Then I sneak out after work and pick a ripe one.

"You take for yourself, you bad!"

Pol Pot girl catch me.

*

My little sister is sick. She not hungry but she is very skin. Some kind of food she eat, it makes her go to the bathroom all the time. It's awful.

Bump of soil all around the fields really good place to catch crab. Stick my hand under the water, feel a pinch, I get it! Another one, another one. I'm good at catch crabs. Have to get them for my sister. But have to watch out nobody see, that's a punishment.

My father's lighter, I still have it. It has a battery in it. So I can make a little secret fire in the hut. Still allow to keep one pot to boil the water to drink. I cook those crab for my sister. But she cannot eat.

My little brother get sick after my sister a couple of weeks. All four of us children cannot stay home from work. Children must not be sick. This is the rule. I have to walk an hour and a half to work with my group. So late it dark when we finish, can't see my sister and brother until we sleep.

Sometimes, when I dig the crab, I feel it must be a snake run over my feet. One time I know it, oh, I almost faint away! Reach down and pull it out, I throw it far as I can away, black snake. Uggh!

My sister's body look like an old dry chicken, the skin hangs off, all wrinkly. My little brother swell up so much he can't walk. The sadness it give me to look at them, there is nothing to compare with it.

They cut the food for my sister and brother because they can't work. "Keep moving all the time"—that is the rule. They say all the sick people are lazy and pretending to be sick. Whoever stop, must be destroy.

Meals always rice soup. Three ways. More rice than water—for strong ones. More water than rice—for weak ones. For sick ones, maybe one spoon of rice in water. Or nothing.

I take out the rice and try to push it into my sister's mouth. She make a sound so dry, like palm leaves rattle. The rice come back out. My brother is numb and swollen. His face only bone, sunk in like a monkey. Maybe no use.

One time I run to the village where my aunt stay. Back in Phnom Penh she have a fine house and a car and her husband is a teacher, high up. I ask her for some vitamins for my sister and brother, they so sick. She say she doesn't have it. She look at me like she hardly know me, the wife of my mother's brother. I can't believe it.

My little brother get worse and worse. So my older brother stay home to take care of them. I have to work more or no food for us.

Now I have to go away on a children's work team to harvest rice. Two or three villages away, in a cart. There's a river. A lot of children try to run away because they miss their parents. Some children jump in the river, try to swim across to shore. I don't know how to swim, I have to go the land way to see my brother and sister.

Then my big brother decide he going to take them to the hospital. I tell him, "Why? You know how Pol Pot people got to be a doctor? They don't even know how to read. They never go to real school. The medicine they have is nothing. Pol Pot hospital is a killing place."

He doesn't listen to me. My older brother never listen me, I just a littl girl. He go to the hospital with them. He doesn't have to go.

*

I like to get up early in harvest time. Hear the palm tree rattle, bird-song everywhere, smell the toasty brown fields. I have a little pocket I sew inside my pants. To hide the crabs I catch in the night field. No one know.

All day throw rice in the wind, comb it out, work is hard. Have to wait for dark and catch the crab and hide them. Start running.

Nobody put an eye on me. I walk and run, almost all the way back to my old village, almost. Suddenly—Oooww!—something pull up my head by the hair.

"Stop! Where you think you going!"

He's a Pol Pot guard. Truth come spilling out. I don't know how to make up stories then.

"I catch many girls like you," he say. "I hear that kind of story a lot. And I don't believe it."

I can't speak. Scared, shaking. Still shy then. Just smile. Just pray he have a nice warm heart.

"Are you sure you're not taking a letter to somebody?" he say.

"I tell the truth," I say.

He laugh at me. He has big teeth, stick out like a bird beak. "You think you're a god or something? You can make your brother and sister well?"

"No, just a little child," I say.

"Children cannot be sick. Cannot complain. Complain, they asking for punishment."

I put my hand in that bag of crabs under my sarong to keep them still. They pinch. Cannot show it. "I promise not to run away ever again. Please, let me go."

"Go," he say at last. "But don't say anybody caught you. And don't say you ran from that direction."

"Oh, thank you, *bou,* you are the best leader."

I run away quick. I have only the night and so far to walk, maybe ten kilometers. I walk as fast as if I fly and my soul float ahead to my sister and brother. The crabs I have get heavy, so many of them. Must be hundreds of them. All the food my sister and brother need to get well. I feel that big bag of crabs go bump bump against my leg, I am happy! Face so hot. Keep running.

But here's what happen when I get there. Where are all the crabs? I think I have hundreds, have only three! Scratch and scratch in that bag. Tear it to pieces. Tears boil up inside me. Three little crabs, that's all. All three of them dead.

I can't look at my little sister and brother. Lie in their own water. I have nothing to give them.

*

The children I live with, they know. Some of them younger than me work in the village, they know before I do. They run up to me in the eating place, excited, like little children act with any news.

"Your sister die! In the hospital. Your brother die a few hours later!"

I don't believe it. Pretend I don't hear. I do hear but I don't want to hear more—what, when, anything. I sort of have no feeling.

I don't want to ask them, how bad is it when you're dead?

Start walking.

Maybe they not all the way dead yet. What to take? More crabs? Yes, crabs, and flowers to please the spirit. In my imagine I see the funeral procession, the long white car moving slowly through Phnom Penh, two young women behind it throwing white popcorn and rice into the road to scatter the bad spirits away. Car belong to a different world now.

I run and run until I meet my older brother and my grandfather. Their faces all shadow. My grandfather cannot speak.

"Where are our sister and brother!"

"We have to take them before the hospital throw them away," my brother say finally. "Cannot bury. Cannot make a spirit house for the ashes. No religion allowed."

"But where are our sister and brother!" I think I'm screaming now.

"We dig a hole."

I cannot speak. I cannot cry. Because if I speak what I think, Pol Pot kill me. If I cry, Pol Pot step on my face. So I take the few crabs out of the bag and fill my own mouth with them, suck the life out of them, like sucking out the little bits of meat left in the sockets of my brother and sister, they die on me, they don't wait.

I don't even want to see the place where they dig the hole. Can't tell which hole is my sister or brother anyway. Lots of funny bumps in the ground with wet soil on top. I can't believe my brother throw the last of our family away like dead fish. Why doesn't he wait for me!

*

My grandpa, I try to spend time with him when I'm not working. But he have no more spirit to live. Hard for him to stand on, look, and he cannot stop any of it—he a grandfather but he has no more authority. Now his wife, his son, his nephew, so many grandson and granddaughter, all his family die without reason. He cannot talk, cannot help, cannot keep anybody with him. The least of his dreams dry up inside. Later he give up his blood, he die too.

My mother gone, my father gone, my sister, my brother, my grandma, my grandpa . . . so that's the end of my dream of family.

I know it from the day they take my grandma. I have to survive myself. No help from anyone. I think there's no way I can survive long. I don't know much, I'm young.

You can't even cry. Can't cry when you see it every day. So much things worse than cry.

The Prince of Darkness—
Pol Pot

A Yugoslavian news team reported in 1978 seeing not a single poster or image of Cambodia's new leaders—"the phantoms," as they were called. The Yugoslavs filmed perhaps the only TV interview with the man whose nom de guerre, Pol Pot, would become synonymous with a reign of terror and stalking death.[1] A short round man with a brush cut, he smiled incessantly as he spoke in the film, an immense, gummy smile:

> I come from a peasant family, like my parents. According to custom, I lived for six years in a pagoda. For two years I was a monk. I couldn't enter college immediately as I had failed my exam. I later graduated from technical school. I was given a scholarship to study in France. I was a first-year graduate student, but later I spent much time in the student movement; they took the scholarship away.

In fact, the man later known as Pol Pot was born Saloth Sar to a family of well-to-do landowners who employed forty laborers and who had earlier had relatives in the royal court. In France he attended the undistinguished École du Livre, a school for typesetters and printers; later he halfheartedly studied radio engineering. In Cambodia, a country of diploma snobbery, Pol Pot was a dropout. He left France with no diploma but in love with Marx and politics.[2]

Ieng Sary, also from a family of well-off landowners, did not get beyond his second baccalaureate exam in Paris. Khieu Samphan was the only one of the leaders-to-be who could qualify as an "intellectual"; he had written a doctoral dissertation, although his grades were only average.[3]

It was these three and the wives of Pol Pot and Ieng Sary, politically rivalrous sisters, together with four other men who had failed even their entrance exams, who formed the leadership of the Khmer Rouge.[4] Dubious scholars all, this group of left-wing Khmer students in Paris in the early 1950s took literally the French Marxist canon "The bourgeoisie must be eliminated." Prince Sihanouk, who later became allied with and exploited by them, described their intentions: "We want to have our name in history as the ones who can reach total communism with one leap forward. So we have to be more extremist than Madame Mao. . . . We want to be known as the only communist party to communize a country without a step-by-step policy, without going through socialism."[5] The logic, Sihanouk advised, was to be found in the library of the Sorbonne, in Khieu Samphan's doctoral dissertation.

The method they chose was genocide. The means they employed were mass killings, forced starvation, and untreated disease. Neither pragmatism nor humanity ever tempered that plan. Cambodia had the misfortune to become the first human experiment in instant communism.

It was a program that had less to do with ideology than with the lust for power of C-minus students who had mixed together the slogans of café communism with mail-order Maoism—understanding nothing and having experience with nothing. Nor could the genocide be marked down to a single deranged leader. It was not madness but logic, albeit a logic of simple minds and megalomaniacal proportions, that destroyed Cambodia.

*

But how, if the Khmer Rouge numbered only a few thousand in 1970, did their strength grow to between 100,000 and 180,000 by 1975, enough to subdue a country of 7 to 8 million? Pol Pot began by ingratiating his movement with the Other Cambodia—but, as noted, that was not a countryside of miserable, dirt-poor peasants ripe for the communist message.

To be sure, the vast majority of the Khmer had remained rural and "outside history,"[6] operating small and medium-sized family farms. And not all of them did that well.[7] The image of Cambodia as a gentle Buddhist paradise of smiling, rice-growing peasants was appropriate only for that broad central region of the country blessed by annual innundations of six months of rain and overflow from the great Mekong. Many Khmer in the outlying provinces of the east and southwest worked the poorest soil in Southeast Asia.[8] There was no discernible difference between the rural technology of the 1970s, with its hoes and sickles, ox carts and water buffalo, and scenes carved on the twelfth-century bas reliefs of Angkor.[9] The peasants had no access to modern medicine or to schooling beyond the rudiments. Often, they didn't have even a temple or monks; hence their religion was reduced to animism and superstition.[10] Yet still they were not ripe for communism.

Private ownership of land was widespread among the peasants of Cambodia, and it had been so since the nineteenth century. Moreover, even where conditions were bad, the peasants did not live in abject poverty.[11] Most important, Cambodia had never even come close to having an indigenous peasant uprising, and individualism was relatively strong. Although the individual was part of an extended family and a village, those organizations were weak (in comparison to those of China, Vietnam, or India) and exercised little discipline. Once a rural inhabitant had paid his taxes to the state, he was under little constraint.[12]

Apolitical and hostile to strangers, many peasants were suspicious even of people from villages more than five kilometers away.[13] And for the older generation, "I am a peasant and I am always going to be a peasant" was the dominant mode of thought. It was almost unimaginable to think of changing one's status in *this* life. To Buddhists, one's lot in life had been determined by the merits, or debits, one had stored up in a previous life. The peasant of the older generation hoped only for a peaceful repetition of nature's cycles. He wanted nothing more than to be left alone.

When Pol Pot, Khieu Samphan and Ieng Sary returned from Paris to Cambodia, they activated the small cadres* of revolutionaries who had been hiding out in the jungles. Through the sixties they also recruited from the margins of society: the social outcasts, the most remote hill tribes, and the youngest and poorest peasant boys whose greatest status symbol was the gold in their front teeth. Offering these ten- to thirteen-year-olds the far more potent status of belonging to a secret army, the Khmer Rouge remade their recruits into toughs, unencumbered by any emotion save total devotion to their faceless, suppos-

---

* A cadre is a group or organization that assumes leadership and indoctrinates others.

edly supernaturally powerful commanders. No study of Mao's thought and no awareness of the Cultural Revolution sweeping China were provided their students by Saloth Sar and his colleagues. As one student in the jungle reported, "We listened to Radio Beijing and picked up slogans from China, such as 'Paper Tiger.' . . ."[14] Recruits were promised that at the end of the revolution they could have their pick of the prettiest girls and return to their peaceful villages.

Pol Pot later admitted that he was proud of using these "national minorities" as his "backing base."[15] When government soldiers later found themselves fighting their wild and belligerent brothers of Khmer blood, the taste for battle dissipated. Often their government didn't pay them anyway.

In the outlying provinces, the Khmer Rouge organized small groups of volunteer work teams, very roughly equivalent to our VISTA. The recruits followed orders to ingratiate themselves with the villagers by helping them raise a dam or build a dike or harvest rice. Their leaders imposed no political message at first, and they were fiercely puritanical: "Making free" with peasant girls was severely punished.[16] As people began to feel friendly toward the leaders of these work teams, the political lectures commenced.

The lectures elicited anger from people against their own countrymen by comparing the lives of peasants with those of the "exploiting classes" of the cities. "Even students are exploiting you" the line went. "They just sit in a room with books having an easy life, while you work all day so hard under the sun."[17] Another target for whipping up anger was the evil foreign power, the United States.

Anger was an emotion that Cambodians, as Buddhists, were trained from birth not to express and so had little experience in controlling. Buddhism and aggression of any sort are entirely incompatible. But every human being can be convinced that someone is out to hurt him —and once that cultural interpretation is accepted, people can become good and angry. The Khmer Rouge channeled that anger into socially sanctioned violence.

Suddenly, sometime in 1972, the helpful, dedicated young group leaders began to crack down on the rural population. They arrested local village chiefs and set fire to their houses and let it be known that there was to be no further question about who was in control. Many peasants turned against the Khmer Rouge and some escaped to Thailand, but for most it was too late.

Purges of Pol Pot leadership groups began in 1973 and continued throughout the Khmer Rouge regime in repetitive waves. No sooner did clandestine training programs produce new and tougher cadres than the leaders of old groups were replaced and usually executed.[18] That is why the Khmer Rouge, on takeover, was headed by such young and malevolent leaders. Their commanders fueled and justified their malice by reminding them of the hard times they had endured living so long in the jungle or mountains. American bombing was blamed for killing their families and destroying their rice fields. "The peasants under Pol Pot could not attack the Americans, so they turned their hatred on the Khmer people who supported the Americans," one survivor explained.[19]

Hanoi hailed the Khmer Rouge takeover and its "radiant prospects of . . . advance for the Khmer people," for which a government newspaper editorial took considerable credit, lauding "the fraternal solidarity in combat that unites the Khmer, Lao and Vietnamese peoples."[20] But virtually from the moment the Pol Pot group seized control of Cambodia, that expedient solidarity knit between brothers in the great anticolonialist struggle began to unravel. Hanoi claims that the Khmer Rouge mounted attacks across the border in Vietnam in the first month after their takeover of Cambodia. And Cambodian communist leaders were quoted as announcing, "We have to fight Vietnam because there are eighteen of our provinces there, including Prey Nokor [Saigon]" and "We are going to liberate Vietnamese territory because it is all our territory."[21] Pol Pot, Ieng Sary, and Khieu Samphan became increasingly hostile to the Vietnamese communist movement, and from 1975 to 1979, those among their lieutenants suspected of being the slightest bit sympathetic toward the Vietnamese were mercilessly eliminated.

The Pol Pot group had brought Sihanouk back to Cambodia in April 1973, just long enough to be photographed for international distribution beaming and hugging Khmer Rouge leaders.[22] A few months later, Sihanouk correctly predicted that the Khmer Rouge would suck him dry and then "spit me out like a cherrystone."[23] Once the Khmer Rouge were victorious, Sihanouk and his wife were placed under house arrest and several of his relatives were killed. He was said to be dejected over having been denied "the position he deserved."[24]

So it was that eight men ran the country after 1975 in a remarkably decentralized manner—probably one of the secrets to destabilizing the population. Cambodia was divided into eight zones, which bore no relationship to her former provinces: A zone commander was assigned to each, supported by regional commanders and so on, down to leader of the "solidarity group"—several villages, something over a thousand people, combined for purposes of work production. Within each solidarity group there was an "action leader" who organized the work force, a "political leader" charged with "keeping everyone happy," an "economics leader" for supplies, etc.[25] These local leaders, chosen from among the Old People, enjoyed few discernible special privileges and worked along with the New People. The shrewdest and most loyal were chosen to be *kawng chhlop* or spies; young girls turned out to be the most effective. The Khmer Rouge soldiers and security forces themselves were not seen at the work sites and were never identified by personal names.[26]

Psychological weaponry was exceptionally potent. "Property sacrifice" meant one gave up all of one's belongings, including mental property. Holding on to the memory of loved ones eliminated as "enemies," or to any former emotional possessions for that matter, was construed as a dangerous disease, called, in effect, "memory sickness."

Women's hair was cut severely: all wore the red-checkered *krama* around their neck or head. Fierce egalitarianism dictated no distinction in dress for men, women, or children. People were required to work at least nine hours a day, every day. The three rest days in a month were set aside for large political meetings. Smaller group meetings were also compulsory several nights a week. The content was slogans and personal criticism; there was almost no political education or explanation of the regime's purposes.

One of the few clear statements of economic policy by the Pol Pot regime appeared in 1976, in a state magazine:[27]

> City people do not know what farming is, do not know what a cow is, do not know what harvesting is. Now they know and understand, they are no longer scared of cows and buffaloes. Our lesson's subject is real work. . . . When we have the food, we will expand simultaneously into the learning of reading, writing, and arithmetic.

The goal of the regime was to set up self-reliant worker groups of about a thousand people, each group producing a different crop or commodity. Over the next five years the plan projected that the groups would barter. But Khmer Rouge policies never resulted in enough food to barter, and they never did begin the teaching of reading and writing.

Irrigation works took precedence over everything. In the Western Zone, there might be twenty thousand young people working on a dam; ten thousand more brought in mobile brigades to dig a canal through virgin forest. Few workers had enough rice to stay alive. Why this obsession with irrigation?

The Khmer Rouge leaders wanted to prove they were heirs to the great god-kings of Angkor, whose kingdom flourished from the seventh century until the fifteenth century when, in its fullest efflorescence, the inhabitants abandoned its capital and their brilliant culture was swallowed by the jungle without a trace. As spectacular as were its kingdom's cities of stone and vast sculpted walls, the real triumph of the civilization had been its water works.

The larger and better regulated the irrigation system in a rice-growing country, the more people can be supported. During the thirteenth-century reign of Jayavaraman VII, over a million people were attached to his court; his territory may have encompassed as many as thirty million people.[28] A vast network of concentric irrigation terraces surrounded the main temple complex. Immense reservoirs constructed in the interior allowed the king and his predecessors to build magnificent roads and rest houses and hospitals for passing caravans. The massive national irrigation system was the source of the civilization's remarkable prosperity and the rulers' control.[29]

Pol Pot himself often spoke of building a new era "more glorious than Angkor."[30] He described his victory over Lon Nol in supernatural terms, as "a great success unknown before in the whole world,"[31] and often referred to his goal of recovering Cambodia's "lost territories."[32] By casting himself as the rightful descendant of Cambodia's fabulous kings, Pol Pot was building a case for his own *barami*—greater merit owing to past lives of royal work or privilege.

How cruel the irony. Indeed, the grand irrigation system created by the Angkorean god-kings had become so large and elaborate that by the fourteenth century, the labor force could no longer maintain it. Sapped by the effort, the king's men were not well trained as soldiers and were weakened by a series of wars. If Pol Pot's clique had read to the end of their textbooks, they would have learned that Jayavaraman's reign was the last burst of glory. "The demands of the water system proved to be a major factor contributing to the downfall of the Khmer state."[33] In the superficial scholarship of the Khmer Rouge lay the second destruction of Cambodia.

*

The captive population was kept in ignorance about policy, including the policy on executions. General orders were issued by the leaders in Phnom Penh to eliminate former government officers and bureaucrats and the "bourgeosie enemies." It was left to local party committees to finger the specific individuals. People simply disappeared. There was no arrest, no notice; the disappearances usually occurred at night.

Relatives were afraid to ask what had happened, knowing the local cadre would consider it a criticism. If group leaders were asked, they mostly lied. "Oh, your father was sent away to another group to work." In one zone, the euphemism for people who were taken to be killed was "They sent him to cut the bamboo." Rumors would circulate, whispers about a killing overheard during the night, but because people also were moved summarily to another work site as normal practice, no one knew for sure what a family member's disappearance meant. The constant uncertainty was an effective means of spreading psychological destabilization.

The whole purpose behind smashing family ties and scattering family members all over the country was to decimate the very old extended-family tradition. When it became apparent to the leaders that one of the most important weapons of resistance was love, the Khmer Rouge stepped up punishments for its expression.[34] Children were forced to watch discovered lovers beaten, mothers to watch babies tortured. Showing any sympathy for victims was punished; a person could be killed for shedding a tear.

The reality for middle- and upper-class adults was unrelentingly grim. A survivor named Wind Song, formerly a product representative for a U.S. tractor firm, described the dilemma facing parents:

To please the communists, so that they wouldn't send your children too far away, so that children might come to visit the parents once in a while, some parents secretly offered their gold or diamonds, whatever they buried in the ground to keep. Even some pretty mothers offered their bodies for the leader. If they were caught, the chief and the mother were both destroyed.

A person who broke—who even so much as wept or screamed when a loved one was killed—was as good as dead himself. Jintana Lee, then the thirteen-year-old daughter of a major general in the Lon Nol army, saw the Khmer Rouge leader who led her father to his death. Months later, when her brother was taken away, Jintana put on an impassive face. But she could not persuade her adult sister to suspend reality long enough to save herself:

> My sister run to tell me, "They just kill our brother! They kill our parents. Why don't they kill me!" I try to tell her, "Quiet. Pretend." But she keep screaming until the KR come. That's it. She die.

Later, Jintana's father's killer presented himself to her, face to face, testing her, tormenting her: "What do you say about it?" he demanded. Nothing, she had nothing to say. Jintana looked blankly at the man and walked away.[35]

Not surprisingly, the combination of forced apathy, exhausting work, and a near-starvation diet was effective in sapping people's will. Indeed, so crushing was the psychological pressure that some people began to believe in *Angka*. It was as complete as the ontological argument for the existence of God, or the devotion to past kings—there was no discussion; one could only immerse oneself within it.

The Khmer Rouge sanctioned killing one's countrymen and identified the targets with slogans that had to be memorized, like prayers:

> "Intellectuals are evil."
> *"Bonzes* are bloodsuckers."
> "Whatever is impure must be cut out."

The lust for blood was excited with songs whose lyrics were sometimes almost orgiastic, like "The Red Flag":[36]

> Glittering red blood blankets the earth—
> blood given up to liberate the people:
> blood of workers, peasants and intellectuals;
> blood of young men, Buddhist monks and girls.
> The blood swirls away, and flows upward,
> gently, into the sky, turning into a
> red, revolutionary flag.

Along with the blood-soaked flag, *Angka* offered a substitute for the family:[37]

> O solidarity group, you are a new kind of family,
> special, beautiful and unique.

Everywhere there were the "killing grounds." A survivor, Arn Chorn, described one next to a former Buddhist temple in Battambang that had been turned into a shelter for orphans.

> Every day they take people to the square at five-thirty and tell them to dig their graves. At six o'clock, they killed them.
> Most of the time by the ax, hitting on the back of the head. It sounds like banging a coconut, but harder. Sometimes they hit a person once, they not die. Okay, they bury them anyway. Children, too. Bloody everywhere. Fifteen thousand people they say they kill in that place. The children, they live in fear all day, all night. Screaming in the darkness from nightmare. No sleep, even though they work very hard, carrying soil and rocks. . . .
> The Khmer Rouge in my district play games. Two of them toss a baby back and forth until they drop it. A lot of time, they make the children watch the killing. You could not speak, not cry out. Just watch. The killing was right in front of me. My eyes saw, but my mind somewhere else. I didn't feel anything. Everybody else was probably the same. My mind just worried about food. Sometimes I think, "If you give me one big bowl of rice, then you can kill me."

Mohm was resettled many times between 1975 and early 1979, but probably only within the provinces of Kompote and Takeo. They happened to be in the Southwest Zone, which spawned the severest branch of Pol Pot's leadership—the Nearat Dai. Much of the work of the Nearat Dai was to kill off the bourgeosie. Survivors from the central provinces of the country report that the Khmer Rouge leaders in their region pursued a less drastic policy for remaking the society than the Nearat Dai in Mohm's zone. They, too, killed anyone who had served the Lon Nol government, but usually they refrained from executing the wives and children of the accused.

The Nearat Dai became the select. In nine separate purges over the course of the regime, the commander of a region and his lieutenants would be called to Phnom Penh and a whole new hierarchy, recruited from the Nearat Dai, would be sent to the region.

When it became evident that the Khmer Rouge regime was brutalizing most of the people, why didn't the people resist? One survivor, at the time in his twenties, offers an explanation of sorts:[38]

People were terrified and soon became too weak to attack. They knew they were going to be killed, and hoped only to die easily. So we just let them lead us by the nose, day by day, in hope we would die without torture.

Children's Mobile Work Team, 1976–1977

After my sister and brother die, they change my town again. Now the bad times really start.

They send my older brother away to work on a moving team with a group of strong boys. I go to a group of girls. All children have to leave their parents, the ones who still have parents.

No more town, no more store, no more money. They kill a lot of men. I don't know why; they afraid the men going to fight back, I guess.

You go to a special school at the beginning, about two month. Just one room. They don't know how to teach anything well. It's not school really, no teaching letters or numbers, just politic.

They say everybody must work for *Angka. Angka* is same as Pol Pot. They always say *Angka* doesn't like you to speak when you work or when you eat. *Angka* say you're not allowed to have private feelings.

Children belong to *Angka.* That's what they say. *Angka* feed them and *Angka* train them and their parents have no rights. Parents can't teach their children any new thing, can't give them rules, can't punish them, can't do anything with them like normal parents do.

They treat children different than adults. Because children have the new mind. They can train children into their political way.

They put all children the same age together, children from the city and children of the Old People. More of them than us, though. About ten of us in our group, some six year old, some ten. We work together, sleep in the same place made of palm leaves and bamboo.

Children the same age always fight, that's natural. But the Pol Pot children, they really hate the children from Phnom Penh. It seem people from the city much smarter than people from the countryside.

They're really afraid of us. They always think we're older, because we seem to know everything.

I'm seven or eight years old now, something like that, but I'm small. Really really small. Children like us have to do heavy lifting when we're very young and our bones are soft, so we can't grow tall. Carrying heavy loads of soil or rocks make my body very short.

They have a *Me-krum* (leader) to keep us. She is like a teacher but not smart, she never been to school at all. She's about sixteen years old. The *Me-krum* get to be import because they work before for Pol Pot in the countryside. They hate that we talk good language, we can talk much better than they do. They've never been anything. They speak badly. They always mean to you. They tell you what to do and you cannot say a word back. It's like you're people in jail.

Our *Me-krum* take a big diamond away from one of the New People and put it in her gas lamp. She says she likes to look at the sparkle. She doesn't know what she has, that's how dummy she is.

Me-krum have a section leader above her. The big leader only come once a year to see if everybody follow the rule. Maybe the big leader keep his power, but the other leaders they change all the time. Some are really dumb and not so tight, some little bit smart and nasty. *Me-krum* and the other leaders only ones can live with their family. Everybody else they separate. Even families of Old People they separate. Have to live with your work group.

You're not allowed to talk, not allowed to eat, not allowed to sing, not allowed to do anything. They have no rule book or religion book. Just make up whatever rule they feel like saying.

Pol Pot children work the same as us, but they want to be better than us. They threaten the New People children, make fun of us, act obnoxious. They could always act bigger than us because their father is higher up so they are protected. You can't really do anything back to them.

Send us to a wild place. Not a town. Beside the forest. Daytime, we get up at 4:30 and walk to work where other people are, in the rice fields. We have to march two by two, all black like pair of crows, and chant the song they give us.

Nighttime, nobody to take care. We go back alone, to the wild place. It's like going into the jungle, black jungle sun and white bone trees and night birds calling their lonely call. Wild things in that forest, I don't know what, they whine and scream.

Everybody afraid of ghosts. When I have to go out at night, I always walk backwards. I keep looking at the speck of light from the lamp, I look for my mother in the doorway. Walk backwards, fall down, keep looking for my mother—she gets smaller and smaller—as long as I still see her in my mind the ghost can't get me.

When I go to sleep in the forest, it's really scary, the ghosts, the children crying. Some nights I can't sleep. I try to remember about my family. Not all the time, but part of the time. Sometimes I think about it and I go crazy and then I think of nothing.

One night I bring up God. I see God's hand always there to protect children like me. Nobody's going to take me away. God always near me and take care of me. So I listen to the wind and go to sleep in his hand. And the daytime, I start to survive myself again.

Only now begin to think about how to survive from day to day. To prepare for the next day. You hurt, but you cannot cry.

Children in my age group cannot carry a gun, too young. But some places, like maybe where they send my brother—with older boys and girls, eleven, twelve, thirteen, fourteen—those are the best ages for training their minds to believe like Pol Pot, to carry a gun and be soldiers. Some of them learn so well, they turn around and kill their parents. It happen many times, I hear it.

*

The leader in the town where they take my grandmother away, he kill many people. Hundreds, I don't know. All I know, by the end of rainy season about six families left alive, that's all.

He's a short man. Really small. Black skin, very dark, but he has a small delicate face. He act educated, sound like the sweeter man you can imagine. If I come from another country, I won't believe what he is. He says, "I speak the true." Not many can see into his mind, where his truth changes the good to bad, cooperation to slavery. I would believe him too, if I don't look at his eyes.

His eyes are redshot. They jump on you like a monster. His eyes so bloody because he eat the livers from the people he kills. Everybody say that. To make him strong.

I can feel the pain in everyone's eyes. If I could bring back the ones they've lost, I would! Does he care? Can he feel? I always think as a child anybody who can take another human being's life is not human, it must be some kind of creature come from another world. It takes human form, but deep down its heart is still animal.

When I see the leader, I want to say, "Don't put your eye on me! I don't want it! Keep away!"

But a lot of Pol Pot families love him.

He live in a big wooden house. Belong to somebody else. The Old People, they can take the good houses with the pointed roofs from the old time. The leader doesn't even carry a gun. He doesn't have to. People protect him all the time. Nobody is going to do anything to him.

*

Every time I see a baby with its mother in the working field, I think about it. Babies supposed to stay in the child center with the old women; mothers can't feed them in the field. But sometimes, when a baby is sick, the mother puts him in a scarf and hangs it from two sticks, close to her while she works. One Pol Pot guard, just a wild boy, he try to act so big, he brag about it. He say, "It's so easy to kill a baby, just hit it against a tree."

I don't see him do it, but I remember the baby who fall down in the street in Phnom Penh, so soft and tender. Babies don't have a hard head yet like grown-ups, not like a coconut. Baby's head hit the ground like a ripe mango tumble down from the tree, all the sweetness gush out. But I think something must be left. Their eyes are left. Babies' eyes are so bright, like new stars. They could still see. They could roll out of the working field, and up over the sugar palms, and find the way through the forest, and back up past the clouds. They could pin that baby's little soul back in the sky—he never did anything wrong yet. He could be a night star.

Cambodia is so beautiful, when I think of it. Everything natural, fruit fall off the trees into your hand. Leaves so big they look like dinner plates for giants, and the short little people. People sweet, talk softly, smile at everybody. How can they make Cambodia so ugly?

I try to remember the story my grandma tell about the Middle World. She say there's many worlds, above and below us, the highest one is all light and air and peace where you don't want for anything. But it takes many lives to reach there. And sometime you have to go to the Middle World; it's a stinking place in between. People terrible to each other there. Maybe we are born again into the Middle World. It's no time here. All the bloody days the same, the same night, night after night. It's like being born again into a new world. A new and terrible world.

*

Nighttime I play a game with another girl. We try to catch the flies that make light. So many, they're everywhere, like stars just born out. Their tiny white light goes on and off as fast as a blink. But their light doesn't really go off; it's just us, we're human. We're like giants to them. Anyway, we can't see the pure light for long.

I try to catch them and keep their light in a jar. I run and jump up, this way and that, fast as I can close my hand! I catch them, hundred of them, but I can't keep the light. Why not? Every night I try. Next morning, only dead flies in the jar. Human hand is too rough, I guess.

Then I think, oh, no, those tiny lights might be the dead babies' eyes. They're just flying over. They're not strong enough yet to make a full light. But if they lucky, if nobody try to catch them, maybe one or two can make it to be stars.

I'm never going to catch the flies that make light again.

*

A worker for the kitchen lady shows me how to climb up the sugar palms. To get the sugar. It feels good to learn something new. A million palm trees in Cambodia, tall and skin, I love how their floppy leaves make a giant bird high in the sky. The sweet juice drips right out like water. The man say if I help him do this, I can scrape the sides of the pot when they cook it to sugar.

I try to carry the sugar container; it's so heavy. Can't hold in my teeth. Have to hold in one arm. I come down the rope backward way. Start falling. Falling. Okay, but don't spill the sugar! Hang on tight, when I hit the ground. Everything spin around, I'm so dizzy. But when I can see again, the cooking lady tell me I have good luck. Nothing spill. I can come and lick the sugar.

I hope she's not cooking dog. It smell terrible. Old People like to make curry out of dog. Black dogs are the hardest to kill. That's what the cooking lady say.

She tell me she hit a black dog in the head. He fall down. Few minutes later he get up with the blood dripping down his face, go right over and lick her. She hit him again, hit him again, keep doing it over and over. She leave him on the ground, not moving at all; she's sure he must be dead now. She go away to do something else. Then he's gone. But next day he come back, looking for her. Black dogs always come back.

I don't know if true. I think just a black dog story.

Then I remember our family dog, in Phnom Penh. We keep him behind our house but the neighbors complain, he makes too much noise. So we put him in the front behind our big wall. But we forget to close the gate. Somebody come by on a bicycle and throw a rope over his head. Drag our dog away. I see the tracks where he's dragged. Why does anybody drag a dog away? Nobody tell. Then my friend tell me it's the village people come to stay in the city because of the war. They eat black dog. My dog is black. They must really kill him hard because he doesn't come back.

They don't serve that dog curry here in the eating place. Thank God! It's the most disgustingest smell. They only give it to themselves.

*

Once a month, they have a big education meeting. Everybody have to go. You don't have to work that day, so it's good. The other kind of meeting is just for your group. For example, I'm in a children's group. That kind we have a lot.

The *Me-krum* talk first, talk about new work assignments, what you did wrong, who stole something. Then what happen, the *Me-krum* ask if anybody knows about one who did wrong today. They love you to criticize others. That way they get information.

One child tell that he saw another child pick fruit from a tree. "I see Seanna stealing from *Angka.*" *Angka* own the trees, the land. Lot of time the person who criticize make it sound worse. You have no right to defend yourself in the meeting. You can't fight back.

They say, "You're bad, you're the city. City is a black cloud. *Angka* break up that black cloud."

They say, "Your parents are criminals. Have to kill them because they're army."

I don't know how to make up stories yet. I have to accept the criticism. I always accept. You say a wrong word, they hit you. Everybody must accept. Except once I don't.

A girl name Sophal stand up in criticism meeting and accuse me. She say I steal her blouse from her. I decide to take a big chance.

I say back, "*Angka* say you must tell the truth. Is this true?"

"Of course it's true, or I don't say it in the meeting," she say back.

They go into my place and check it out. They find Sophal's blouse. They say, "See, it's true! You must be punish." Sophal sneak me a smile. She's a tricky one.

I have to stand in the sun for thirty minutes on one leg. I just pray they don't put the red ants on me. I see them do it to grown-ups. They stink so bad. Crawl all over the skin and sting until the people start shaking, a fever comes on them. But no ants for me. I just stand. Keep changing my leg. I start to laugh. Later, I tell them that's a fun punishment.

Someday the children in that meeting will lie about you. They will. So many times I tell a secret to one of them, they go around behind my back and use it against me. They always say your secrets out loud in the meeting. They not a good friend at all, not somebody to talk with, share with, no, I been through it so many times.

I live two years with those children, never make a friend.

Children are very clever; they want you to get in trouble so they feel higher than you. In the beginning, everyone take advantage of me. I too shy to say anything back. After a while I get so mad, I learn how to make up things to get them back.

It's like a game. Just have to understand the rules. After they take my parents away I don't care anymore. I make up anything. Then I see this works very well. As soon as they criticize me, I accept it. Then I criticize them back, badder.

For example, the Pol Pot children mess up our house just to be mean. Our leader have a strict rule against that, because it takes time away from work to clean up. I can fake it. Next meeting I stand up.

"Sophal is not giving all her loyalty to *Angka*. She go into our house and mess it all up. Also, I see her picking up yams in the field for herself, she doesn't share with others. She is not the best example to us."

The *Me-krum* speak sharply to Sophal. She say next time she give her a punishment.

After a while, it's fun!

I find out how to scare back Sophal. Before the meeting I get her alone. I tell her she better not criticize me.

"Why not!" she say. She scratch at her face. It's round and blank as a melon, except it has dark spots all over it; she never wash.

"God will see." That's what I say to her.

"What God is?" She sticks out her hip; it's big and bumpy like a tree stump.

"Bigger than *Angka*. God sees everything that you do."

She laugh. "What can some dumb god do?"

"You see. When Pol Pot runs away."

"You don't know nothing."

"I know, I do know."

She doesn't show if she believes me, but I think she's a little scared inside. So next time I scare her more.

"When Pol Pot runs away, God will come in the night and take your head off."

Her watery eyes blink.

"So you better treat me well," I say, and I walk away.

She doesn't say anything about me in the next meeting.

One meeting the leader tells us, "You born out of a grain of rice. City is rotten; money in the city. In the countryside, you can eat rice you grow yourself."

I don't say what is in my heart. *I not born out of a grain of rice. I born out of the Lord Buddha.*

I bathe all the time in the ponds beside the road. My hair is always wet. A Pol Pot girl tell me, "No time to wash!" She asks why I wash my hair so much. "Were you rich before?" They really hate us.

Before dinner, they count your name off. They want others to say how bad or good you are. If someone hate you, she can say a lie about you too. You have to say a nice thing about them, otherwise they count your name off to say you're bad. Bad two times, they send you for a lot of study. Bad three or four times, maybe they kill you. They don't say how they punish if you run away. Nobody try it.

*

Then I learn to make up ghost stories to frighten the Pol Pot children. I tell them about ghosts in the forest. I scare them, I do.

I tell about the Great Naga, king of the snakes. He lives in a huge cave under the ground. The only sound there is snake hiss. The Great Naga has seven heads, each one with tongues that suck out your blood. His body is so long, it takes fifty demons to uncoil it and carry him when he wants to come up from his cave to get you.

The Pol Pot children know what I'm talking about; everybody know about the Naga. He's like a god from the olden time of Cambodia.

I tell them some of the demons have eyes half hang out and all boil white like a dead fish in the sun; some have breath that smell worse than dead crabs rot in the black mud. "Better watch out if the Great Naga hear about you being cruel to children. You open your eye one night and you going to see something strange. Maybe you think it's a big banyan leaf, but it's not. It's the seven heads of the snake king."

Some of them don't really believe my stories but they still a little scared inside, they try not to show it. I just make up that the ghost come in during the night and take one of them back to the forest. They want to hear more about the ghosts. I try to remember all the stories my grandma tell me. My grandma, I think she have second sight.

You see, I tell them, the king that come many years later, he's supposed to be faithful to the Great Naga's daughter. Every night he's supposed to go to the snake princess, and she changes out of seven heads into a beautiful woman. You see, gods can change to be people. Then the king can go to his wives and dancing girls. But if he forgets the snake princess, disaster comes.

One day the king decide to have a ride through the countryside. He make a big ceremony of it. Everybody know when they hear the sound of conch shells and skin drums. They get ready to see all the wonderful silk and jewels and the elephants in gold braid. First come the dancing girls, so many of them, jingle the bracelets on their ankles. Each one wears a gold-pointy helmet and flowers in her hair. They carry tall candles. Then come the young girls, hundreds of them; they carry trays of jewels like big rocks and ropes made of pearl. Next come the lady giants, twice bigger than the men; they carry the king on their shoulders in a gold chair. His soldiers stand up on elephants. All the people bow down when they see this amazing parade. They cannot put an eye on the face of the king, so they lay their face on the ground until he pass.

But he's so enjoy himself, he forget about the snake princess.

She is back in the palace all alone. She's the god; the king is just a man and all his people only human, not supposed to act like gods. The Great Naga hear about it; he's very angry. First he throw out a spell over those people. Then he crawl under the ground to the elephant terrace around the king's palace. He spring up with his seven huge heads and push a mountain over to bury the people.

So if you stand at the edge of the forest, and look into the black and green, you probably can see their ghosts. The king and the lady giants and the weeping dancing girls and the soldiers stand up on their elephants, all in a spell. They ride through the forest every night, look for their dead city. They cry to the god to call them out.

At the end of the story, I say, "If you don't want those ghosts to drag you into the forest tonight, you better not threaten me." Every night I give them these frightening stories.

Sometimes, even I scare myself. Then I cannot sleep at night. I hear the crashing of animals through the bamboo, I think it must be elephants dancing. The tiger smell is on the wind. I think maybe there really are cities lost in that forest, from ancient time, like my grandmother tell me. Giants build those cities, they make sculpture of themselves big as gods, they do anything they want. The gods don't like it, so they put a spell on those giants and bury them under a big mountain. They fall to sleep for hundred of years. Still in there, those giants, waiting to be called out. And that's why there are so many ghosts in the forest. They just wander around, wander around, crying to the gods to let them go on to another life—even as a black dog—so they can learn their lesson and gain merit.

Funny, though. When my grandma tell these stories to me, I keep thinking I see all of it before. I think I see that city carve out of stone, that beautiful calm pond with the water lilies on it; I think I ride on an elephant across the stone way. Somehow, when I hear her tell about the dancing girls, I know it all before she tells.

Maybe I live back then, but I'm called out. I don't know how many others still bury under the mountain, but I think a lot. Maybe a thousand of million, who know? That's why there are so many ghosts in the forest.

Most of time the children believe me. We can even play together, pretend to be the dancing girl or blow the conch. But if they treat the other new children meanly, or make fun of them, two or three of us go to see them and say, "You better stop that or else, you know, the ghosts—"

Sometimes I lose. If I scare them too much, a few of the Pol Pot children get mad and go to the counselor, make up stories about me. Of course, the counselor believes them before me. But I would better die than they look down at me.

*

My work change to feeding the animals. All kinds. Pig the most fun. You cannot catch pig very easily, but pig cannot hurt you at all. That's the good thing about it. Rabbit you feed with grass. But rabbit won't drink the water. I have to put water on a leaf and hold it out to the rabbit, very gently. I like this work.

Only thing is, I smell something terrible. Out by the forest. Where I graze cow. The ground is turn white there, must be somebody dig it. I ask the *Me-krum* what it is. She say, nothing, keep moving, you have no time to smell.

*

In the beginning I just feel left out; I have nobody to talk to, nobody to care, feel alone, feel so down. The work I doing a whole year long is just something I have to do.

They have a list, a blacklist. If they dislike you, the way you talk, the way you smile too much, it could be anything, a mark goes against your name on the list.

But after I live with the same children all this time, I begin to feel part of something, not so lonely, not left out. It's a group. You work together. We all proud, happy with what we did. The leader won't give you any reward when the project is good. Only the leader doesn't think you're useless. It's just so you won't have a terrible time.

Work time is equal. Hair equal, clothes equal, all black so easy to wash. But of course, the leader always has some favorite.

It's not a real feeling. They just using the children as a favorite. It doesn't do any real good for those children. But they see something in you that they can use.

They use people to spy on other families. A lot of people do it. Especially children. Even they spy on their own family. Because the family stop being a real family; it's all broken up.

One boy, I think fifteen or something, he act like a big shot. He do everything Pol Pot like—he walk around tough, never show feeling in his face. He act like he doesn't care for his own life, he do anything to please *Angka*. Probably the communists take over his mind. That boy find out his older brother fall in love with a girl in the camp. The two brothers both from New People but they strong. Strong counts the most. Communists like them. The girl is New People. The man and girl really love each other. At the end, they find the girl is pregnant.

The little brother big shot, he ask all around, "Who is the father!" Then the older brother comes forward.

"I am the father," he says. "Why don't I have a right to get married with her, because I love her?"

Little big shot say, "No one has right to choose. *Angka* choose marriage for you. You break the rule. You have to pay. We make an example of you for the group." So he take his big brother out by the forest. Tell him to dig a hole. The brother dig a hole for himself. Children must come to watch the lesson. The girl that love him, she have to watch too.

Pol Pot soldiers and the little big shot play a game. They push that young man back and forth, bang him on the head with bamboo sticks, back and forth, each one bang his head many times. They shout, "Ask for your life!" That man scream out his prayers. "God, please help me!"

I pray too. I can't speak, can't cry, can't show any feelings. The soldiers laugh, like just playing a game. After a while, that young man fall down still.

Little big shot kick him into the pit. He leave his brother without covering him, not even dead yet. I just stand there, wait for that killer to change into another form, a snake or a dragon or something, as I used to think. He just stand there, nothing in his eyes. For the first time in my life I realize that a human being can be as evil as any other animal.

I hear that young man crying and all night I cannot sleep.

Next morning, I go near the pit. Grazing the cow. Look down. I see that man's eyes open, white and cloudy, like dead fish eyes. I put some soil on top of him. I just pray for him, suffering for him. Then I give him some flowers. I think maybe my father die like that. I say to God, can you not let his spirit fly around forever? Give it a place to rest? Why does he die like an animal?

*

Next time I graze the cow, I stare at that pit and the place just past it. The ground raise up a little higher over that place. Now it smell so terrible I can't stand it.

Next day I see something push up through the soil, like it explode. Wild animals snorting like pigs around it, so excited. I climb up on the cow to see what it is. Oh, no! Bodies. Human bodies, blow up like balloons, pushing up through the dirt. Now I see why the sandy soil have dark spots—curds of thick blood. I see a wild animal chew on a neck. I can't look.

People say be careful where you walk when you graze the animals. Sometimes you might walk into the bodies who die and your feet go right through them.

Just try not to think how terrible it all is, because from now on it's going to be like this all the time. After days and days, you just forget. You can see the picture, see people cut up and kill in front of your eyes; you turn around and think nothing. Pretend you don't understand. Nothing is going to be better if I cry or I get sad or I think how terrible it all is. Doesn't do anything good for me at all. So what I do is just turn around and walk away.

*

Sometimes I can't feel I am there. It's really strange. I don't feel hungry, but I know my bones are like sticks. I feel like I'm floating sometimes; I can see everything, but I'm not really there, not touching the ground.

A lot of times I look down at my feet under water in the rice field, I see the toes go all wiggly. They grow longer and longer, like little snakes. I can't stop them. Behind me I have the idea there's a deep pit, dark one. If my toes keep growing, I'm going to fall backward into that dark pit.

They accuse me in the criticism of being the child of a criminal. The *Me-krum*, dummy one, say she know why my father die. She say they find his military medal with my mother's private things. She say they know my father is an officer with Lon Nol, so he an enemy of the people.

I say nothing.

Anyway, in my secret little mind, I always believe I have two fathers. Ever since I'm a little little girl, when anyone ask, I give my godfather's name first, then my real father. My godfather is the Kru Khmer of my father. Kru Khmer means teacher, but a special kind of teacher, spiritual teacher.* The Kru has magic, too.

One time, I remember, my whole family go to the country, I don't know why—my mother is going to born my baby sister. It's a big big rain. I want to take a rain shower; it's really fun, play and run around and the rain take all the hot and itchy out of your skin. My father go down to check the water jars under the house.

A big thunderlight come down and jump across the ground. I scream and my mother come running out. My father fall down on his back; he lie there stiff like he's a dead tree. My mother drag him under the house. She call the Kru Khmer right away.

He come and drag my father up the steep stairs to the top room in the house. He lay him down and put a big white sheet over him, like it's a dead person. Then he build a fire out of special wood, smell like the forest, and he blow the smoke on my father. He say magic and do charms over my father. After he pray awhile, my father sit up. He can't talk. He walk like an empty shell, to one wall. Then he turn around—it's hard to explain—and his spirit walks through that point. He come back to life.

It's really complicated to explain about the spirits. Once I see one in the shower room, the long-haired lady, and I scream. My brother come and say, "There's no one here." I'm the only one who see it. Sometimes my mother see it too. It's hard for a man to see it. But the Kru Khmer tell about all things like that. Sometimes it's a good spirit, sometimes a bad spirit. If two spirits start fighting, it can knock you down. It seem funny now, but it wasn't funny then; it was real.

When I'm little, I never see what my father's face look like. It's not polite for children to look at a grown-up in the eye. Anyway, my father a soldier; he's away a lot. Sometimes, my mother send me to stay with my father's Kru Khmer. He is like my second father.

But he's a really strong Kru Khmer. A lot of people come to him when they have snakebites, get hit by lightning, all that thing. And

* Kru comes from the same Sanskrit root as guru.

when somebody start screaming and crying and laughing, all at once, when somebody is sick like that, we call it *khmah chou*. It's when a ghost leaps inside your body and tries to take your spirit. You can't remember what you do before, what you say. People say a ghost go inside and make the person do strange things. You can't get them back. That's why we believe in ghosts. There's a lot of people have that; it's really scary.

Doctor cannot help with that. Only a Kru Khmer take care of that. A doctor just say there's nothing wrong, sick. Not body sick. But the Kru know about it. Kru Khmer is more special even than a doctor in Cambodia.

I tell people, "My father is a Kru Khmer." He's a big figure in my childhood, like a god to me. Maybe he even save my life.

When I born out, I remember my whole life from before. I always want to know about my old life. Why do I have one tooth so long? It come out of my lip like a lion. My relative all tease me. My aunt come over and say, "Oh, no, she's a ghost!" I hate that. So I cry and when my father's teacher come, I tell him.

He look at my tooth. It got much longer. He smile. All my aunts sit around me. He calls me his daughter.

"You will see," he say, "you will be as good as my daughter," and he cut off the tooth so fast, I didn't even see. I look in the mirror and it's all gone.

Before Pol Pot, when I don't feel well, the Kru Khmer come to my house. He give me herbs to drink. He give me a magic shower with special water, say magic things over me. He's trying to talk to the spirit and see what it wants. I feel shaky when he does it. Something pulling me back, won't let go, but the Kru, he's trying to save me for this life. He spurts the magic water through his teeth in a fine cool shower; it's to take all the bad luck away and bring in beautiful things to dream about. It seems strange to you, I know; it's hard to believe unless you see. The Kru stay with me about two days, and I feel better.

I learn from my father's spirit teacher how sometimes you can hide yourself so other people can't see you—just enter the magic world. I wish I can do that in Pol Pot time.

Then one day, I'm eight or nine, it just all come back. The old life.

*

It's a day so hot, sun like fire on your skin. I'm looking down at my feet in the water and my toes go all snaky again. Everything go dark. I can't see anything. I can hear the other children playing, throwing things at each other, but I can't move. I say to myself, "Keep standing straight." If I move even a teeny bit, I'm going to fall back into that big black hole. I walk out at rest time and find a banyan tree, trunk so big and cool and silver. Lean against it. I put my hand in the crack. My mind goes all dark. I feel something pulling me, into the tree, down a hole, into another world.

You know how long a time I stand by that tree? Four hour, maybe five hour. I just stand there like a sculpture. The *Me-krum* think I'm sick. The other girls, some of them think I'm dead.

But when I come back, I say something very strange. It come out in a different language. Like the language on temple walls. I don't know what I'm saying. I don't know what it means either. It just come out.

Two or three other girls say, "What's that supposed to mean?" They believe that some spirit took over me.

I'm shaking so much, I try to talk and I can't. I try to tell them what happen to me. I go back to my old life in the garden of a temple, it's peace and beauty everywhere, lotus flowers on the lake and dancing girls. Only thing is, I cannot go outside the garden. Nobody believe me.

"Don't be stupid," Sophal say. "You stand there five hours, you don't go anywhere." But she look funny at me.

In that minute, I'm not afraid anymore. I know I've been in that temple garden before; I just don't know when. I feel a new power. Feel it running in my arms and legs, I think I know what it is—I must have very good *veseana** if I come from the king. I look at the Pol Pot children and smile.

"Don't ever threaten me again," I say. "Or I use my special power on you."

"Yeah, you just try to scare us," they say.

"It's not to scare, it's true."

"I'm going to tell about you," Sophal threaten me. "You talk another language." Before she can say anymore, I leap on her and pin her arms in the dirt. She's the same age and much bigger, but I feel her go limp like a rice-stalk doll under my hand. I push my thumb into her throat.

"You tell, girl, and you'll never get away from my hand."

* Destiny, predetermined luck or life force.

*

After that, it happen to me many times, whenever I look down and see my feet turn snaky. I try to stay with other children around me. Not just alone. But when I go away into another world, sometimes it's wonderful, sometimes it's really scary. I have to bite my hand, something that really hurts, to bring myself back.

*

Sometimes they give children a very old egg to escape from the memory of their old life. But what I have, you can't escape from it.

Sometime now I feel I know what is happening really and then I don't. Sometime I feel like I have people around me and sometime I don't. Each hour it change. It's like living in a dream.

Myth, Mores, and Madness

For centuries myth and religion have cast their spell over the Cambodian mind. Many myths derive from their lost civilization. Combining creativity and intellect with the gifts nature bestowed on the basin they inhabited, beginning as early as the first century A.D., the Khmer cultivated the most brilliant civilization ever recorded in Southeast Asia. It flourished during the Kambuja, or Angkor, Period, beginning in 802 and lasting until the sudden, desolating capture of Angkor by the Siamese in 1431. The capital was abandoned and its marvelous culture vanished without a trace inside Cambodia for the next four hundred years. Another civilization gradually developed in the south, with Phnom Penh as its capital, but it was beset by wars and internal strife; finally its leaders invited the French to take Cambodia under its wing as a protectorate in 1885.

The figures who gave life to the fabulous Angkorean epoch have been assimilated by most peasant Khmer into their spiritual universe, a place where Buddha and the ancient gods commingle, together with good and bad spirits, ghosts, fantastic animals, and mythic heroes.[1] Many Cambodians still place faith in magic doctors and other spiritual advisers and are inclined to see in every event a sign or omen. Their subjective life is still haunted by spirits and shadows of the past.

This "mythic infatuation" has been blamed for much of Cambodia's weakness; indeed, some observers see it as a veritable national psychosis.[2] But under extreme conditions, it may be a primary source of strength. Myth and fantasy may have served children particularly well during the first year or two under Pol Pot, faced as they were with the mystifying separation from or disappearance of their parents, stunning scenes of brutality, and a totally inverted system of reward and punishment. Mystical beliefs offered another, inner world, a refuge where a child could not be watched or punished. For minutes or hours, the real world with its inexplicable cruelties and terrifying impersonality simply ceased to exist.

Traditional Cambodians have no concept of mental illness. Whatever symptoms cannot be ascribed to physical causes are assigned to troubled spirits or ancestral ghosts trying to possess the sufferer's mind. Curing that is the province of religion or magic; either a monk or a Kru Khmer, one of Cambodia's traditional healers, is called to perform a ceremony of exorcism. But no such practices were permitted under the rule of Pol Pot.

It is not hard to imagine Mohm mesmerized by the hot sun in the wringing heat of the rainy season, when the clouds come tumbling across Cambodia's sky like a menagerie of fantastic animals; any number of the tales she had heard from her grandmother might have been evoked. Stories about the Naga king and sleeping giants from Cambodia's glorious past, stories now half forgotten, may have been stored in her subconscious memory and later retrieved to link her with the glory of Angkor.

The ghost stories Mohm told were rooted in Khmer folklore and superstition. If she had consciously designed a tactic of counterintimidation, she could not more cleverly have preyed on the subconscious fears of many Khmer than by spinning ghost stories and ancient myths. When Mohm described the arrogant giants who offended the gods by making colossal sculptures of themselves, and how they were put under a spell, she was relating one of many versions of the mythology used to explain the mysterious downfall of Angkor. And the tale she related of the Cambodian king who owed his existence to the snake monarch is not only Cambodia's traditional creation myth—equivalent to our Genesis—but scholars say the story is not without historical foundation.

Although the creation myth has many versions, it goes essentially like this:[3]

*

A *juju* worker (magic man) named Dak the Forest Dweller had a dream. It was revealed that he should plant a new kind of grain on the bank of the great river, then give up war and hunting and sit quietly to see what magic might spring up. Dak had great misgivings, but one did not flout the wishes of the serpents that controlled human destiny.

When Dak looked up from his planting, he saw a stranger wrapped in layers of white cloth.

"My name is Kambu," the stranger said. "I am Prince of Arya Deca. And Siva, the great god, is my father-in-law."

Dak protested. "The great god is not Siva. It is the King of the Nagas, whose name I shouldn't dare to repeat even if I remembered it."

The stranger inquired about the bit of grain in Dak's hand.

"It's magic," Dak replied. "I was instructed in a dream to plant it and this is the result. Maybe I should throw it away."

"Oh, no!" Kambu implored. "It is more potent magic than you suspect. All the world about is sere and desert. In my own land, hot winds have withered everything that people might eat and all are dead. When I look at this magic you have, I can see into the future: I see a nation growing here in this valley—a nation with great palaces and temples."

Then Kambu asked the magic worker to describe the King of the Nagas. Dak revealed that the snake god lived by a great lake in a cave surrounded by cobras as big as pythons. The stranger exhorted the sorcerer, "Help me make a craft that will withstand any whim of the water gods."

On the point of refusing, Dak recalled the rest of his dream. He was to lead some prince to the court of the serpents. The thought of trespassing in the kingdom of the Nagas terrified him. No mortal had ever dared journey into that stony country. Not a tree or a reed of grass grew there, it was said, and the sun beat down in a continual flame.

Kambu assured him, "I had a vision too, and I have been given a magic crossbow for our journey." And so Dak helped Kambu lash together a log craft. Almost immediately, a great wind surged about them. Their craft bobbed and dipped crazily on a course all its own. Kambu and Dak surrendered themselves to nature. They were blown across India's Bay of Bengal and through the Malaccan Straits, around the peninsula now known as Singapore, and up the South China Sea to the coast of a place later called Indochina.

The winds stopped. Their spirits rose. Stretched before them lay an emerald strip of land. And all at once, speeding toward them sleek and resolute as a water serpent, was an exquisite canoe.

Spellbound, Kambu stared at the vessel and was shocked to see a maiden maneuvering it—a maiden of incomparable beauty.

The next thing they knew, arrows were zinging past their ears. Kambu snatched his magic crossbow and returned the hostile greeting.

Each time he fired, the maiden's canoe spun faster and faster. Her last arrow released, she cried, "What would you have of me?"

"Nothing but to be guided to the great King of the Nagas."

"Never!" she hissed.

So Kambu hit her canoe broadside. As she began to disappear under great swallows of water, Kambu lifted her into his craft. Awed by a peer in magic powers, she said, "No one has outmaneuvered the Naga Princess. How is it you have such powers?"

"No doubt because I come only in friendship," Kambu replied. And then he produced shimmering Indian silks, jewels, and ivory.

"Come," she consented, "I will take you to my father, the King of all Snakes."

When they came to the entrance of a cave, Kambu entered and wandered down a long cool passage where crystals rose up from the floor and hung in spearpoints from the top. All about him were hissing sounds but he could see nothing. The passage opened into a large chamber, but the moment he entered, Kambu was surrounded by hissing serpents, each of which lifted seven heads in a fan to look at him more closely. The largest, a horrifying hooded snake, spoke.

"Before you are put to death, what excuse do you have for invading the land of the Nagas?"

"I come to ask for help," Kambu replied simply. "Siva the Destroyer had one of his whims and blotted out the crops in my land and my people died. Siva even took back my wife. My grief overwhelmed me. So I wandered on toward the East, until I came here to the great river, and there I found a magician named Dak with a talisman in his hand, which is called Rice. If it is your will, I should like to settle here and make use of the Rice to raise up a nation of servants to the high gods. If not, then kill me for I can go no farther."

For some days the King of the Nagas thought over the stranger's proposal. His daughter, who meantime had fallen in love with Kambu, pleaded with her father to spare the prince. At last, the snake monarch summoned the stranger.

"All rules indicate that you should be put to death," he said, "but for the sake of peace in my own household, I shall have to overlook your error in coming here. We shall make a marriage for you. And we shall find a fine wife to reward Dak. You, as a mortal, cannot take our shape, but my daughter will not mind taking yours, and in her human appearance she is said to be even more beautiful than she is as a Naga." The snake king added, "I shall look with interest on your experiment of building a nation."

And as grandmothers told generations of Cambodian children . . . after the Princess of the Nagas married the brave Indian adventurer, they settled down in the valley of the great river to make a new kingdom. They gave birth to the beautiful race of Kambujas, the children of Kambu. Eventually, that name was distorted by the tongues of foreigners into Cambodge, or Cambodia. And later, by the Khmer Rouge, into Kampuchea.

According to scholars, the story is not without foundation. Mainland Southeast Asia did have an indigenous race called the Mon-Khmer and a relatively sophisticated culture in the prehistoric era.[4] Rice, it is believed, was first cultivated in the Mekong delta of the Mon-Khmer,[5] a region with plentiful fish and forests that were a riot of game, rare trees, and spices. The early Khmers were a cultivated people as well as warriors. And Indian navigators did come upon this peaceful El Dorado. They saw in its gushing abundance and exotic goods the potential for more profitable trade within the Mediterranean region, and soon Indian merchants came in great numbers. There were probably a number of regional kings. And it did also happen more than once that an Indian adventurer or exiled prince would seek to marry the daughter of a Mon-Khmer king and succeed to the throne.

The Khmer welcomed contact with people from this superior civilization and over the next several centuries assimilated the alphabet, literary language, mathematics, astronomy, aesthetics, and religion of India.[6] Unlike the Chinese influence imposed by force on neighboring Vietnam, the Indianization of Cambodia did not produce an identity crisis.[7] Indeed, later monarchs—each one a usurper[8] and therefore needing a good story—liked to trace their ancestry to the mythical Kambu and his Naga princess. It was said to represent a marriage between culture and nature.[9]

Clearly, the Khmer's self-confidence, early myths, and animistic beliefs were indigenous. Accepting Indian culture as the fountainhead, they were able to build up their water kingdom to a brilliant civilization —rivaling in some aspects the magnificence of ancient Egypt, Greece, and Rome.

*

Religion has always ordered the lives of the Khmer, but creativity is evident there as well. The animistic beliefs of the indigenous Mon-Khmer were combined with Indian Buddhist beliefs to form a unique folk religion.[10] Buddhism came to its fullest expression in Cambodia under her most illustrious king, Jayavaraman VII, when his two wives converted him to Theravada Buddhism. Hundreds of thousands of ordinary people, the inscriptions tell us, labored to build Jaya's opulent city, Angkor Thom, on the assumption that it would deliver them, in another life, from pain. Surely it caused them great pain to drag huge stones out of the jungles, but they took the long view.

Throughout the next six hundred years of war, decline, and colonialism, Buddhism survived in Cambodia[11]; from the fourteenth century onward it was virtually the national religion. But by the mid-twentieth century, Buddhism was less a formal religious faith than a vestige of tradition.[12]

As a rite of passage to young manhood, it was customary for a boy to shave his head and spend several months before his eighteenth year living in a temple or *wat* as an acolyte to the monks. Otherwise, religion was like bathing: Everyone participated at least now and then in a ceremony, but it was a natural function, not a studied system of thought.[13]

There is one formal Buddhist belief that remains unchanged in the Khmer's folk religion: the concept of merit. Power, ability, riches, or good luck are seen as rewards for previous existences lived virtuously. Thus, society is a natural pyramid. Because there is no hope of changing one's circumstances for the better in this life, the only way to play the game is to obey one's superiors and store up acts of merit toward the next rebirth.

Given this belief, how does one explain the independent spirit attributed to the Khmer? It refers to the cultivation of an inner liberation. A person can be free of all anger and sorrow and spite provided he or she masters the passions. This helps to explain why Cambodians so easily accept death and destruction. Better to die than to remain miserably alive; at least death offers the chance for another, better possibility.

The Khmer infatuation with myth and the glorious past could explain much of the appeal of Pol Pot to the forest-dwelling boys and girls who formed his base. He claimed that after "two thousand years of exploitation," the country's history would begin again with the building of a new era "more glorious than Angkor."[14]

Chouk, Kompote Province,
1977–1978

New place. Near the sea [Gulf of Thailand]. Harder work. So dry here. I can't see any hill, any sugar palms. They say there are mountains in the west, and waterfalls, but all I see is flat and gray like ashes.

Many children here, about fifty groups. Maybe more than a thousand build irrigation terraces. *Me-krum* here are nicer. They teach songs and children can sing and clap hands, have some fun. Not really freedom, but not so tight.

Rice fields don't grow well here. New work is to dig the soil—Kompote have special termite hills to make the rice field rich—and then mix with, ugh! animal dung.

I try not to breathe. A girl in our group laughs at me. "You gray as a monkey!"

My work is thirty trips a day with two baskets on a pole over my shoulder. I'm so small, my legs are too short; I'm always the last one. Can't carry those heavy baskets of soil. I keep getting shorter, I think.

The rainy season is much easier. Then I don't have to carry anything. I do get a lot of blisters on my hands, pulling up rice shoots, and you have to stand in the water hour after hour, worry about leeches get on you. You get so itchy, red skin, that comes from the rice leaf. But dry season, sun stay on all the time. You walk, carry, walk, carry. People same as water buffalo.

New leader coming. People look forward to better times.

New leader calls a big meeting. Everybody go. He say don't worry; you are lucky people to have me as your new leader; the killing is over. He ask people to come forward, tell if they educated what can they do; *Angka* will love them. Some people cry like little children, so happy, want the leader to like them. They say, "Yes, I can do this for you; I know mathematics!" Everybody relax, get happy, say "We're lucky."

People keep asking one another, "Maybe one more week we can eat rice, think so?" A lot of people say, "I don't care if we eat rice or not; what I care is they stop the killing."

The first two or three days, it's fine. People don't have to work as hard as they used to. The leader just document everybody. Everything is going to be fine—they always say that.

But it never really happen. Two or three weeks and it get worse. It's a double trick. They trick the people to find out who is educated, and they trick each other to get the power by making the people think the new leader is better than the old one. But Pol Pot leader all the same.

They send some people to the prison. That's where they try to get answers you can't give. They don't kill you right away in the prison. They don't kill until they get the right answers.

Many people running now from one settlement to another one. They run at nighttime through the forest. When they come into our place, they just make up a story. Pol Pot doesn't have any real government or real law, so you can write a letter and pretend your *Me-krum* write it, pretend you are sick and can't keep up with your work so you have to go to another settlement.

*

I see a monk I recognize from Phnom Penh. But his head is grow with hair, and he is force to work like everyone else. He digs in the dung hill. I wait until he pass by. Just for his eyes, I give a very tiny bow, a message to say, "I know who you are, I respect you, and I do feel for your suffering." Then I turn and walk away.

One day that monk disappear.

It's a trick. The new leader just lie. Lots of people start to disappear again. The ones who tell the true all disappear.

My parents believe in God. My father say thank you to Buddha every time he come back from war. My mother always pray. But I don't know anymore. Maybe what the *Me-krum* said is right: There isn't any real god.

If there is a god, can he ever open his eyes and look down to see what people do to other people? Can he ever stand being seen? Is he in the dung pile the monk has to shovel? Can he ever see the baby the soldier throw against the tree? Where is a god who cannot see these things?

You cannot look forward, there is nothing out there, only emptiness and hurt, no one to take care, no one to love. It takes a long time to get the idea that I the only one left. To stop blame myself. To think it would give my parents joy to know that I stay alive.

I begin to see what it's like being alive but letting all your feelings die off. I think that must happen to everybody who survives.

But little things happen each day; you make friends, you find something to laugh about. I begin to see that not all of life will be terrible things happening to me. I begin to see what is it like to be alone. It won't be always and only suffering with nobody to care about me.

*

I'm more skin than all the children. A lot of children younger than me but bigger than me. And they can work harder. I look like fish bones. They don't care about how small you are, still have to work same as your age group. After a while have to climb higher and higher to get to the top terrace. On that carrying job I'm always the last one. If you don't finish, you can't rest until dinner. Every day I'm more slow, more weak. Pole is like a wall on top of me, pound me down in the earth. Every day I get smaller, thinner. Sometime no dinner too, too tired to eat.

Me-krum look disgust with me. Maybe they wait till I drop down sick, then no more food for me.

I think I hear the bomb sound. Not close by.

My mind going all dark. Some days I can't feel if I'm really here. Maybe all my nerves are going. Sometimes I can't tell if it's real or it's a dream.

*

I guess they're tired of me, too small. They send me back to the town. I have to work in the house, carry water and take care a little child. But I have to work harder in the house. Wake up in the night when the baby cry. That baby get sick. First they scratch his forehead with a coin; they say to scratch out the bad wind. Then they cut slits in his skin to suck out the bad blood. Poor baby cry and cry. A lot of time I have no sleep. And I feel badder than when I work with the group.

Move us to another town. I hear about a big ceremony in that town.

A hundred pair come for marry all at once. I ask if I can go. I never see one of their weddings.

The Old People can marry anybody they can take advantage of. *Kawng chhlop* [spies] and *yu vea'chon* [unmarried young males], whatever wife they want they can have it. The leader can even let him pick from the New People.

It's a meeting for the whole town—not for children, but I can go anyway because I'm taking care of her baby. They come from many different places around for this ceremony; marry two hundred people all in one day, I guess not to waste time from work. They want everybody to have equal ceremony, nothing special. Not like our weddings with everything colorful and three days of dancing and the most wonderful things to eat and even a pig's head.

It's a hundred people all in a line. They never meet each other before. A lot of the men have no legs; soldiers, I guess. Somebody just push them up to the place where they shake hands, and there they go. Each one of them wear black and a checkered scarf around their neck. The man and woman step up to where the microphone is and shake hands. Leader make them man and wife, their way—*Angka* say it. They go together for a day.

The girl can't say no. Many New People girls force to marry with a *yu vea'chon* or a *kawng chhlop*. After the wedding, they still have to work, but they can stay in the village, give them a house—they don't have to go away on the work team anymore. They become sort of civilized adults.

To marry somebody you hate—ugh! I imagine myself, I don't think I can live with it. I think I rather die than take that pressure. But I not really worry, I so young.

Actually, I do worry. I hope that I never grow up.

A Separate Planet of Death

Time is a flattened landscape for the survivor of extremity. There are no fixed landmarks in one's existence; there is no personal narrative that continues in orderly progression, accumulating clarity and wisdom. One day is indistinguishable from the next. There is no hope for light at the end of the tunnel—there is no end—since future does not exist. People drift suspended, clamped inside an endless present.

Such may have been the subjective reality for Cambodia's hostage population between 1977 and 1979, the last two ghoulish years of Pol Pot's "superleap forward" to communism. Already there had been the forced relocation of people to formerly uninhabited forest land with the most primitive living conditions. In these new zones, married women were separated from their husbands, who were sent to different regions to work. Among the unmarried New People, no one had the right to choose a spouse. In the view of the Khmer Rouge, women of the New People were weak, shy, and spoiled. They had to be remade.

Now considered equals, women did most of the work. Men of the Old People had to serve mostly as soldiers at Cambodia's heavily guarded borders, and men from the New People were being killed or were dying out from disease or starvation in greater numbers than the women. As time went on, it became the norm for women to stop menstruating and for nursing mothers—the few who were left—to see their milk dry up.

Children from the age of six were placed in special work brigades; at eight they were sent on mobile teams. The few remaining factories were operated by children, standing on boxes. Monks were also drafted into the labor force, often made to work on dung piles as punishment for having been "bloodsuckers" before.

For Mohm, the move in 1978 to Chouk on the Gulf of Thailand

meant little improvement. The sea had no romantic associations in those years. The sea was just another place to work, a salt supply.

In 1977, new policies were put into effect, but things only grew worse. All children over the age of six were housed in village communal halls or a long distance from their parents, whom they rarely saw again. Groups of more than two people were forbidden to assemble. The radio carried only political speeches and revolutionary music. Mass executions of New People began. Although the Khmer Rouge top leadership gleefully announced that the "bourgeosie" had been driven from the cities and subordinated to the worker-peasants, they were still uneasy about having them around. As their Black Book noted:[1]

Their economic foundation has already collapsed but *their views remain, their aspirations still remain.* [Emphasis in the original]

The dragnet became even broader now, condemning anyone who could not or would not fill the work quotas that were established. The worker drones had to complete digging a section of dike or a fixed number of trips from dung pile to irrigation terrace before they could stop for rest or soup. If they fell short, they were punished or killed. But the crueler death was by starvation. Rations were cut in 1977 to one small tin of rice soup per day.[2] Withholding food from the population could not be explained only by the increase in rice being bartered with China for weapons and supplies. Pol Pot outlawed medicines, presumably for the same reason: Only the supremely strong were meant to survive.[3]

Blacklists were drawn up. In areas where most of the men had already been killed, the widows were rounded up. One woman had shaved her head to mourn her husband's death, as was the old custom. When the Khmer Rouge accused her of expressing emotion, she said coolly, "No, it is only evidence that I have a lot of head lice."[4]

But at night, when the moon appeared, they would gather the people on their "phantom list." I knew from the spies who kept trying to catch me in a slip that I was on the list. One would ask, "Can you give me directions to that town, near Phnom Penh?" If I knew north from south, that would mark me as educated. Another would ask, "Can you add five hundred and seven hundred for me?" I would just count on my fingers—one, two, three—like an illiterate, and come up with the wrong answer. But at night, when the moon shone and they came around with the plastic hoods and rope, I always felt the terror.

Rare glimpses filmed early in 1978 by fellow communists from Yugoslavia showed the legendary *joie de vivre* of the Cambodian people frozen. Long rows of densely packed forced-labor groups worked like automatons, their bodies gaunt and their faces drained of all expression.

Some among the captive population appeared to be walking in a trance, dreamlike; some floated, starving, turning slowly into air. Young men reduced to ropy muscles and not a sixteenth of an inch of flesh labored hard, driven by some invisible engine. There were reminders enough of the penalty for weakness—a shrunken man with hands and feet bound and hung from a pole upside down, carted past the others like a barbecue. Women with sunken cheeks showed facial tics from the fierce effort of repressing all emotion. As they walked, their pelvic girdles looked slack, brittle, detached from any force of creation. And everywhere the eyes were lightless, pits of dull pain. People moved as if possessed.

For the first two years, most of the hatred whipped up by Khmer Rouge leaders had been unleashed on the New People. By 1977 their suspicions turned inward. A "second expulsion" of the population was ordered in 1978. Those in the east were sent to the west and vice versa in a massive reshuffling, as the paranoia of the Khmer Rouge top leadership escalated. Pol Pot personally toured the country to direct executions among his political cadres and his troops. Merely because of their proximity to Pol Pot's nemesis, Vietnam, these people were suspected of fighting on the side of the Vietnamese. Many of them were not given a chance to prove loyalty.

What had been happening, beginning in January 1977 and unknown to the captive population, was a series of large-scale purges within the Khmer Rouge at every level from village to zone. In nine purges carried out across Cambodia during the course of the regime, the pattern was repeated: The commander of a district would be summoned to Phnom Penh together with his lieutenants, ostensibly for new orders. The group would be dragged off to a former school on the outskirts of Phnom Penh, Tuol Sleng, and tortured until they signed confessions to being agents of either the Vietnamese, the KGB, or the CIA, and then executed. The next day a new cadre would be sent to the district to replace the "soft" ones; usually its members were recruited from the "tough" Nearat Dai.[5] The equivalent would be if President Reagan invited the governor of New York, together with his entire staff and all the state's mayors, down to Washington, blew them away, and the next day sent in a bunch of ex-cons to run the state.

So it was that new leaders would appear suddenly, try to subdue the populace by promising a more humane policy, and then elicit more confessions from those who had successfully disguised their identities. Killing quotas were handed down from above, say a thousand people to be executed in two months. If a new leader did not show sufficient commitment, he, too, would be scheduled for a "holiday" at Tuol Sleng, where the victims, in addition to discredited Khmer Rouge, were civil servants, teachers, actors, students, technicians.

Some of the Khmer Rouge did start out as sincere revolutionaries, not monsters. But the cannibalizing of their own ranks ensured that terror spread to every corner of the country and wormed into every heart.

At that Asian Auschwitz called Tuol Sleng, the Khmer Rouge photographed each victim as he or she was brought to the schoolhouse and again as that person was being mutilated, hanged, drowned, disemboweled, or electrocuted. No one ever escaped from Tuol Sleng. Twelve thousand died there.[6]

*

Pol Pot's determination to build a state whose independence would be "total, definitive and clean" brought on further destruction.[7] Even as the broader purges left him supreme within the party, and busts and posters began for the first time to appear of him, round-faced and smiling, he turned in full fury on the Vietnamese. From December 1977 on, constant, fierce, and brutal clashes created a full-scale war between Cambodia and Vietnam. On May 10, 1978, Radio Phnom Penh announced, "We could sacrifice two million Kampucheans in order to exterminate the fifty million Vietnamese—and we shall still be six million. . . ."[8]

Given that maniacal ambition, virtually every male over the age of ten had to be forced into military service. Orders went out to relax killings of New People. Khmer teenagers with no training were handed AK-47s and M-15s and told, "You go, or you die." Guns behind them to cut them down if they faltered, they rushed to their deaths in increasing numbers, but not before they had slaughtered some Vietnamese.[9] Arn Chorn, a refugee now living in Jefferson, New Hampshire, who was thirteen at the time, recalls:[10]

> I was one year with the gun. A lot of children had to fight in the front line; they died first. I had some food to eat, for a change. Sometimes they praised us for being very brave. But the Vietnamese soldiers were well trained. The children died easily. We didn't know how to operate those guns. I just shot bullets like rain.

*

Thus, the Khmer Rouge had nearly perfected a particular form of social reconstruction—auto-genocide—defined as the murder of more than one quarter of a nation's population by its brothers. Mass graves were later found outside almost every village. In one just outside Phnom Penh, a total of 8,985 victims had been blindfolded, their necks broken with iron hoes, and their bodies dropped into pits. Ammunition was saved for use against the Vietnamese. Moreover, the Khmer Rouge were instructed that the people they annihilated were not worthy of the cost required to kill them by a round of bullets.

In four years, that separate planet of death had decimated Cambodia's gene pool. Of 70,000 monks, more than 65,000 were killed. Of the 367 physicians who were practicing in Cambodia in 1971, 48 survived, and almost all of those fled to the West.[11] If "intellectual" may be defined as anyone with some college education, there are fewer than a hundred intellectuals in Cambodia today.[12] Soth Polin, a novelist living now in California, is the only well-known member of the intelligentsia who escaped massacre. Of the painters, musicians, singers, dancers, and artists of any repute, only a tiny number survived.[13]

The final death toll is a careless estimate of two million—roughly one quarter of the population.

Vietnamese War in Cambodia . . . 1979

The bomb drop near me while I'm eating. Surprise attack. Everybody in the dining hall runs. To tell the truth, I don't feel frightened at all. Just keep on eating.

We hear bomb noise before, over there, some other village. But nobody know when it's going to come here, if— There's no letters, no cars, so how can people know anything?

First, nobody run away. Where I live now there are not many New People; all kill off. So the whole town stay under control of the Pol Pot; the leader say everybody must stay. Rumor go around the "enemy" going to take over. I don't know who the enemy is, except what I hear from the rumors. People begin to whisper in their huts about how the enemy going to bring terror. I never hear anything good about the enemy so I'm scared to death if they take over. The leaders don't want the people to know about it. They have a big meeting to say it's never going to happen, calm down. But I can see the leaders are a little shaky, too.

Another attack comes. Bomb after bomb, then soldiers march into the village. We run with the gunshots just behind us. People scream for their children, "Hurry up!" People scatter in different direction. I'm looking for somebody I know, somebody I can go off with. I don't see anybody I know.

The Khmer Rouge carry pigs and chickens and pots and pans and everything they need with them; don't ask me how they get it. But they move the whole town from place to place and keep control of many people. We move very near the edge of a forest.

*

Run. Have to run alone. But where do you run, when you don't know where you belong? I walk around, walk around, just wandering, stop where people are eating, where people rest. I'm looking for somebody I know, for my mother or my brothers, somebody like that.

I try to remember again why my mother and father die. Where is my older brother? Why didn't I keep my little sister alive? She can come with me now and I find a way for us to live.

Bomb sound like thunder all day, until the sun goes down. Then you hear the monkeys. Monkeys in the forest are so big, almost as big as a man, with long long fingers. At sunset they sing a high scream, sad one, like a person looking for something lost. Must be all kind of wild animal in this place—flying squirrels, flying foxes, wild pig. Sometimes a terrible smell passes over me, like a soup of hair and blood; is it the smell of tiger? Is that elephants crashing through the bamboo?

In the forest, I'm lost but I'm free. Like a bird, I go from one person to another and fly off. All Pol Pot people. Some want to share food with me but I don't trust. I don't eat. You can trust the animals, they're not like people.

The monkeys make funny faces and try to make friend with me. They're always with their families. I watch the monkey mother give a bath to her baby, she put the baby between her two feet and splash water over its back. Same as my mother do to my little sister.

I make friends with the monkeys. They climb to the top of the fruit trees and pick the best fruit. They drop down some to me. I eat what they eat, that way I know it's not poison.

One night it's late. I haven't hear a shot for about two hour. I finish the fruit and I'm looking for a place to sleep when I see him—a boy look like my father, carrying a gun.

His eyes see me. He cannot say the name but his eyes say I am his sister. I'm really happy to see him alive, my brother.

We cannot say much at all, cannot.

I say, "Why don't you come with me?"

He say, "I cannot."

I say, "Why can't you?"

He say he's supposed to take care of the cows for the Pol Pot soldiers. There's no way for him to get out.

I say, "Take me with you, then."

He say he's going to a real bad place. I, his sister, would get punish too.

He's nervous, keeps looking around to see who watching us. It's only a minute or two we have to talk.

Then he whisper to me, "You don't have to stay around these Pol Pot people anymore. They can't stop you now."

I ask him one more time, please, let's run together. Then on the way we can find someplace to stay and we can always be a family. But my brother never does listen to me, I'm just a little girl.

He tell me, "Go to a place you think is good for you to live. If I die, still you. If you die, still me. That's a good way to do it."

*

After a while I find a group of New People. About ten people attach to it, they smart. We walk out of the forest and keep walking to a place where the Vietnamese haven't taken over yet. It's just a dry-up place where nothing much really grows. There's nothing to do! Except cut out some of the trees and start over.

Fighting again. Bomb fall in middle of where we stay. Pol Pot soldiers find us. They don't know where we come from, don't know anything about us; they just see our faces are a little lighter and they say, "So, you are New People." They tell us, "You have to work here. This is your group."

This place gives me a very bad feeling. Everything is disorganize; even the soldiers seem unsure. This is maybe the last place under their control. We're back under a Pol Pot leader, eating in the same kind of communal hall, the food is less and less, and in the end they probably plan to kill us all.

Why else do they tell us to dig the big hole?

All day dig and dig, roots like strong arms pulling me down, I don't trust it. We're down in the pit and they tell us keep digging, a hole about twenty feet long, ten feet wide. A hole like that, I know what it's for. We're digging our own grave.

Now we get all together, our group, and two men have an idea. We have to play a trick to get out.

We get two people who work nearby to pretend they're messengers, coming from our old village. They go to the leader's house and two of our group go with them. We hide outside, trying to hear what will happen. The men say, "Their old leader wants them back. He send us with the order." I guess they give him a fake letter.

The new leader is silent. He doesn't know to believe or not. Maybe he's going to stick us in the pit and crack our necks and call the wild pigs on us!

The two from our group come out of the leader's house. Their heads nod. We can go. They ask, how many? So we count up—only the ones we know we can trust, about fifteen. We pack all our things and slip out in the evening.

Just walk quietly as if everything normal. Try to lose ourselves between all the people coming and going to trade. But inside my heart race ahead, pounding and pounding. Just pray that nobody tell the leader our trick. Just hope they don't notice we have nothing to trade.

Gunshot, many gunshot we hear, come from that place we just leave. All the people that stay back there, they must be die.

As soon as the dark come down, we run, run fast. It's a lot of fighting out here. Growly bomb sounds, short pepper of soldiers' guns, we don't even bother to look. But the bombs fright me now, the first time, I don't know why.

It's very confusing because people going in every different direction. We're desperate for supply to help us get to the next place. That's when I give up my last earring. I hide it long ago. Sew it up inside my black pant. One drop out before, but I have one left. Real gold. Who know when I'm just one year old and my grandmother give it to me what that earring is going to mean. We trade it for rice. The men in our group say now we have enough supply to get to Mong.

*

Mong is outside Battambang City, supposed to be a real town. That's funny, I haven't seen town in so long, what is town? Somebody tell me the Vietnamese already take over Mong. I'm afraid of the Vietnamese. But still I follow this group. I tell myself, they save us from Pol Pot with a trick, they know better than I.

When we get to Mong, the town is empty. Roof on the houses all fall in and bush growing out of bedroom windows; the street is like a river of dirt. Town is no people.

Then a lot of people come to trade. They can live any way they want, do anything they want, kind of wild, because there's nobody to rule over.

At that time, gold just spring out. Everybody seem to have some gold. I don't know where they hide it all the Pol Pot time. Our group has nothing to trade, nothing to sell, not enough food.

This one boy, he only care about money. He buy gold the New People have left over and sneak into Thailand, sell it to buy clothes and shoes, then he bring back all those old things. Everybody buy and sell. It makes me a little sick. We call those people *rhutbhun* [smuggler]. But one day this boy say something interesting to me. He say there's a New Camp over there. Just over the border into Thailand. Keep you safe from the bombs, from the Vietnamese. And you can make a little business or go out to another country.

I think it sound like a good idea.

One lady is ready to take the chance. She ask everybody in our group. Nobody want to go. So many story people tell about that border —soldiers, bombs in the ground, danger. A lot of people want to go into Thailand. But Thailand doesn't accept those people. Many don't make it.

I think about it. Remember what my brother say. I have to try other places to see if I can live. I don't feel at home here. I have nothing. I take so much chance already. Why not one more?

*

Running in the bomb sound. Many mountains. Mean sharp mountains, rake your arms, tear your feet. Lot of people run this same way. Many mothers run with a baby, maybe two children tuck up under each arm; they look so tired. Everybody have to walk on their bare feet just like Pol Pot time. From mountain you drop down into deep ravine. People are just walking and they step on a punji stick, a pointy thing, poison on the tip, it push up through their foot like meat you put on a stick to grill. The pain is terrible, I guess you have to get the poison out before it run all through your body. A lot of people step on them. Some cry to be carry, some don't even cry. Too tired.

Children always cry, "Pick me up! My feet, the blisters!"

First have to cross Pol Pot soldiers' camp. They shoot if you make a sound. Whenever a baby cries, everybody freeze—will it give us away?

At night I dig a hole to crawl away from the bomb and cover up my body with soil and leaf. Lie there and watch the stars shake. Maybe God is so angry he's going to pull the stars out from the sky and throw them at the enemy but I don't think so.

Light again. Run again, fall, empty, no food. Green sun pound through the twisty trees, it can put you to sleep walking. Too much people. The babies always cry, can't keep them quiet.

Some old people can't really do it. Just we put a little bottle of water and put the blanket on them and they sit there and can't go anymore. Sit there. Some people sit there until you see their skull. So tired, can't walk anymore, stop for sleep, just die there. So many so many so many —I feel awful they have to give up now, after all they work to survive. But they can't do it. The mountain is just too big, and so many mountain to get to the border.

Then I drop my little suitcase, it's just two pair of clothes. I drop it near where an old lady give up.

That old lady tell me, she say, "God going to help you. Don't give up. I am an old lady and I can't go any farther. But you're young. Life. Someday might be you get to a place where you can go to school and be a normal girl."

When I hear that, it give me hope. I say to myself, "Oh, my God, what did I do?" I run back to the top of the mountain, and I run on, as fast as I can.

When I sleep overnight, I begin to think: There's no water. Only here a little spring water come out of the ground, but on the way so many people get sick on bad water. I look around and around and I find an old water jar left over from the soldiers. Fill it up with fresh water, we can carry with us. Now okay, we have water for a long time.

Is it something I think or dream? I don't know. I wake up in the morning with a thought so clear, it's like spring water: *Stop blame yourself. If your sister still alive, you cannot survive. She cannot make the mountain; her feet would get blister. You'd have to stop, you must not leave her. You'd give up.*

I don't want to give up! I want to live.

Moment of Choice

During "Pol Pot time," there was almost no possibility of fleeing Cambodia. It was a country held hostage. All that changed when Vietnamese forces invaded Cambodia in late 1978. Phnom Penh fell to the Vietnamese in January of 1979. After a year of war, the Vietnamese army drove the last remnants of the Khmer Rouge into the mountains along the borders of Thailand and Laos.

For the exhausted survivors, the assault on their apathy was almost too much. Many Cambodians later described their condition of protective indifference much as did a former schoolteacher who lost his family:[1]

I had a different life at one time, bigger dreams. But under Pol Pot I forgot, forgot everything, stopped seeing the killing, stopped feeling the suffering. I left some of my mind behind.

For a year the Khmer Rouge was on the run, its guerrilla army trying to ride herd on its captive population while a far more sophisticated fighting force—the Vietnamese, flush with military hardware left over from the American withdrawal—tracked them with fighter planes, tanks, heavy artillery, and division after division of infantrymen.

In the midst of this chaos, people confronted a terrible moment of choice. Rather like hurling a spear into oblivion, each individual had a chance to cast his fate. That moment is the crucible for the survivor.

Some saw no choice but to remain under the control of the Khmer Rouge, who warned constantly, "Don't go with the Viets! They trick you and kill you." Herding as many Cambodians as they could intimidate, Pol Pot's forces fled the villages and rice plains in the wake of the advancing Vietnamese, and led their captives through forest and jungle, their food supplies dwindling, finally finding refuge in the mountains of western Cambodia. Those who were not cowed into following the retreating Pol Pot forces spent the next several months wandering their country in search of surviving family members.

A vast, dazed transmigration back to their houses and farms began. But farmers found their rice paddies sick and 60 percent of their draft animals dead of neglect. Those who walked back to their town or city faced temples and fine buildings in ruins, streets decayed, pigs and packs of wild dogs nuzzling through the underbrush, and a gush of vegetation snaking through their houses and out the windows and over the verandas where they used to sit at night and gossip. And the silence. Phnom Penh, Battambang, Siem Reap, Skun, these were truly ghost towns.

So staggering a burden of reconstruction faced the Cambodian people that even the ancient instinct of the Asian peasant, whose existence repeats in an endless circle like the seasons and traditionally ignores war and politics, even that continuity was broken. The paddies of Cambodia were not planted that spring of 1979.[2]

Others in that moment of choice decided to run behind the Vietnamese for protection. A woman named Mom-Mom explained her choice:[3]

Just before the fall of Phnom Penh, Mom-Mom was a pretty young single woman with a pleasant job in a French boutique. Her brother worked for the U.S. Embassy and had offered in April 1975 to take her out with him when the Americans left. But she declined. She had a mother who was old and sick and who needed her.

The Khmer Rouge controlled her area near the Thai border until April 1979.

When the Pol Pot soldiers ran away, I started to walk back to Phnom Penh. Rich men gave gold to Vietnamese soldiers and got a ride in the truck. But I have no ring, no watch, no gold. No brother, no mother—she was dead by then. Only one is me.

Human guideposts were left along the roads by the retreating Khmer Rouge to impress upon deserting civilians the folly of their choice.

I see from the women lying dead, the Pol Pot soldiers cut off their breast, or cut out down here [indicating her crotch]. It was too terrible to take a chance to run to Thailand.

Having found her way back to Phnom Penh, and fearing imprisonment by the new government if they knew of her background, Mom-Mom sought work as a street sweeper. Four years later she would be a receptionist in a government hotel in Phnom Penh, so desperate to get out of Cambodia that she was ready to flee overland with a guide she would pay in advance, risking that he would rob, rape, and desert her along the way. Many other survivors, particularly former government employees, were arrested and "reeducated" into submission by the occupying Vietnamese.

*

Some struck out alone. Boreth, the widow of a professor of English, carried one child in her womb and one in her arms; another daughter of six ran beside her. When her labor pains began in the midst of the advancing destruction, she tried to ignore them but she fainted outside a remote village. The next sensation of which Boreth was aware was burning—a greasy, fat-sweet odor swam around her and her back throbbed with pain. She was lying on a bamboo bed over a burning wood fire.

"They broiled me!" Telling her story three years later in Providence, Rhode Island, Boreth lifted her blouse to show a network of purplish scars on her back.

It was the practice of peasants to place a wood fire under a woman for three days after delivery, to draw off the "bad blood" and improve her circulation so she would heal more quickly. Customarily, her husband watched the fire. But with Boreth, there was no husband, and the baby would not emerge, and so the fire had been set early to encourage birth. She had writhed on that fiery bed in labor for twenty hours. When at last the child was pulled out, one of the peasants held it upside down and spanked it. But there was no sound. Boreth's child died three hours later. It was a small death, unheroic, but it hung heavily on her and she did not wait for her back to heal from its burns. She got up that same day, gathered her two remaining children, and once again she struck out alone.

Four years later Boreth was an auto mechanic in Providence with enough money saved to move to Southern California.

But who can know in that desperate moment of choice which is the right way to run?

As these two women were making their choices, Mohm was picking her way toward Mong. The flock of Cambodians camping in temporary rest camps just inside the Thai border began to swell into the thousands. In June 1979, the Thai government panicked.

*

Army officers used loudspeakers to summon them. Buses roared up. Soldiers in combat gear ordered everyone onto the buses: They were going to a camp where the housing and food would be better, they were told. When the Cambodians hesitated, soldiers began to drag old people and children onto the buses and their relatives followed.[4]

Crammed with Cambodian refugees from rest camps all along the Thai border, hundreds of buses stopped in a mountainous area shrouded in fog. It was after dark. Soldiers pushed the people to the edge of a mountain escarpment so steep a human could descend it only by ropes or vines. Those who panicked at the edge and tried to run back were shot. Over the course of several days, more than forty thousand Cambodians were forced at gunpoint over the precipice. The screaming and gunshots and the smell of burned flesh from human corpses were carried on the wind as a warning to each batch of new arrivals.

Rumor traveled fast about this forced repatriation. It may have deterred even larger migrations to Thailand for the next few months. It did slow down the group with which Mohm traveled. As it was, American Embassy observers saw as many as 100,000 Cambodians crawling toward the border during that summer of 1979. But it must have been like finding the way out of one of the circles in Dante's inferno. No more than 60,000 actually made it across; most of the others were presumed dead. The American ambassador in Bangkok, Morton Abramowitz, pleaded with the Thai prime minister to admit anyone who made it to the border. The Thais refused, fearing admission would confer on the Cambodians refugee status, and the Thais would be stuck with them indefinitely.

*

Americans had not tuned back in to Southeast Asia until January 3, 1978. After the long news blackout that followed the bitter U.S. withdrawal from Vietnam, our voluntary amnesia was lifted by a *CBS Evening News* broadcast:

> Good evening. The bitter memories of the Vietnam war, which have been receding for the past two and a half years, were awakened today with reports of intense fighting in the region—this time between the communist governments of Vietnam and Cambodia.

Correspondent Marvin Kalb reported that "experts believe the Vietnamese have no intention of advancing beyond the disputed border territory." Ironically, the United States had been exploring normalization of relations with the new government in Hanoi. But by late 1978, Hanoi lost patience with the Khmer Rouge and invaded. The U.S. State Department watched, openmouthed, as the Vietnamese gobbled up the whole of Cambodia.

By October 1979, half a million Cambodians were perched along the border or en route to it through treacherous mountains and malarial swamps. Mohm was among the latter. What people referred to as "the border" was worthy of *Terry and the Pirates*, dominated by local warlords and petty bandits, smugglers and deserters. Murders and rapes flourished alongside scenes of private jubilation as people embraced family members newly emerged from the interior and until then thought dead.

In that wild and lawless territory, where the air crackled with crossfire between the Vietnamese and guerrilla factions, the uprooted noncombatants fell into one mind set or another—leading to fateful choices.

Many seized the moment. Thousands plied the roads between Battambang and the border carrying on black-market trade, buying up hidden objects and sneaking into Thailand to sell them at a profit, then returning to hawk Thai products to finance their next journey.

After years under the colorless, possessionless Khmer Rouge yoke, it came as a shock to some people to see vast open-air traders' and smugglers' markets offering sandals, fishhooks, firearms, lipsticks, pop music, hypodermic needles—you name it. The goods were a magnet for gold that had been hidden ingeniously and often refound by other than its original owners. On good days, in bracelets or brooches or ingots, half a million dollars' worth of gold spilled out of Cambodia.[5]

Some of the border camps were controlled by the Khmer Serai, or free Khmer, trained earlier by U.S. Special Forces. One such place, opposite the village of Nong Samet, was dubbed by the American volunteers and medics who worked there "007." It was known to Mohm only as *Chomrom Thmei*—New Camp.

The majority of Khmer remained on the border, waiting and hoping for a time when they could return. But tens of thousands more risked crossing into Thailand, seeking the relative safety of "holding centers" like Sakeo, which were being established by the United Nations High Commissioner for Refugees (UNHCR). Rumors flew back of what to expect: food rations, medical care, protection from border fighting, and the chance for resettlement in a "third country." For those who chose to cross, that bitter grace would be bought by a total break with their own country.

For such people, about the only thing keeping them going as they dodged Vietnamese artillery, Khmer Rouge patrols, Thai border guards, and the land mines was a mysterious possibility, something the *barang* called "future."

The UNHCR took a head-in-the-sand position. They were determined to give Hanoi the benefit of the doubt, preaching peaceful repatriation for displaced Cambodians. But the Vietnamese were the real Spartans of Southeast Asia. Their business was war, and their historical design for dominating all of Vietnam, Laos and Cambodia was now within grasp. They isolated themselves from the world community, deaf to its protests against occupying Cambodia, blind to its own government's need for international economic aid. All those who had "voted with their feet" by crossing the border out of Cambodia were not then, nor would they ever be, welcomed back.

Dominated by aristocratic Europeans, however, the UNHCR bias continued to be that the worst choice would be to send these people to the USA, the ultimate cultural deformity. That brought Ambassador Abramowitz's blood to a boil. He prayed for some event that would turn world attention to the emergency. Yet even those who prophesied a mass exodus from Cambodia were unable to take in the full hallucinatory spectacle of that October in 1979.

*

Through a narrow pass in the mountains straddling Cambodia and Thailand, a long, slow line of creatures began to emerge. Wasted by malnutrition and malaria, they kept coming. With bodies shedding life as nonchalantly as feathers dropping, they kept pouring out of the narrow pass and across the Faustian border.

Their entry point was Ta Prik, a major Khmer Rouge encampment along the border. That mountain stronghold had been encircled by the Vietnamese, and now the Cambodians were being driven down the mountain by the Khmer Rouge—apparently as bait to attract world food aid for Pol Pot's crippled army. It worked. For the first time, world attention was attracted to the crisis in Cambodia. The irony was overshadowed only by the tragedy.

One of the first witnesses to enter Ta Prik, Dr. Pierre Perrin of the French organization Médecins Sans Frontières, found twenty thousand people, their faces devoid of animation, their minds frozen. Death or life—it did not seem to make any difference to them. The years of malaria and acute malnutrition, the months of being on the run and ruled by fear, had left most in anemic shock—a rare phenomenon.[6]

"These people are not in our world," the stunned doctor said then. "They are still in the world they came from."

*

Rosalynn Carter was in the air halfway between Washington and Bangkok when her Secret Service men were informed of the dicey situation. The camp she was scheduled to visit was controlled by the Khmer Rouge. That meant the wife of the president of the United States, in full view of global TV cameras, would be surrounded by hordes of starving communist insurgents. But it was too late to turn back.[7]

Ambassador Abramowitz was adamant that it did not matter. A staggering humanitarian task demanded an immediate response. Only after President Carter, Secretary of State Cyrus Vance, Assistant Secretary of State Richard Holbrooke, and Ambassador Abramowitz each personally assured the Thai government that it would not have to *keep* these castoffs, did the Thais agree to a new policy—the "Open Door" policy. Clearly, if the United States had not pressed hard, things would have been much worse. A holding center, Sakeo I, was opened at last inside Thailand. And rumors about it traveled like lightning to refugees huddled along the border between two hostile armies.

Crossing the Border,
December 1979

They say this is the border. But this isn't the end. Soldiers on the other side waiting to shoot you. We meet a trader. He tell us we have to walk along the border to find a camp, maybe another week. We have to pass O Chrau [Deep River], it used to be a big trading place, and find the bridge into Thailand.

"What's that?" I ask the woman I go with. It's a bamboo stuck in the ground with a leaf on top of it.

She say it's good luck. But it smell bad here, funny greasy burning smell. Then I see it. The leg. Just a leg, lie there, black from sun, no person to go with it. Oh, no! Over there is a man without the leg.

"Mines."

The lady say it's a danger place. People go through here before us, they leave two or three bamboo sticks as a mark. This is a trail of the dead. See another body. Another, another. Their own body leaves a mark so we know when the mines are there. Sometime we don't know if the body is dead or they fall asleep or they still alive. Just keep running.

Mine blow up in front of us—phhsssh-swok! See a hand floating out of the air, it looks so natural, then a finger float by. Natural as a leaf blowing in the wind.

Always scare now, all the time. My hands shake every minute. Big gun noise overhead—blam! blam! blam!—hear fighting all the time. Even when I sleep, I dream it's still happening. Imagine myself walking around a mine, imagine myself dropping down fast because a bomb just explode. It's in your mind all the time. If I don't have all that thing to think about, I don't know if I can go on.

You become accustom to it. You even see people kill in front of your face, shot by the big gun or blow up; you see it all the time. Your eyes see but your mind, it's not like a human mind anymore, it doesn't care what it sees.

Even I see a head come off a body.

They tell us to run on top of the bodies. You can't step on a mine if you walk on the bodies that already fall. Can I do it? I just want to get it over.

It funny. Doesn't bother me that much.

Pass O Chrau. See the river! Across the river, little Thailand house. Bridge is destroy by the time we get there. Just put some tree across . . . have to go . . . keep go.

New Camp,
December 1979

"**W**ant to buy ice cream? Sarong? I have beautiful earring."

I never think the New Camp be this way. People having their families all together, people making money, clothes a million different color, people have gold, shoe, earring—I don't see these things for so long. Never see ice cream in my life. So I go a little sick in that New Camp.

Really, really sick. So skinny my feet are swollen. I'm so pale. But I'm not as bad as a lot of people. I can still walk. Sleep all the day. So dizzy, I don't eat for a long, long time. Have nothing to trade for food. All the grass is dead here. No fruit tree to pick. There's one small pool of muddy rainwater people use for bathing and drinking. After awhile I have the diarrhea, because I keep drinking that water. Everything fall apart after that.

The lady I run with from Mong, she find me. She has a little food stand, she wants me to help her. She has her own real daughters, older than me, but they're not smart. She tell me to make a fireplace with rocks, find the wood, set out a couple of chairs and little tables. She stir-fry the noodles and I take the money, Thai money, two baht a plate. But that lady pretend to people I'm her daughter. She use me to make better business.

"See my lovely daughter?" the lady call out. "Stop here, my sweet daughter serve you."

Every morning I wake up dizzy, everything around me is fake, not a real family, not a real town, not a real mother. The woman's voice so kind when the people around. But at night when she count the money, she never talk to me, never look at me, I'm nothing to her.

A man and wife come to our food stand every day, I guess they begin to understand that lady is not really my mother. They pass on the gossip—tell me there's a place for children without parents way on the other side of camp. Sometime a bus come there and pick up children, take them to another camp in Thailand. They can be support and live safe there, maybe they even have the chance to go to another country.

I'm desperate. I do anything to get away. I wait for a good chance. One morning in the dark I run away. I don't have any real family so I should find some way I want to live, I want to make something out of life.

I find the children place. It's a long tin roof over mats. Ten children there, one older girl. The housemother is young and beautiful. I think, "How lucky I am!" The housemother is nice to me. Not many days pass and I feel a little bit close to her.

One day she tell me a secret. She know a woman in the camp who want children, she like pretty girl best. I don't say no or yes. The housemother take me to the house of that woman. I don't like the look of it right away.

It's a permanent home, not a tent like everyone else. They must be really rich. The woman invite me in and the first thing I see is bright silky pillows. Yes, and curtains, like walls of soft silk, dividing the bedrooms, I don't know how many but more than two bedrooms. The woman has a man with her, they kind of old, but she has three girls all young and pretty.

She gives me lunch, smoked fish from Thailand, and sausage and all kind of expensive things on a fine plate. The smell of fish sauce, oh, how it pinch my nose with its sharp rottish smell, the smell of my old life! I almost faint, fall back in the silken pillow. Then I hear that woman say sweet things in my ear. She always want another daughter, she say, another pretty little daughter . . . but why should anyone want me? I'm not pretty. I'm skin and yellow and sick, just a pathetic little thing. She say never mind.

The other girls don't call her mother. Something is strange. I don't sleep that whole night. I don't know what I'm falling into.

The next day I'm resting in a hammock outside the house. I go inside to get a handkerchief, and all of a sudden I see the housemother —the old woman is handing her money. Just a quick motion. They don't see me. I slip outside. I feel sick.

The older girl from the children's place happen to come with the housemother. "Are you going to live in this place?" she ask me. "It doesn't look normal, you know."

"I know." I don't say, but I think that housemother try to sell me.

"Attack is coming," the older girl warn me. "Vietnamese. We're leaving today. A truck is going to pick up children who want to go to another camp, in Thailand."

It's the last minute—I have to choose. I don't know who's telling lie, who's telling true. What kind of life are you going to get—who can know? Have to make a decision.

The housemother come out and say to the older girl. "Time to go. But Mohm is going to stay, isn't she." She doesn't put it as a question.

"No," I say.

"What?" She surprised.

"I'm not staying here."

She say, "Why?"

I don't answer. I'm scared but I can't show it.

They all look at each other. They must know they can't force me to stay.

"Fine, then," the housemother say lightly. I see—just a quick motion again—but I think I see her slip the money into the woman's hand back.

Everybody get separate. I'm alone again. Back in the children place, people are packing up their little things. The girls I know are leaving. One asks me to take her leftover rice and run to the market, see what I can get for her to eat on the ride. I go alone. Run from one stall to another, hold up the girl's little ration bag. "Please, what can I buy with this rice money?"

No one look at me. Maybe I so small now, no one can see me. It's so hot, my head is spinning.

Somebody behind me scream, "Move!"

I just wish it's all a dream.

"Move, hurry! It's your last chance before attack!" The older girl come to get me. She say something about the truck, it's the last truck, I'm so dizzy I can't put the words together.

"Run, Mohm!"

I run, fall down, run I don't know where, the truck . . .

Feel a hand reach under me, scoop me up like a dead little vegetable. It's a man. It's the truck. Maybe it's a better chance. All I'm looking for is a chance.

New York, 1979

What trivial crisis was I absorbed in while Mohm walked that butchered land, praying she would not be gored by a poison stick or lulled by the breathless heat of the forest into stumbling on one of the pits full of bodies, boiled to the surface by the flame of the sun? But she found she could walk on a tightrope of corpses to avoid the buried death of mines. She was a survivor.

*

My crisis? I have been attempting to talk to Clay about having a child.

He is scared; the conversations are elliptical, fragmented; a true exchange never really gets started. He says I'd be impossible if I had another child. But now I have the financial freedom to continue writing *and* have a family life, without the same pressures I had as a struggling writer and a single parent with Maura. I try to be honest about the work involved in having a child. He snaps back, "I have no intention of giving up my job to stay home to take care of a child." "But whoever said—?" I try to talk about how a child touches him, how he can relax his defenses, be tender and playful; I see him doing it with Maura. I want that for him. He says he'll think about it and we'll talk later.

But we didn't, not really. Oh, it drifted piecemeal into subsequent conversations, like a romanticized acquaintance who assures you whenever you meet, "I'm definitely going to call you," but he never does, and you knew he wouldn't. We never fully discussed it, never openly. Instead, I hinted, made innuendoes, and occasionally landed on him as the heel of the Western world for slinking away from a family commitment. I wish I had not lost the time.

*

"And do you have a family, Ms. Sheehy?"

"Oh, yes."

"How many children?"

"Maura, the one I told you about."

"That's it?"

"And a dog."

"And you're divorced?"

"I have a . . . there's a man I share my life with."

I am not handling this newspaper interview well. This is the Midwest and I come from Manhattan. They expect me to have a one-testicle voice and fish-scale disco pants and a theory for how-to-have-it-all. But like many women, I carry the human baggage of an adult life begun with a different set of premises. Premises, premises.

*

Easter. I want a puppy. My sixteen-year-old daughter says it's impractical.

I tell her about the little fluff ball of a Lhasa apso I saw in the window of the pet store. It's the spitting image of our own Tibetan terrier, same black and white swayback, same flop of hair over the eyes, same impudent little face with the lion fang's sticking up over the black lips—

"Oh God, Mother."

I try to tell her what it felt like when I held the puppy to my chest and it stopped wriggling and lay there, perfectly still.

"How could you want *another* dog to feed and walk and leave hair balls all over?"

"I don't know. I just want it."

"Okay, but *you* clean up when it poops on the new carpet."

*

The word *marriage* does not come up much these days. Probably it's been sent out to that great Edsel parking lot where they keep words like *poise* and *togetherness* until they're needed again, along with temporarily junked cultural artifacts such as breezeways, DC-10 cargo doors, Pintos, Murphy beds, and garter belts. People don't know what they believe anymore and so they are strident about stating their beliefs. Young women say they want to get laid and they'll call you sometime. Young men say they want to be "loving." Children are in charge of the culture.

I am keeping lists:

Expect period.

Register for jazz dancing class.

See specialist in late pregnancies. Keep temp. chart.

The new dog is pregnant. Impregnated by a Schnauzer four times her size. She comes into my bed, pushes her cotton candy pink-stretched belly against my backside, whimpers. There must be six German storm troopers practicing manuevers inside her delicate Tibetan-china womb.

*

In January 1980 an invitation comes from the White House. Rosalynn Carter is forming an emergency National Cambodia Crisis Committee. The letter says one hundred prominent Americans, from the business, labor, media, entertainment, religious, and voluntary communities, will be responsible for mobilizing private-sector support for relief efforts.

I am both flattered and chagrined. What do I know about the "Cambodia crisis"? I see grainy indistinct pictures in the occasional *New York Times* article: a sea of tuberous bodies stranded in a dust-scape, starving, diffident; why did they just stand there around their little plastic tents? Usually there was a mother in the foreground, cradling her child, still unable to stare back with even a silent reproach. The more memories of the war in Southeast Asia blurred like a bad Xerox copy, the more those photographs screamed silently for explanation.

So we sat on gilt chairs in the East Room, under eight hundred pounds of cut-glass chandeliers and fluted pilasters, and we discussed how to get rice and seed and medicine across "land bridges" and past the Vietnamese political blockade. The blockade already had allowed forty thousand tons of food sent from the West to rot in warehouses. We wanted to reach survivors in the interior of Cambodia—a land that had disappeared from Western consciousness for four years and that no Westerner or American had glimpsed, filmed, entered, or could even be truly certain was still there.

The Last Kilometer

The survivors kept coming out. In November 1979 a second mammoth holding center had been opened for them: Khao-I-Dang camp. Cambodians picked up by U.N. personnel who cruised the northern border were stacked upright like sticks in the back of rice trucks. These were mostly middle-class survivors of Phnom Penh, and their physical condition appeared to be marginally better than that of the wretched who had walked into Sakeo I camp. But the same desolation seemed to rattle within their bodies and blow out in front of them like a deadly draft, turning the volunteers who met them numb. They had to be taken off the trucks like rag dolls; the Prince of Death seemed still to have their souls clamped in his vise.

Mohm was among them.

Khao-I-Dang
Camp,
January 1980

I so lucky I make it to this place. Amazing place. Nice and clean. You
have a proper house. Everyone sick like I am. I have a new feeling. This
is where I belong.

The first day they give us cracker and milk. I never taste milk. I hate
it but by then I'll eat anything. Then they give us a skirt, a blouse,
shoe, a little round blue mirror. I don't want to look at my face. Somehow, I forget how to use all those girly things.

They put all the children without parents together, in a center by
ourself, with wire all around. Like our own village. I'm in "Sancette B"
with the little girls and boys. We have a long dormitory with a roof of
woven palm leaf and bamboo beds raise up off the ground. They even
give us a shelf over the bed to put your cup on.

This is a place I can't imagine. We have water, three tank of it.
Sometime I just sit to watch for the water truck, watch it fill up the
tank with more water than we use up in a whole day. I can't remember
much of how I get here. Every time I open my mouth, the words I
want scramble around. Can't say anything. I don't go out of the children center for a pretty long time. I'm really scared of going out.

Sometime at night I hear shooting. Shouts, screams. In the morning
you see the people who get hurt, everything they have is stolen. Happens night after night. People say it's the Thai. Can't sleep without
hear scream.

My hair begin to fall out. I guess I'm sick in many ways. One day
I'm alone in the dormitory. Sun flash on the little blue mirror children
hang over their bed; I decide to take a look at myself. That face, I can't

ever forget it. It still give me nightmares. For so long I never really look at myself—in Pol Pot time even I forget if I'm a boy or a girl. Now I see a face, it doesn't even look human. It's an old face, drag down under the eye, pale and yellow. The head is bare except for about fifty hairs, hanging like whiskers from an old man's chin.

The children come back; they're singing a song, playing, making fun. I lay down and turn my face to the wall. I feel the lice hopping over those few hairs; the itch make me wild before but not now. I lay quiet, hoping the lice chew up all the rest of the hairs. Then I be like some little crab fall out of its shell; no one ever notice me again.

Every night the bad dream take me away. The world in that dream is a long hall with a heavy door at the end of it. The trees are unsure where they supposed to stand. Once in a while, I hear a loud noise smashing. It could be an exploding bomb. I cry for help, but it's hopeless. I am all alone, like a little cat inside a boat in the middle of the ocean. And when the wave rock the boat, it carries the boat farther and farther away. As if the world has no doors.

About a month after I come, they finish the school. I think it going to be so exciting. I go to the tent and sit in front of the paper book. It feel strange. I don't know how to read. Must be I'm stupid. It's not exciting. I can't keep my mind on that paper. My mind is filled with something else, I don't know what it is. Feel like punching someone, hard.

I touch my head. Funny, a patch of new hair is grow in one place, another place. But most of my head is bare, feels like ground too sick and tired to grow a good crop. The camp mother help me. She cut off the long hairs. She say it's better to even it up.

I like to play games, boy games. I get into fights. So many fights. Girls, boys, anybody who say something nasty, I just punch and hit and scratch and shout. One day a big boy, Thy, he's playing volleyball with us.

"I catch you, you're cheating!" I shout.

"Am not."

"Am so."

"What you going to do about it?"

I jump on him. That big boy so surprised, he just go flying into the dust. He get up and walk away.

Next day we play again. Thy say it to me in front of all the others: "You're not a girl."

"I am so."

"You look just like a boy."

"Do not."

"Do so."

"I know what I am," I say very quiet.

"If you're so sure," he say in a big voice, "why don't you take off your clothes and show everybody."

My head swim all red I want to kill him I hate him so much how can he say such a thing he might as well bury my face in the dirt. I run away I never speak to that horrible Thy again in my whole life.

*

Gossip come around that my relative still alive. She's in another part of the camp. I don't know who it is for sure, but I can guess. I wait until the water truck come so I can take some water to her. When I find her, it's the woman pretend to be my mother, the woman I run away from on the border. She speak to me as if nothing happen. She doesn't ask me to stay with her. I'm glad.

The camp mother for children without parents come to talk to me. She say maybe it be better for me if I forget about everything that happen and try to live my own life instead of in the past. You can't have all those things again.

I think about it. Maybe she is right. So I try to let my mind go. Forget everything. That was the past. Both my parents die. Don't think about it. If some of my relative still alive, let them bother somebody else. I just want to live a simple life, not own anything, not think about anything.

The one thing I miss is my brother. My blood. My closest blood. If I can only find him again, that's the only thing I wish. Just to have a piece of our family left. He know just what to tell me so I survive, and now there's still me. But I don't even know—is there still him?

I have a new dream. It's a river, I'm on one side. She's on the other side. Her hair hanging down on her neck while she works, I know it is her, her beautiful hair, dancing side to side on her sweet narrow shoulders, the bright sun shining into her hair and she's so alive! I have to do something to make her turn around. I jump into the river, punch and kick and thrash all around, but I can't go, can't swim, the river keep pushing me back to my side. I get out and throw a little rock at her. Please, turn around, see me . . . Mother!

She turn and look at me. I look back at her. She have no teeth and her face is all wrinkle. She is old as death. She does not know me.

*

I stop trying to remember why my parents die.

PART II

In Transit

A lotus indeed.
But a lotus without a stem.
—EIGHTH CENTURY CAMBODIAN INSCRIPTION
FROM ANGKOR THOM

Khao-I-Dang Camp . . . January–June 1980

The process by which those dead souls in Khao-I-Dang camp came back to vitality astounded volunteers with its rapidity. During the first two or three months the survivors appeared to reexperience the past stage by stage. At first, many described being haunted by spirits of those who had died. Children often awoke convulsed with visions of being called to join their dead parents or grandparents, sometimes at gunpoint.

"Why do they want to shoot you?" volunteers would ask. The children's eyes would sink back as if seeking blindness by an act of will. Only when the Kru Khmer held ceremonies asking the spirits to excuse the children for whatever evil acts they had seen or committed did these seizures subside.

The first actual release of emotion came through singing. One night from the loudspeaker a gentle, beautiful wailing floated over the camp. It was a woman's voice, singing of the past sorrows. People came out of their huts and lifted their eyes to the sound and let the tears leak out of their sealed hearts. Tears, of course, like the old songs, had been forbidden under Pol Pot.

Others begged for listeners to hear their stories, but there were not enough volunteers to absorb a fraction of their pain. People turned then to drawing. On blank brown pages they began imprinting the grooves of agony like woodcuts from the unconscious.

The first drawings were of chaos. No earth, no sky or trees, no right side up; only a cockeyed spin of children, parents, soldiers, spurting blood. Tentatively, some of the furniture of life reappeared in the drawings—huts, eating halls, working fields—and gradually the barbarities of the Pol Pot regime were depicted with increasing realism. One drawing would show a man trying futilely to blow life into a fire while another carried to him a rat, for cooking, by the tail. Another drawing would depict the carcass of a live prisoner, tied upside down by hands and feet to a pole, being carted off like a side of half-eaten beef. Brutish labor, torture, starvation, mass graves: These were the ubiquitous subjects.

Abruptly, from an obsession with the recent past, the drawings shifted subject to the future, or rather, to fantasies of the future. Placid scenes of families beside stilt houses at sunset or a boy and girl paddling a sampan along a still river were set, apparently, in a new and peaceful Cambodia. There was not a single drawing of camp life, not a moment lost dwelling on the intractable present. The characteristic Khmer weakness for fantasy was in full flower.

By early 1980, less than two months after it had opened, Khao-I-Dang camp bulged with 130,000 refugees—then the largest concentration of Khmer in the world outside of Cambodia. Overwhelmed, the Thai government declared its Open Door policy closed. Three layers of barbed wire fended off the camp from new arrivals. Paramilitary guards patrolled the camp perimeter, swinging M-16 automatics. But the refugees kept coming.

*

Schooling had to start, in every sense, from a *tabula rasa*. The daunting task was undertaken by one of the few Cambodian educators to survive, a high-school principal from Battambang named Sok Bun Heng, assisted by an American college student who happened to be passing through, Peter Rainer. Neither of them knew the first thing about construction.

They began with tents and bamboo tables and thirty thousand children whose minds for five years had been suspended in ignorance. Apart from calculating the tactics of survival, mental activity had lain in hibernation. These children simply had not developed the habit of thinking. Would they, could they, ever catch up? Of the thirty thousand, only five thousand children could read, and even they had attained no more than third-grade level before the Khmer Rouge abolished schools. All were barefoot, shirtless; some were naked. But for all the heroic efforts, teachers were few and inconsistent, textbooks nonexistent, and when the sun fumed through the plastic tents, children often fainted. The smaller ones often were suffering the effects of prolonged malnutrition; the only weight they registered on a scale came from their bones. Others swooned from recurrences of malaria, twitched from eye infections, suffered from bone TB. And some were too nervous to leave their compounds. First grades were set up for these children in each section of the camp. Schoolrooms ran eight hours a day on double sessions. It was imperative to supplement the children's diets and to construct more humane school structures. Sheppie Abramowitz, wife of the American ambassador, took a keen interest in Khao-I-Dang, and before long, she had scared up construction materials from the United States and encouraged a Thai agency, CEBERS, to supplement the children's diet with eggs, fruit, vegetables, and even chicken and meat. Sok Bun Heng had to appeal to many international agencies to provide the rudiments—shirts and trousers—before even asking for such niceties as pencils and crayons. The French contributed slippers, the Japanese flip-flops; other agencies donated fabric, and soon two old warhorse machines were stitching up children's clothes around the clock.

The International Rescue Committee assisted the Khmer teachers to establish a vast school system numbering over eleven thousand children. IRC helped in printing textbooks, procuring teaching materials, and organizing the teaching staff. For most of the children it was the first schooling they had had in over five years.

The children learned fast. In only three or four months, most of those over the age of ten had grasped reading. They were then considered advanced students and sent to the School Center, which went to the fifth grade. Those who became confident about reading Khmer were started right away on English. Other subjects, taught from hand-stenciled pages, were arithmetic, health, and basic biology. There was no time to teach history, and no attempt made to give the children a world view. Most had no idea of what "America" meant, or "Canada" or even "France"; children could not tell one foreign volunteer from another. And probably none had a concept of the universe. What Western educators would call the study of science was consigned, according to traditional Cambodian educational practice, to the province of religion.

Mohm was ten years old when she entered Khao-I-Dang, but in her six months there she did not learn to read. Her concentration was poor. By all accounts, she showed signs of depression. And depression after loss is a period when the brain, searching frantically for a solution to problems that are temporarily insoluble, exhausts itself. Much of the information stored in the brain may be blocked, temporarily irretrievable, until a way is found to accept the losses and find substitutes. Only then is the brain able to reorganize stored information in such a way that access may be gained to it for the purpose of new learning.

Depression was as common as the common cold among the camp population, according to the Khmer health technicians who had been exposed to Western medical theory. But to the Khmer themselves, whose traditional belief system offered no concept of mental illness, there was no way to explain that depression was a normal stage of the mourning process, that it probably would give way to anger, and that these states of emotion were nothing to be ashamed of, not a punishment for bad deeds. Lacking the means to communicate such reassurances, relief workers found many survivors mired in Mohm's predicament.

If one can imagine the survivor's mind as a volcano, filled with the ash of years of servitude and shame, one can imagine the palisades of anger to be uncovered, the white-hot walls of humiliation waiting to rupture. Now that her captors could no longer force her into a position of helplessness, Mohm's initial depression and fearfulness gave way to aggression. Any surrogate for her former tormentors became fair game. She sought out rough boy's play and overreacted to the slightest injustice—attacking without warning, incapable of forgiveness.

This is also to be expected. Under the conditions of extremity during Pol Pot time, the emotional life of orphaned children must have regressed to the atavistic. Survival instincts informed every act. There were no distinctions, no nuances. One operated from a single imperative: Submit or be killed. Although such extreme reactions were no longer appropriate, survival instincts continued to dominate social behavior. The children were rough, unruly, quick to anger. Their speech patterns were crude and their moods volatile. Gusts of laughter could twist in no time into a corkscrew of anger.

But what mostly occupied Mohm's mind for the first half year in the refugee camp, as she later recounted, were nightmares of remembering. After she took her camp mother's advice to let go of the past, gradually, gratefully, she discovered the emollient of forgetting. After five months, Mohm was called to her first interview.

*

"What is your family name?" asked the camp official.

Her mind was suddenly a blank slate, the name wiped away like chalk with a rag. She had known it yesterday.

"I don't remember."

"Do you remember your father?"

A silhouette flickered in her mind's eye—a tall man slung with a rifle
—then it was gone. There was no face.

"Do you remember his name?"

"Phat. But that's not real; he fakes it."

"What was his real name?"

"I can't—I don't—"

"Can you remember your mother's family name?"

"I don't remember."

"Then do you remember the name of the foster mother who
brought you to the border?"

"No."

All she produced were the given names of her family members. And
so, on a dossier form provided by the UNHCR, the bare bones of
Mohm's first ten years of family history were recorded:

RELATION	NAME	OCCUPATION	COMMENTS
FATHER:	Phat (Alias)	soldier	killed by P.P.
MOTHER:	Kim	housewife	ditto
BROTHER:	Heng	pupil	forced by Khmer Rouge to fight with them during Vietnamese attack
BROTHER:	Kgnel	age 3	starvation
SISTER:	Pou	age 2	ditto

Comments/General impression of minor: Very mature behavior.
Education—starting here. Is interested in literature. Hopes to become a teacher. Minor was brought to the border by a family she
traveled and lived with. Minor does not recall any of their names
and would not like to find them. Misses her older brother (who
may still be alive) but would go to any country. Definitely does *not*
want to return to Cambodia.

Sakeo II Camp . . .
August 1980–
December 1981

In the wet gluey heat of August, Mohm was transferred to a new refugee camp, Sakeo II. The children feared being separated, so accustomed had they become to helping one another, but benevolently, the three children's units from Khao-I-Dang were transferred intact. At Sakeo, the children's center was neatly fenced off and the wooden houses arranged in a quadrangle. With no evidence of phantom control by the Khmer Rouge, Mohm could relax her vigilance. She determined to teach herself to read.

Poring over picture books, she matched the words to the drawings. She played with the words on her tongue. Some days it was like walking through a door into a fantastic kingdom, a vast territory filled with amazing creatures and people to look at from a safe distance. She could read alone; she liked that. She asked for more books. Her housemother sent her to the camp library, where new storybooks were being run off on the mimeograph machine every week. Giddily indiscriminate, she read alphabetically through Khmer kings and Lon Nol and marriage customs among the Malays and menstruation. Imagine that! Babies weren't dropped into their mother's arms by a giant-beaked bird, as she had always thought. Cambodian mothers did not discuss such things with their daughters; that must be what books were for.

When books from the camp library ran thin, she found the Christian evangelical center and began reading pamphlets about someone called Jesus Christ. She found the story unbearably sad. The evangelicals were eager to have Mohm come to their services. She attended a few, but the English made no sense. They gave her a Bible translated into

Khmer. She read a little . . . about a god who makes a flood to destroy every living thing on the face of the earth, a god who orders a man to burn up his own son . . . what a cruel god these Christians had! She did not want to read anymore about death. She went back to reread the romantic stories of Cambodia's ancient past.

Hungrily devouring tale after tale, Mohm became, without noticing it, almost mute.

> I don't care what people talk about anymore. I hear the voices but I don't try to understand the words. I don't talk to anyone. Stop talking. I just read. Only I want to take the words on the pages of my books and keep them inside me, where no one can change them or twist them or use them to trick.

A Khmer temple sprang up, and monks emerged. A traditional medicine center was started and Kru Khmer began collecting herbs and bark and leaves to prepare remedies for treating headaches, asthma, lesions, and all sorts of what Westerners would call mental problems. Like many others, Mohm gravitated back to the familiar cultural supports that had traditionally served to interpret the mysteries of life and death.

But some of the Christian evangelical groups were insistent in offering their services. Their practitioners planted the suggestion among the Khmer that God had not heard their prayers during the suffering under Pol Pot because they were not Christians. If they were to have any hope of a positive answer to their prayers to be resettled in a third country, they would have to accept Christ.

Waves of conversions began in the camp. Some of the children who had lost their families identified readily with their Christian benefactors, learning to reject their degraded origins. And then the seizures started.

A woman suddenly began wandering aimlessly around the camp. She had lost all her children but until this abrupt change had appeared normal. Her hair and dress became disheveled; her speech grew incoherent. Sometimes she would just sit in the middle of the road and squeeze her exhausted breasts as if for mother's milk and babble endlessly about Jesus; she became an embarrassment to the camp leaders. A U.N. official took her personally to the TMC, the traditional medical center. But she told the Kru Khmer she was a Christian.

Some of the Western physicians recognized the therapeutic value of

these traditional healers and suggested that many patients might benefit from a combined approach. But there were Christian missionaries
who warned their converts never to see such physicians, calling them
"doctors who speak in the devil's tongue." The miserable woman
would not request treatment from her own kind, and the Kru Khmer
would not force it. She became known as the "Mad Christian."

Passing the TMC on her way back from school one day, Mohm
thought she saw the Mad Christian. Her body was shaking all over.
The Kru Khmer stood some distance from her, holding a candle and
incense sticks and saying magic words over a jar of lustral water. Presently, he sprayed the water some distance. Mohm suddenly remembered the meaning of the ceremony. Power had been conferred on that
water by the magic words, and showering it over a person drove away
any evil spirit and freed the person from seizures. But the woman
would not come close enough; the water did not touch her. She trembled, began to coil and uncoil like a snake, slithering down to her knees,
rising up again, then twisting violently, as if she were trying to crawl
out of her own skin. Mohm walked around to see her face. The eyes
were a child's, huge and wobbling and almost, it seemed, ready to fall
out of that shrunken face. Mohm ran back inside the safety of the
children's center. If the Kru ever did drive that evil spirit out of the
woman, Mohm didn't want it to land on her!

*

One night Mohm awoke and sat bolt upright in pain. Her head was
pounding. Her stomach shuddered with cramps.

After school the next day, she sought out the Kru Khmer. He gave
her an herbal remedy for the stomachache and monkey balm for her
headache. She applied the camphory balm to her temples before clos-
ing her eyes that night. But she slept only fitfully. And once again she
awoke writhing with violent cramps. It felt to her as if somebody were
kicking at her innards, the way the kitchen lady used to kick the black
dog, and then she knew who it was. It must be her grandmother. The
monks had taught children that if they did not go to the temple and
honor their dead ancestors, their grandparents would kick them in the
stomach.

She opened her mouth to cry out—*Grandmother, I remember you!*—

but no sound came. She tried again. All at once she realized she could not speak.

One day she gathered the nerve to go inside the TMC. The air was fragrant with delicate herbs being boiled in big black cauldrons. Old women with shaven heads were grinding herbs from the forest while men chopped rubber wood to fire furnaces for steam treatments. There was more than one Kru Khmer, but they were busy. One was making an amulet out of silver, engraving it with magic formulas for protection from mines. A screaming baby was set before another healer, who chewed a mouthful of red betel and yellow areca nuts and then, in a fine, slow-motion spray, spat the medicament at a wound on the baby's arm.

Mohm approached a Kru who wore a jogging jacket over his white *krama*. Addressing him respectfully as "Om Om," or uncle, she pointed at her stomach and moaned. She used gestures to ask for a massage.

A sinewy woman was assigned to her. Mohm lay facedown and let her head swim in the light musk of cardamom and coriander, camphor and coconut. The woman began. A spear of pain shot down her arm, another dagger dug into her neck and traveled across her shoulders, and before she could catch her breath the woman was grinding her lower back with the ball of her foot. Khmer massage follows the nerves and blood vessels (unlike Western massage, which follows the muscles). Mohm could not wait until it was over.

On the next visit, the Kru Khmer said, "No massage. Magic." She was afraid. She wanted to resist. But the Kru, a man with a deep, pained tuck between his brows, began murmuring incantations. Hot waves swept over her. She slipped into a state beyond conscious description. Involuntary sounds came from her throat.

The Kru would have interpreted the sounds escaping from Mohm as a sign that she was being visited by the spirit of a dead parent or grandparent. It was not Mohm speaking, but the spirit speaking through her. He would have asked the sufferer to join with him as he attempted to intercede in the conversation, inquiring of the dead relative, "What are you angry about?" The dead relative might communicate: "Why do you never take food to the temple or light a candle to honor me; why do you never remember me before you go to bed?" The spirit might be so angry, it would demand immediate appeasement: The child should cross over and join it in the next world. In an effort to stave off fatal convulsions or suicide, the Kru would try to negotiate a more reasonable settlement, saying for example, "If your grandchild makes offerings for you in the temple, and remembers you every night, will you give her permission to live out her life and join you at the end?"

Some children responded to such ceremonies by trembling and twitching for hours in a fevered trancelike state. Family members and friends would stand vigil over the youngster, supporting the struggle sometimes for a day and night. And then, as if miraculously, the tension of guilt would break. The trembling would stop. And the child would sit up with a calm, radiant smile.[1]

But no such overnight cure came to Mohm.

*

Perhaps, she thought, the spirit was taking her back piece by piece. It was the children's duty to make offerings for dead parents or grandparents, but what had she offered, what had any of them offered? For all she knew, her mother had been left in a pit, staring with open eyes like the dead fish she found the day of her mother's disappearance. And her grandmother, what honor had she given her grandmother?

> I see my grandmother in that line . . . soldiers pointing their guns . . . people tie to people like cows . . . the soldiers lead them down the road to the forest. I don't go to my grandmother. I let them take her to kill.

She became as fascinated as she was fearful about what the spirit might do. After taking her voice, perhaps it would take her eyes. It could change itself into a bird and pluck out her eyes like berries; then it could carry them in its beak over all the forests and rivers and mountains, using them as another pair of eyes, pure clear mirrors, allowing it to see everything anew as a child would see it.

Maybe it would replace her eyes with the eyes that had fallen out of the Mad Christian woman. Then she would be old before she ever knew what menstruation and marriage were like.

Mohm's headaches, stomach pains, and muteness persisted. She returned to the Kru for magic showers.

But her hair fell out; she could not eat, could not sleep. She lived in a constant state of tension, her mind unable for a moment to relax. The unthinkable thought, the black suggestion hovering always like a bat poised to dive at her head and carry off her mind, was that it had all been her fault.

*

It was at this stage, roughly six months after their arrival in Thailand, that the effects of prolonged trauma became evident in many refugees like Mohm. Some camp inhabitants began exhibiting bizarre behavior. Like the Mad Christian, they would slip from apparent normalcy to trembling, or to complaining that they could not breathe or get up from bed because a ghost was standing on their chest (the equivalent to an anxiety attack in Western terms). Others began wandering about talking to themselves, or to invisible voices. To Western-trained eyes, the last were classical symptoms of schizophrenia.

Many such people were diagnosed as psychotic.[2] Western medical practitioners hurriedly opened a psychiatric ward. The result was that the extended family, normally very effective in providing emotional support during mental crises, pulled away from those relatives branded "abnormal" and hospitalized. Their own reserves exhausted, many were just as glad to have one less family member to worry about.

*

A small-eyed, scarlet-blotched pig's head is fished out of the boiling cauldron. It is placed next to another pig's head on the altar of offerings, face up, and its tail is stuffed into its mouth. A murmur of appreciation runs through the emotionally troubled who have assembled for the ceremony in the TMC—this is High Magic, of a magnitude seldom seen since before Pol Pot time.

When men finish plucking two freshly killed black chickens, the fowl too are laid on a shelf of an altar that glows as if with an inner light. Much fuss has been made to find the youngest, unripe sugar palms to wrap as a glossy skin around banana-tree trunks; the result are columns resembling pale green marble. Coconut-tree branches are bent into arches on either side, their fronds looking like huge curved green fish bones. The Kru Khmer chants in Pali, a royal language. He is asking the spirits to help clear the minds of those seated before him.

Other freshly dressed offerings are laid out: huge watermelons, bowls of limes, banana-leaf cones, and candles in lucky clusters of threes and fives. Flying birds made of golden palm flutter above and sprays of orchids festoon the steps full of offerings. Above all hangs a pastel image of the Buddha.

The late afternoon sun finds slots in the bamboo curtains and flutters across the cool darkness of the traditional medicine center. Above the few dozen still figures, deep in meditation, the only movement is the swinging of a gauzy white kite. And then the orchestra breaks into an exultant sound. Brass bells lighten the mood, a double xylophone chimes in along with a wind instrument played by a blind man. A drummer smoking a cheroot uncorks a bottle of lustral water and sprays it over the offerings; then he flings the water over the assembled sufferers. An astringent scent slices through the cardamom-soft candled air.

Some of the people rub themselves vigorously. The Kru throws out more of the water and people shake and toss their heads. Each from his or her own private hell has come for spiritual cleansing.

*

Dr. Jean-Pierre Higel, a French psychoanalyst who persuaded the Knights of Malta to support a traditional medicine center at Khao-I-Dang, draws parallels between Western and Southeast Asian phenomenology. The Khmer use the concept of possession by spirits to reduce or relieve guilt. When a person commits a socially deviant act—a married woman falls in love with another man, or a child acts destructively toward his brothers and sisters—that, too, may be laid to intervention by a troubled spirit. The traditional healer asks the spirit to speak out and then drives it away. The individual need not take personal blame for "bad" feelings or unacceptable wishes; he has been possessed.

*

At camp Dr. Higel urged a collaboration between the two medical traditions. Khmer and American health practitioners together held mixed meetings to sort out emergency cases—spinal meningitis went to the West, asthma attacks to the East. Interviews with immigration officers, particularly as final judgment on a case for resettlement came closer, often caused profound stress. Not uncommonly, fear of rejection brought on an acute mental breakdown. The refugees welcomed hypodermic needles and miracle drugs, but it was when these methods were supplemented by the magic showers, herbal remedies, and exorcisms of the Kru that many difficult cases were cured.

*

The tracing program for family members of the unaccompanied minors got under way in the fall of 1980. Each child's photograph was run off on posters along with all the available information. Mohm's picture was smudge-eyed but smiling; with her one inch of hair she looked like a little boy. She was identified simply as: MOM, AGE TEN, FEMALE, BORN 1970. Beneath that was the chart of skimpy data about her family members. The International Rescue Committee, in charge of delivering these posters to operatives on the Cambodian border, saw to it that they found their way into the interior.

On October 19, 1980, eleven months after crossing into Thailand, Mohm was reinterviewed about the possibility of living relatives to whom she might be returned in Cambodia:

> Minor claims she has had no news from relatives while she has been in the camp. No visitors or letters. Claims she has no cousins or aunts or other relatives. Minor studies Khmer and is able to read and write a little. Seems to be secure and happy in the children's center. Wants to continue to live with her friends. Minor never speaks about the future, except to say she does not want to return to Kampuchea.

Mohm went back and back again for magic showers. One day the Kru told her "ban," it's finished. She later recalled the change she experienced:

> One year pass, and I can't believe I can forget so many things. Memories so strong, but I completely forgot all about them. I just give up the whole thing and I don't want to think. I can always have a good little dream when thinking of my future. I'm only thinking now how I want to make my life better. Until I forget my own name.

After she had read virtually every book in the camp, Mohm looked in the mirror again and caught her breath, astonished. Her hair had all grown back. Her face was altogether different: She was a child again. She ran outside to find the children and join in their games. She began to play badminton and developed considerable skill. Hitting, winning, joining in the team spirit and forgetting herself, she began to feel like a different person. One day, at the end of an exciting game, she found herself shouting out loud.

Imagine that! Her voice had returned as suddenly as it departed; it flew out of her mouth and back into her and out again just as naturally as a bird gliding from tree to tree—her voice.

The spirit must have been satisfied. She was to be freed after all. It was as if someone had wrapped a cord around her head and had been pulling tight for months, but suddenly the cord had been released. Her head cleared. She stopped thinking so hard. The terrible tension in her mind relaxed. And then, as she felt it, a new and wonderful life force surged within her. It was like fresh seed, pulsing under the dung hill, pushing against its seed case with a reckless energy. She was ready to reinvent herself.

*

Living with children of all ages, Mohm made friends with older girls and boys and with the housemother, Bun Soeun, and her boyfriend. The housemother insisted she take iron tablets every day. Her body began to fill out in proportion: The legs and arms were still elongated and rail-like, but she developed a waist, a tiny swell of hips, and at last a stomach appeared.

One day, behind her back, she heard Bun Soeun say to her boyfriend, "Mohm is pretty, isn't she?"

"I'm going to engage Mohm to my son," he said. Everybody laughed. His son was only five years old.

But not long after, a boy named Phroh, big and strong—probably seventeen—said in front of others, "When Mohm grows up, *I'm* going to marry her." He was teasing, of course, but at least they didn't confuse her anymore with a boy. She began to take a keen interest in her appearance.

*

Cambodian classical dance was being taught. Finding her fingers to be double-jointed and her body able easily to bend and sway to her command, Mohm worked hard at learning the movements. One could never learn them all—two thousand positions for the hands alone! But here was something precise, something she could control. She grew her nails as long and strong as spoons, and every night she cracked her fingers so they would bend farther back.

Her parents used to say that dancers were not good girls; she didn't have to be a dancer to attract attention. Now she found herself wanting fervently to show they were wrong.

And I do it. I do turn into a dancer, and still I am a good girl.

From dancing she moved on to acting. A young playwright in the camp was turning out three-hour Khmer operettas every week. Mohm usually got the part of the young princess in the Khmer king's court. They had a performing platform, huge amplifiers, a microphone, pre-1975 Khmer popular-music tapes, even costumes—and the audiences! Every afternoon people would gather in the dust block and watch the rehearsals, then stay and cheer for the performance. It was a thrill beyond description. The child who had felt a bug beneath the foot of *Angka*, the pathetic cringing little minor who had lost her voice, was now flinging out her voice across a thousand heads—as if by magic!

So engrossed did Mohm become with the performing arts, in fact, she forgot many days about going to school. Her housemother had to report her to Darvy Heder.

"Why don't you go to school?" the Cambodian director asked her.

Click click, she flicked her nails.

Mohm held her stubborn silence through one after another of Darvy's lectures. At last, she burst out with what most of the minors were feeling:

"What good is it for me to go to school!"

Darvy made an announcement to all those in the children's center: "We have to study hard; no fooling around with things like acting. Girls must learn well so they never have to be dependent on a man." Darvy, having experienced divorce, had a strong point of view. But

Mohm decided to show Darvy just as she had "shown" her parents. For the next few months, she scarcely went near school. Day and night she devoted herself to the acting troupe.

> I learned and I was good and everyone in the camp clapped when I did the shows. I won my point, halfway. Sometimes I go too far.

Mohm grew her hair so long she could sit on it. One night she twisted her straight hair into dozens of tiny braids, and in the morning when she brushed it out, she looked like a foreign movie star—whoever saw an Asian girl with a huge cloud of curls!

The boy who had taunted her in Khao-I-Dang about looking like a boy began to say, "You look more like a girl now." But the minute she let down her guard, he called out, "Ha ha, girls are weak. See if you can catch me!" She dropped the game they were playing and walked away, vowing again to hate Thy for the rest of her life.

She went to the karate teacher and told him she wanted to learn. He didn't teach girls, he said. So Mohm watched him from outside the tent day after day and mimicked his moves. When the teacher noticed her, he criticized her movements harshly. Months later, he acknowledged that she could do as well as a boy.

> Sakeo is the happiest time I ever have. I like playing a lot of boy's games. If I were back in Cambodia, girls have to stay behind their mother in the kitchen. But dancing and acting, I feel special, people notice me, I'm not just a little bug.

The American director of the children's center, Margie de Monchy, remembered Mohm out of the thousand or so minors she saw in two years. "She was never afraid. She always made contact. I close my eyes and see Mohm coming in to say hello, always carrying one of the houseparent's little babies on her hip, always eager to talk. She wanted to be noticed. She captured your attention."

*

Sometimes when the American volunteers had a party, they asked Mohm and her friend, Peng Rann, to dance for their entertainment. They gave her a hundred baht. This meant she could support a little family. She kept a cat and named it the Khmer for "sweetheart." She added a chicken and later a fish. When the egg was passed out once a week to children as supplemental protein, Mohm traded hers back to the housemother. And every morning before school, she would hurry to the market to buy food from her earnings for her family of animals. Often she fed her own rice to her cat, her shellfish to her pet fish. No chances could be taken. This time she would keep her charges alive.

*

After two years in the camps, Mohm's tracing card still bore the same notation: NO LIVING RELATIVES FOUND.

The time had passed when physical survival and locating lost relatives were the children's chief concerns. By the end of 1981, most of the minors were fending off a wall of despair. As foreign visitors came and went inexplicably, the children pitched between highs of anxiety and sloughs of apathy. They were told they had to stay in tracing for two full years, only to watch "special cases" leave much sooner. They heard the Thai were going to send everyone back to the border, that France had gone communist. They didn't know anymore whom to believe. But the most persistent rumor had it that once a minor was interviewed by a foreigner, he or she would get out of the camp.

And so, on that day when the newspaper lady came to Sakeo, it seemed to Mohm that her lucky star was at its zenith.

First Meeting . . .
December 1981

They come to find a girl for the newspaper lady. Not me. Darvy doesn't choose me. Probably she wants to punish me for the acting. She choose Peng Rann.

Darvy comes into the children's quad to call her, but nobody can find Rann. The housemother tell Darvy she at a dance class. I'm supposed to go to that dance class too, but that day I don't go. I take a shower and wash my hair and clean my nails, I'm just sitting outside Peng Rann's dorm when Darvy comes by.

She look at me. I smile at her back.

"Mom," Darvy say, "how old are you?"

"Twelve." I don't really know the year I'm born. Sometimes I tell the interviewer I'm born in the Year of the Monkey, because that make me a big girl, fourteen, so maybe I can leave sooner. But now I guess they want twelve.

"The newspaper lady wants to interview a girl from Phnom Penh about her past history and what she went through during Pol Pot time," Darvy say. "I have Rann for her, but Rann is busy."

"I know."

"Are you willing?"

I shake my head yes.

When we walk to the administration center, some other children look at me; they're jealous I think. Darvy tell me, "Go in now."

I see a French. She has light skin and light hair, the newspaper lady. All the people like that, they come from a different world. I hear somebody call them *barang* and I look it up in the camp dictionary; it say "French." That's how I know everybody who has light skin and light hair is a French.

She smile at me a lot. She has a T-shirt on and trousers with a zipper like a boy, but she is not very big. Small like me. I look at her eyes. It's not polite to look at the face of an older person but I can't stop it. Amazing eyes! I think everybody has black eyes. But she has eyes like shallow seawater. So light, so blue, so strange.

She ask me about my family. But it's not like the other interviews, not like a test. I don't know what the words mean; it's English. But I don't pay attention to the words people say anyway. I pay attention to the feeling behind the words. I keep looking into her eyes.

I don't know—but I think—I have a feeling halfway in that interview—maybe the newspaper lady is interested in me.

I feel like crying the whole time. I never feel like this for a long time. But it's so natural, the way it goes. She ask about my mother and my father. I don't know why, it's the first time I can open, allow myself to open about the past.

She ask me if I see anybody get kill. I want to tell it. I start to tell. Oh, no. I feel it coming. Like an ocean wave crash down on me and my head split open and all the tear from so many years I don't cry . . .

Can't stop.

Try to stop.

Maybe can't ever stop.

I feel somebody rub my back.

I think that lady say something like "I can help you."

Darvy ask her if she wants me. But I don't think I'm important to her at all. Sometime they just say they help you and then gone forever.

New York City . . . Spring and Summer, 1982

"**S**he got it!"

Clay was handing me my letters and the air-mail envelope fluttered out. I scarcely noticed his large shy form filling up my doorway, unexpectedly in the morning; all my attention was riveted on the reply from "Mom." She had received my first letter after all. And answered. I could almost hear her soft, monotonic voice speaking the words as I read aloud . . .

No one can help me and make me happy but just you, which I can put much depend on. I am looking forward to your sponsorship paper day and night. I cross both my hands to God for whatever will make you happy.

"It's fine to try and help, honey," Clay advised. "But you help by being the kind of writer you are."

"At least I can try and find a real family who'll sponsor her."

"Watch out. You'll get sucked in."

I dropped the subject with Clay.

*

Not one social agency in all of New York City was set up to sponsor a Cambodian refugee. "Why?" I pressed the city's refugee coordinator.

"No one ever asked before."

After many inquiries about Mom, I was able to trace her full name. According to Cambodian custom the family name came first—Phat Mom. I tried to get another letter to her, letting her know that I would try to sponsor her myself. I told almost no one. It had to be closely held, this delicious, implausible secret.

But communication between Mom and me through intermediaries faltered. It was a tiny private echo, I soon discovered by reporting the story, of the general deafness our State Department had developed where Cambodian survivors were concerned.

The new Reagan administration had drastically lowered the ceiling on intake of all Indochinese refugees. As for Cambodians, a web of cynical motives among the international powers combined to discriminate persistently against them. Our State Department's motives were mixed, chief among them the intention that Cambodian survivors use Thailand as an R&R station and then return to fight against the Vietnamese. Given the dismal state of the American economy in 1982, hard-liners in State, Congress, and the INS believed they would be vindicated by keeping the resettlement pipeline shut down; a large share of the Cambodians, they insisted, could return to their country without persecution. New INS researches disproved that, but there was still no movement. The obstacle was obviously higher up, the general policy toward refugees set by the president.

A New York spring passed by. No word from Thailand. In early April, I interviewed the man President Reagan had appointed special ambassador for refugees. Richard Vine insisted that the country's irritation with Southeast Asians was growing. (I had just been told by another senior State Department official, De Saix Anderson, that the fifty thousand Cambodians already resettled in the United States had adjusted as quickly and successfully as any immigrants we've ever had.)

Did the irritation come from their being Southeast Asians, I asked Ambassador Vine, or from the fact that people were fed up with sharing with refugees under strained economic conditions?

"I don't hear it about other refugees," he answered. "It must be because they cluster together."

Hadn't we encouraged cluster settlements? I inquired.

"They move into the same apartment house and produce little ghettoes with strange smells, strange language, the way they act . . ."

"Is that different from what they said about the Puerto Ricans, or the Italians, the Jews, the Irish?"

"I'm just telling you, I think they're different," our special ambassador for refugees said.

*

Word got around about our interview. I kept hearing that the State Department was having a fit. A week later, on April 13, a cable was sent to Bangkok by Ambassador Vine authorizing the embassy to begin "calling out" Cambodians again to be considered for resettlement in America. The suddenness of this apparent policy relaxation stunned many people. But the Catch-22 was already in place. An embassy official tipped me off that cowboy immigration officers in Bangkok were boasting that they intended to reject 90 percent. Even as the right hand was opening the door, the left was poised to slam it.

In June of 1982, *The Washington Post* ran my long article on Cambodian refugees, "The People America Forgot," under an eight-column headline. It included the interview with Vine and reported the cynical callout.

No matter how absorbed I became in this activist journalism, I was still unable to forget the little girl who could not cry. But a few weeks after my article appeared, the bottom dropped out of my personal dream. Word was passed through embassy channels that the child had changed her mind; she did not want to be resettled in a third country; the whole idea was out of the question. Hiding my disappointment, I wrote a careful letter to Phat Mom encouraging her to stick to her guns if she had any hope of returning to Cambodia. She never received it.

*

The new dog is pregnant again. How could she have gotten herself pregnant a second time by the same Schnauzer—all they did was sniff noses. Where did I go wrong?

*

"Clay? Oh, you frightened me. C'mon up." Buzzer, dash for the bathroom mirror, splash of cold water on puffy pink eyes, lift the chain, uncollar the Medeco, draw back the dead bolt. Letting someone into a New York apartment late at night is like coming back from the grave.

He comes in with his rakish smile and his clean male smell. He says he can't stay over. My bed, the way I've got it sticking out in the middle of the room, he can't get a decent night's sleep . . .

"Then what are you doing here anyway? If my bed isn't good enough for you."

"You know I didn't mean that; it's just that I don't sleep well—"

"Neither do I. Not with you coming and going whenever the mood strikes you. . . ."

"I thought you were glad to see me."

"I was, I mean, oh God, Clay"—spilling it now, not having meant to, what's the point of arguing over a horse that's already dead— "they're going to keep me from getting her out."

"Who?"

"I don't know, the State Department, the Immigration people, I don't know who exactly but they're going to punish me for my *Washington Post* piece—"

"Getting who out?"

"Mom."

"Agghh, God, Gail." He's up and pulling on his clothes with that air men get when something is revealed as out of their control. "Why would you try to do something like that anyway?"

"Because it feels right. Because I have room. In my home, and in my heart."

"What room?"

"Maura's room."

"That's terrible, Gail."

"What?"

"How is Maura going to feel when she comes home from college?"

"Well, obviously, in a Manhattan apartment it's pretty extravagant to keep a child's room as a shrine."

"Not obviously. I want to tell you something, Gail. This, I mean, it's not a good idea." He can't find his sock; the dog has a thing about socks.

I put on his shirt and walk barefoot out onto the terrace. Oh, what a night, deepened into silky summer black, with a veil of clouds. "Okay, where's the sock, c'mon." The dog lifts her rump and lowers her nose, clamping her vestigial devil-dog teeth up over her black lip—ghrrr— dying to play.

"What're you doing out there?"

"Planting tulip bulbs." Oh, I'm on a tear now.

"I just want to say good night."

The avenue nine floors below is quiet, the trees of Central Park full and spongy; how incredibly lucky I am to have a terrace over the park, how sad and stupid it would be to live here all alone. I look up the terrace steps at him: Maybe he isn't, after all, the man of my life. "I thought you saw the little miracle it could be. You got me started on Cambodian orphans, but I, I guess you don't—it doesn't really mean the same thing to you."

"The reason that I—"

"There's a real fear for you in getting close, Clay."

"You're wrong about that."

Suddenly he's talking about a book review he read, telling me, with that infuriating tone of authority adopted by male shrinks and priests when categorizing women's weaknesses, about the premenopausal panic that afflicts women at a certain "time of life."

"Don't analyze me!"

"Well, it just shows how desperate you are, to consider taking in a teenage child from another culture."

"Desperate? Because I fell in love? With a child?"

"Everyone knows that women get irrational when they're afraid of losing their looks."

"It's not my looks—"

"Not that *you*, I mean, you're prettier than ever—"

"It's the family you would never agree to have—"

"Don't attack me!"

"*You* want to be the child!"

He runs for the door as if for the DMZ. We have about exhausted our tolerance for open warfare.

He says at the door: "It's really very simple."

"What?"

"The reason we haven't gotten married. You know."

"I don't know."

"I need you to pay more attention to me."

"Why don't you get a nanny!"

"Okay, I'm going home," he says.

"You know what I think? I think we ought to take a vacation from each other."

"Fine. Good."

"I mean it."

"So do I."

Slam, chenk, glonk-glonk, dead bolt in, chain back on. I snuggled that night with the dogs, small hairy lumps of blind animal affection.

*

The next morning I awoke feeling lighter, feeling I had to move quickly. There was a party in Washington that night, a P.R. event for media types and politicians; I had planned to fly down. But the cab driver warned me the Bos-Wash corridor was awash with rain. At the airport they said freakish lightning was on its way. Nothing, that night, was going to fly. I walked back to the same Yellow Cab, grounded, glum.

"Tough luck," the cabbie said.

"Yup." Now what—home to eat sprouts and clean out the drawers of Clay's jogging togs?

As the cab crowned the Triborough and cut over toward the Manhattan exit, I said, "What would it cost to drive to Washington?"

"Two hundred and dinner—I got a sister lives there."

"Let's go."

Three and three-quarter hours later, the cab pulled up to the door of the restaurant where the party was in full swing. Action stopped dead. People peered through the rain at the incredible sight of a Manhattan Yellow Cab on a quiet street in Georgetown. I must have looked as corny as Cinderella stepping out of the pumpkin. But the cabbie was carried inside on a brace of shoulders and plied with drink, and I, within moments, was being chatted up by a handsome senator who said he'd read my books and happened to be divorced. At four o'clock in the morning he swept me off in his convertible—the air was dry and June-sweet by then. It just hit him, he said, the Capitol's so gorgeous by night, why don't we walk through and look at the art? He waltzed me up the white marble steps and showed his pass to the guard and then talked me through the portraits, arm pinching my waist, as if through his private gallery. I didn't even mind that he must have conducted this spontaneous tour a dozen times before; practice makes perfect. He dropped me at my hotel and kissed me good night. An evening worth a two-hundred-dollar cab ride? Offhand, I'd say yes.

Enormous changes seemed in order—toss all the pieces in the air and see where they fall. I decided to take a year out and try playwriting. Plunge in by kibitzing at the Eugene O'Neill Playwrights Conference. So it was that in July I pulled into a New London motor court and put my pathetic bags of groceries away and then sat down at a plastic tablecloth to hear myself chew Grape-Nuts for dinner, alone. The more I tried not to think of him, the more I thought of Clay.

At eleven, I went outside to the pay phone and called Maura.

"Mom, it's childish to conclude on the basis of six weeks being unattached that the only kinds of men are the ones who want to take care of you but you don't want and the ones who make you laugh and tingle but who disappear on you."

"Have you found any other kind?"

"Not yet, but . . ."

She was breaking up with her boyfriend, too. Our roles flipped as easily as a pushbutton cassette, and we talked about her problems. But she seemed to be taking it better; she was young. After the age of forty, one should probably figure one's shelf life the way one counts a dog's age. That would add up to a year on the shelf for yours truly, already. . . .

"What did I call it in my book? Mutual love, hmm, sounded fine at the time, but let's face it—where is one going to meet the man who will find a successful, tuition-paying, sexy, but somewhat shopworn older woman preferable to a cupcake?"

"The one thing certain about finding someone to fall in love with is —there's nothing certain about it," she said.

"Like a new strain of flu."

"It'll happen when you least expect it, and it will be like nothing you had in mind."

"WRITER TO HAVE SPACE ALIEN'S BABY!"

"C'mon, Mom. Don't give up on yourself because the first few men haven't worked out well. You didn't give up on yourself as an author when the first few books didn't become hits, did you?"

"Maybe I can't fall in love because I am already."

"Oh, God, Mom, don't talk to me about Clay. Please. I've put in six credits already. When my college adviser asked me 'What's been your extracurricular activity over the years, Miss Sheehy?,' I wanted to say 'Analyzing My Mother's Fifteen-Year Relationship.' "

We laughed. Even across a long-distance phone wire Maura was a warm, sunny, sustaining presence—if only because she wanted so desperately to be loved—she always gave out of the center of herself;

"On April 17, 1975 the Khmer Rouge took Phnom Penh. They chased the people out of their lovely homes." Drawing by fourteen-year-old Cambodian refugee

"Why were these people killed by the Khmer Rouge soldiers? What had they done wrong?" Drawing by thirteen-year-old Cambodian refugee

David Hawk

One of hundreds of mass graves: Tonle Bati, Cambodia

Ousted Pol Pot "resting" in Cambodian jungle, June 1982

AP/Wide World Photos

AP/Wide World Photos: Eddie Adams

One small victim of Pol Pot's regime clutches his baby sister at Sakeo Camp in Thailand, November 1979.

Phat Mohm
at Sakeo Camp,
Thailand, 1982

The author at home in New York
with her Lhasa apso, 1980.

Forest camp, like 007, on Cambodian border, October 1979

Mohm's arrival in America, September 30, 1982

Moment of first meeting: author and Mohm

Mohm looks down on her new life in Manhattan.

New sisters at Thanksgiving
in Long Island

Shopping in Chinatown, week two:
author, her daughter
Maura, and Mohm

First Christmas, with an extended family

First pizza, with friend Brie Williams

Clay and Gail's wedding,
with Maura and Mohm, at which Mohm said,
"And now I feel like I have
everything I ever needed."

people felt it right away. I vowed never to burden her with my romantic problems again, never.

The new dog has been spayed. She lives quietly now, with my other Lhasa, also female, ten years her senior and going blind. Two spinster sisters.

*

Time for self-help. Let your friends know you're free, Gail. See that? Now you have an invitation to a book party and the hostess has a man flying in to meet you, a sweet, supportive type. Clearly the way to go.

"So, you're a psychiatrist?"

"Mmhmm, and I write a few articles."

"Oh." Alarm bells. "You're a *writing* psychiatrist."

"Not really. No, in fact, I don't know how to write well, I can't really write."

"Thank God for that."

He laughs so easily. He understands everything. He buys spectacular seats at the opera. He performs the lindy expertly: throws you out and snaps you in, throws you out, 'Hey, neat, what kinda dance is that?' say the kids at the Red Garter. Slow dancing, he nibbles your ear just like your Lhasas do. You are underwhelmed.

He tries harder, giving you extravagant metaphors: You are my beautiful mermaid. (Does this mean your butt is too wide?) He preserves you with his Leica, your milky midriff at the beach, your greenish freckles on the first autumn day in the park, your pets, your hallway, your flower arangements; he puts you up on his walls like shelves full of canned goods against the snowed-in winter of your departure.

*

The spayed dog is humping her sister. Is this where we're all headed?

*

I had a book and author dinner in Nashville. They put me on a TV talk show opposite a country singer famous for rising out of poverty, rape, and drugs to seven-figure success. She lugged into the studio wearing a bicycle-chain belt, mean and dikey-looking.

"Isn't *she* one of your pathfinders, Ms. Sheehy?" the host asked on camera.

I looked into the woman's frosted violet contact lenses. She wasn't there.

"Uh, well, it isn't *just* change that makes a pathfinder. . . ."

*

In late August a two-sentence letter arrives from Phat Mom. This time it is in her own handwritten Khmer. The translation above reads simply: *I miss you. I want to live with you in America.*

Exhilarated and utterly frustrated, I make calls to the social agencies. Can't anyone help me co-sponsor a Cambodian refugee? Catholic Guardian Society in Brooklyn promises to look into it. Prospects dubious at best.

*

On the nineteenth of September I drove Maura to college. A stepped withdrawal; we stayed a night at her father's, another night at her grandmother's, then on to Providence where we shopped for bedspreads and books and then at last it was all unpacked: a selected inventory from her old life as a child to be integrated with the streamlined, institutional possessions of her new student life. We had a last, civilized talk, during which I suggested that she try Greek while everyone else was studying computer science, and she exclaimed, "Imagine if I could read Homer and Plato in the original!" We hugged and the last of her childhood slipped out of my arms. She walked me to the elevator of her dorm. "Would you like me to walk you around to the car?" "No, thanks." It was time.

I pulled the car out onto the leafy college street, knowing that she would flourish there. So much of life is sitting around and waiting for someone else to make his move. You tell yourself, I'm not going to just sit around and wait, nosirree, life's too short, but you find it difficult even to start a new train of thought. As the turnpike peeled away the miles, singing along with Lionel Ritchie . . . *can't slow down* . . . I felt almost a weightlessness. I wondered if Ella had remembered to get my fall clothes out of storage.

*

Three weeks after leaving Maura at college, I walked across the street after a dinner at the typewriter and sat beside the rowing lake in Central Park. I gazed at the lovers enjoying their postprandial idylls and felt inconsolably alone.

*

Back in the apartment, a halfhearted check of messages on my answering machine turned up an unfamiliar voice.

What? Who? When? WHEN? I listened again. Yes, I must have heard the astonishing message correctly:

PHAT MOM ARRIVING TOMORROW NIGHT, SEPT. 30, NORTHWEST AIRLINES, FLIGHT 8, JFK, 8:30 PM.

Just like that, a new life began.

PART III

A Time to Love

Never seek to tell thy love
Love that never told can be;
For the gentle wind does move
Silently, invisibly.
—WILLIAM BLAKE

Sakeo . . .
August
1982

I'm scared. Two and a half year I wait, then I see a lot of minors leaving—why not me? Must be the newspaper lady forget about me.

One day in the IRC office I see my name, chalk on a board—Phat Mom is on the list! At the top they put the name of the country that call you out—mine say "USA." I don't know what it mean or where it is but I'm so excited I don't care.

September 15, I'm supposed to leave Sakeo and go to a "transit camp" in Chonburi—the last test. I have fifteen interview already. But everybody says the last interview in Chonburi is the important one. They talk very fast. You have to answer very fast.

*

"The swearing officer with all the gold" is what the refugees called the chief interviewer for the U.S. Immigration and Naturalization Service. A 250-pound sirloin of a man decorated with gold chains and tattoos, his name was Prokopowiez, and, as he later told me, he saw it as his job "to grate [sic] these people."[1] Most of his field officers had earned their stripes flying spotter planes over the Rio Grande to catch illegal aliens. The job of the INS officers was to determine whether or not the applicant qualified for the status of refugee. The sole criterion was evidence of persecution. Their questions were usually loud and accusatory.[2]

Describe your life before you left Cambodia.
Can't remember.

Why did you leave Cambodia?
  No food, bomb.
Did you come for money?
  Have no money, only one earring I sell.
Did you travel with anyone else?
  Have no one else.
How many family members did you lose under Pol Pot?
  All my family.
Oh yeah? We know different.
  All my family dead.
Did they really take your parents away?
  Yes.
You sure?
  Yes.
No, no, no, we know about your family. Actually, you just ran away; you made up that story.
  I not run away.
We know all about you. It's not the way you say.

They're just testing you, to see if you're the person you say you are. Many children get scared. That's when you fail.
  If I fail here, I have to stay in the transit camp forever.

New York City . . . September 1982

The anticipation was tainted with rumors. "Expect lice." "Assume she's been raped repeatedly." "Probably lied about her age." "They're very manipulative, you know, refugees are, and maybe even violent."

It was true I knew next to nothing. Who was Phat Mom anyway? There had been only two formal letters and one hour of contact through a translator, and the eyes.

Maura was at once thrilled and concerned for her. "She'll be landing on Mars!" Were we really doing her a favor with such a drastic dislocation?

I called Clay with the news. He echoed Maura's doubts.

My mother was wonderful. "Don't let anyone talk you out of it," she said over the phone from Florida. "Listen to your heart." She had mothered me well and exuberantly and I suppose passed on the affinity for children, but neither that nor her unfailingly sunny nature made me discount her advice. My mother had demonstrated that the best way to defeat the numbing ambivalence of middle age is to surprise yourself—by pulling off some cartwheel of thought or action never even imagined at a younger age. At forty, my mother had seemed old. But at fifty, divorced by my father for a younger woman, my mother had bounced back, begun a new business, dropped three dress sizes, and within a few years had been courted by and remarried to the love of her life. Not a few times had she pulled me out of my anomie by chirping, "If I could start a new life at fifty-three, why you, honey, with what you've got to offer [etc. etc.]—and besides, you're young!"

Despite the doubts others expressed, I had an oddly strong intuition that this child was meant to move on, that she had the will to endure another transmigration, that the adventure would be right for both of us. As my preparations grew more feverish, a calmness expanded inside me. Underneath, I was singing.

*

Wash my hair a hundred time so they don't find any head lice. Early morning, the bus comes. Thai guard tell us, "We take you to a better camp." But no American on the bus. No food. No one explains. It's the first time alone with the Thai. We're all afraid.

I think it's a trick. The road is so far—where are they taking us! So long since I've been outside a camp I feel afraid every minute. I stare at the Thai guard sitting up front; he smokes a lot of cigarettes, he looks nervous—probably he's taking us to the mountaintop and we have to climb over into Cambodia! So then we'll die and that will be that.

*

Three hours left to prepare. What were the essentials? Nightgown, toothbrush, a Khmer-English dictionary . . . self-respect. I dashed to Asia House to buy a poster of Angkor Wat. In the last moments I found a globe. Mohm would have at least two points of reference—one in twelfth-century Cambodia, another in the modern world.

General Chana, Thailand's former ambassador to Cambodia and a devoted friend to refugees, left a phone message. "I would like to help with the girl. May I ride with you to the airport and translate?" Knowing that the photographer-writer Jill Krementz was longing to adopt a child, I invited her along too. And my dear sister, Pat Henion Klein, who had her own first child only a year before, at the panicky age of thirty-five. I was afraid to invite Clay, whom I had not seen for three months.

Margie de Monchy, the former American director of the children's center in Sakeo, called to reassure me. No matter how traumatic the transition, resettlement was the only alternative left.

"If she had gone back to the border, what would her fate have been?" I wanted to know.

"She'd be used as a food card. Women and children are the only ones eligible for rations from the international agencies. She'd be used to work for a family. She'd have to watch all the time about her own life. Oh, and just before I left Sakeo, child abuse was up incredibly. The unaccompanied minors were the easiest targets."

"But what should I feed her?"

"Have a bowl of rice ready. And Gail," she added, "be calm. Enjoy the arrival. It happens so quickly."

*

Halfway around the earth, a small orphaned survivor who already had walked across the border of the damned took another risk. She gave away her six sarongs to the children left behind. She found homes for her bird, her cat, her fish; she said good-bye to the only stable home she had known in seven years and stepped off the edge of her world. She did it all for a crazy hope called "future." The chances were equally good that the abyss would laugh back.

The pipeline to America opened for twenty-four hours—the last day before the fiscal year ended and the ceiling for refugees expired—and in Bangkok, Mohm was hustled with fourteen others onto a Japan Airlines jet. The officials gave her no name, no address, no fix in the galaxy to set her internal compass for, nothing but a mimeographed map of America and the magic words "New York."

Worlds to Go Before I Sleep

When I step onto the airplane, I feel good. That's it—I passed everything!

I never fly before, never travel to another country. I don't know there is anyplace else. I know there's Thailand, but you could walk to it. We sit in the back of the airplane, all fifteen minors. One other girl, Suon Unn, sits next to me. The fly lady stands up front and waves her arms around. And then the back of the airplane drops down and—ooohh—my stomach!

Children all around me start throwing up.

Stand up, walk around, relax, think about what makes me happy . . . a lily pond in Cambodia . . . to take my mind out.

Quick try to find my monkey balm, rub it on.

They take us off the plane to sleep for a while and then they take us on another airplane. This time the fly ladies all have white faces, must be American.

"What is it?" Unn holds up the bag of food.

"Don't ask me. I live in the city, but I never see that before."

I try it. Hard, salty. The fly lady says, "Peanut." She gives me a cup: "Coke, good, try it!" It's more sweet than a sugarcane stick. I guess this is American dinner.

They bring a tray with sticky yellow stuff and gooey white stuff and dark brown stuff—no fruit or vegetable, nothing I ever see before. Unn is very sick. I show her how to put her head in the little sick bag.

Look out the window. I see the sun rise and after a few hours, the sun set—up, down, day and night passing so fast—time is speeding. I keep wondering, "Where does the sky end?" because I know the world is flat.

Unn's little sister has to go to the bathroom. She asks me to guard the door for her. So long she stays in there, the plane is bumping, the fly lady wants me to sit down. "Come out!" I call. She doesn't come. I sit down and after a while I forget about her. Suddenly I hear her, she's screaming. She's locked inside. She can't get out! I stand outside the door and tell her what to do—don't ask me how I know. Finally she opens it a crack. Poor girl. She is standing up on top of the seat and trying to pour water down the hole from a paper cup. That's how the bathroom works in Cambodia. But it's different here. It's too disgusting to tell her about.

The plane stops somewhere [in Seattle]. They call my name first, and all the children have to get off. Some go this way, some that, suddenly all my friends are gone. "I'm Customs," the man says. "Have to look inside your bag and check your identification." I show inside my plastic bag. I want to show my letter from the newspaper lady but he doesn't want it. I have the feeling it's going to be important at some point. It's like a ticket—to show somebody wants me.

A woman leads us to the next airplane, three of us left. Unn, myself, and a boy. What happened to all the others? It's so sad. I don't know where I am, how long we have to go or how short.

Only a few hours I sleep but when I wake up the sun rose again. Time speeding past. "Oh, my God," I think, "now I'm in a different world!"

The fly lady makes an announcement, I don't know what, but then I hear the words—*New York*—what beautiful words! That's the world I'm supposed to go to. But I don't know if anybody is going to be there.

*

At 9:42 P.M., E.S.T., a slip of a girl with hungry eyes and torn rubber sandals emerged from the flight canopy at Northwest Airlines. The world around me shrank to a soundless concentration. Our eyes met. A smile exploded in her face. I waved. She waved. Something wonderful stirred in my private regions of creation, and I felt tears of happiness flush down my face.

Our eyes bobbed between the thicknesses of other people until we reached each other. I embraced her and felt her meagerness. She looked up at me. Her eyes were immense, filled with light and hope, a child's eyes in a face no longer a child's.

As if from a great distance, I heard my sister saying, "She's beautiful, Gail."

                              *

Catholic Guardian Society had sent a bilingual social worker, Mr. Sao, who prompted me to try the few scraps I had of her language. *"Chum riap sua."* Hello. *"Nea' khlien bai te?"* Do you want to eat? No. *"Nea' chawng tau dek te?"* Do you want to sleep? No. *"Neh chawng tau bangkun te?"* Do you want to go to the bathroom? No. I asked if she was cold. Yes. Good. I had brought one of Maura's sweaters for her. I introduced my *bong srei*—"sister." Then I tried the phrase that means in Khmer "I love you."

"Knhom sralanh nea'."

Her face whirled up at me, astonishment in it. Such an intimacy from a near stranger must have seemed very odd. But her face seemed to melt.

"I think you said the right thing," whispered Mr. Sao. He asked Mohm how she felt.

"Sok sabai," she said, an expression that sounds exactly like what it means: calm, content, well in spirit.

She slipped her arm around my waist and we began to walk briskly into the bedlam of Kennedy Airport. Her long legs fell into synchrony with mine. It was a good sign. We were in step from the start.

                              *

I see her face, I know her face. She comes right to me and hugs me. That second I was so happy! But in the next second it was gone. I'm sure that happened to everybody.

What she says makes no sense to me. I never hear an accent before. Suddenly it's a different language, different people, some with faces white as cabbage, some with spots, some the color of soil—everything is different. Just pretend, "Oh well, it's normal."

She says, "I love you." It's funny to hear, it's wonderful. The man [Mr. Sao] tells me to call her "Mom." That's funny, too. Her name sounds like the way these people say my name. Mom. Is it the name for every woman here?

"Mom" drives her own car. She must be import. She has a sister who looks part Asia—she has short straight hair and her eyes are a little slanty—and she has a friend called General Chana; he can speak Khmer. "Mom" tells him how I will live and he tells me. She has one daughter and two dogs, they live in the city but they have a porch over a park.

I think everybody in that car lives with her. But one by one they disappear. Just the two of us left. I cannot believe it. My idea was I would live with children from the camp. But no children. No one I know. Nothing I can speak. I don't know what it is, this big city. I don't who she is—"Mom." I don't know what I'm going to turn out to be.

Sickening feeling . . . air so greasy, things fly around in the air you can't see, cars come together in a blind of light, screamy sirens, big trucks, buildings as tall as mountains fall over on us from both sides, oh no, I can't look . . .

*

She was sick in the car. Of course. Travel by automobile was strange to her, as were most of the accouterments of urban life—elevators, intercoms, chains and locks and leashed dogs, not to mention shower taps and the magic instrument one holds to the ear and it talks back in a human voice.

At home, I showed her the terrace first. She seemed to like seeing all the trees across the street. I picked a flower for her. She picked a flower for me, copying my movements precisely. But I'd forgotten the rice! My sister went for takeout.

I showed her the room that would be hers, all to herself. She looked amazed. Gravitating to the picture of Maura, she must have grasped that this would be her sister, and she smiled. We turned on the light inside the new globe, and I traced her flight path from Bangkok to Tokyo to Seattle and across the United States. A frown rippled across her forehead. Then, recognition. She ventured her first English words. "New . . . New Yawk!"

She wanted to know about the two little animals who kept sniffing at her sandals. I gave her their names and we looked up the word *dog* in the dictionary. My sister returned with the container of Chinese rice, but Mohm looked at it as if at a well-meant mistake. I knew I had a lot to learn about marginal differences among Asian cultures, but rice—at least rice was a universal in the Orient, wasn't it?

"Show her the nightgown," my sister coached.

Mohm studied the granny gown, then pulled it over her fully clothed body. I coaxed off the sweater underneath and suggested she remove her jeans. She dipped her head modestly. I had to leave the room.

Maura telephoned from college. "Snuggle with her."

"I don't know, maybe she'd like to feel a little bit separate at first."

"Mom, she's only eight."

"I don't know what she is, her papers say fourteen."

"Oh, wow."

Suddenly I felt an arm slip around my waist from behind—Mohm. "I've gotta go, honey," I told Maura. "Call you tomorrow." Mohm was still fully clothed under the nightgown. Her body represented all the privacy she had; it would be fiercely guarded.

We took off the bedcovers together and I tucked her in. The dog jumped up and worked her rump into the crook of Mohm's waist. Would she like the dogs to sleep with her? I indicated. Her expression read as if I'd suggested she sleep in a tree. One thing I did know: Physical demonstrations of affection were severely inhibited in her culture. The head must not be touched; being the part of the body closest to God, it is sacred. And so, that first night, fully aware I was taking a chance but unable to restrain myself, I brushed her cheek with my lips.

"Goodnight, angel."

*

It's not what I expect, at all. I think America has log cabins with lots of land in between, I see a book about it. But this isn't even like Phnom Penh. Here the buildings have a thousand million little yellow windows, each one looks alike.

She show me the bathroom. It's as pretty as a house. I don't know how to push down the handle on the toilet, but I don't want to try anyway. We know from the letters minors send back how machines do everything in America. In American bathrooms you're supposed to sit on a seat and push a handle, and a hand comes out and cleans you! Disgusting!

She show me in the big word book the Khmer word *chkai*. She tell me it's the word for "dog." When I say the word after her, she clap her hands. Is that good? Is she angry?

A room alone, a bed alone. A dress to wear to bed. Where are my friends? Where is Unn? It's so different than Sakeo. We all sleep together there, seven or eight of us on little mats all in a row, together. If I close my eyes here, everything I know from before might fly away, I can never catch it again.

*

I poured myself a glass of wine and sat down to look through the plastic bag that represented the sum total of her worldly possessions. She had come with a tin spoon and the torn half of a file card stamped by the U.S. Immigration Service. Finding a certificate with her picture on it, pronouncing her a *theatre artiste* from Sakeo Holding Center Khmer Theatre, I smiled; this was a child who would not settle, no matter where she landed, for being a nobody. Underneath a parka issued by IRC was a notebook in which she had been doing lessons, an elementary school book about the human body, and an envelope with three photographs—images of her housemother from Sakeo, Margie de Monchy, and Buddha. That was all she had, and she had abandoned it. On a dossier form provided by the UNHCR, the bare bones of her family history were recorded.

Zipped up inside a tiny red plastic pocketbook was a cloth, and inside the cloth, worn and folded and handled to a limp relic, I found the first letter from me. I wept.

What if I had been away on a trip? What if I hadn't listened to my messages? Her papers said nothing about a sponsor, my name was nowhere, the only address given was 80 Lafayette Street—the New York City Welfare Bureau. What if I hadn't shown up at the airport?

How was it possible that this child had come through genocide to a refugee camp and from there to an apartment on Fifth Avenue? Call it determination, call it luck; maybe it was destiny. But whatever help she may have had from fate, clearly this child had the soul of a survivor.

From her documents and possessions, it seemed virtually impossible to reconstruct the history of a survivor, from a family almost totally wiped out, from the wasteland of a country, from the habit of aliases and the patches of protective amnesia. I knew I would have to deal with her past eventually, but who was she *now?* What could I help her to become?

She was one of the first Cambodian refugees to be settled in New York State. And, among the thirteen co-sponsored by Catholic Guardian Society, she was the only girl. Plucky. I was infatuated with Mohm, but would I like her? Would she like me? Because the government did not yet permit one to adopt a refugee, she was officially a foster child, meaning that either of us could declare the "placement" hadn't worked out. But what was important now was not the rules of bureaucracy; it was the act of bonding, which we would have to do without a common language.

Discovering
Mohm

At least for the first day, I was determined to keep the frenzy of the city at bay. It was ice-cream-melting mild for the beginning of October and as I looked across the vast, green stretch of the park, I noticed how the steel and glass spires of Manhattan receded behind lollipop trees. That was it—we would go rowing on Central Park Lake. Rowing did not require words, and it came as close as anything I could imagine to the pace of her country.

Within moments Mohm had mastered the stroke and we were pulling oars together, in unison again, just as we had fallen in step walking through the airport. Being culturally a whole metronome apart, this seemed the right way to start—side by side, trying to bring our bodily rhythms into synchrony.

As our little boat glided under the wishing bridge, light filtered through the stone cutouts and played like eyelet over her face; she smiled. We lay back to rest and gazed up at the trees. People in other boats nodded at us approvingly. There was even an occasional Asian face. It reminded me all over again of one of the things I love about New York: It embraces differentness.

*

Rowboating, I like. It's the first thing we do that connects to my old life . . . nature, water, trees, some bending over close to the water, so beautiful and peaceful . . . not big trucks and screamy sirens. It's the first time I can feel sort of relaxed.

*

As we spooned our way through the green-cheese water from east side to west and back, both smiling and content, I thought, "Maybe this is the answer to urban stress. We'll simply travel by family sampan."

In a puddle of sun on a green promontory we spread a blanket to have a picnic. I bought her what I thought would be her first American treat—a hot dog.

"Hot—dog?" she repeated, quizzically.

"Yes, hot dog, okay American, try it?"

With a wan smile she accepted it, took a bite, a few bites in fact, but in between held the specimen away from her body the way a child does a dead snake. I went to find her ice cream, and walking back with the two cones, seeing her run to help me, bright and exuberant, I thought of the rags and bones from a buried childhood I had seen laid out on a bleak dossier the night before.

*

She call it "hot dog." Same as the word she tell me last night for the two dogs live with her. Why does she eat dog? I try it, can't stand it, think I'm going to faint away. If I don't eat dog, can she still like me?

*

It wasn't dawn yet when she appeared in my doorway: still as a statue, afraid to intrude. I went to her and caressed her face; it was as warm and smooth as a glass of tea. With a gesture I invited her to share my bed, but no sooner did she lie down than she popped upright expectantly. Of course, jet lag. What was morning for me was the end of afternoon for Mohm.

We found her one school book and crawled back under the comforter to flip through it, stopping at the drawing of a man: an anatomy lesson.

"Head," she said perfectly.

"Yes."

"Eye. Noh. Mou."

"Very good!"

But rummaging around in her ragbag of English, that was all I found. So we made a game of singing the body parts, and when "face" came out "safe," I had her pull out my bottom lip until she felt the air funnel that creates an *f*. Once having mastered "head" to "foot," she began looking eagerly around the room, ready to extend her control. I found her a box of labels. Would she like to—?

"Jah."

She caught on quickly. Sticking the labels all over my bedroom, she sounded out the words—"light," "wall," "floor," "door"—as she wrote their Khmer equivalent above. She came back under the comforter to review the body parts. Mozart was playing softly on the radio. Language, which gives voice to one's uniqueness, which is the very structure of thought, language is one's mother. If I did nothing else, I had to give Mohm a voice.

Now she walked delightedly around the room, pointing to the labels and pronouncing the words intelligibly, or if not, making penciled adjustments in her phonetic Khmer when I corrected her. Together in this windowless shell-pink haven at six in the morning, listening to her voice, soft as a sigh, repeating my prompts, it seemed to me that not even Mozart in all his delicate discipline could surpass this performance.

The first concept that helped her to venture beyond the tiny learned word pile to the vast unlearned forest of foreign words was alike and not alike. At the end of our first session, she asked me, "Shelf—like safe?"

"You mean 'face'?"

"Jah," and with a contortion of her lips she produced "face."

"Face no like shelf," I replied.

"Oh. No like face."

"Oh, you no like my face?" I pushed up my nose and dragged down my eyes in one of those idiot faces. A giggle escaped through her intentness. "But *your* face—I like!" I clowned. Her giggle cascaded into a glissando. Here was another good sign. She had a sense of the ridiculous.

*

"Hi, I'm Ella."

Mohm looked startled. I was on the phone.

A great smile spread across the raisin-black face of my housekeeper. I hadn't known how to prepare Mohm for meeting Ella Council. Ella was smart as a whip and pretty and warm, and she had worked for me for almost ten years through joys and heartaches and deadlines and tantrums; we had come through it all as mutually dependent as sisters. But to an Asian child, there was something out of place. Like most Cambodians, Mohm probably thought "American" meant the only kind of Americans she had ever met, volunteers in the camps: light-haired and white.

*

I see a black face. Give me a shock. She must not be American. She open the white box and point to their strange food. Egg, okay, yes. But she put the egg raw right into the pan—disgusting! Feel so sick, so tired, I try not to be sick on that egg with no shell.

*

For Mohm's second night in America, a celebration dinner was planned with Peter Pond, the minister from New Hampshire who had been so helpful on my trips to the camps, and who, being a frenetic activist, was only too happy to barrel down from his home in New Hampshire in a huge van with his brood of five Cambodian children. Before then, it was off to the stores to find two more essentials for Mohm—a dress, and fish sauce. Nice Cambodian girls simply didn't run around in short skirts or rump-revealing pants, and Mohm had let me know that through pantomime. I found her a violet-sprigged print with a lace collar and long sleeves—from Ramayana to Victoriana in a day. Not so much fun was buying the fish sauce. The stuff is as ubiquitous in Cambodian cooking as olive oil is in Italian, and I was delighted to find a Korean grocer who carried it, but opening the jar at home, I almost swooned. Anchovy-based, it smelled to a Western nose like rotten fish. So I held my nose as I whipped up some Japanese-style noodles and doused them with fish sauce, and left Mohm happily eating with Ella while I left for playwriting class.

In all the excitement I had almost forgotten what I had decided to spend my time on before I had any idea that Mohm was coming—a master's degree in dramatic writing at NYU. I knew you couldn't be taught to write plays, but it seemed important to study the form and to have an amateur milieu in which to try out my embarrassing experiments. Now I would have two uncharted territories to explore—how to write a play and how to make Mohm my child.

*

"So, how does your daughter like school?"

"She hasn't started school yet."

"No, your *daughter.*"

"Oh, you mean my daughter *Maura.*"

It wasn't something I had decided I was going to say. It slipped out. I hadn't known until that moment that already I thought of Mohm as my daughter.

We had bumped into the Pond family on First Avenue. The four Cambodian boys, all strong, handsome teenagers in jackets and ties, had gathered around Mohm as if a startlingly delicate bloom had broken cement and pushed up through the grimy sidewalk.

"Oh, oh, she's so pretty!" they exclaimed.

"Look at her fingernails!"

"She gave me a hug!"

Apparently hugging was all right among friends close in age. Then the beautiful girl of the Pond brood, Jintana Lee, stepped forward. Suddenly, squeals of delight erupted. "I know her! From Cambodia!"

Jintana's father had been a major in the Cambodian army. The two families had visited one another on Chinese New Year; that was how she knew Mohm was part-Chinese. And she thought Mohm's father had been a major general. Each dot of information the youngsters unearthed to fill in Mohm's sketchy silhouette prompted more squeals and laughter. Mohm was only twelve, not fourteen as her papers stated. And there was a reason her fingers bent back like lilies; they told me she had trained in the camps as a classical Cambodian dancer.

I was glad I had taken the time to brush out her long hair. It gleamed under the lights of the Thai restaurant like a moonlit river, and her large onyx eyes danced; the child was blessed with a lovely face and a well-formed (if now frail) body, and she knew these attributes clearly were part of her armamentarium for survival. The only obvious evidence of her past showed up in her feet and her ears. Trying various old shoes on her before dinner, I noticed that her feet appeared splayed and flattened, probably from the heavy carrying work; nothing was bearable except the torn rubber sandals. Through her ears were small wooden sticks. When I had puzzled over those peculiar studs, she explained by pointing at the gold hoops in my own pierced ears and wagging her finger: "Pol Pot, no no." I had tried to lend her my earrings, but she seemed apprehensive; the authoritarian hand was not so far behind.

But none of that seemed to matter right now. Now, she was wholly concentrated on sitting up straight at a restaurant table with her napkin unfolded in the lap of her violet-sprigged dress, eating daintily, and moving dextrously from chopsticks to a fork. Throughout, she kept up an animated conversation in Khmer.

Halfway through dinner, the boys expressed another kind of surprise. "She's smart!"

"How do you know?" I asked.

"Most Cambodian girls, they don't talk much because they are afraid they have nothing good enough to say. Mohm is different."

"Explain."

"She is not shy."

*

Jintana came home to stay over with Mohm. I asked her to communicate some fundamentals. "Can you tell her that I will do everything I can to take care of her?" "Tell her if she is ever hungry, there's a basket of fruit in the window; she can help herself." "Tell her—" The list was long but still seemed incomplete. "Oh yes, can you ask if she ever has nightmares?"

A shadow passed over Mohm's face when she was asked. Jintana replied for her, "Yes, sometimes, of the past."

"Can you tell her that dreams are called the wastebasket of the mind. Thoughts or memories that we can't bear to think about are thrown into that wastebasket. Sometimes, they wake us up in the middle of the night. It's upsetting, but it's also a way of beginning to put the past behind us."

While Mohm seemed to comprehend this heavy Freudian concept, she quite obviously did not want to dwell on bad dreams. I had the impression that to her dreams were like ghosts: If you thought about them, they could float through the door of your mind.

It was time to break and be active. I suggested that Jintana show Mohm how to use the shower. This produced furious giggling.

"She cannot use the shower here," Jintana said finally.

"Why not?"

"She does not have a sarong."

"But in the shower you don't wear—or do you?"

Jintana mustered enough self-control to explain that Cambodian girls are very modest. They don't like to take off their clothes, even to see their own bodies. The way they are taught to bathe is to wrap themselves in a sarong and pour water from a jar held overhead. Afterward, they wrap a dry sarong around the outside and slip off the wet one. "But Mohm says she gave away all her sarongs," Jintana reported.

"Then I guess she'll have to shower in her jeans!"

Jintana translated and we all laughed.

On the pullout couch, the two girls snuggled together and were still whispering when I went to bed. As I bent to kiss Mohm good night, it occurred to me to ask Jintana to find out how Mohm felt about this. Gently, indirectly, she let me know that Cambodians do not kiss—at least, not the way Westerners do, not with the lips. I asked her what they did, and she attempted to demonstrate. Amid giggling from the two girls, Jintana brushed her nose against my cheek and with quick, successive sniffs, imparted a slightly pleasant tickling sensation. It seemed to me like a cross between an Eskimo kiss and a head cold. I could not imagine it becoming a comfortable habit, so I bent to touch Mohm's cheek with my lips anyway.

*

I tell Jintana how the first days, my heart sink. I feel like nothing. I think I won't have the spirit to go on. But I'm so happy to see her, I know her face from my old life, I pretend she is my big sister.

I ask Jintana, "Why do I have to call her 'Mom,' same as Americans say my name?" Then I start learning. "Oh, 'Mom' means mother."

I can tell Jintana my secret. I was happy I made it to this place. What is it like here—I wanted to find out. But if you don't know anything, don't know how to talk or go anyplace, you feel like a dummy. It's not what you used to be—you're not yourself anymore.

Jintana tell me everybody feel scared at first. She say when people ask her a question in English, the whole first year she can only giggle back.

I tell her when I was acting in Sakeo I was really happy with who I am. An actor is special. You know you are interesting. And I read a lot of books in the camp, I always know the answer. So I feel important to other people. That's what I want to feel.

*

In the morning Jintana confided, "Mohm thinks it's strange when you put your kiss on her face. But I think it's good."

It was Saturday, and we found a Buddhist center in midtown where we took off our shoes and nosed around until we happened upon a Cambodian woman able and willing to tutor Mohm in the basics of English. Mrs. San So, formerly a director of language studies at a lycée in Phnom Penh, was a bit dour but offered to come by later that very afternoon.

*

At the temple all I can think about is what has been taken away. Friendships, all I used to have, especially the language . . . Cannot even open my mouth to speak to Mrs. San So or I would start crying. Cannot open my mind to the Buddha or think of the temple, my cheeks fill up with tears, but I swallow them back.

*

Lurching up Madison Avenue traffic in a taxi, Mohm broke off in the middle of reciting words and pointed to her forehead. "Headache, sweetheart?" I massaged her temples; she liked that, but looked sicker. Why not? I thought. New York cabs do to people approximately what food processors do to vegetables. We would walk from here. Mohm smiled gratefully as we got out. It was noon, hot, diamonds of hard light flashed off the store windows, and all the mannequins were hair-less to suggest the sexual ambiguity just becoming stylish that season.

For which of the reasons stated above I never knew, but Mohm swooned. Her head fell on my shoulder and she allowed herself to be propelled up the avenue like a limp doll. I began to sense the daunting journey we both had ahead. In the course of her twenty-five-hour hegira from Southeast Asia, she had rocketed through at least fifty years of technological advances and cultural change. Would she ever be able to catch up? Should one begin by explaining transistor radios and jet travel, or start with home computers and homosexuality and work back-ward?

An hour's nap did wonders. Not only did Mohm bounce back quickly, she greeted Mrs. San So with impeccable manners and helped set out a platter of what must have been baffling "cold cuts." Some-what severely, the Cambodian woman questioned Mohm about her experiences. She translated for me the saga of one death after another, related by Mohm in a tone that sounded almost casual but that I had begun to suspect was deliberately emptied of emotion. Mohm spoke not like a participant but like a good reporter. I asked if she had ever been punished.

"She never made a mistake!" was the indignant reply.

I understood then that the mind police were still operating inside her. Why should she confide in me? Treachery was the norm she had observed up to now, not the exception.

"Wait a second," I said at one point, "didn't the Khmer Rouge tell people they would be killed if they tried to escape?"

Mrs. San So consulted Mohm. "Yes, many thought they could not go anywhere, because of Pol Pot."

"But she—"

"She ran away alone."

That was a different kind of child, I thought, a survivor by will, not chance. What was such a child made of? I wondered if there were many such children. Did it take a war to make them? And once cast as survivors, I worried, now with intense personal interest, could they ever go back to being normal, trusting children?

Mrs. San So questioned Mohm about her schooling.

"Can you estimate her grade level?" I asked hesitantly, almost not wanting to know.

Mrs. San So gave Mohm what sounded like the third degree. After-ward, she sat back and clucked her tongue a few times. "She can add.

She had to know multiplication. And she's all right in her own language. Between 1980 and 1982, I think she studied up through third grade."

"And if that were translated into an American grade level?"

"I think second grade."

The anger surged through me. I thought of Pol Pot and Chairman Mao and murderous dictators like Somoza and the Shah and Khomeini and Botha and Marcos and on and on. When the revolution was all over what was left was a generation of deformed children.

To lighten the mood, I put on a record of Khmer classical music. "Can she dance?" Mrs. San So inquired. Immediately Mohm took off her sandals and began to move to the music; slow, graceful, highly controlled movements. Mrs. San So allowed herself a slight smile of cultural pride.

For the rest of the afternoon the two of them worked. When at last Mrs. San So left Mohm's room, she said, "She's not stupid, Gail. She picks up fast."

"Should I find her a tutor, enroll her in Berlitz, what?"

"Wait and see how she can cope with the beginning of her life here," Mrs. San So advised.

"Did you get the impression she's overwhelmed?"

Mrs. San So said she had asked Mohm one question: Would she like to stay here or go back home? "She said, 'I don't know yet. If many of my friends go back, then I want to go back.' But for the time being, she likes to learn."

"That's the best attitude one could hope for."

"I told her she has lost so many years, she must work hard to catch up."

"Mrs. San So, frankly, how long do you think that will take?"

Mercifully, the precise Cambodian woman became vague: "The barrier is the language."

"We'll get started on Monday," I vowed.

I asked Mrs. San So to teach me a little about Khmer, the national language of Cambodia, which derived from Sanskrit and has been in written form for about fourteen hundred years. There is nothing in the language that corresponds to our plurals, and the verbs have no past or future tense; a rearrangement of words is required to designate a quantity of more than one or past or future. That explained why Cambodians struggling with English speak almost exclusively in the singular and in the present tense. But that was not to say that Khmer was a simple language. It had sixty-six consonants and thirty vowels, nearly a world record. It should be a relatively easy matter for Mohm to absorb our skimpy twenty-six characters, I thought, and decided not to attempt to learn more than shorthand Khmer. Let Mohm learn our common language while I worked on decoding her culture.

By the end of that day, Mohm had gobbled up the entire English alphabet and converted from Sanskrit to Arabic numerals. The next day, Sunday, I took her to the zoo and began teaching her how to ride a bike. When we came home, and I sat down at the typewriter, she immediately wanted to learn how to type the alphabet.

It was like having a high-speed baby.

*

That evening, I suddenly remembered the speech I had to make the next day, in Miami.

*

It was like being yanked out of one kind of time—people time—and locked back into scheduled time. How lovely it had been the past four days, letting myself tune in to sense the tempo Mohm brought with her and trying to adjust city life accordingly. It was natural; that's why it felt so good. People time, which I think of as elastic and responsive to the people around you, also responds to the unpredictable, and Mohm's arrival had been nothing if not unpredictable. Yet I had learned well how to function in the straitjacket of scheduled time—compartmentalizing the mind, ignoring others' needs, skipping sleep, and cheating my body with stimulants in order to perform. The tension between the two kinds of time, of course, is the eternal battleground of any career mother's life. Oh, sure, as professionals we all learn how to depend on planning calendars and answering machines and the rest of it (just to meet someone for lunch in midtown Manhattan requires logistical planning worthy of the secret invasion of a Caribbean island). But sacrificing a person to suit a schedule is a stratagem men must have invented; when women do it, we know we're committing a silent crime. If only I could take off the next few months and concentrate on this surprise child. . . .

I made some phone calls to see if I could conscionably get out of giving the speech, but it was impossible. While I talked, Mohm knelt at my feet and rested her head on my knees. The tenderness of her gesture was almost unbearably sweet.

We went out to walk the dogs together. I gave her more nouns. "Car." "Bus." "Taxi." "Sidewalk." "Tree." "Central Park." She repeated until she had them right. I pointed to the angle between curb and street: "Dog bathroom." When I bent to pinch the dog's leavings into a paper towel, Mohm drew back. I tried to pantomime the reason for this practice, poised with an unsuspecting foot over a pile of dog turds. The expression on Mohm's face made me think of some colonial queen contemplating the native practices of Wagadugu—that same, pitying noncomprehension.

*

In America, people sleep with dog, people eat dog, then people pick up dog bathroom. I think I can never understand them.

*

When Mohm was the learner, her voice had been a whispery carbon copy. But when she schooled me, her own strong personality began to surface.

She gave me the Khmer word for "mother": *mad-dai*. I ran it together. She drilled me with a deliberateness bordering on authoritarianism: "Mah-*dai*, mah-*dai*."

"Ok-*ai*, ok-*ai*." I made mistakes, so she knew that she could make mistakes.

The next morning we made coffee together, tea for her. It was strange, my taking pleasure in these simple repetitive tasks, watching her observe each motion and commit it to memory. I set her up at the typewriter to practice her alphabet while I was away—but seeing her there, the tiny strands of trust binding her to me still so tentative, I could not bear to leave her. I had an idea—call up Mrs. San So and have her ask Mohm *her* wishes.

"Mommy has to go on a trip on an airplane to work," I asked her to translate into Khmer. "She says she will miss you if she has to leave you home. Do you want to go with her?"

"I go."

Boom, no hesitation. This child is an adventurer, I thought. Chop-chop, pack her new dress, zip, zip, no time for breakfast, grab a cab. We were on time, if counting minutes, when the driver missed the ramp.

If Mohm hadn't been with me, I would have had a full-dress tantrum. We hit the Delta ramp running, and shot down the flight canopy just as they were about to close the door.

"Pleeeze—can we use my first-class ticket for both of us in tourist?"

The flight attendant looked at this wild-eyed woman and composed child. "C'mon aboard," she drawled, "y'all look like you've earned it."

Thus was Mohm baptized into my kind of time.

We stepped out of the plane into steamy Miami. A squeal of delight broke through Mohm's proper demeanor when she saw the first palm tree. "Oooh, Cambodia!"

Our hotel room overlooked a bay, and beneath us was a promenade lined with banana trees. I had two newspaper interviews, back to back. All through the trooping in and out of people falling over themselves to please the sweet little refugee with bunches of flowers and fruit, all Mohm wanted to do was to stare down at those banana trees.

*

I am so excited. This is almost exactly like Cambodia. Just looking at the banana tree and dreaming of nature, it makes me so happy. But then I am sad. Because I know it's not Cambodia and the people all around are not like me.

*

After the program, people came up to her at a reception in the hotel lounge, speaking to her as if she were hard of hearing, and to each one she gave the response, "My name is Mohm Phat."

"Isn't that cuute? Well, honey, how long have you been in America?" Her eyes searched me out—that answer we had not rehearsed—and pretty soon she was replying, "Four day."

*

Mommy make a speech and now they going to take her picture. I feel big to be with her. I don't make any mistakes at the party. I decide not to do anything the way it makes sense to me, I just going to do things the way people here do them. That way, I won't make any mistakes.

*

Summoned to the next room for a photograph, I had to leave Mohm in the smoky, mirrored cocktail lounge for ten minutes. When I returned, the smirk of pride spread all through me. This child—who made friends with monkeys so she could share their fruit, whose only eating implement for the past six years had been a tin spoon—now stood balancing a plate of hors d'oeuvres with one hand and spearing Swedish meatballs with the other. She had figured out how to handle herself at a cocktail party, because she had to.

You Can't
Live
in a World
Alone

"**S**he's probably filled with intestinal parasites," the doctor snapped. "And I'll have to do a patch test for TB. We see it all the time with these refugees."

I was accustomed to the brusque manner of Maura's pediatrician, but this was different. She referred to Mohm only in the third person and kept her at arm's length. Mohm shrank into a corner.

"Tell her she'll have to take off her clothes."

I pantomimed the doctor's instructions. Mohm's face colored. As gently as I could, I helped ease off her polo shirt and jeans.

"The undershirt, too."

"That's all, though," I said.

Mohm stood in her training bra and panties against the wall like a prisoner waiting to be shot. The doctor pointed to the scale. Mohm stepped up, wrapping her arms around her chest. She weighed eighty-eight pounds and stood four foot nine.

"Hmmm, she doesn't look bad, Gail." It was the kind of remark one makes about a melon after pushing a finger into its stump. But nothing could detract from what I was seeing for the first time with my own eyes: well-formed limbs, a long back straight as a chair, narrowing to a tiny girlish waist, only a hint of hips—she was no more than twelve, the doctor agreed—and skin uniformly satiny with scarcely a mark on it. Except for a few scars from leeches and boils, the child's body was perfect. Thank you, God.

Mohm dressed quickly. I meant not to leave without registering a note of disdain, but before I could, Mohm bowed her head and made the prayer sign with her hands.

"Sank you, very, doc-tuh," she said.

"Hmm." The doctor's brows shot up over her eyeglass rims. "That's a nice child, Gail."

We stopped at Woolworth's to buy Mohm a treat to eat. "You must be starved," I said, and then winced at my casual American hyperbole. She knew about starved. I pointed to the candy rack. She smiled but shook her head and nodded toward a jar of peanuts. Her eyes widened in disbelief when I bought the whole jar. But outside, struggling to unscrew the top, I clumsily spilled a handful on the ground. Mohm dropped to her knees and scrambled to pick up every last nut. She squirreled the soiled ones away in her pocket, and then ate, slowly, one at a time, out of the jar.

Arriving home, she offered the precious jar of nuts to Ella.

*

Suddenly realizing I had a long-standing dinner party invitation, I jumped up to dress. Needing to know why, Mohm composed her first English sentence.

"What you go, Mommy?"

My dinner host was a former hostage in Iran. The discussion of Mohm at dinner that night turned sharp and unsettling. When I described how Mohm's voice changed from the soft and passive learner to the strict teacher, one of the guests, a lawyer, mumbled "Maybe she was a trusty."

"What's that?"

"Prison lingo. Trusties are prisoners used by the authorities to keep the other prisoners in line."

The former hostage nodded. "You may find she went over to the other side."

"But, if you met her—" I was too stunned to speak.

"She survived, didn't she?" he said.

The former captive Foreign Service officer had emerged as a leader among those held four hundred and forty-four days in Iran, and his tone was nonjudgmental. "They used to razz me as a hostage for acting like a Harvard man and ordering our captors around as if they were waiters. But it turned out to be essential. Anyone in a situation like that will reach for whatever he has to feel momentarily superior."

The first doubt pierced at the haze of euphoria through which I had been seeing Mohm's every move. Was I being naïve?

*

Mohm was persistent about reaching out to her Cambodian friends, but we had only one name, the girl with whom she had traveled to New York. Every time we passed a pay phone, Mohm would point and repeat "Suon Unn." At last, I thought I had tracked the child down. "Hello, may I speak to Suon Unn?" I asked.

"Yes." Ah, relief.

I handed the telephone to Mohm.

"Hello?" she said expectantly. A frown darkened her face. She held the phone away and pointed at it. "Boy," she said, barely disguising her indignation. "Suon Unn"—she pointed at herself—"girl."

*

I don't understand anything at all. I don't know where to start. Everybody is a stranger. I don't know the words, the way they think, the way they do. Are they angry? What do they expect from me?

If I could only see Cambodian children. Before, they didn't seem that important to me. Suon Unn became my best friend in one week—that's how desperate I was! The reason I made such good friends with her is both her parents died, the same horrible experience that I go through. How she was dealing with her problem was the message that got to me. We humans seem to send those messages to each other. As long as there's somebody there, you can always change from bad to good. But you can't live in a world alone. I think I've lost Unn forever. All the Cambodian children—I'll never see them again. It makes me so sad, I can't cry.

*

She could always laugh. After ten sessions with her first tutor, Mohm hid in the kitchen when she heard the doorbell. Although vastly generous, Mrs. San So appeared to be suspicious of the quality of charm and suffered from little of her own. Mohm had to be summoned.

Mrs. San So glared as Mohm knelt dutifully at her feet. I inquired why the Cambodian woman never greeted the girl.

"It is not our custom," she said. "We have no word for hello."

"But there is a way to communicate in any language 'I am happy to see you.'"

"She must do it first," the tutor smiled condescendingly. "Anyway, it doesn't matter."

"It matters," I said, whereupon the tutor began admonishing Mohm for not greeting her first.

Mohm looked straight at me, and with one large, cartoon-clear gesture, she winked. Her wink said, "Nice try, Mom."

No matter what, we were on the same side.

The Circle Widens

At the end of my second week as a new mother, I awoke tingling with the expectation of Maura's first homecoming. What a delight it would be to have her a part of the next startling discoveries. It is hard to explain what it is a child brings to the day. As adults, we spend so much energy planning for what we hope will be and replaying what might have been, we have little left over to live the moments. A child is the moments.

When the doorbell rang, Mohm flung open the door and immediately recognized her new sister. Maura wrapped her arms around the child and hugged and hugged her. Mohm responded with an uncharacteristic gesture of intimacy, nestling her head on Maura's shoulder. Maura tried on Mohm the title of *bong srei*. Mohm seemed delighted. When these first spontaneous gratuities were in danger of dissolving in the language gap that quickly opened up, Maura found her old hand puppets and created an imaginary world of trolls and hairy monsters where she and Mohm could explore each other without a word of English. It was Maura's special magic to be able to reach into people, even on first meeting, even into her most formidable elders, and touch their essence. She opened Mohm up from the start.

The formidable Mrs. San So arrived, removing Mohm for a time. Maura had plans to go out with her boyfriend. Surprisingly, she consulted me about her clothes, then decided on the velvet skirt, and with her beautiful hair dancing red and brown, went off to dinner. The initial meeting of the two girls had gone so well, I didn't want to think about the problems ahead. With no time to make room for Mohm, I'd literally taken room away from Maura.

If I were to recount what we did on Saturday—Maura and I and two friends of mine took Mohm to Chinatown, bought her shoes, had dinner, taught her to hit a tennis ball, and rode home with Mohm asleep on Maura's lap—the events themselves would be unremarkable.

It was the thousand tiny strokes of shared sensation that mattered: the moment, for example, when Mohm first comprehended the concept of choice.

Passing a store window, she pointed at a pair of Etonics and exclaimed, "Jogger, jogger!" We all nodded approval, but when the first pair turned out to be too small, she replaced them on the shelf and sat back in her chair, resigned. The notion that you could have one or the other instead of nothing was foreign to her. We had to urge her to make direct statements—"I like" and "Not like"—then build to the notion of comparison—"Like a little bit," "Like a lot"—and finally, triumphantly, she understood that it was acceptable to make a choice among many: "I like *this.*"

It occurred to me that I had no idea what Mohm did like. The only request she had allowed herself was through the bilingual social worker: She hoped to learn a sport the boys played in the camps. "Tennis," he had translated. Tennis? Some preppie refugee, I thought. But I scrounged up a Prince racket and some clunky sneakers so Mohm could join my Saturday morning tennis game, and Mohm was soon being told how to hold her wrist stiff, drop the ball, and swing through . . . she looked utterly mystified.

*

So strange, how they play this game here. Everything is heavy and dragging you down, the shoe, the racket. Playing badminton in America feels like playing under water.

*

We swung down Canal Street, Maura pouring herself into the child in every way she could invent, the two of them joking and laughing nonstop. We all sniffed at the Oriental vegetables in the street stalls for scents of Mohm's old home. Oh, yes, ginger, and Chinese broccoli, and —"I like this!"—Mohm passed me a dried root with a peppery citrus scent. Lemon grass! We'd asked everywhere for it, for this was the smell of Cambodia.

In the midst of the pleasant confusion, Mohm noticed Maura leaning against a light pole, pensive, for the first time standing apart. She went over and threaded her arm around her new sister's waist. A flush of surprise spread over Maura's cheeks and reddened into delight.

Seeing them, I felt *sok sabai*.

"That was the moment we became close," Maura told me later that evening.

Maura and I discussed possible private schools for Mohm. Our neighborhood elementary school had stonewalled me. Mohm was fourteen on paper. "Legally, we don't have to touch her," the principal said. In New York State a child is placed in a grade according to age and fourteen was junior-high age. The fact that Mohm had had only two and a half years of spotty schooling mollified the bureaucratic temperament not at all. So I walked her past the junior high to see her reaction. Whenever she had seen on our walks a class of elementary-school children skip by holding hands, she had followed them wistfully. Approaching the junior-high-school playground, she again came alive. But when we leaned on the fence, she looked bewildered. The children were easily twice her size. Where her gestures were classically Oriental —graceful, contained, self-effacing—theirs were large, wild, explosive. Some of the boys had slouched over near us and spat expletives. The girls walking by behind us, the ones they were trying to impress, shouted back, "Yeah, your mutha." These were not children. Mohm had looked defeated.

What about The Brearley School? It had been wonderful for Maura.

"For me, yes, but don't forget, Mohm walked across a jungle to survive. There were Brearley mothers who wouldn't let their daughters cross from the East Side to the West to play with me."

"There must be a right place for her—" I was musing, when Maura blurted, "Oh, I'm so glad to have a sister! It's as good as I always dreamed it would be. I only wish it had happened six years ago."

The sentiments she expressed were genuine; to Maura, nothing was more important than family connections. But when it came time to go to bed, my first daughter was without a room.

"Honey, I had nowhere else to put her—"

"Never mind." Maura, stepping on the next words evenly as she dragged her sleeping bag out of the hall closet and laid it on the floor: "I won't be coming home much anymore."

*

Clay felt left out too, even though officially we still were not seeing each other.

He called. "Why did you forget my birthday again?"

"I wasn't thinking about you, it's true. I'm sorry. I was thinking about Mohm."

"How is she?"

"She's magic."

"I'm terribly excited about meeting her." His tone was honest and sweet.

"You should have come to the airport," I said, unfairly.

"You didn't invite me."

"I didn't want anything to mar that moment." Then my better nature triumphed. "But I'd love you to meet her now."

It was like him to bring an inspired gift, a big book about ancient Cambodia with a lovely inscription:

For Mohm:
Welcome to your new home. Here are some beautiful scenes from
your other country. Now you have two home countries, the U.S.A.
and Cambodia. I hope you will love it here as everyone will love
you.

Clay

She gave him back the sort of undiluted attention that American men have mostly given up trying to command from their women. She even danced for him. He was, of course, enchanted.

*

But how do you communicate? my friends naturally wanted to know.

At first, through empathy.

Lacking all but the most primitive language, we had no choice but to become keenly aware of each other's needs and moods. When she didn't know the next move, Mohm scanned my face like a forest creature instinctively sniffing out the invisible signals necessary for survival. It made me realize what vast nonverbal resources we squander—the paintbox of the face with its many shadings; the language of the body that spells out when we are receptive, guarded, hurt; the keyboard of voice tones so exquisitely tuned to express nuances of mood and the precise level of intimacy. Taken together, these nonverbal cues must account for at least 60 percent of the messages we communicate. There must be an alert receiver, however, as well as a willing sender. A nonverbal message is not successful unless it is received.

As with many survivors, one of Mohm's strongest defenses, and one that became evident quickly, was a sense of humor. One day on the sidewalk we had to jump out of the way of a man being pulled by ten leashed, straining, snorting, drooling, unevenly trotting dogs—a dog walker. I burst out laughing, and a second later, Mohm laughed too, uproariously. Another day a race-walker passed us, and when I mimicked his turkey-lurch, again the laughter rushed out of her like a buried spring suddenly unearthed. So I began to seek out the ridiculous. We would mimic the sights together—a greedy gibbon at the zoo, a petulant squirrel in the park. Normally, such sights might have been worth a chuckle, no more, not the cascades of mirth that shook Mohm from head to toe. But there was something healing about it, I knew that for certain, as if such spontaneous absurdities and the license to laugh at them were, each one, precious gifts.

We gradually broke the ice by poking fun at each other. Having observed me standing at six in the morning (or evening) in a stupor by the stove, waiting for my liquid caffeine to heat, she began serving me cups of the stuff unrequested: "Here, Miss Coffee." I noticed her picking out and eating the meat or fish in the Asian concoctions I tried to make and repeatedly turning up her nose at the rice.

One night I cocked my head, "You don't like rice—what kind of Cambodian are you?"

She howled with laughter. It was coming along nicely, the chemistry between us. She even seemed prepared to accept at face value the peculiar habits of these natives of New York, who stepped around mountains of bulging black plastic garbage on their sidewalks but who bent down to scrape up their dogs' excrement.

Even as the composure of her face enchanted people, I could see her eyes sweeping others' faces for every crumb of meaning. The sanctions of her own culture against looking people in the face, particularly adults, were overridden by the urgent need to understand, to read people, to respond correctly to the challenge of their inscrutable sounds.

Notwithstanding, there is no substitute for language. Amputated of the ability to communicate, we lose the very foundation of our identity. There is no way to say, "This is who I am," or "This is what I can do," which makes it vital to find proofs in action that will communicate our particularity. On her second day of learning to ride a bicycle, Mohm wobbled down the hill and called to my huffing figure, "OK, Mommy, I go now! Hello, tree!"

Each time we walked the dog I drilled her, and every night I could hear her roll the empty words over and over in her mind until she sank mercifully into sleep . . . "bus, car, taxi, airplane, street, apartment, check, computer . . ." words that reflected her fate in dropping out of the sky into the fast lane of a sophisticated Western megalopolis. I didn't know how Mohm felt inside, but she was showing me that iron motivation was her shield.

*

Before, I always have something I'm looking forward to, something I'd like to be—like an actor. It's something to work hard on. Something to hang on to. Without that I feel like nothing.

But now I get to the place I want to be, and I can't speak the language to her. I don't know what Mommy wants. I don't know what I want. I can't speak so I have to show how I feel in other ways. But I don't know if I can care about other people again. I don't really understand Mommy much, the way her life goes. I just have to figure out some way to get along.

All my life is torn up. I left all the people I made friends with in the camps—they were my family, so precious to me I didn't even know it until I lost them—to come to this strange place. When you have so much sorrow inside you, you can see or hear something and not even know what it means, but you can laugh. Normally, it might not be funny to others. But because *you* want so much to get out of your sorrow, to be happy, to live, you burst out laughing.

*

"The principal has hung up on me three times." It was Joanne Baterfalvy of Catholic Guardian Society calling to report on her efforts with the public school.

"Can't we get an appointment so he can *see* that Mohm's twelve? The doctor even said so."

Joanne said, "Gail, I've taken it to a higher court—the Board of Ed itself—and they're going strictly by the guidelines. The central office told me she could be bused to another district—Harlem."

A chill went through me. I had written about the war over busing and neighborhood schools in Boston, but now I felt the atavistic fear those parents had felt, on both sides. What if that were my only choice?

This was not just my problem. Mohm had added two years to her age, but many Indochinese refugee children had lowered their ages in the immigration process, fearing they might ripen to eighteen before they were called out for resettlement and be left in the camps to rot. The result in New York State, as I later saw, was Cambodian boys with bulging muscles and fuzz above their lips and girls who felt too ashamed to ask the nurse for a sanitary napkin, sitting in classes next to eight- and nine-year-olds, all because the educational bureaucracy insisted upon going by the book. The ages of all these refugees were approximate; after genocide, there are no papers.

My oldest friend, Sue, a soul mate since kindergarten, came down from Boston to spend the night. We looked in on Mohm. In sleep, she appeared like a still glass pond. Her arm was a long thin reed bent back over her head, the hand cupped open and the fingers tapered like lotus petals. But behind those serenely shut eyes, what diabolic images might be ambushing her dreams was anyone's guess.

I shut the door and saw the tear rolling down Sue's cheek. "Oh, God, Gail, *that* child . . . that angel . . . saw what you said . . . the horror . . . I can't stand it." She hugged me and we rocked and wept together, and then I remembered the poem that had presaged Mohm's arrival.

"Maybe that's what she is—one more angel," I said. "Sent to show us something."

The Silent Period

Week three. I noted in my journal: There is only one catch. So expert is she at surviving, she gives no hint of her feelings.

One afternoon when I returned, Mohm had a faraway look. We had begun making the rounds of private schools. At each one Mohm scanned the faces almost frantically for someone like her, and each day she grew more despondent. "No Cambodians," she would say as we walked home.

At the U.N. School, which looked like an immense luxury liner jutting out into the East River, we were told about its own theater, its five different orchestras, the faculty from forty-nine different countries —and yet nowhere in that wondrous ark could Mohm find a single Cambodian face to mirror hers. We were asked to see the guidance counselor. They wanted to give the child some neurological tests.

A mellow-voiced Afghanistani in short sleeves asked her, "Do you speak any English?"

Mohm frowned.

"Do you understand me?"

Mohm froze.

"Remember, sweetheart, *a, b, c, d*—" I prompted her.

Nothing.

"Can you tell me her story?" the counselor asked.

I tried to mute it by using a factual monotone, but even then, I could see the man's expression gather alarm.

The counselor motioned Mohm to sit on the floor. She hesitated. She was wearing a brand-new, light-blue denim dress, I told myself, and she doesn't want to dirty it, that's all. She found a plastic stool. He asked her to copy the stick figure he was drawing on the blackboard. Her hand moved hesitantly. He sat her at a desk and gave her shapes to replicate. There was no light in her face, none.

I began shaking. Gruesome equations coursed through my mind.

How many bowls of rice soup does it take to keep brain cells alive? How much protein in a beetle? How long can one live in the jungle on monkey discards and remain fully human?

"Have you seen her perform any complex motor activity?"

Think, Gail, think. "Yes, we taught her to hit a tennis ball in less than an hour!"

"Can you write your name?" he asked Mohm softly.

She picked up the pencil and wrote "Mom" in elaborate Khmer script and then in blunt English.

"Beautiful."

The counselor came over to me. "What I was afraid of was brain damage, given her terrible experiences. But I see no evidence at all. She is nervous, that's to be expected."

He explained things I knew but in my maternal panic had forgotten. Almost all neural development is completed by the end of the second year. "Emotional shocks cannot affect that development, although prolonged malnutrition can result in dullness or retardation," he said. "But if she picked up tennis—"

Then Mohm looked up, blinked, and recited lickety-split the English alphabet.

The counselor smiled. He studied Mohm. After a while he said, "It will take her some time to realize this new life is not a dream, it's reality." He told me his own story of flight from Afghanistan. And then he said, "What she has seen is unique. When she can admit what she has seen to mind, maybe she will tell her story for others to understand."

The reception at other private schools was decidedly chillier. At one, the principal told me after our first interview, "Frankly, the faculty is divided on whether we can handle her or not." He looked down his long Anglo-Saxon nose at the Asian child as if from a spire of the Church of England, and shook his head. "We would, of course, have to suspend traditional educational goals in her case. All we could provide is a rich social setting, in which she could learn what it is to be an American teenager."

"She might even have something to teach them," I said.

"Mmm, perhaps. She would also need a Khmer-speaking tutor to be with her throughout the schoolday at first. Would you provide that?"

He was, of course, raising the ante to an impossible level. Mohm had been sent off with some of the children to the lunchroom. I found her standing by a globe with several curious girls and boys. One was saying, "Cambodia—is that, like, Vietnam?"

A girl with a hundred-watt smile introduced herself as Lorisa—"a Spanish name"—and reported to me that the kids had made pictures to help in talking with Mohm. They had drawn a mother and father and asked her if she lived with them. She said no. They had drawn a brother and sister and asked her if she lived with them. She said no.

"Well, actually, Lorisa," I said, "Mohm is an orphan. Her mother and father were killed in a war."

The child's face dropped in disbelief. Why not? This generation of American children knows nothing of war, and so long as most refugees can be in effect "quarantined" apart, in pockets of a few inner cities, young Americans' illusions about the world will be kept intact.

Outside, before I could even ask, Mohm said emphatically, "I don't like this school."

"Why?"

"No Cambodians."

"Did you like Lorisa?"

"Vietnamese." A cold hard sound.

"Lorisa? No, honey, she's Spanish."

"No. Vietnamese."

The helpful little Spanish girl's mere use of the word seemed to have marked her indelibly. Rejection has a way of generating rejection. I wanted to go back and tell that headmaster: *It's your loss; someday this child will be fabulous.*

*

The next morning she did not get up. I went in to reawaken her several times; we had another interview. "Chop-chop, really!"

"Not go," she said and rolled over.

Her face looked heavy and pale. I sat on the edge of her bed and remembered what Margie had told me: After the first few weeks of trying to please, there is often a depression and they may refuse to come out of their rooms, escape into TV, or sleep all the time. I lifted Mohm's head in my hand. "Sweetheart, why won't you get up?"

"Tired," Mohm said. It was a problem as simple as that. Why not? Anytime I sat down now for more than a few moments at a time, in a bus, a class, a waiting room, I dozed off. My body screamed for sleep. I carried a thermos of black coffee everywhere. It had been three weeks of heavy lifting for both of us.

Another private school called. "It's not good news; we cannot increase the class size," said the woman in officialese, and then her voice dropped to a whisper. "There's a crying need for places for these children. If I could persuade my husband, I would do just what you did."

I turned in frustration to Maura's former adviser at the Brearley School. She suggested Friends Seminary, an old and estimable Quaker establishment. "It's a gentle school," she said.

And it was. From the moment we approached the brownstone scale of Friends from a tree-lined street downtown, I saw Mohm relax a little. We made our way through its unpretentious corridors, discovering the basement that had been used in the 1800s as a stop along the Underground Railroad. All at once Mohm flew from my side and down the hall after two girls with gleaming black hair and amber skin, shrieking, "Same me!"

They were indeed two Cambodians. It seemed that members of the Brooklyn Quakers had learned that the new refugee children were languishing in the public school there and sent them here. Why was Friends so ready to reach out? One answer was the school's link to the American Friends Service Committee, a voluntary agency that works with refugees around the world. But the headmistress, Joyce Macrae, a woman with the raspy warmth of hot cross buns in the morning, gave me a subtler answer. Quakers believe "there is that of God in every person, that divine spark," and thus develop their educational goals to emphasize the individual. "Competition doesn't fit into the Quaker concept," the headmistress told me. "Children have got to feel safe first—then they will flourish." The school was also committed to instilling in young people the concept of service, and not just lip service. From seventh grade through graduation, students were required to give a block of time either to other students or in community hospitals, courts, or housing projects.

It was as sound an educational philosophy as I had heard. And the results were evident even to a superficial observer. Although the children dressed to reflect a vast range of individuality, they didn't make a game of exclusion; they seemed nice, and nice to one another, more so than at the usual private school.

"I *like*," Mohm said outside.

The rest of the day she was unnaturally euphoric, and the next day subdued and sluggish. As we walked home from yet another command performance, Mohm resisted for the first time our word games. The fragments of conversation we could manage had become suddenly unsatisfactory.

"Tired," she said. I felt the loneliness surging through her. If she had at that point been able to quote from Shakespeare, she might have chosen, from *The Comedy of Errors*, the soliloquy of Antipholus of Syracuse, who was separated as a baby from his twin brother and mother when their ship broke in half during a storm:

> I to the world am like a drop of water
> That in the ocean seeks another drop. . . .
> So I, to find a mother and a brother,
> In quest of them, unhappy, lose myself.

At home Mohm drifted onto the terrace and walked in circles. I went out to give her a Pepsi. She thanked me politely, then leaned over the railing and turned her face away hoping to hide the last futile contortions before her face seemed to disassemble, separating into plates of fear, of anguish, or was it fury? slipping then into a leer, a sardonic flash—it was a face of masks. Whatever wild elusive discord of spirit those masks covered, I could not look her full in the face. Not then. And she could not succumb to tears. I wrapped my arms around her, but her body felt like broken bird bones in my embrace.

She put a foot up on the railing. I shuddered. Here in her glass and gilt prison, separated from her culture, so lost, she must have thought of me as her jailer. I could almost read her thoughts, and months later she was able to describe them. . . .

*

I don't like to live here, all Americans, all big apartments, no children, and I can't speak. Everything I know seems so far away, cannot ever get it back. My family is all gone, part of me torn away, I'm already broken. But I healed some of that wound, brought some of those parts back together and made the beginning of a new life in the camps. And then, it was torn away from me again. Maybe I have to go the rest of my life without seeing anybody I love.

It's not going to change. I can't learn the things I want to. I'm not good enough. I'm not even myself anymore. Never ever can I bring all the parts back together and be myself. I don't think I want to go on.

*

It grew dark and cold on the terrace. "Will you come inside, sweetheart?" I coaxed.

"No."

She had left me. I could not reach into the tunnel of silence to pull her out. I knew then that I cared for Mohm unfathomably.

Her former camp director chose that moment to arrive. Margie quickly sized up the situation and went out to talk to Mohm, but the child was too far away to respond even to her. They stood for what seemed an eternity side by side, silent, Mohm hanging over the railing, Margie giving her unlimited time. Seven o'clock came and went. Margie began to talk again. I couldn't understand the Khmer. For the first time Mohm looked at Margie and her eyes blinked and a gurgle of laughter began in her throat. She laughed and pointed down in the street and laughed some more.

"What did you say to her?" I couldn't wait to find out.

Margie had simply talked about how she herself felt on her first visit to New York—overwhelmed—how everybody else seemed to know which bus to get on and which turn to take at the corner and how they all walk so fast you don't even dare to stop somebody and ask where you're going. Mohm wasn't the only stray bird lost in New York, and once reassured, she could laugh.

"She has such presence," Margie said. "It's easy to forget that another part of her also has all these needs."

"Is she angry with me?" I asked.

"No, that's what is lovely about Mohm and a lot of these kids. They understand it's circumstance. I didn't feel any anger from her. Just the sadness. The loneliness. Not seeing enough Cambodians. She said it was nice with Maura. But she only came once. There's only so far you can go with the excitement of newness."

Then Clay was at the door. I almost asked him to come back another time. He looked at Mohm out on the terrace. "My God, what's wrong?"

"Let's show her the book you brought."

We coaxed her inside. Clay and Mohm sat side by side on the sofa to look at the book of monuments of ancient Cambodia.[1] I slipped in on the other side. The book seemed to transport her to the deepest layers of memory and fantasy. She devoured it page by page, gasping at the towers that leapt out of the photographs with an almost touchable psoriasis of age, and through those pictures she narrated the zenith and decline of her culture, its religious legends, the desertion of Angkor Wat, right up to its desecration under Pol Pot. All this gushed forth in rapid-fire, emphatic Khmer. We were compelled to listen. She was taking us on a journey to the spiritual axis of the Cambodian kingdom.

The temples of Angkor were one of the largest religious creations in the world. Like the pyramids, they were built for human monarchs as monuments to their own divinity, and since each "god-king" was in fact a usurper, they also served to proclaim legitimacy. One sensed those massive stones were not joined with easy plaster but with blood and flesh. Suffering to praise their Buddha by building the king's city was believed to assure the workers of less suffering and greater content-ment in the next life. I wondered if the captive population of the Khmer Rouge had labored under the same rationalization. Present-day Cambodians were probably the self-same people depicted in the bas-reliefs of Angkor, according to the preeminent French scholar.[2] That meant they were descendants not only of rulers of compassion and builders of one of the most sublime wonders of the world, but of butchers of exceptional malevolence.

Mohm pored over the visions of hell carved into those sandstone temples, which were precise as evening news footage in depicting Pol Pot's regime of terror—people being yanked up by the hair, blud-geoned with shovels, led away in chains. I sensed that she was wonder-ing about patterns of repetition herself. Drawing a finger across her throat, she let us know more of what she had seen. She had seen people's heads lopped off like fruit and tossed in mass pits. There was no escape. "No go, kill." Simple as that.

One thing I did grasp for certain: The condition of Angkor Wat symbolized for Mohm the condition of her country's soul. Each picture in which a limb or a head was missing on a statue would bring forth a moan, "Ohh," or a lament for things broken apart. She believed this damage was all the work of the Khmer Rouge, and that the Vietnamese were now allowing what was left of Angkor to strangle in the grip of the jungle.

I tried to convey through Margie that Angkor had not been destroyed by Pol Pot; in fact, I'd read somewhere that only one of the hundreds of *apsaras* had been damaged.

Mohm breathed, "Oh, God, that is so good."

Before midnight, she climbed out of despair. The book had served as an instrument of healing. And by morning, the storm had passed.

*

As I look back, there seem to be four distinct stages through which one must pass to regain identity and flourish in a new culture, and the centerpiece of all of them relates to learning the language. During the first, the *rote period,* one simply repeats words and phrases and begins programming the brain. A new learner in the rote period is a stumbler in the dark, no light, no map. He or she must proceed by sound. But any new language *sounds* unnatural, its words arbitrary. Who would ever think of calling a mother "Mom" (which in Khmer is slang for a young girl) or calling a *seh* a "horse" when *seh* so obviously sounds nicer? Or as comedian Steve Martin expresses the frustration of this stage: "The French, they have a different word for everything!"

It is impossible to produce cogent speech until enough examples of the new language have been stored to make associations with the structure of one's native tongue, whereupon the new learner can produce some sort of language. While that difficult work is being done one enters a *silent period.* For Mohm, it was at the end of the third week that her facade began to crumble. The mute weeks or months that must follow are like being in a tunnel, all alone, surrounded by cacophony. As Mohm later described it:

*

Sometimes, I feel like I'm outside them all and looking in through a glass—I notice they walk around the same way, they move their lips and laugh and lie down to sleep—but I cannot hear anything they say, I don't know what they're thinking, I don't know if they're really human or not. It's like being trapped on Mars.

*

At the end of the tunnel of silence is a wall. If one cannot get up the courage to crash through it, to stumble and fall and make terrible mistakes, one will never communicate—period. Many refugees become stuck here. Out of self-doubt or impatience or simply lack of time, their speech becomes fossilized at this insecure level and learning stops. The trick is to be willing to throw around the words and phrases one has stored. That takes the new learner into a *reckless period*. The sentences gush out and half the words are half-breeds or backward but it doesn't matter because one is communicating. And getting messages back! That makes it worth living with the fear of saying something that may be all wrong. What's more, the emphasis now can be on the meaning of words rather than on the mechanical production of sounds.

The responses one gets back in the reckless period help in making corrections, and more quirks of the language are, if not satisfactorily explained, at least exposed. ("They tell you to put *s* on everything that's more than one. Like eyes and ears. Then why does Mom always say she's brushing her *hair* when anyone can see she has hundreds of *hairs?*") This, too, is the stage at which the values and attitudes of one's new culture or new family can be internalized, or rejected, or eventually synthesized. Beyond the sheer euphoria of having found the key to unlock one's new culture, a reckless period should lead the new learner toward the crucial, self-critical *revising period*.

Here, the learner hikes straight into the forest of language and forms hypotheses about where things belong in a sentence and how to talk one's way back out of a thought, discovering rules and relationships among word groups and responding to *context*. The skill needed here is one the experts call *inferencing*[3]—a process of constantly organizing and reorganizing—until one gradually makes the structure of the new language one's own. Inferencing is now thought of as far more important than the rote memory once said to be the hallmark of able language learners, although one does not reach this level of confidence in a new language just by saturation. The revising period demands systematic and purposeful work.[4]

But while I thought I understood the stages, I had no idea of their duration. Even as Mohm was entering the fearful silent period, she was starved for contact with other children.

Searching for Cambodia
in Brooklyn

All that silent weekend I flew back and forth across the Brooklyn Bridge to drop Mohm into a pocket of Cambodian culture. I had found the principal teacher of Prince Sihanouk's Ballet Royale, said to be one of four or five surviving dancers trained in the royal palace[1]—alive and well on Flatbush Avenue! Madame Kamel had a performing troupe, and she agreed to try out Mohm. At the same time, Mohm was introduced to the social archaeology of America's inner cities.

By mid-Saturday afternoon, the streets of the Flatbush section of Brooklyn were wavy with drivers mellowed by drink or drugs, who start and stop in their own fantasy time. We walked up the stairs of a once-proud prewar apartment house, past the scent of gefilte fish to the top floors where the newest arrivals, the Cambodians, were swallowed in darkness and the scent of lemon grass. Many of them were virtually under siege by young blacks, whose defeated aspirations had found a new focus of rage. The Cambodian refugees resettled in inner cities were often better served by social-service people than some black residents, I had learned. It wasn't hard to understand why: Even their teenagers smiled and said "sank you." This favoritism only fueled further resentment by American blacks.

Mohm was welcomed into the home of a courtly, educated family. Madame Kamel was a quiet, tired woman whose suffering under Pol Pot had been preserved in the deep furrows around her pretty features. At least half of the royal ballet dancers had been killed, she said, but she was determined to continue a school of dance to bring the dying art form back to life. Classical Cambodian dance, more than a thousand years old and steeped in Indian influence, had been displaced at least once before. When the great capital of Angkor was sacked by the Siamese in the fifteenth century, its performers, along with the rest of the court and the language, had been abducted or their movements copied to become the core culture of the new state of Thailand. By the time Cambodian dance was returned to its homeland in the nineteenth century, the roughly two thousand movements of the bare-breasted, hip-swaying women enshrined on the walls of Angkor Wat as heavenly *apsaras* had been reduced to no more than thirty.

Madame Kamel's own life had followed the dictates of palace dancers as preserved throughout Prince Sihanouk's monarchy. Sent at the age of six to the palace ballet school, girls were trained until the age of twelve or thirteen, when they first appeared before the king. If he took a fancy to a child, she would be brought to his bed where she would remain until he tired of her. Thereafter, she might be allowed to resume dancing and, if she was from a good family, be married off to one of the king's officers. Otherwise, she would become a teacher or be demoted to servant. Madame Kamel showed me a snapshot of herself that she had buried during Pol Pot time, resplendent in a gold headdress, performing for the prince on a sun-dappled pavilion.

"This method of dance, slow and gentle, is Cambodia's soul," she said. "If we lose the dance, we lose the soul of Cambodia."

Madame Kamel asked Mohm how much she had danced. Eyes downcast, Mohm whispered her reply. "Never mind," said Madame, and she assessed the girl for the first requirement: charm. The second was a supple body. She instructed Mohm to bend her body backward. Crack, crack. The teacher admonished her to bend every day. Meanwhile, she would give the girl a tryout. I left Mohm with a half dozen other girls to dance for two hours.

*

Everyone here is a stranger, too, and they look at me like a piece of nothing, but still it brings joy to me. I am seeing Cambodian people, the same skin, the same hair, the same blood as I am, and it makes me happy just to see them.

*

On my return, I found her squeezed into a string of children on the sofa, swaying to the endless loop of Cambodian music.

"Mohm can be a fine classical dancer," Madame Kamel told me. "She is doing well. But we must ask—is she serious?"

Mohm nodded.

"We have a performance on November twelfth," said the teacher, "so you have only two more weeks to rehearse."

"Oh, my," I said. "Where?"

Lifting her chin with phantom pride, Madame Kamel said, "Here. We have no other place."

At home Mohm wrote the words of a Khmer song on her blackboard and sang in a sweet whisper for two hours. Then she got out the screwdriver to install the new videogame in our TV set. With the instincts of her generation, she hooked up the game box to the UHF outlets, plugged in the joysticks, and beat me by seven hundred points at Space Invaders.

I began to understand how vital it is to provide an immigrant with two tracks to put down a new life: the shiny new track that demands one learn to think in a new language, and the memory track that permits trips back to the cultural symbols around which a person's core identity was formed.

We made that round trip across the Brooklyn Bridge every Saturday and Sunday. Sometimes we listened to tapes of Shakespeare and other times to Khmer music. Eventually I perceived a different sort of beat, a pulsing of repetitive notes in shifting rhythmic layers. The layers of sound created a sense of space and elasticity, as if beckoning the listener into a realm of timelessness. I began to understand that to the Khmer, music was a form of worship.

I suggested Mohm keep a diary. She began making voluminous entries in her own language, double dating them in Arabic and Sanskrit. The diary proved to be a precious mirror for her thoughts during the silent period.

But whenever that ocean of loneliness seemed about to swamp her again, she would go into her room and turn on the tape of Khmer music and sing to herself. Waves of girlish soprano, celestial and tender, flowed out softly through the half-open door. She had found in music a means beyond language, to heal herself.

The crisis of the silent period had passed.

*

Already I could see in Mohm one of the hallmarks of the victorious personality. Despite the unfamiliarity or chaos of the conditions she found herself in, no matter how distressed or disoriented she was, she had a knack for making the *other* person feel comfortable.

"I had hundreds of kids at Sakeo," Margie had told me, "and the two kinds I remember are the kids who had a lot of problems and those who would come in and just capture my attention. That was Mohm. She was never afraid to make contact. She knew I was studying Khmer so she'd stop by wanting to talk. She always *acknowledged me.* As a result, she was always noticed."

I remembered the same pattern from my own first meeting with Mohm. When I had raised her hopes falsely, she went out of her way to make *me* feel better.

Something I'd read about invulnerable children came to mind. When the social worker would call on a home in utter chaos—mother drunk, father just home from jail and slapping her around, six kids sitting clam-eyed before the TV or crayoning on the walls, kitchen an excrescence of old barbecue containers—there would be one child who would come forward, introduce himself or herself, and bring the worker lemonade. That was the victorious personality.

In the same way, Mohm extended herself to people whose goodwill she needed. Standing before a doctor who had offended her sense of modesty, Mohm, instead of sulking or becoming hostile, had disarmed the doctor. She had danced for Mrs. San So, reached out for Maura, read a book with Clay. Using whatever she had to work with, she touched people.

The elasticity of Mohm's behavior also amazed me. She could be amazingly blasé holding her plate of hors d'oeuvres and mimicking the crowd at a Miami cocktail party, but instantly on alert to save the last peanut when threatened with loss. She lived intensely in the moment. Survivors must, I supposed. But it was as though her mind were hooked up to some super radar that allowed her to sense and adapt immediately to changing circumstance.

So far, so good. She had survived for months on the run in the Cambodian jungle, but would she survive the first months on her own hook in the jungle of New York City?

Firsts

The great buzzing confusion of her first day of school turned Mohm's face nearly incandescent. It was her fourth week in this country. At last she was with kids, packs of kids. We sat in the high-ceilinged meeting room for the silent time that begins each school day at Friends. The American children swung their feet and fussed with their big black digital watches. Mohm sat stock-still. But when it came time for her first class, gym, she hurtled up and down the basketball court letting off weeks of steam.

*

My teacher is a man, nice one. His face is white. Teacher for math is black. Teacher for gym has hair all curly, the nurse has blue hair, and some of the children have red—I guess you can have whatever kind of hair you want in America.

Everyone smells like milk.

The children all say "Hi!" to me. It must mean something nice. Some of the girls wear shirts big as tents and three earrings in one ear. And some of their shirts look like underwear, so tight! One of the boys talks all the time even when the teacher gives the lesson. I lean forward to catch what the teacher is saying.

Psss, chhh, ppt, shhh, tsss . . .

There's a hiss on the end of every word they say. That's how it sounds to me, anyway. I never heard those sounds before.

I'm so glad the Cambodian girl is in my class. Sarouen is her name. She showed me how to push the tray around the tracks in the eating hall. But the food! They call it *pizzz*—I can't pronounce it.

*

The first day Mohm came home with Sarouen. The older, larger Cambodian girl seemed to be taking an aggressively proprietary interest in Mohm. We all sat on the bed to put together her first looseleaf notebook. Fifth graders today may learn to "access data bases" before they learn about the Fertile Crescent (which topic had introduced me to the concept of boredom), but it was reassuring to go through the timeless ritual: to snap open the big ring binder, then fold back the tabs along the perforations and print the subject names—Math, English, History, Science—and slip them inside the pretty colored plastic windows. But tension developed almost immediately between Sarouen and me over who would set the rules for Mohm.

"No bed till eleven," said Sarouen.

"Bed here must be at ten."

"Too early!" Sarouen scowled.

"Sorry, Mohm needs her sleep. Ten for her, okay?"

Sarouen smiled. But no amount of shushing their muffled chatter could get the two girls to sleep before midnight.

The next day, Sarouen arrived home with Mohm again. I asked if she had called her mother. She simply smiled.

"Okay, we're off to your first party!" I said as we walked past the doorman.

"Why don't you get sunthin to protek dose girls?" the nice Dominican doorman called after me.

"I'm counting on my vicious devil dogs."

"You need a gun. Listen, I get for you. Yus a leetle gun."

"So I only have to commit a little murder?"

They walked in front of me to the car, two proud Oriental princesses preening in their new ruffles and high white socks. We drove across the Queensboro Bridge and I heard them gasp. As far as the eye could see the city was webbed with bridges, spinning out a tapestry of moonlight on the black water. Mohm thrust her arm through the open sun roof and exclaimed, "Moon!"

At the Catholic Guardian Society home in Amityville we were welcomed into separate rooms for children and parents to discuss the adjustment from those opposite points of view.

It wasn't the sort of crowd that shops at Brooks Brothers or Bendel's and I doubted if anyone there had a tax shelter. The foster fathers were for the most part beefy blond milkmen and bearded Hispanic baggage handlers and the women were the sort of mothers who make do with the scroungy jogging shoes their eldest child has just grown out of. Not a few were immigrants themselves. I loved them for opening their hearts and homes. They hadn't had a clue about what they were getting into, as their stories revealed.

A bulkily-built bus driver described his apprehensiveness as he and his wife arrived at the airport to pick up their two Cambodian foster children. All they had been told was that most of the refugees were male adolescents and did not speak any English.

"So I'm lookin' at my wife, and she knows what I'm thinkin'. Will it be a monster? Will it carry a gun? So this guy comes off the plane, see, and he's OLD, I mean, he looks like he's been through a WAR. I say to my wife, 'Do me a favor . . .' "

The room erupted in laughter. All of us there had been through those last-minute panics.

"So we drive home with the two of them in the backseat. I say to my wife, 'We just had two baby boys, age fifteen, and there's nothing we can talk about.' "

With four months of foster parenting behind him, the man was now wreathed in smiles. "My boys are, well, what the hell, I'll say it—beautiful." The rest of the parents were just as enthusiastic. Some had fostered a Vietnamese child earlier and were pleasantly surprised to find the Cambodians more emotionally forthcoming. Everyone remarked on their *joie de vivre*.

On the way home the two girls fell into dense chatter in Khmer, but before the ride was over, Sarouen informed me that Mohm had told her not to speak to her in Khmer at school anymore. "She tell me speak to her in English!"

"Bravo, Mohm!"

"Mohm is my best friend," Sarouen announced possessively. "The other kids, they're mean to me."

The third afternoon I picked Mohm up at school, heading off Sarouen while I consulted the school nurse. "Sarouen worked on a road gang under the Khmer Rouge," the nurse told me, explaining that she had arrived in America without yet being literate in her own language. "I took her home one day to read with her. Her pronunciation was almost flawless; even her spelling was fine. The problem was, I discovered, she had no idea what the words meant. She was lost." The fifteen-year-old had been put back from seventh to fifth grade. The nurse, who made me think of Cinderella's godmother, confided her own feeling of failure. "We're in a terrible position with Sarouen, because she goes home to Cambodia every afternoon." Like so many adolescent refugees, Sarouen was the only one in the house who spoke any English. She had to be the go-between for her parents to the new culture, reversing roles of authority at just the age a youngster wants someone to fall back on when the challenges of the adult world become overwhelming.

I told the nurse I was having trouble finding a way to tell Sarouen that she couldn't live with us.

"She won't say no. She will nod and give you a wonderfully open smile, and then she'll walk away and do as she pleases." The nurse was only confirming a profound cultural difference I had already come up against. An order or a personal question was interpreted by an Asian as an insult. But rather than argue back like American teenagers, these youngsters used indirect negatives.

"It's almost impossible for us to challenge that tactic," the nurse added with a wink. "So I warn you from the start. Mohm will win."

Everyone at school was frantic on the fifth day. Before I could pick her up at three o'clock, Mohm had disappeared.

"Let's give her an hour," I urged the school authorities, "and see what she does with it," and I took a cab home.

An hour later, like clockwork, in strolled Mohm, her brows innocently lifted as if to say, *See what I can do.*

"I go bus," she said. She had figured out how to board the public bus, count out her fare, ride sixty blocks, and walk the last five blocks home, on her own.

"Any problem?"

"No problem."

She was announcing that she did not want so much help. After all, she had been operating without parents for at least five years; she had figured out for herself how to walk around mines and across enemy lines; her independence was the most precious possession she had. That she had been reduced to a toddler where speaking was concerned made it all the more important that she demonstrate her many other capacities. The survivor needed room to show her stuff.

Physical challenges were the easiest place to start gaining a sense of mastery. Maura came home and took over the bicycle coaching. I watched her and her boyfriend, one on either side, cheeks pinched pink with November air, tirelessly pushing the wobbly but persistent stranger until she took over the two wheels on her own, and I knew that we all were learning. To this imperishable child everything new was good. Different was intriguing. Change was approached with relish rather than apprehension. Had she always been that way? I wondered. I had a hunch not.

On the next bike-riding lesson, Mohm began by perfecting a gentle grade. A member of the park-bench parent-surveillance police, those old pretzels who like to point out that you are letting your child play in the rat poison, volunteered the directive: "This place is no good for her, over there the hill's steeper."

Mohm caught the cue and went flying down the path beneath Dog Hill, disappeared into the underpass, catapulted out of the tunnel, jammed on the brakes, and of course went over the handlebars.

At home, an ice pack on her elbow, she was more determined than ever.

"Do you want to go back and learn more bicycle tomorrow?"

"Of course. I not afraid!"

By the fifth week she told her social worker she was very happy in her new home.

But she wasn't sure whether or not to approve.

Shocked by seeing me casually kiss my friends of both sexes hello and good-bye, she wagged her finger when the same behavior turned up on a TV program. "No Cambodia, no," she scolded. "Mommy and Daddy," she pointed to the bedroom, "okay. Not this, this, this," and she pointed to chairs around the room.

She would bring out a picture of Maura with her father and two half brothers. "Maura hab two brothers. Maura hab two mommies?" It got worse. "Where is Maura's Daddy?" And then, of course, she wanted to know who was the ardent young male person who so often accompanied Maura.

"Why, that's Maura's friend."

"But he a *boy*."

In Cambodia, if a girl so much as accepted an invitation from a boy, she was pledged to him for life. Her mother did the marriage brokering. And she would never have walked through a rice field alone with her intended until the end of the three-day wedding feast. Men and women in Cambodia touched each other only when they were married and then only behind closed doors. The discrepancies between our cultures threatened to cast something of a pall on my social life. How to explain?

Whenever my friend and then-editor, Hill, came by, I tried to beat Mohm to the door but usually lost. Hill knew all about the proscription against touching the head of a Cambodian; he was simply constitutionally incapable of coming through the door without his body pitched forward, lips puckered, hands outstretched, ready to touch and tousle and tuck Mohm up under his shoulder like a father hen.

It got so I would give a little squeal of warning and he'd arrest himself in mid-lunge, rear back, "Aahhh!" and throw his hands up in the air like a burglar surprised in the act. Mohm howled with laughter. This, she apprehended, was truly a well-meaning American man.

The concept of divorce was as exotic to Mohm as Americans' premarital habits. Everyone knew his place in the hierarchy of her culture; here everything was so maddeningly *un*discriminating. She was determined to sort it out. Not daring to push me any farther, she worked Ella over.

"Mommy hab nice friend, gib book." She pointed to the book Clay had given her. A half-hour later she came into the kitchen and inquired nonchalantly: "Clay, Mommy's friend-boy?"

Ella giggled. "No, Clay Mommy's friend."

"I sink friend-boy."

Ella resorted to her usual trick under interrogation: "Me no speak Cambodian."

"No Cambodian, I speaking English!"

Finally, I took a crack at explaining divorce. Shortly thereafter Mohm came home from school to report, "Ebreybody divorce. Children, all go to Daddy's house on Saturday."

"Not *all*."

"Most. And Cambodian minors, same same, new family no father, too. American man no good. He throw woman away."

What her sample lacked in statistical validity, it made up for in chilling brevity.

Having done divorce, it seemed only appropriate that we do mugging. One night when we were walking the dogs, we could see the Conservatory pond below the street with its jazzy silver stripes across the patent black and she asked if we could go into the park.

"Park in day, okay. Night, not okay."

"Why?"

"Bad people in park. Bop you on head."

She giggled. And practiced by giving me a karate chop.

*

She pointed to Ella's hair and then to the telephone cord, making our sign for "alike." Then she would point at me torturing my poker straight hair with the curling iron. The absence of standardization in skin and hair baffled her, even seemed to offend her. And when I was gone, she often balked at Ella's authority. "No!"

The next time her bilingual social worker came, I reminded him that Mohm did not know about black people in the United States. "We must explain to her that this is a place where we welcome everybody. We have black people, white people, brown- and yellow-skinned people, and everybody has to have the idea of helping one another."

Dutifully, he translated. Mohm showed no reaction.

"Would you ask her how she feels about Ella?"

He demurred, too direct.

"I tell her she has two mothers," he whispered, "she has so much love from them. I tell her try this home, it is very good for you."

Then I asked a remarkably stupid question. "Can you ask her, if she could live the way she wished, how would she choose?"

"She doesn't know how to answer." Mr. Sao lowered his voice. "You know, many of these children do not know the concept of 'fun.' We have to instill these things again—the emotions of living."

*

When at last we did locate her plane friend, Suon Unn, I spoke to the child's foster mother in Sullivan County. It was a rural community, and Unn, together with her two sisters, were the only refugee children in the school. Her foster mother, a dog breeder, having had a bad experience with a Vietnamese refugee and runaway phone bills, wouldn't permit Unn near the telephone.

"Suon Unn live far?" said Mohm, disappointed.

"I'm afraid so."

Dimensions of space and time were even more difficult to put across than those of social distance. At least she had Unn's address. Mohm sat down to write her first letter. The reply a week later shook her up.

"Suon Unn have no English. Mommy and Daddy have no Khmer. Suon Unn not understand." Mohm indicated that her friend was very busy looking after her two younger sisters and had no time to study. She found the word for it all in her Khmer phrase book:

"Sad."

There was something else, important, that she wanted to communicate about her friend. It wasn't in the phrase book. She ran for the big English-Khmer dictionary. Nothing. She flipped through all one hundred mimeographed sheets from Mrs. San So. After forty minutes, she called out, "Somesing like this!"

Pointing to the Khmer word for "think of a person, remember," she added, "Suon Unn, me."

I made a lonely, yearning face.

"Yes."

So I quickly turned in the phrase book to the word *miss*. She shook her head, no, because of course the translation must have been only "unmarried female." Back to the big dictionary. At last, under the fifth meaning of *miss*, we found: "to miss someone loved."

"Yes! Suon Unn miss Mohm."

But when Clay and I took Mohm to see her first movie—*E.T.*—I wept, she didn't.

"Not sad, Mom," she corrected me, "not like Pol Pot time. Just a story."

Unlike many Americans, Mohm knew the difference between special effects and the real thing. But Mohm's view of the world was something else. I had no inkling of how disoriented she still was until the day she came home from school to study for a test on the solar system.

Mars, Venus, Pluto—she quickly memorized all the planets by rote —but what was this world we lived on? She led me to her new globe. "Show me?"

*

Mommy calls it "earth." Funny, it's round. And it's really a little tiny place. Anyway, it's another world from Cambodia. I know that for sure, because in Cambodia the world is flat. Well, sort of square, like a rice field. In my eye it's thousands and millions of rice fields stretching as far as you can imagine, and past that, only ocean. So now I know what is the new world I've come to—they call it "earth."

*

"Do the children at your school know anything about Cambodia?" I asked.

"Oh, no."

I pointed to her country on the globe, a butterfly shape. She asked which was Vietnam. I traced the long red shape that pinches the eastern border of Cambodia like a pair of lobster claws. "Vietnam."

"Ohhh," she groaned softly. "Thailand?"

I traced the large gold wings that hover over the Western side of Cambodia, then the vast blue mass that hangs over them all: China.

"Oh," in dismay. "China too big. Cambodia too small."

She ran her finger around the soft pink border of her country, crooning softly, then pantomimed the position that Cambodia is in—a butterfly with hungry beasts on all sides waiting to swallow it up. She sighed and shook her head. She had seen her homeland from an entirely new perspective, and it was helpless.

"United States, lucky," I interjected. (We looked up *lucky.*) She observed the huge oceans on both sides: "No Vietnam, no Thailand, no China, only water, water, water." She shook her head up and down vigorously. "And no soldier. United States, I *like.*"

*

So each country must have its own planet. My mind is still in my little world, of the camp, where you could walk to everything. Anything you need, you could just call out for it and people will hear you and you can hear them. When I walk down the street in New York, there's another street like it and another and another as far as I look—it's endless. But I'm beginning to know which direction is right and wrong. I want to try to find my way.

*

Reading every book on Cambodia I could find emphasized still further how vastly different were the cosmologies from which Mohm and I viewed existence. It was evident even in the architecture. Western constructions with their thrusting verticality—whether the pointed spires of Westminster or the nose cones of rockets—represent the aspirations of the individual, the desperate Daedalus ambition to "come out on top." This emphasis on the singular vertical thrust could be an obsession of cultures where this life is generally believed the be-all and end-all.

The architecture of Cambodia, by contrast, mirrors a system of thought based on the assumption of multiple lives and the transmigration of the soul. Even the ancient kings created gentle temple mountains that mimicked the Cambodian landscape, with their multiple tiers and terraces representing a series of worlds, a series of lives. The individual is moving always through planes of good and evil on a trajectory inscrutably guided by his karma. And given the belief in karma—that the deeds of a past life influence the conditions of one's present life—there is no fixed point of forgiveness or safety to be hoped for, nor final judgment day to fear, only restless spirits and dead ancestors to be appeased so that one's path through this life may not be strewn with unlucky accidents.

I wondered if Mohm would come to believe that the individual can control experience. She would need a long period of continuity in her daily life before she could even consider such a notion.

Every day now she seemed eager, infectiously enthusiastic, ready to try it, write it, sing it, plunge into her new world and take big juicy bites and wash it all down with humor. But she was still—and perhaps always would be—running.

*

On November 12, Madame Kamel's dance troupe gave a performance at the Friends School. Backstage, I found a painted child-woman, with smoky eye shadow, rouged cheeks, and crimson lips, a face I scarcely recognized as Mohm's. "Maura here?" she wanted to know immediately. "Maura's brothers?" The two boys (Maura's half brothers, twelve-year-old Duff and ten-year-old Ean) had chosen this occasion to come to New York and meet their exotic new relation.

The performance began. Boys boldly costumed as monkey kings or crocodiles played out Indian myths with girls dressed up as mermaids or angels. The girls' expressions remained hauntingly composed, the flicker of a smile perhaps; the roll of jet eyes was tantalizing but untelling; the tapered fingers were always moving, unfolding as flowers, bending into fantastical shapes, drawing one's eyes into their trance.

Maura's brothers sat forward, transfixed. When Mohm appeared,

Madame Kamel's daughter was right next to her and occasionally guided her hand this way or that. Mohm caught my eye. Her smile flickered wider. She was obviously enjoying this, a magic moment encapsulated within ancient Cambodian music and movement, surrounded by legendary characters out of the *Bramacharyi*.

Afterward, we went to a coffee shop with Maura and her brothers. The boys explained that they lived in the country and had horses.

"Horses, two?" Mohm guessed.

"How did you know?"

"In Cambodia, *seh pi*—'horse two,' " she taught them.

The boys then enumerated all their animals, Cambodian style, putting the number second: "Chickens twenty, cats two, dogs three, no, *cats* three." It was agreed that Mohm would have to visit their house and count them for herself. As the boys reluctantly bid us good-bye, Ean said solemnly, "Will she be our sister, too?"

*

After six weeks, this child who had squatted in fields all night while the fireworks of death screamed around her was waking up with a Mickey Mouse doll in her arms. She awoke to a mother with the strange habit of touching her cheek with her lips. Her eyes would pop open, she'd check her precious watch, synchronize it with the digital clock, march into the bathroom for a ritual of soaps and creams, and emerge in jeans to wash down her vitamin with a treat of ice water. Off down the street to meet her subway escort, buoyant in her jogging shoes and buckled into a book bag, she delighted in a breakfast of finger food—salami with soy sauce. In six weeks Mohm seemed to have reached a working equilibrium with this new world called "earth."

*

On Thanksgiving weekend, Maura drove us to Long Island. As we turned down a dirt road toward the water, the sky yawned and a flock of dark birds flew out of its mouth, then the sun flared and ran into a stream of gold. We parked and sprinted to the top of the sand dunes. Mohm gasped and staggered back. There it was. The first ocean ever created—the thunder of God rolling the earth this way and that, rocking the world from one end to the other as far as the eye could see.

"Who is it?" Mohm shrieked.

"Ocean," I called. "Whenever you see the ocean, you have to run." We broke into a dead run toward the surf.

"Oshun! Oshun!" Mohm cried, jubilant, "Run, oshun!"

The sea lapped up her sneakers and the spindrift tickled her face and her laughter came close to hysteria. Mohm mimicked the gulls, climbing and diving in a frenzy of feeding, until she was turning somersaults and flipping over a palisade of sand into the wash of receding surf.

*

Ocean—it's the same! I'm so happy to see it! Same taste of salt. Oh, I love the white part. It looks just like Chouk where I stay by the ocean in Pol Pot time. At least one thing is the same. Same ocean in this world and my old world.

I asked Mommy is there really an end to the sky or not. She doesn't know. I'm not sure anybody can find it. But I'm sure it ends someplace we don't know. Maybe it ends where the ocean of the United States and the ocean of Cambodia come together. I want to believe that.

*

On the jetty we discovered another wonder, a honeycomb of barnacles, then another and another. Maura and Mohm and I all marveled at the over-and-over-againness of the same clinging mollusk. Whether a shiny black shell or a dried husk, their shape, their atomic structure, their symbiotic relationship to the rocks showed off nature's nonchalant repetition of form; it made me wonder if we all came from a uniform blueprint. For all the striking differences in our racial and cultural heritage, Mohm seemed sometimes more like me than my own daughter. And we seemed both to intuit, that day, that we were two souls meant to come together, two people who could give each other the gift of a new life.

*

In the course of the weekend, my whole family gathered at the house. Everyone marveled at how rapidly Mohm seemed to be acclimating. She liked saying grace over the big turkey dinner, and she enjoyed the story of the hungry Pilgrims being given food by the native Indians. But beneath that jubilant exterior, excited by the warmth of a holiday occasion, were patches of agony.

*

This is family. I love family. I'm only sad not to have my family of children from the camps with me. The younger ones, I cooked for them, I nursed them; it made me feel needed. I took those children for granted then. You don't realize how precious a time in your life is until you leave it all—then you look back. It's like the other half of you, torn apart from you.

*

The first night, Maura went around the room kissing the family good night: her grandmother, aunt, nephew, and then her step-grandfather and uncle. Back in the bedroom they shared, with a tinge of disapproval in her voice, Mohm questioned Maura.

"Why you kiss the men?"

"Honey, they're not *men*. They're family."

Maura asked if there was something Mohm would like to read with her. "Yes, I get it." Mohm came back with what looked like a colorful picture book, *Children of Kampuchea*, published by the International Rescue Committee. "Great, I'd love to look at it," said Maura, cuddling next to Mohm on the sofa the way a big sister does with a little kid who brings home a favorite book. They turned the pages.

The first drawings showed children playing tug-of-war, then walking down a street filled with cars in Phnom Penh, then climbing the ladder to a fine country house on stilts.

"Like my family," Mohm said proudly.

Abruptly, the next page pictured people running and the next showed soldiers chasing them and blowing up bridges behind them, and in another, women with children were being forced out of their lovely homes in Phnom Penh.

In a dry monotone Mohm commented on each picture. The next one showed a double line of people stretching into infinity, their mouths howls, all awaiting the same fate as a man tied to a tree being tortured to death by a soldier with a knife. Blood poured from the man's mouth. In the foreground was a pit filled with human skulls and bones.

"Dog." Mohm pointed to the face of one of the soldiers. The child-artist had drawn the Khmer Rouge soldier's face as a dog. "Baby." She indicated the form of an infant, which another soldier was literally tearing apart limb by limb. It started out as coldly as that. Maura hadn't yet had time to learn much about the Khmer Rouge regime. Confronted with these graphic scenes of incomprehensible cruelty, the blood drained quickly from her face. Mohm was intense. I came through the living room and knew that something momentous was passing between them.

"This how they tie people, hand back," Mohm was saying.

The picture showed a line of young and old tied together like cattle and being herded to a blood lake, where young toughs were smashing a boy over the head with a gun butt.

"We see this ebrey day ebrey day."

The caption by the fourteen-year-old artist read: *Why were these people killed by the Khmer Rouge soldiers? What had they done wrong?*

Maura's face crumbled. Even Mohm's eyes seemed to be leaking tears.

"You know, sweetheart, we don't need to look at this," Maura said. "Do you think it's helpful?"

Mohm couldn't speak. She asked to go to her room. When she didn't return, Maura went in and found the child on her bed, sobbing. Maura wrapped the little girl in her arms.

"Let's put the book away."

"Yes, put away! Too sad."

They found a high drawer in the desk with a lock on it and hid the book.

Maura kept rocking the little girl. She had always been able to talk people out of their dark corners. Always, before. After a while Mohm confided in her that she had never cried—not once—since the beginning of Pol Pot time. She felt desperately sad inside all the time but she dared not cry; it would be like the ocean, it would drown her. So she tried to look pleasant all the time. And nobody knew.

"Don't tell Mommy," she pleaded.

"Okay," Maura agreed. "I know I don't understand what happened to you and I can't even imagine it, but if you ever want to talk about these things to me, or if you just want to cry . . ." and that was all she could say. She could find no point of common experience, no pertinent words of comfort; she could do nothing more than be there, laying out all the love she had to give.

"Oh, Mohm, I hope we can make you happy," Maura said, and from then on, with Mohm's consent, she was the only one permitted to kiss the little girl good night on the lips.

Mohm did not cry again for more than a year.

The Reckless Period

One Sunday night we took Mohm to see *Bambi* and afterward stopped for ice cream.

"It's called a sundae," Clay began resolutely as the waiter set a confection before her.

"If I have ice cream on Monday, is it call a Monday?"

This was only the second month but already Mohm was throwing her English around, even playing with words. Her curiosity rushed out before she could line up the sentence: "Who is it mean?" She had arrived at the reckless period.

*

We found a new tutor, Kim Cox, a sweet, diminutive student with a nice sense of humor, who was determined to teach herself how to help Asian second-language students (the New York education establishment wasn't much interested). Kim advised that this period of indulgence in the intoxicating new language be stretched out as long as possible, so I didn't bother to correct Mohm. When speaking to her I didn't sprinkle in all those confusing bread crumb words like *an, in, on, the,* and *that,* and I took pains to stay out of what Tom Wolfe calls the whichey thickets. Many current experts frown on using telegraphic speech with new learners, but it seemed to give Mohm the confidence to continue splurging on new words, so it couldn't be all bad.

Something had to be done about her name. Kids in school pronounced *Mom* as in "Mom's apple pie." (It actually rhymes with "home.") And of course the aspirated *h* in *Phat* was lost on the inevitable gum-chewing goad at school who liked to call down the hall, "Hey, Mom Fat!" "I've got it!" Maura said one day. "If the *h* is causing a problem, why not move it?" We decided to take the *h* out of *Phat* and drop it into her first name—Mohm Pat—how was that? She liked it. And if that didn't fix things, we'd make up T-shirts.

But although she seemed herself to be enjoying the word play, letters arriving from other newly resettled minors worried her. Many were struggling desperately with English and feeling depressed.

"Would you like to go and visit and try to help them?"

"Oh, yes!"

It seemed vital that she find out she was not isolated. What's more, she needed an adventure. What could be worse than to have earned the wily instincts of a survivor only to be domesticated into a lap dog? And what quicker way to begin to grasp concepts of time and distance on this immense continent than to try to get from here to there on one's own? So off went the little goodwill ambassador by herself on a shuttle to Boston.

"I go see Margie," she announced proudly to Ella. "No you, no Mommy, plane Mohm—plane to Massashoosut." She punched out every last syllable.

She phoned me from Boston. "Thirty minute to get here, Mom. So easy, I like travel, a lot!"

On return from Boston, she was exuberant. She had seen her own kind; she had compared herself and registered pride in her progress; she had felt needed. Finding that some of the minors who had been resettled with siblings or in cluster sites were still clinging to one another and their native language, she had coaxed them not to be shy.

"I tell them it's okay to make mistakes in America, they don't hurt you here."

Giggling, she reported that people in Boston don't speak like people in New York. "They say 'caahr'!"

"It's called a different accent," I told her. "You know how taxi drivers in New York speak sometimes—"

"Hi little goyle!" She flushed with pleasure in her own powers of mimicry. "You see, Battambang people not speak like Phnom Penh," and she imitated the accents in Cambodia's two major cities. "Battambang people say Phnom Penh people, uh, crazy!"

Driving to visit friends in small towns outside Boston, Mohm also had seen how some other American children under the age of eighteen live, in poverty (22 percent of them).[1] The value of living in New York, with all its educational and cultural stimulation, was beginning to dawn on her. Her world had some bounds and in other ways was boundlessly exciting.

"There's been a tremendous breakthrough," her tutor, Kim, reported. "I don't know what happened in Boston, but Mohm is ripping through her exercises twice as fast as before."

*

I love seeing my own friends and my culture. We care about each other. It's not many children who think the way we do. As long as you can be around others who have been through the same experience you have, you can send messages and know they are received. Giving the message back and forth tells you that you're still alive.

After that trip, I can speak. It's getting a lot better. Things begin to fall into place little by little. And I'm not scared anymore of doing things, that I'll make a bad mistake. Even I'm able to communicate with people, a little bit.

It isn't going to be as bad as I think. I have the feeling if I want to be myself badly enough, I can be someday—but not soon. Life is not as ugly as I think. It could be as beautiful as I want, if I make it.

*

More complex conversation between us became possible. She stopped calling me "Mommy," having gathered from her peers that it was babyish. The more recklessly spontaneous she became in her observations, the more often her sentences would end with a dimpled frown and the double beat "Right, Mom?" And now she was able to initiate her first request.

"Thursday, Friday, no school. I go visit Suon Unn?"

I suggested she look up the address in her new book.

She came running back, "Jeffer-son-ville."

"Oh, dear, that's three or four hours away," I said.

"Maybe I walk?" she offered.

"You'd better start now," I teased. "It's two hundred miles."

So she took the bus to upstate New York. She found her best friend shrugging off school and ashamed to attempt English because all the kids laughed at her. Mohm urged Unn not to fall back on speaking Khmer. "Don't let the school say it's too hard for you. Tell them, 'Why not just let me try? Even if you don't do well at first, still got to try.'"

The feedback from her trips to Boston and Jeffersonville allowed Mohm to bask in a partly recovered sense of self-worth: At least she could be a good friend. "We couldn't believe it when we sat down with Mohm," wrote one American foster mother. "We could have a conversation with her!" Unn's foster mother wrote: "Mohm made us realize that shyness has to be discarded." There was negative feedback, too. Margie de Monchy was run ragged driving Mohm around to see her friends. Despite Margie's obvious overwork with other refugees, Mohm had continued all weekend to be demanding and self-centered. When Margie blew up at her, she sulked.

"Look, Gail," I was told by Peter Pond, "you have to *assume* they can't care at first. At least about us." Arn, one of his refugee sons, routinely told the Cambodian kids he visited, "Okay, you have a broken heart. What is your program for repairing it, so you can care again about others?"

She did pick up thereafter on the stunning gaps between the haves and have-nots among us. I remember the gasp that escaped from her when we first passed one of New York's thousands of homeless sleeping on a park bench. "Who takes care when no job?" she wanted to know. "Government," I said, "sometimes yes, but sometimes no." She wanted to know why the government didn't simply give out enough money so everybody could have a home and food. This was not an easy moment. She remembered what Mr. Sao had told her about democracy: Everybody has to have the idea to help everyone else. So why . . . ?

How could one explain the chasm between the fabulous towers of Fifth Avenue's rich and talented and the cold, rheumy reality of those sacks of flesh curled on the benches just across the street? Somehow it wouldn't square with the saga of the Pilgrims, or of all the immigrants who followed them. It wasn't going to be all that easy to sell her on the benevolence of democracy.

*

Christmas holidays brought the joy of many more firsts. The first circus —"I love New York! Everything happens in New York!"

The first snow. A great white muffle had already fallen over the city when I awoke one morning at six. I couldn't wait to show Mohm. She ran out on the terrace barefoot and scooped up the fluff, but by some prestidigitation, more magic even than in Cambodia, it disappeared! She packed more together, made a big round snow pizza of it and held it up over her head in triumph—"It snow!"—then crumbled it all over her face and caught the magic crystals on her tongue.

"I sink if it snow so much in Cambodia," she breathed in awe, "children sink they are born into a new life."

*

The first Hanukkah. It was a Friday night, Shabbat. She took a present for Jonathan, the fourteen-year-old son of my friend Elaine, who had made a project of Mohm by taking her for Big Macs and teaching her to play Pac Man. Elaine explained the story behind lighting the first candle of eight nights. "We are Jewish people, and this is our holiday." She spoke very slowly, conscious of the fact that she was responsible for giving Mohm an *exposure.* "Your mother is Christian, and she celebrates Christmas. But you are Buddhist, and it's a special privilege to have all three religious beliefs in one place." The blessing was delivered in Hebrew, by Jonathan. We all noted the look of utter bewilderment on Mohm's face but we had no idea what was going through her mind. And then it was time for the traditional potato pancakes with applesauce. "De-lishush," she managed to communicate.

*

I like the candles. I understand about giving food to say thanks to God. But three languages! All speaking in one room at the same time! How can they do it? I can't even speak two. And Jonathan, only one year older than me, he's so smart he's like a monk. Can I ever read English like he reads from his book? Are boys smarter than girls?

*

When we talked about plans for the future, rather, when I painted pretty pictures of what it would be like when we went on holiday, when spring came, when school let out, Mohm would inevitably freeze up. I tried harder to evoke her enthusiasm.

"Oh, Mohm, I *wish* summer were here so I could show you all the fun we'll have in the country."

"No wish!"

I had hit a wall.

"I don't have any wish," she insisted.

"Didn't you wish to come to America?" I tried.

"I *know* I come to America," she said.

With the slight impatience of a teacher faced with a sentimental child, Mohm explained the facts of life:

"You can't wait for a wish to come. You got to keep going. Maybe the wish never comes, can't think about that."

Wishing was a luxury available only to those who believe that life is fair and that people have the right to pursue happiness. Mohm lived on a literal level: What you see is what you get, or don't. Study, repetition, getting it right, these were the critical things to Mohm, as if she suspected that only good work habits could be relied upon for salvation.

Christmas, I hoped, might begin to moderate that. If I couldn't get a wish out of Mohm, perhaps Santa Claus could.

Trying to preserve the mystery, my friend Ginette and I had to sweep her past the pathetic, twiggy specimen got up in a Santa suit and ringing his bell outside Macy's, and up to the toy department, where, in the midst of that mobbed frenzy of consumerism, she maintained a maddening self-restraint. At the rockets and dollhouses and dozens of likenesses of E.T., she took only a standoffish look, and when the life-sized stuffed elephant was pointed out, she picked up the price tag and sniffed disdainfully. It was nothing like what an American parent would expect, not until her eyes came to rest on the display of dolls. There, on the top shelf, frothed in white lace, satin-slippered, with the illusion veil streaming like moonbeams around her face and grazing her impossibly long lashes, was an artifact that must be indelibly feminine in its effect. A squeal of longing erupted from Mohm, and she stood, rapt, studying the apparition. No explanation was needed. We simply gave her the two words: bride doll.

"Let's go see Santa Claus!" we exhorted. This one had an authentic corpulence and a silky beard that flopped up and down as he moved his lips, bidding Mohm to come closer. She hung back. "Go on, honey, you can sit on Santa's knee," I coaxed.

"Aren't you going to tell Santa what you want for Christmas?" he kept asking. She giggled and produced no request. He tried again and again. "No wish at all?" She shook her head no. *(Weird kid,* one could imagine Santa thinking. *What is she, some kinda commie?)* At last, a squeak. "What was that, little girl? *Tell* Santa." Mohm's cheeks shone and she dipped her head modestly.

"Bri-doll."

"Wayall, aww*right!*" Santa bellowed and rocked her in his pudgy arms, all of us reassured in our American bourgeoisie conviction that every soul has a material lining.

Mohm was asked later, "Well, so you went to Macy's, and what did you do?"

"I sit on fat man."

*

The coming of Mohm also prompted me to reach out to people who had at one time been of central importance in my life, and I in theirs, so that our memories were past sorting out. I accepted an invitation to spend Christmas day with Maura at her father's house.

In the hushed final moments of Christmas Eve a champagne cork popped and all the grown-ups sat back gratefully on their heels to take a break from wrapping presents. Two bright black eyes peeped around the doorway to the living room: Mohm, of course, establishing to her satisfaction that despite the propaganda barrage of recent days there was no Santa Claus.

The next morning, however, in the scramble of children and dogs and importunings from hearing-impaired grandmas—"Turn the kaleidoscope—no, you have to *turn* it, honey"—Mohm did melt into the general rejoicing of the holiday. Maura's grandmother asked if she knew the story of Jesus. I had taken her to my church once, where I hoped the lovely Episcopalian service would interest her, but she was bored silly. Notwithstanding, after three months in a Christian country she came up with a pretty fair synopsis of that most heavenly-minded tale and left us chuckling with the all-too-mortal punch line.

"All the people pray to Jesus and some tell King, but King angry. King say, 'I'm the big one here,' so he take Jesus to the mountain to kill him."

Mohm was the sacrament that Christmas. She brought us together as one big happy extended family.

*

There was a surprise package waiting for her when we returned home to New York. Clay was there to witness the event but as the perpetrator was definitely in the clear—hadn't he unlocked the door with us? Mohm looked truly mystified as she undid the wrappings. Slowly, the box cover released its hold on the contents. As she peeled back the tissue paper, Mohm's face shivered all over like a pond into which a stone has been thrown. Then she shrieked.

"Fat man bring me bri-doll!"

Her first wish had been answered.

*

I wangled a ticket for her to accompany me on a publicity trip to Los Angeles. Entering a plane (now on her seventh flight) Mohm peered into the pilot's cabin, fascinated. She asked me what jobs a woman could do. "I sink woman little under man," she tested. "Not for smart, but woman only cook, teacher, work in office, not do ebrything man do?"

"That's because men made the rules," I explained, "but in America, women can do just about anything men can do, even fly a plane."

"Really? I sink I like to be a pilot."

A beat, then a devilish grin spread over her face. "Go moon!"

What a natural resource refugees bring us, I thought. They create the American dream all over again, as if it had never been dreamt before, nor despoiled, disparaged, taken for granted. What is a dream anyway, if not a concatenation of our childhood wishes? When the European and the Russian and Jewish and Irish immigrants prepared to leave behind their lives in Zagreb and Minsk and Berlin and Belfast, what did they all believe—that money ran in the streets of America, that one didn't even have to work? The American dream was and always will be a child's fantasy, a myth that cannot be expected to "cost out" against reality for third-generation workers now accustomed to a hundred dollars a day. But every culture needs a myth to live by. The engines of hope brought to America by the immigrant waves of the nineteenth century have been replaced in the latter half of the twentieth century with the raw determination of refugees. By revaluing the freedom to work to better oneself, they can make Americans believe in our beliefs again.

But behind those joyful moments a shadow followed us, and when we were least expecting it, gulped up the gaiety. It had happened the first time we watched fireworks together. "See, isn't it beautiful, Mohm?" But the child had cringed. The gunpowder that shoots stars into the sky makes a sound indistinguishable from bombs. And now it happened at Disneyland. As our boat passed through Pirate Land, on both sides of us rose up realistic tableaux of leering, red-scarved outlaws who grabbed people by the hair and put flashing blades to their throats.

"Just like Pol Pot time," Mohm said. Such familiar scenes must have held for her a morbid fascination; she wanted to go on the ride again.

To watch my appearance on *The Merv Griffin Show* Mohm was given a seat in the studio audience. She saw Merv hold up a copy of my book and say, "Number one from coast to coast, will you welcome— Gail Sheehy!" It was her first taste of our culture's determination to promote everything, including authors, like breakfast cereal. All the way home on the plane, in a voice just loud enough to embarrass me, Mohm teased:

"Miss Gail Sheehy, Number One Delicious!"

If she was already able to satirize her new culture, she would probably survive it.

Dancing to American Time

O ur first fight was about time.

"Chop-chop!"

My usual morning exhortations to rev her up to tempo began to lose effectiveness as winter set in and her sack hound of a subway partner called more and more often to report, "I'm running a little late." Being no prizewinner for punctuality myself, I had even less tolerance than your average New York rush-hour robot when something interrupted my morning routine. "Chop-chop! C'mon, we must go *now*, I *mean* it!"

By the sharp tone of my voice she knew she had done something wrong, but what was it? Having dutifully incorporated the chores of personal hygiene I had given her, she could not understand why she was being scolded for performing all of them. She felt something wadding up in her throat, some new bitter herb of remembrance beyond the sadness. Whatever it was, it began to worm out of her and the face it wore was a ferocious scowl.

She set a cold turbulent silence against me. "Bagel?" Silence. "English muffin?" Mute indignation. "How about some nice hot noodles this morning?" Her scowl lasted for days. It began to look as if this might become a major hunger strike. (As it was, she had subsisted for her first four months here largely on grapes and peanuts.)

*

I think we can walk out late one time, it's not the end of the world and I just have too many things in my mind about what I have to do, read this, do that. All you want to hear is a nice voice. When the angry voice comes out, it just makes it worse than what was meant. It cuts off the good things you did and makes you feel far away.

*

One night I put my arms around her and crooned to her, about how she did so many things beautifully, about how she was an angel. The actual words she could not absorb, but as containers for the soothing sounds of approval and affection they served well enough, at least superficially. Her good humor returned.

The concept of "hurry up" had been a hard one to put across from the very start. The notion of an individual "schedule" or "appointment" was utterly foreign in "Pol Pot time." There were no clocks or watches. People were summoned to rise for work by the cock's crow; everyone ate, rested, and finished work at the same time. Larger dimensions of time were purposely distorted to suit the Khmer Rouge political program; their whole notion of taking Cambodia back to "ground zero" was meant to obliterate the past. As in almost any situation of extremity—being taken hostage, or sent to a forced labor camp—people were confined in a slow relentless now.

There had followed two and a half years in refugee camps, where one was suspended again in unmarked time and severely limited space. Mohm had no notion of "If we don't hurry, something might not be there." In the camps everything was there, and there was nowhere else. It was incomprehensible to her at first that friends' voices could be summoned up on the telephone and sound as if they were in the next room but it might take four hours to be beside them in person. Unless one took an airplane, in which case it might take only an hour. What was time, anyway? It kept changing. And just when you thought you'd mastered it, they gave you an extra hour to put on your day or, when you flew to California, took three away.

I began to grasp that the cultural differences between the ways Americans and Southeast Asians look at time were much more fundamental. American time runs in a straight line. Like our calendar, it has a beginning and an end and moves between them from point to precisely dissected point. As a result, for us, time must be scheduled, time must not be "lost," time is always "running out." Southeast Asian time runs in a circle. From moon to sun to moon, from rainy season to dry season and back to rainy season, from life to death and rebirth to life again, it returns always to where it started. So time cannot run out.

Mohm would watch in disbelief as I leapt up to answer phone calls in mid-meal. Inside I began to feel a twinge. Why do we live this way? Constantly plugging in through multiple outlets to our noisy world, no sooner starting one train of thought than being interrupted by something else—do we really get more done? I watched Mohm. Whatever she did, she did with her whole body and mind. She *concentrated* on the moment. And by concentrating her energy on the everyday things, one thing at a time, she seemed able to absorb a thousand and one new sounds and sights and tastes and subtleties of feeling each day, to select and master those bytes of information that were in her immediate vital interest, and still manage to disarm her detractors and charm her supporters every step of the way.

"How does she do it?" I pondered in my journal. "She seems to know exactly, what she needs. Maybe it's what they call 'Buddha nature.' " From what I had read about Buddha, he was not interested in grand metaphysical theories; he was concerned about how he himself existed in the moment. That was his point, the basis of Zen, and so much of Mohm.

If only her new mother would be as concentrated as she. But that new mother had no time, no leeway. Or did she? It became clear that one's approach to time went to the heart of my own problems in balancing a satisfying family life with a serious professional life. I had a great deal to learn, and life with Mohm could teach me if I let it.

But as everyone expressed concern at how "far behind" she was and how hard she would have to work to "catch up," Mohm herself began adopting a hyper-Western orientation to time. She asked constantly about the expectations here.

"How long Maura take to learn bicycle?"

"A few weeks."

"I have to hurry then."

Next it was, "How long you think I take to learn to read English, Mom?"

"Oh, probably six months."

"I think maybe four month. Better."

If there was a skill to learn or an obstacle to overcome, she determined not only to master it—as a survivor she never knew when it might be needed—but she began imposing on herself rigid time limits. And this applied no matter how ludicrous the skill she was being expected to learn. For example, skiing.

We took her to Utah over spring vacation. She looked up at the jagged mountains heaped with hundreds of inches of snow and the tiny figures scissoring down on little sticks; she was not enthusiastic. After two days shut up in the lodge under an avalanche alert, Maura and I got her outdoors in a cold gray blizzard on the practice hill, urging, "Try it, it's not as hard as it looks, really. You don't have to like it but you probably will."

She let us nudge her downhill, she took the rope tow up, and each time before going downhill again, she stood with her legs strapped to the moon boots and scowled.

*

I am going nuts to do this. After all the things I've been through, the one thing still okay is my body. Do I have to break it now for what they call "fun"?

*

We told her that Clay had been a beginner, too, only a few years before. And it didn't take him long to learn. . . .

"How long it take Clay to learn ski?"

"Oh, it took about a week."

Click. The point at which she resolved to learn the sport happened when we had our backs turned. She didn't come back at the end of the day. We went out to the practice hill, worried; there was the solitary figure, sidestepping all the way, pushing off to carve perfect arcs through the blue shadows on the chewed white snow, skiing. So there, smartie Clay!

*

We celebrated her thirteenth birthday in American time. (To satisfy bureaucratic requirements, we'd made up a birthday. Mohm remembered that she had been born shortly before Cambodian New Year, though it was not Cambodian custom to celebrate the day. She had chosen April fourth.) Still under avalanche alert, none of the guests was permitted to drive the roads so the possibility of surprising her with a cake seemed remote. We secreted a few small gifts under the dinner table and friends treated Mohm to a Shirley Temple cocktail. As we were finishing dinner, the kitchen staff threw open the door and paraded out with a pink and white confection they had sneaked down to town to obtain, singing "Happy Birthday." Maura lit the candles and I explained the ritual of making a wish. Excitement rippled through the room. People called out their good wishes. Mohm was radiant. Her eyes filled up with the light and her breath came in gusts of "ohhh" and "ahhh," and she was transformed into a child again. We knew it when she forgot herself and made a wish.

"My very first birthday," she kept saying. "I *love* it."

*

Even as Mohm began to adjust to a Western tempo, I became more acutely aware of my own problems with time. In January I'd had five speaking engagements in different parts of the country. The last one was in Bartlesville, Oklahoma, a remote dustscape dominated by the headquarters of Phillips Petroleum. Any speaker from a metropolitan area is made to feel like a shot of adrenaline to the bright bees confined to such a place. Because of the kind of books I write, and the kind of people who come to my lectures, and the compression of time, there is often an atmosphere of crash intimacy. I'm a one-night friend.

So it was in Bartlesville. The hostess who gave a reception after my talk confided that my speech had given her an insight into the nightmare she had been through: the abrupt descent of her daughter, a lovely and talented ballerina, into a mental institution at the age of nineteen. The ordeal had devastated every member of her family, but that night the mother realized that all of them had been strengthened as a result of the trauma. With her hand clasping mine, she called her husband over and told him of her insight. He looked at her with limitless devotion. I knew I had been a catalyst to that intense and memorable moment, but I also knew I was not a part of that family. Having served my purpose, I felt out of place, oddly empty.

"It's all fragments," I told Maura later as we sat in a sushi restaurant. "I have a wonderful life, but it's so compartmentalized. And I never seem to have enough time."

"Oh, Mom, you would be such a delightful person if you'd give yourself more time for an inner life. But that would mean convincing yourself that you're not being lazy or not sacrificing an important cause."

I heard myself sigh deeply.

"I mean," and she looked into me with her sweet, solemn eyes, "solving the world's problems gives you a good feeling, but isn't it nicer just to see the people around you, your friends and Clay and me, happy because of your giving?"

"I know, but we don't live in the world alone," I said.

Yet even as I was about to launch into a drill on the importance of addressing the issues of our times, I knew another truth. I was famished for some good old personal gratification. I *would* be happier if I could make Maura and Clay happier. I wanted—after all the years devoted to proving I didn't depend on it—a husband and family.

Clay's words at the end of our major rupture still rang in my ears: "You don't have enough time for me." We had seen each other off and on, mostly off, since the arrival of Mohm, but with no continuity of attention on either side, we were assured only of committing unintended slights and overreacting to them. Whenever I saw his shape hulked up in the fisheye of my door, he looked about as relaxed as a goalie for the New York Rangers.

I certainly didn't expect him to turn up at the Women's Campaign Fund Dinner. These are pseudo-intimate fund-raisers. Someone donates their home and a media name is asked to be the dog and pony act. The guests, having paid a hundred dollars a head, not only come with an agenda, each one thinks he or she owns a piece of you. Clay wasn't speaking to me at the time, or I wasn't speaking to him, one or the other, but it must have been the other because that night he had bought a ticket to my dinner so he could be sure of sitting next to me and I would be honor bound to speak to him.

The hostess, however, had placed Clay as far away from me as the seating plan would allow. He sat through dinner poker-faced, forcing himself to make polite chatter to strangers. After dinner, I was monopolized by people who wanted to know how to get an agent, how to write a play, how to get a haircut like mine. Around the outskirts of this taut circle Clay prowled, all but rabid, helpless to approach his prey. Once, feigning innocence, I glanced up at him with a "What? you're still here?" look. Wicked, that's all it was. Not until the host brought my coat did Clay have a chance to assert any territorial perogative. "*I'm* taking Gail home."

Walking up Park Avenue, he behaved so correctly I had all I could do not to laugh. He asked how my play was coming. (The seed of it had been his idea—just as he had planted the seed of Mohm.) I didn't have to say much about the problems I was having; Clay is all but clairvoyant about writers. He is able to tease out of hundreds of disparate personalities their particular quirky point of view, affirm it as worthwhile, tug at it, poke holes in it, praise it, until eventually he finds just the right subject for that writer and connects them and the two are off —like a cart hooked up to a charging tiger.

"I wish you'd hurry up and finish," he said, "so we can get back together."

A beat. I was seeing another man. "But we're not going to get back together."

He looked as though I had struck him. He took me home, stroked my cheek, and left. I tried to pretend I didn't tingle where he had touched me.

*

This was not the person I wanted to be. I wanted to learn how to be *available* to the people I loved. And I knew that was the kind of time that could not be scheduled. It had to be conjured up out of smoke and mirrors *then*—when the other person needed it.

Nothing had brought me more joy than to open up time to try to divine the nature of this new child. And each instance where I was able to improvise another link in the complex support network she needed, I felt like a million. I was learning that "people time" paid off in a currency that could not be counted. Call it inner gold.

*

But time had to be made for another trip to Thailand, where the situation for the remaining Cambodian refugees had worsened dramatically. Mohm let me know she felt a little guilty. "All the children you interview when you come to the camp think you pick them to come to this country," she told me. Some of Mohm's friends were still stranded there, together with about a thousand more unaccompanied minors and tens of thousands of adults. Churches were clamoring to sponsor them, New York City's Refugee Entrant Assistance Program was beating on the doors for another thousand to resettle, hopeful foster parents were sending telegrams to the State Department, but all of it seemed to be falling once again on deaf ears. I couldn't sit back smugly and enjoy my good fortune.

President Reagan's new handpicked ambassador for refugees, Eugene Douglas, had been silent for months about the charges of abuses of the refugee code by immigration officers with respect to the Cambodian applicants. When members of his own Religious Advisory Committee made noises about going to Thailand to see for themselves, Douglas exhorted them not to focus public attention on the issue. Three Lutheran bishops went anyway, organized by Peter Pond. With his customary hyperbole, Peter urged me to go along. "Just the mention of your name by now causes trembling."

What we found at Kamput Camp was appalling. The first of eight thousand Cambodian refugees were being herded onto buses to be returned to Khao-I-Dang Camp. Eight months before, those same people had been among the twenty-one thousand Cambodians "called out" to begin processing for entry to the United States. Their files showed they were of "special interest" because they had served the United States as soldiers or civilian operatives under the Lon Nol government, or because they had relatives in the States. I had written then that the call-out was a cynical trick to take the heat off the administration. U.S. Immigration officers had been boasting back then that they intended to reject 80 percent of the applicants. Having relented under pressure and admitted thirteen thousand, they had again become arbitrarily heavy-handed.

"Why did you come to the border of Thailand in the first place?" applicants were asked.

Confined by intimidating officers to a single answer, most applicants said: "I was starving."

Rejected. Not a refugee. Economic migrant. The term, decoded by the U.N. to mean a person moved exclusively by economic considerations, was first coined in the Nazi era when it was used to describe German Jews denied status as refugees.

The immigration officers, quartered at a luxury beachfront hotel and paid about $40,000 a year for "hazardous duty," proceeded to use against them the very criteria that had qualified many of the applicants to be called out. Thousands of those with family in America were said to be using their relatives as "anchors."

An official at UNHCR described the position in which these people had been placed. "Having applied for resettlement and been singled out to go to the United States," he said, "any return to their country would be extremely dangerous." A simple test had been given as a directive by some INS officials in Washington as the best way to decide: "Would I want to go back if what the applicant says is true?"

From our meeting with INS officer-in-charge Jack Fortner, we gleaned that new instructions from Washington to be more empathetic were being flagrantly disregarded.

"The Cambodians are nice people, but, really, they're not sophisticated," Fortner told us in the condescending tone his officers had adopted. He insisted that most of their stories demonstrated merely "subjective fear."

General Gerhardt Hyatt, formerly chief army chaplain in Vietnam, lashed out at Fortner: "Thirty years in the military and I've never seen power like this, not even in the President. It's close to God."

Jack Fortner giggled. "I don't place myself in that position," he said. "Everyone has a boss."

The American ambassador in Bangkok, John Gunther Dean, held a very different subjective attitude about refugees. "A man who walks across the border is a man who's made a choice—a man who can't go back," he told us when pressed. Dean acknowledged that the refugees' acceptance was determined by domestic politics. But Dean himself was a survivor, having fled Nazi Germany as a twelve-year-old refugee. Acutely aware of the fate of his predecessor, Morton Abramowitz, who stuck out his neck for the refugees' cause and had his career pinned back, Dean had proclaimed before taking up the post in Bangkok, "I'm not going out there as ambassador to refugees."

After three years of waiting, the Cambodians had been told by the American government they were not refugees after all. Trembling and exhausted, the only identity they had left hanging from them by a safety pin on a plastic I.D. card, they filed onto buses and pressed their faces against the windows, searching the dirt road for clues essential to their next act of survival.

Believing their hopes for resettlement were finished, many among the eight thousand rejects were considering going back to border camps controlled by resistance forces. The Vietnamese army had been pounding those forces ever since the coalition had been formed by the followers of Prince Sihanouk, former Prime Minister Son Sann, and the remains of the Khmer Rouge.

A week after I got home, the Vietnamese socked in Nong Chan

border camp with artillery and rockets and then burned it to the ground. Women, children, and noncombatants—fifty-three thousand of them—fled into the jungle.

At least I was able to bring home a marvelous gift for Mohm. General Chana, the former Thai ambassador to Cambodia, believed he knew her father and that he had been a major general in the Lon Nol army. I waited for the right moment to tell her. Clay and I were sitting with her at a Thai restaurant.

"I think I've found the name of your father," I said quietly. "Tia Ben Eng."

"Tia *Bun* Eng!" It burst out of her before she knew what she was saying. But having said it, she became still. "I forgot everything before I come to America," she said under her breath. "I don't want to think about it, just let it all go."

"Do you remember what your father looked like?" I encouraged her.

"I never look at his face. I keep my eyes down out of respect," she said. And then, dropping her head, she mumbled miserably, "It's so stupid."

"Tell us more about him," we probed.

She had adopted her father's nickname, was all she could say. In a miserable hush she admitted she didn't know even her own name. "Mohm" was nothing more than the commonly used sobriquet meaning "young girl."

She could see us staring at her, puzzled. We didn't know what to think, and she must have picked that up. She lowered her eyelids and was silent and miserable all the way home.

Why couldn't Mohm remember her father's face; why didn't she want to talk about him? Could her mother still be alive? Had she lied about being an unaccompanied minor in order to get out? Over all hung the unspeakable question: Had Mohm played any part in the spying and killing? Would she ever be able to forgive and forget, to give and accept love again? Or would she always be running?

The answers, if they ever came, would not come quickly.

Out of This World

Five months after Mohm's arrival, gas tanks blew up in New Jersey in the middle of the night, with an explosion that shook our apartment. I asked in the morning if she had heard it.

"No." She hung her head and pulled at her hair. The little outburst that followed was the first of many brief and enigmatic confessions over the next months. She told what it was like being on the run under the Vietnamese bombing.

"Ebreybody afraid, maybe wake up dead, so they not sleep. I hear bomb in the day when I run. But when dark come, I dig a hole and get in, cover myself with soil, then I go right to sleep." Hushed now, she confided a curiosity, perhaps a terrible flaw. "I don't hear bomb, don't hear people, don't hear them cry—I don't know why, Mom! Sleep till little bit sun, then quick quick I jump out, start to hear again. Start to run again."

"You weren't scared, Mohm?"

"I can't fig it out, Mom. Maybe something wrong with me."

"No, sweetheart, you're fine, you're good."

"You see, children like me, lose mommy and daddy, we don't hab anybody to take care, so okay run run." She hesitated. "Isn't it?"

I tried to reassure her that it was no crime to look out for yourself, especially if you were ten years old and all alone. But the stark image of what it was to be a survivor left me chilled. How would I have behaved? Perhaps a lot worse. The very fact that she could disengage from the disaster around her and take what she needed—sleep, in this case—was why she was here, or at least one of the reasons. But now? In Mohm's little riff was the sound of a child who had nothing left to lose. Survivors, they say, afterward become aggressive and almost defiantly incautious. They are sustained by the superstition that lightning doesn't strike twice.

During the refining period (which I hoped would begin soon for

Mohm) the rational tasks would be to learn to read and write her new language, but the harder tasks were to give up some of that survivor behavior and begin to mend the heart that had learned not to care. I realized that more room had to be left for her to relive the terrors of the past through writing about them and dreaming. And talking. Despite Mohm's proscription against wishing, I wished that summer would hurry.

*

Coming now were the first nightmares of Pol Pot time, leaving ugly little shards around the edges of her calm facade in the morning. Some were intense dreams she locked back up, unwilling or unable to describe. Some were fragments of events or remembered sensations. The line between what she had seen and what she had imagined was a hazy one. But there was another line, more perplexing to me and haunting to her, I sensed—the taut, frayed line between power and submission that may run through the center of all our psyches. She had not been solely a victim.

*

I go into my room and shut the door tight and get under the blanket and close my eyes and try not to think about anything, but it's impossible to go to sleep. In the back of my mind I think I'm terrified of being alone, in the dark.

When I do finally fall asleep, the night terrors take me away, far away. I don't think I can ever come back. But then I wake up and Mom's face is over me. Just to see somebody smile at you, it makes you think there's one human being in the world who understands you.

*

The nightmarish vignettes she did describe ran on in an endless loop of uninflected free verse, no sentences, no emotional coloring. It was far more difficult to understand than her everyday speech, which I had caught onto, with its abrupt attack on the beginnings of words and fadeout halfway through into vague endings—*Viet*namee for Vietnamese; *sol*yer for soldier. Naturally her speech became Americanized before she could speak English properly. She picked up the easy memo forms of communication—"Y'know" and "No way!"—and of course the curse words. Because they were not, for her, freighted with lifelong prohibitions, she tossed them out with casual merriment at the dinner table. One night we were talking about how to respond to heckling from boys.

"I think the best thing is to ignore them and walk away," I commented smugly. "How do you handle it, Mohm?"

"I tell them 'fuck you, sank you.' "

Clay choked on his salad. "WHAT?"

"That what *they* say."

"I know but, honey, you can't come down to—"

"Mohm, nice girls don't talk that way—" Clay began.

"*You* the one teach me all the bad thing," she retorted, laughing at the rise she'd gotten out of him.

"Me?"

" 'Phony' I learn from you; 'idiot' I learn from you."

"But didn't I also teach you 'innocent' and 'demure'?"

"Clay," and she leveled on him a look as droll as if she'd been bantering in English all her life, "you are *highly* illogical."

Clay roared with laughter. "Your mother sends you down to that nice religious school and you learn all the dirty words in English," he needled. "You better watch out; we'll get the vocabulary police after you."

From then on their conversation was a running banter, always funny, sometimes fierce, occasionally a porthole through which one glimpsed the much deeper furies that swam beneath her placid surface.

The only other time those furies appeared was when we wrestled. She loved to roughhouse, throwing me down on the bed and pinning my arms behind my head, whereupon the dogs would jump up, ostensibly to save the innocent, and invariably start biting the victim. If I could maneuver her onto her side and start tickling, she would dissolve in helpless giggles. But more often, she asserted herself until I was twisted into contortions from which there was no escape, only the plea for mercy. In this reversal of roles she took great pleasure. Through play, she could ape the vocabulary of violence, take the part of the torturer but turn out to be good. Apart from those private exhibitions of raw hostile exuberance, however, Mohm's movements were almost robotlike. She was always polite. She made every effort to copy my speech to the letter.

But she never hugged. She allowed herself to be hugged. When I gave her her allowance she did attempt a distant skeletal embrace, but with all the days and nights of closeness, she never displayed her feelings. Does she have feelings? I began to wonder in frustration. True, Buddhists are encouraged never to display extreme feelings, but if only there were some warmth in her embrace. There was only duty.

*

All I do is try to make sense of what happens. I never really know what Mom is thinking. That's the scary part. I never know if what I do is wrong. Is it reasonable? Is it selfish? Mom tells me sometimes but I don't really understand the words. Even when I know what the words mean, it's like when you don't know the language and children give you all the curse words. They could be the most disgusting things in the world but you say them and you don't feel it, because they have no meaning for you—at least, not yet, not until you learn the culture.

All I'm trying to do is fit in with the group. By the tone of a person's voice I know that something I did is wrong, but what is it? What *is* wrong, what is right in this place?

Everything that my body did during that time, my mind was someplace else. I don't remember the feelings—happy feelings or sad feelings or any feelings at all. I wasn't really there.

*

Words were obviously the treasure in my household, enshrined as they were in bookcases along almost every wall. As Mohm became increasingly attentive to her diary and adventurous in writing stories for school, she said, "Mom, you used to give me harder words; give me some more hard words." The words were gifts to her. They were steps to put one's feet on, they had texture and dimension, they particularized things, taking thoughts out of the realm of multiple lives and superstitions where spirits flew around and left one helpless; words made experience concrete.

One night I was late coming home to help Mohm write a composition. Necessity sponsored creation.

"I so happy, finish story!"

"I know just how you feel."

Her grammar was atrocious, of course, but her prose projected the apocalyptic world that remains in the mind of a refugee, no matter how safely resettled. Mohm was still thinking and dreaming in Pol Pot time, still running.

All the people went to jobs, to play, all the children happy went to school. Three day later a war coming. Peggy said to her friend Marie, "Do you remember we live in city, go to school, things were good? Oh God, please give me fun again." We did not want to cry anymore. Apartment all fire, people die everyday. Peggy look for her mother. "Mother, mother, I'm waiting for you. Are you okay?"

But the bombs coming, bomb bomb! Mother died. Marie said, "You can't cry. The war is not over. If you stay here, you got to die too."

Peggy and Marie lived with no clothes and no food. One night Peggy she did not sleep. Cry all night. "Mother, why did God let people died? Why?"

Yet there was an optimism in her that surfaced from time to time. When we picked out a cockateel to replace the bird she'd left in the camp, she turned the gentlest attentions on the creature. This was not a user-friendly bird, it turned out, but nothing daunted her patient efforts to turn that imperious, biting, squawking brat into a civilized pet. Even as she showed a limitless patience with animals, when it came to expectations of people her temper was not sanguine. It came as no surprise to Mohm, for instance, when, walking out of Madame Kamel's apartment in the Flatbush section of Brooklyn one Saturday, we found the window on the car smashed and the radio stolen. Cambodians in that section had been preyed upon so mercilessly by poor black teenagers, some virtually held hostage in their apartments, that thirteen families had had to relocate to Pennsylvania. The dog-eat-dog code of America's inner cities was something Mohm understood too well. And yet, and yet, she would screech on the brakes of her bicycle to avoid squashing a mindless beetle crossing the path.

*

How far I had to stretch to begin to understand this remarkable human being I wasn't aware until one weekend in April. We drove to the country with Madame Kamel's daughter Runcie as company for Mohm. There was lots of laughter when we stopped at the hot dog stand and Mohm asked if she could have a "hot cat" instead.

After dinner we made a fire in the living room and the girls sat on cushions. Through the penumbra of wine beginning to eclipse my brain I heard them talking about Cambodian New Year.

"What do you do on Cambodian New Year?" I asked them.

They described making special dishes and taking them to the monk. He would pray over the food for their good fortune. The girls were concerned that they might not be able to find all the ingredients here. I asked if bringing American food would count. Mohm frowned briefly. Then, across the broad, smooth plane of her face spread a devilish grin.

"Big Macs! We'll take Big Macs to the monk."

"Don't forget hot dogs," I put in.

"And hot cat!" Mohm added, savoring our private joke.

"What do you say in your prayers?" I asked the girls.

"You say about the next life," Runcie replied. "When you die, you want to be better than this life."

Mohm elaborated. "We say in Cambodia that life is never end. I mean, yes, when you die your body goes, but your mind and your spirit is always there. We can't really imagine that you're going to end."

I told them that Christians believe the same thing, but we don't have the notion of actual rebirth into a new person.

"Sometimes animal!" Mohm reminded me.

Runcie spoke up. "Rules say when you die, if you want to be better than this life you have to remember five rules. One is, don't drink wine."

"Whoops, guess that means I'll be reborn as a monkey," I blurted.

"Mom, you American!" Mohm exclaimed, dissolving in giggles with Runcie.

I put on a record of Cambodian music. It gurgled strangely in that hyper-American farmhouse of a room. Quickly, Mohm's mood changed. I was altogether unprepared for what she told me next. She spoke quietly.

"When I born out, I remember my past life."

"I do, too," Runcie said.

"What do you remember about your old life?" I ventured.

"I live in some kind of mountain, temple mountain, in the deep forest," she began. "It's a king there, and lady giants and dancing girls and the solyers, they stand up on their effalan—"

"I think you mean the soldiers rode standing up on their *elephants?*"

"Yes, effa-uh, I mean, they hold the *um*brellah over the king when he make a parade and—"

"Wait a minute, Mohm, it sounds like you're telling me about a past life from a very long time ago."

"Yes, in that time people don't wear clothes yet. It's a garden . . . beautiful flower ebrywhere . . . the pond have water lily and lotus flower all ober it . . . the girls dance at night . . . under moon . . ."

Her voice gradually trailed off like a mist, as if she were being transported back to that mysterious realm.

"Wall . . ." she continued almost imperceptibly, "all around the garden is a wall, can't go out."

I tried to sound unastonished. "Do you think you were part of the court, I mean, the king's family?"

"I sink so."

"What else do you see?"

"Sometime I see my old mother, from old life inside the mountain. I talk to my old mother. I don't remember what we say after, it's like a dream. But my real mother scared of me. She say it's a spirit, try to call me back. You see? After a while I can't feel that I'm alive. I can't tell if I have a body or mind or anything."

"Were you between the old life and the new life?"

"I sink so." Mohm hesitated, not sure I could take this all in. "That's *real* Cambodian religion."

"Let me ask you something hard, Mohm. Do you think the old life you remember could have been, say, hundreds of years ago?"

"Maybe. Old old time. Yes."

Then Runcie broke in. "My mother told about how she went to a palace to dance. When she walked in an old woman called her. 'Come here, lady, I'll give you something.' The old woman broke into two parts, all full of diamonds inside, and then was I born out."

"I always want to know about my old life," Mohm repeated hypnotically. "I talk to my grandma about it."

"What did she say?"

"My grandma tell me about my mother; she have a son but she can't get a daughter. So she pray in temple, pray pray, she call for me."

And then, amazingly, in English that faded in and out of Khmer but with Runcie's help in translation, I heard Mohm describe the sight of her real mother praying for her. Mohm was in one world—it sounded like a beautiful, joyful existence but also sterile and beyond desire—separate from the laughter and secrets of ordinary children. She could only gaze down from her sanctuary at the adventure of full humanity, until the call came from her "real" mother.

"Did you have any choice?" I asked.

"No!" Both the girls tittered at my ignorance. "My old mother decide to give me," Mohm said. "It's my turn."

"Probably they sent you to the Middle World," Runcie said. "Even kings and gods, they have to give their sons and daughters sometimes."

"When I learn how to talk, I didn't call her mother or mommy or anything like that," Mohm said. "That bother her. She tell me, 'You're my daughter, why don't you call me your mother?' I say something about my old mother. My family get so scared, they call the Kru Khmer. They just want me to forget."

"Grown-ups don't like you to remember," Runcie chimed in. "My mother gave me a hundred-year-old egg to eat."

Mohm described being given the sort of magic showers and benign exorcisms I had seen in the camps' traditional medicine centers. Once, her parents had left her with the Kru for several days, after which she seemed to be cured of this "memory sickness."

"It's so strange," Mohm added, "it's like you wake up, you're older now, you don't remember what you did the past two or three year."

I didn't know whether to laugh or gasp. Either these two girls had gifts of fabulation that would challenge any novelist, or Cambodian religion had a catechism that made the Jesus story sound like a second-rate soap opera. And yet, as bizarre as it sounded, I found it on some level credible. I seemed compelled to ask the most disturbing question.

"Mohm, can you ever go back to your old life?"

"No, cannot," she answered soberly.

"Nobody can?"

"To go back, you have to die. And if you die, you don't know what you'll turn out to be."

Ghosts

Mohm's school year ended with encomiums to her determination from all of her teachers. Everyone had noticed a slump when she seemed depressed, which had coincided with my absences for speeches and the trip to Thailand, but she had bounced back nicely. Her English teacher wrote, "Mohm is quite incredible for someone who has been here such a short time. She will continue to need and benefit from all the one-on-one support she can have." She was skipped from fifth to seventh grade—a tremendous boost to her self-confidence.

If our own inner-city kids could be given the benefit of that kind of schooling and that kind of one-on-one support, I kept thinking, how many of them would, could be saved from this society's debris pile?

Summer was officially launched when we made the first fishing trip. It was just warm enough to swim to shore with the towels on our heads and picnic on a spit of beachfront. Famished, my friend Hill and I attacked the potato chips and pickles and beer. Mohm went off with a Cambodian friend to explore. When they didn't come back, we meandered down the beach to look for them. Then I heard a shriek and raced to reach the voice. What I saw was bizarre.

A swarm of fiddler crabs, hundreds of them, each with a single claw held high, was crossing the sand. Scuttling on her hands and feet in their midst was Mohm, frenziedly reaching for them, shrieking every time she paralyzed another by pinching its fiddler claw. There was something desperate about her movements. I was afraid to interrupt.

Finally she saw me. Her eyes were wild. She ran toward me with her hands outstretched, as if to announce, *What a good girl am I,* but her fingertips were alive, wriggling with masses of the creatures.

I shrank back. She looked startled.

She ran toward Hill and offered up her grotesque Medusa-like hands to him. He smiled and found a container for her catch. He knelt beside her at the edge of the water and entered, it seemed, into her hallucination.

A pail full of the fiddlers had to accompany us home, and Mohm's running conversation about them was agitated. She demonstrated how she would hang one little fish on top of another and bring back a string of the shiny morsels. "Hundreds of them."

"Hundreds?"

"Really! I keep some for the family, send some to my grandmother with people go on oxcart. My brother and I, we have a lot of things to catch. Crab, fish, I catch anything, I do every day, I'm good at it!"

The rest of the long weekend it rained. Undaunted, we raised a badminton net and played anyway. Mohm was ecstatic. *"This* is tennis!"

Mohm was adamant about keeping the crabs alive in a tub in the kitchen. Every morning she awoke early and rode her bike to the ocean to fetch jars full of fresh seawater for them; she caught bugs for them as well. Also under her care fell the sickly apple trees, which, after several seasons of assiduous spraying, had produced the previous fall a single Thalidomide apple. Mohm watered them every day until she was drenched. She dug a vegetable garden and squatted on her heels in the fragrant June earth beside her portable cassette player, listening to Khmer music and happily planting as if she had never left the rice fields.

The best part of the country weekends, Mohm observed, was breakfast. One by one, guests would straggle out from deeply refreshed sleeps in the wisteria-laden air and gather around the kitchen butcher block where fresh strawberries and warmed bran muffins were set out. They would stir cream into their coffee and rub their unruly heads of hair and talk about doing laps or jogging but instead stand around telling stories about their childhoods and comparing most embarrassing moments, all very easy and affectionate.

Mohm said, "Every morning people come out, have coffee, stand around the table. It's like a party! I love it." She took an increasingly active part in entertaining, producing dishes that were an aesthetic delight. It seemed vital to her to discard the unnatural self-centeredness forced upon all the children by conditions of survival. She wanted fervently to show that she could be counted on to do her part in the family.

When we were alone, we talked more about the crabs, and again her speech became staccato, the pronunciation deteriorating as she went along.

"I don't know what is a month, when I young, but I think it's about two month after they take my mother and my father away. Then my brother get sick. One week time and my sister get sick, too. And so I have to work very hard, they want to try me, you see? When they take your mother and father away you go down, you're not import, you have to work very hard or they don't bother keep you, you see? And I have far away to walk to my job, I walk I walk, and I can't find anything, you see?"

"You were looking for something to eat, to bring back to your brother and sister?"

"Yes! I pick crab, shrimp, anything, I like crazy! Anything to cook for my sister"—suddenly her speech was speeding, sticking on words— "I find a lot food to eat and I walk walk I walking walking I don't know wha hoppen then it fall away from me, I have all that crab I know I have I have it, you understand?"

"You found a lot of crabs?"

"Yes! I sink a hundred, now I look again only one or two, see? They fall down one one all gone—"

"All gone?"

"All gone! And I say wha hoppen? I couldn't find again I get home I have only three."

"What happened to—"

"I don't know, you see, and after that, my sister have to die."

"I know, sweetheart, but what happened to all the crabs you caught?"

"That could hoppen to you, anybody, you see?" Her words spun now out of control. "I make two trip every day two trip give to my sister, you see? Two trip every day I have a lot lot crab to give her four four then ten ten but wha hoppen to that crab? And after that about, mmm, three week or four week, my brother and my sister, dead the same day."

"The same day! Oh, God . . ."

"You see? They go to hospital very sick and I say, 'Can I stay with my sister?' They say, 'No, you have to work or you don't have food,' you see? don't have food I die, you see?" She raced on. "And so my brother and my sister they sick they don't have any good food don't want to eat, I try give them soup they don't drink, and so, you know wha hoppen . . ." Her voice began to slow with exhaustion and defeat.

"Did you go to the hospital to see them?"

"I can't go!"

"Of course—"

"And I like crazy or something I love them so much, you know? I love them so much, I don't want to hear any about dead anything about that, you see? My big brother have to go. So when they put them in the soil I don't see. I don't see my sister and my brother face, dead."

"I thought you helped your grandfather to dig the soil for them?"

"No, a lot a lot of children dead the same day!"

"The same day?"

"Yes! And you see so many dead, nobody cry."

"People stopped crying."

"Stopped because so much, you have to cry so much, and if people see you they tell soldier Pol Pot. A lot of my family dead nothing I can do my father soldier dead and my brother and sister dead and the soldier Pol Pot get very angry at me, say 'What you cry! You don't have strong heart. You not good!' You see? People don't have anything to say or they take to kill. People have to lie their feelings."

"Of course, you were not allowed to have feelings."

"Not allow catch crab either. How come? When Pol Pot take over, Cambodia have a lot of food. Grow very easy; people don't have to work so hard. But Pol Pot don't give to the people, keep keep. Why? If so much fish live in the water how come Pol Pot keep them all in there, nobody allow catch to eat, why?"

We both had a rueful little laugh over this model of pure communism. "I think, Mohm, they used starvation instead of bullets. It killed people more cheaply."

"That right. Pol Pot family grow potato and vegetable for himself but if one potato fall off the cart, you can't pick it. You pick it, you have to die."

"I see."

"You see, Mom?"

I thought she meant for me to grasp some finer metaphysical point. But no, in the middle of this fraught exchange, Mohm abruptly lifted her arm and puffed up her tiny bicep.

"See, Mom! I play badminton, not so skin now!"

Once again I marveled at her ability to turn away instantaneously

from the bitter toward the blitheful. That is why children are natural
survivors.

*

Later that day we drove a couple of towns away to shop for Mohm's
first bathing suit. I ventured back into the territory she had opened up.

"Was it your grandfather who buried your little sister and brother,
sweetheart?"

"Yes. They say can't keep in the hospital, have to put in the soil right
away, can't see, so . . ." She trailed off into a nervous laugh.

"Oh, Mohm, so you never could say good-bye to them, even say a
prayer over them."

"I never say." A puzzled frown creased her forehead; then a shadow
seemed to fall over her eyes. "When I was young, I don't know how to
help people. When I big I know about that, I have a good head, I can
think about help people, but then I young, maybe I can't help my
brother and sister, I so small too, I can't clean my brother, I can't be
good like my mother but now I feel so sorry—"

"Sweetheart, don't feel bad that you could not help them, because
you were just a little child yourself. And you had to work so hard. No
children ever have to work that hard. All you could think was how to
get from one day to the next day."

"Yes. That's right." Her eyes cleared for a second; then the shadow
was on them again. "Now I think about that, maybe I can't stay. I not
good."

"You are a different person now. You are thinking with a thirteen-
year-old's head back to when you were six or seven years old. You acted
then like a six-year-old child; that's natural. You can't change that."

She laughed nervously.

"You understand?"

"Maybe."

"When you grow older, you can do much more. You are stronger,
you are smarter, and you know how to do so many more things, how to
cook, how to help someone who's sick, how to wait for what you need
until danger passes. When you're only six you can't know those things.
No matter how much you wanted to help, you couldn't do it. Nobody
could."

"Well . . ."

"Nobody."

"A lot of children have to do that. You didn't see, Mom, in the camp?"

"But in the camp they have time, and nobody takes away their food if they fail to work twelve hours a day. It's different."

"We have so much work in Pol Pot time"—and she was off at high speed enumerating the pitiless schedule of it—"it so hard to help when you have to work like that."

"Of course it is. I don't know how you even—you know what a miracle is?"

"No."

"A miracle is something that only God could understand."

"A God doing?"

"A God doing, yes, but the person has to be ready too. A miracle is something that nobody can explain. It's just something wonderful that happens. A miracle is—you didn't die."

Darkly, "Yes, but so many people did die. And they weren't bad people either."

We had run up against the cruelest mystery of all. Why do a thousand virtuous people perish for every one who is spared? Is there anyone up there keeping score? Mohm said she wondered sometimes if whoever was up there saw human life as a game for his own amusement. I had wondered myself. But if God was a manager, His team was losing. I preferred to think of God as the Universe and each of us as carrying a divine spark, capable of contributing to illumination or destruction.

"I think I go a little crazy in Pol Pot time," Mohm whispered. "But I alive now."

"Alive and giving light to other people every day. That's why you're a miracle, Mohm."

"Oh, we here!" She recognized the store we'd once visited. She shucked the sober mood. It was time to shop.

Soon Mohm would be off to summer camp. Before she went, I had to convince her that swimming and canoeing in a sarong might be awkward. We went through the racks of girls' bathing suits with their scanty Spandex diapers and spaghetti straps and peekaboo cutouts. She was scandalized. We found the only one-piece suit in the store and she took it.

"In camp you'll learn how to hold your nose and blow out the air through your mouth when you swim," I chirped on the way home.

"What camp is?" she wanted to know.

"It's a place where you can be with lots of other kids and learn sports and have a lot of fun."

"That's good," she said. "In Cambodia the girls don't want to play sport. It's the way the country is. But I like sport."

During the few days we had alone together, Mohm's thoughts returned to the subject of good and bad.

"First when I come," she said at dinner one evening, "you don't like me so much."

"Me? I liked you right away."

"No."

I laughed. "What do you mean, no?"

"I'm just kidding." She giggled. "But you don't know what I am, and you don't think that I'm good"—she broke off—"you don't know if I'm good or bad, right?"

"Well, that would be true for anybody."

"But a lot of people think, because we have a different language and everything that happen in Cambodia, we're not good. They like to do bad things to us. But if you do good to people, they're not bad at all." She went on to explain the behavior of many of the unaccompanied minors in the camps, how they had turned mean, cursed at girls, shirked studies, and given no evidence of caring much about anything. "But when they come here, they stop all that. They're not bad at all. So why do they change? Because all the American mommy do good to them, give them their own allowance, give them a heart, treat them like a good person. So now they see there's a good life to live! The bad things they did in the camp were because they had nothing else to do, they had no chance to be children, you know?"

"Yes, I know."

"So now they become gooder!"

"I see that every time we're at a get-together of the unaccompanied minors." Then in a teasing tone I asked, "So, Mohm, were you bad in the camp sometimes?"

"No. I mean, I'm not *puffick*, but I not lie and sneak. My mother really hated a sneak." She threaded her fingers nervously through her long hair. "But you don't know if I be a good child or no."

"And you didn't know if I'd be a witch or no, right?"

"Nobody know. But you have to be thinking about that, right?"

I stopped and seriously described what I had thought about her when I first met her in the camp, how I could see her strength, her intelligence, her resilience. "I thought you were strong enough to come to America and learn all the new things and start a new life. How about you? Did you think I would be fun to live with or hard or what?"

"You see, Mom, I can weigh people if I lib with them just one day."

Of course—she was a quick study. She had to be able to scour a person's surface for clues to the true character underneath and do it as fast as if her life depended on it, which, in many instances, it had. It was another of the secrets of survival. That was how she had selected those adults who were key to her own survival. In a jungle crawling with Khmer Rouge and under bombardment by the Vietnamese, she had to decide which group of adults to attach herself to. When it became evident, in the last Khmer Rouge outpost, that she was literally helping to dig her own grave, it was an act of consummate discretion to select and be selected by an escape party without exchanging a word. She had taken a chance on trusting the woman who wanted to make a run from Mong to the border. It had taken her only a night in the silken house of the woman in the New Camp who whispered endearments—"I want you to be my daughter"—to detect that her interest was in sexual commerce. It staggered me to realize how many times Mohm must have been right.

Before summer camp started she was supposed to attend a week-long Khmer Institute for unaccompanied minors, but I kept her in the country an extra couple of days so we could talk. It felt as though we were on the edge of some breakthrough. The closeness between us also seemed to be accelerating.

We biked to the beach with a picnic. Lying back beneath that magical white-brushed light of Eastern Long Island, I could see the dunes with their sprouts of beach grass, and I could see Mohm, staring at the sea as if in a trance.

"What are you thinking about, honey?"

"That day, I know right away something is wrong. I remember clear when my parents come back after that meeting, for a week before they gone, they don't say much. But what they do say, it's like leaving their last words."

She continued. "The other children keep asking me, 'Why won't you play? What happen at home? Did your mother hurt you?' That made me feel so unhappy. I say, 'No, nobody hurt me. But I have to cry.' They kept on. 'Oh, come on, Mohm, play.' So I play, and we laugh, laugh so much I have to sit down, ache. I laugh like crazy. But my heart's not happy, it's like it has a big bomb inside."

"You felt like something terrible was about to happen?"

"Yes. But why do I laugh?"

"You were probably laughing at anything, nothing, just to release your worry."

"Leader of our group give me an ugly look," she went on. "People say to me, 'When you are happy without reason, sometime it turn out to be sad.' "

I tried to reassure her. "But it was good to laugh, Mohm, it was healthy. Because if you'd shown your real feelings—your fear or your anger—the leader would have punished you, right?"

She permitted herself no such simplistic exoneration. "And then I bump into that dead fish. My friends say, 'Oh, oh, Mohm, bad luck.' I say to them somesing like 'Shut up,' but they tell me, 'You have to take it home.' Then I look at my feet, you know, my toes are moving around sort of like snakes, everything get dark and a black hole behind me, if I even try to move I'm going to fall in that hole. . . ."

She told about running to the hut to wait for her parents. The activities of the evening were numbingly normal, with the exception of the unmentioned absence of her mother, but through them all wormed a sense of dread; it was in the air, in the way her father bathed her sister and brother, in the bamboo walls, in the sleeping mat, in the muteness of everyone.

"I try to forget about that fish eye"—she was almost whispering now—"but I keep seeing the dark hole in back of me. I still feel it sometimes now, in back of me, if I not careful I'll drop into that black hole and fall out of this world. Do you know the feeling? Just a nervous feeling you can't tell anybody about . . ."

"Yes, it's called a 'premonition.' "

"That's a good word for it." She seemed to be turning something over in her mind. "Nobody can tell. Even the people our really good friend, nobody can tell why they take my mother away."

"Why couldn't they tell?"

"They're afraid they be punish. Cannot trust anybody in Pol Pot time. Nobody but your family." In a whisper she added, "Maybe not even them."

She was quiet for a while, lost, it seemed, in her dreams.

"My dreams are like a scrambled-up map," she said at last. "I think they take me to where I tried to forget."

I was stunned by the perception and took the chance of pushing it further. "Your dreams probably take you to the place where you stopped trying to remember why your parents died."

"Yes. If I could just figure them out!"

And then she revealed a dream she had had only the night before.

"I see all the minors I live with, we go back to Cambodia to a big place where we sleep under little blankets, everybody wait for all the parents coming back. They call out the minors one by one. They meet their mother, hug, they really happy, bring a present. Everybody find their mother. I look everywhere for my parents. I ask somebody. Nobody know. I start to cry. I can't stand it. Why didn't they come? I know they die. I cry the whole night, I can *feel* it, the crying, it's only in my dream but I can feel the tears—" A sob caught in her throat, stopped, struggled up as a broken laugh.

"Oh, sweetheart, you didn't tell me you had a bad dream." I tried to hug her. She drew away.

All at once she said, "Maybe my parents not die yet."

My face must have jumped.

"What do you know about it?"

"I dunno." She twirled the top of a soft drink can. "I can't say yet." She gulped air. "But maybe she not die yet."

"How will you know?"

Edgy now. "I don't know."

"I thought you said—"

"Just forgot about it. Forgot I say anything."

With studied calm I opened the picnic basket and went about spreading ham sandwiches with mustard. She didn't want to eat. Neither did I. As gently as my alarm would allow, I prodded again. "You should tell what you do know."

"I don't want to tell. Because I can't get a point yet."

"I thought you said your mother was taken away with her hands behind her back."

"I know, sometime they take people that way and put them in a hard place without food, hit them all the time, but if they lucky, still not die." The surf pounded behind her words. She mumbled something else.

"What did you say, Mohm?"

Softly, like the sound of music, she said, "Still I wait for her now."

"Do you think she would know where to find you?"

"Mom, I can't tell you, because I don't know if it's true or no."

"Well, if you tell me what you know, maybe I can help you look for your mother."

"How will you know?"

"I'm hoping to go into Cambodia this year."

"But I don't know where they are. They probably not inside Cambodia anymore. If I'm lucky, maybe they came out."

"Do you think your parents came out of Cambodia alive?"

"I tell you, I can't get a point yet. Everything else I'm sure. But that, I just know a little bit, but is it true or no?"

"Is this a feeling, Mohm, or some information you have?"

"Feeling! Forget about feelings!" Her laugh was a dry rattle. "Nobody's feelings are true."

"Then you should tell me—"

"Mom, I told you, I can't get a point yet, okay?"

Was it my imagination, or was there an edge of cunning in her words?

"I don't know what you mean," I said.

"So, forgot it."

"I don't want to forget it. It's important."

"I know, it's important to *me*," she said possessively.

Suddenly I saw myself as she must see me: with my pale spotted skin and red hair, with my American impatience for facts, pleasantly innocent perhaps, but so quick to believe that facts can solve everything. I saw Mohm's smile, too, in a new light. It was a protective mask, but it was also a weapon to defend against an intruder to her inner world.

I wrestled with my urge to coax more information from her. I knew what I was doing: I was trying to seize control of that vulnerable territory where she had invaded me.

The surf rocked and surged.

"You see, Mom, sometime you can't get a point," she repeated. "It's hard to say about one person's life. Because sometime a person is not dead and not alive. That's what the Kru Khmer say. You understand what I mean?"

"She's in between lives?"

"Yes. So you can't get a point."

"I think I understand now," I said.

The delicately interwoven defenses employed by the mind to deal with inconsolable sadness should make any outsider hesitate before attempting to unwind a single thread. Mohm was not ready to separate the threads of fact from fantasy, and despite the discomfort of uncertainty for me, I knew I should not push her.

We sat for a while, staring into the blur of white light that always hung at the far end of the beach.

"Do you think your father might be alive, too?"

"I'm not sure about that, may not, may not." Her words had the cold ring of a tolling bell. "But my mother . . ." and then her voice trailed off into a region beyond my comprehension.

*

On the way home I pointed out a pond of water lilies. She squealed with pleasure and we got off our bikes. Each white flower stood up like a starched napkin in the center of its green saucer, the saucer leaves spreading rim to rim all over the pond. How like a lagoon in ancient Angkor it looked, the lilies so much like lotus blossoms. We picked out the prettiest bloom along the edge. "Snakes in here, right, Mom?" she said. She shut her eyes and plunged a hand into that snake-slimed pond anyway to tug at the flower. Its tough, twiny stem was anchored far below in the dark water; they all were, and the blooms were unyielding.

*

All at once I imagined how her journey to America might have appeared to Mohm. From a timeless, passive, paradisial existence in the temple of a king, she had been called—the first time—by a woman praying fervently for a daughter. She had answered the call. Perhaps, as she saw it, she had been released by the God-king, a divine body disguised as a newborn child, chosen to illuminate in her new parents the spiritual glory of her first Father. She was "born out" into a new life as the daughter of a beautiful half-Chinese woman married to a Cambodian military officer. But after five years on the new plane of existence —a pleasant world of markets and motorcycles and movie theaters and country houses and grandparents—that world had changed utterly. It had become a stinking, hellish place where time wound down to a slow, relentless now; a place called Middle Earth. And there, the true nature of people was revealed.

But she had escaped the Middle Earth of Pol Pot time. Wandering barefoot through mountains and ravines, when her will to go on began ebbing, an old woman had appeared to her—perhaps, as she would see it, the guardian of her destiny and good luck—and the old woman had pointed the way to something called "future." Thus had Mohm crossed a bridgeless river only to become confined in another sort of in-between world—the refugee camp—where she let the past slip away and waited for the next call.

I thought that I had chosen her, but perhaps she had enchanted me. She may have thought I was another species from an altogether different plane of existence, that by attaching herself to me she could slip out of her world and leave all its danger and misery behind. When I put out the call to her, she was ready. Hadn't she answered the call of a new mother before?

I imagined the thinking that might have preceded her decision: She would place herself in the wheel of chance again, disport herself as she had done before through limitless space and time to a world utterly unknown. If her luck held, she would be "born out" in more benevolent circumstances. But there had been no foretelling what form she would take, nor what demands would be made on this new plane of existence. It could be just another stinking, hellish testing place.

And this time she was alone. Plucked from the gardens of her own kind, she was an exotic bloom borne to a different planet—a place called Earth. Mohm was indeed a lotus, but a lotus without a stem.

But did she know that I, too, was afraid of losing love?

For all the natural sweetness I sensed at her core, and the unfailing politeness that glazed over her ugly moods, still, I wondered sometimes if she weren't driven solely by the cold engines of survival: *You want a daughter, fine, I'll play the role of your daughter—until I have what I need. But when I take a mind to leave . . .*

Why should that disturb me so? What was the nature of this quickening love for a stranger? For now, I knew, I loved her indissolubly.

Women are always yearning for perfect unity with the ones they love. We want to be indispensable to them and to be loved back unconditionally. And isn't this what does happen at first in any romance? Think of the small sweet shocks of discovery and the secrets of self-revelation they unlock, the obsession with each sensory detail that is set buzzing by the mix of two chemistries. The new lovers create a world between them, a world that never existed before, an island protected from intrusion by mistakes of the past or pressures of the future, a suspended state made all the more exquisite by its evanescence.

But the unconditionality of first love between a man and a woman inevitably gives way to the pulls of the world. It becomes encumbered with claims, roles, institutional functions. And so, perhaps, some women seek to reinvent the closed charmed circle with each new child, hoping for something similar to the innocent joy of early love with a man.

If I were very lucky, the affection and trust would grow between Mohm and me, and that would slowly bind us together in a deeper, less idealized way. But if that was not to be, if her natural mother did turn out to be alive, then all the more reason that we should savor each day we could love each other.

The next morning when I awoke, I heard a sweet, faint quivering of violin strings. . . . What was it? I went downstairs. There was Mohm, her palm halfway into the bird cage, and Benjie the cockateel eating out of her hand.

"I finally get him to trust me!" she announced.

"How?"

She pointed to her cassette player. "I find his drug. Mozart."

First Separation

Mohm spent the week before camp started at the Khmer Institute in New Hampshire. For over a hundred Cambodian teenagers now scattered throughout the New England area it was a grateful saturation in their own cultural traditions and a chance to practice familiar mating rites. Mohm had her problems fending off the attentions of one smitten son of Peter Pond's. Although she praised him to me over the phone—"He have a job and he have two banks, one to keep the money and one to take out"—she was not about to be spoken for at this stage; she insistently called him "my brother."

At the farewell luncheon for the children and their foster parents, we sat with the dean of Hampshire College and her Cambodian daughter, Sophal. Eight months before, when we all had had lunch together, the girl's cheeks had been pitted with angry dark berries and she flinched with a nervous tic. All that was gone now. "What did you do?" I asked. "Nothing on the outside," said her devoted mother, smiling. "It's amazing what inner calm can do." It was the same story with Nhep Sarouen, the lively boy who had been my translator in the Thai camps. Having met him in the States several times before, I was happy to see that this time his greeting was less desperate, more relaxed. The American father of two Cambodian boys told me, "It's been like a dream—we've had joy from them since the first day." "No major problems?" I asked. "No minor problems."

But we were all a little hasty. In our eagerness to believe that the benevolence of a free society and loving substitute parents could drive away the traumas of the past, we were not aware that the mourning process had scarcely begun for these lost children. Although we didn't know it then, grieving for their lost families and then for their lost country would dominate their thoughts for at least another year and a half.

*

I couldn't wait to see Mohm's reaction to Aloha summer camp. It had sounded from the brochure like a wholesome, roughing-it experience set in the unspoiled mountains of Vermont. We pulled in at dusk, in time to look at the shivering blue-black lake and to drink in the pure mountain air. I was excited. Mohm's counselor met us and showed us the small, wood-floored tent she would share with two other girls. They would be awakened by reveille at 6:30 A.M., expected to wear uniforms and green ties, or "C.C.C." (Correct Camp Costume), given grades on tent inspections and not permitted to receive gum or candy from parents. They would go canoeing and play tennis and have riding lessons, and on special occasions take three-night hikes high into the mountains.

Mohm made no response during this presentation.

"What fun, Mohm!" I led the cheer. "Now you can do all the things you did in the past, only enjoy them. Right?"

She looked at me oddly.

One of her cabin mates was introduced as Courtney. As we walked down the hill to meet the other groups, every one seemed to have a Courtney, if not a Holly-Krissy-Katie. This camp must be the last bastion of WASP America, I thought with a silent chuckle; well, it would be useful to Mohm to be exposed to America's core culture.

We went to the kitchen to find some leftover supper. I told the camp director I felt it was important, since this was our first separation, that I stick around for a couple of days. I had a motel room across the lake. The director was not enthusiastic but relaxed the rules in our case. So Mohm saw me off and on, showed me her classes, introduced me to her "big sister," and seemed, as we sat together in a rocking chair on the broad dining-room porch the day I was meaning to leave, happy enough to try this odd ritual called "camp." In fact, she was laughing about her first canoe trip.

"Okay, sweetheart, it's time for me to drive home now."

Her head whipped around as if I had struck her.

"The camp really doesn't like parents around," I tried to explain. "We've been lucky to have—"

"I go with you?"

"Well, no, you see—"

"I don't want to stay here my own self. Can't I come home?"

"But there would be nothing for you to do."

"Summer school."

"It's too late."

She grew more agitated. We had to leave the porch so the other campers wouldn't see her face twisted up against tears. Her mood shifted suddenly from panicky to defiant.

"I don't want it!" she almost shouted.

I tried to reason with her. "You can't really know what it's like until you give it one full week. Will you promise me you'll do that?"

"Maybe I have to run away," she muttered.

"That would be foolish, Mohm. C'mon now, we can stand anything for a week, right? I'll call you up every day. And if you are really unhappy at the end of the week, I'll come back and get you."

She didn't yield an inch. A scowl erupted on her face, from what bitter depths I could not discern. I thought I heard her mumble, "I'm going to do something . . . awful."

What could I do? Except for short absences, we had been virtually joined at the hip for the past nine months. It was time to make a break, and wasn't this the most benign sort of break? But with all the rationalizations marshaling themselves neatly in my mind, I felt fainthearted, not knowing with this child where the line lay between natural growing pains and desperation. I stood there, she stood there, in a frozen equipoise of empathy and alienation.

*

When Mom showed me where I'm supposed to stay, I thought, "Oh, my God, sleeping in a tent! This is Pol Pot time all over again!" When they tell how we're going to sleep on the ground and make a fire without matches to cook our food, I want to say "Why do I have to do this! I went through all this already."

This wasn't my idea of "camp" at all. Mom told me there would be lots of children—I thought they'd be Cambodian, not all these strange blondies called Courtney. They don't know anything about me. Now Mom's going to leave me here alone! I didn't know that camp is a place where you stay without your parents.

I'll say anything, I'm desperate, if only the next word she says is "All right, you can come home now."

She doesn't say it.

I feel like everything is draining out of me. Why do I have to go through all this again? It's killing me. A thought comes into my mind for the first time: What is life? What is so precious about it? Is it worth it to go on living?

*

We made an uncertain truce. I squeezed her hand and said my last good-bye. Or so she thought; in fact, I stayed another night in the motel so I could check with the director in the morning to see if Mohm had settled down. I ducked in to leave a long, loving letter in her mailbox before turning the car, with trepidation, back toward New York.

Seeding a
New
Garden

"**I**'m not ready, Mother."

It was Maura's voice, gone suddenly to stone. How it was supposed to be was that Maura would come out to spend a few days with me in the country after Mohm left for camp. It would be a makeup period for all the time that had been soaked up by the new child. Then the phone had rung—let's see, I dashed in from the garden, and—what?—to this day I don't know what went wrong, but it was probably my short temper. Some slip had been made, I must have overreacted, and as suddenly as a foot accidentally puncturing the thin ice of December, I had plunged into the depths of my first daughter's despair.

"And I don't know when I *will* be ready to see you again," Maura was saying over the phone from New York. "Or if."

"What's that supposed to mean?"

"Mom, let's don't talk about it."

I tried to open the dangerous subject we had both successfully avoided. "I know this has been a tough year for you, with Mohm coming and everything—"

"You don't have any idea how tough." Where was my sensitive Maura in that calloused voice?

"I thought—I hoped, oh God, Maura, we're just beginning to make a family. . . ."

Her reply was barely audible. "All I've ever wanted is to be part of a family. But I always feel like the odd man out."

"How can you?"

"You only see your side. The distraught divorced mother, 'losing' your only child. So you go out and find a—" she was beginning to choke up "—perfect child to take my place."

It was the moment of reckoning. "No one could take your place in my heart, Maura, you must know—"

Not hearing, "I didn't think I was abandoning *you* by going to college. *I* felt scared. I didn't really want to give up home."

"I should have made it easier—"

"You made me feel like a terrible person because I was going to leave you. As if I didn't love you enough. Oh, God, Mother, if you knew how much I did—" She broke off, cooled, retreated. "So now everybody thinks you're a hero, you've saved her life, you're all happy, where does that leave me?"

"Sweet darling Maura, you're *part* of it—"

"You might as well have written me a letter: 'Dear Maura, you were a great daughter but now you're gone, so I went out and got someone to take your place.' "

"Stop! No! You're wrong—I love you more than anyone in the world and I only wanted—"

"Don't!" It was too raw between us now to continue. "Just have a nice summer, Momzo, without me."

She hung up.

After consulting with a friend who recently had been over the adolescent rapids with his own daughter, I called Maura back and with every ounce of self-control I could summon, for once I did not try to control her. I told her I understood she needed to be separate for a while, that I was there if and when she wanted to come out, but I wouldn't expect her.

She sounded surprised. "Fine, Mom. I'll call you when I'm ready."

*

I was planting a Shakespeare garden that June. Starting it with rosemary and rue and "cuckoo-buds of yellow hue," and pansies for thought and hot lavender, mints, savory, marjoram and wild thyme and eglantine: It was my first serious garden. I lost myself in the kneegrubbing work of it while my mind was off on flights of whimsy, searching the verses from Shakespeare that might fit on plaques by the appropriate flowers. The England of Shakespeare's day was not so different from Mohm's Cambodia, full of spells and ghosts, witches and mischievous spirits and omens of disaster. As I nudged the dirt around the silver-green rue, thinking of the woeful lines spoken by the gardener in *Richard II* as he pitied the queen her sorrow—"I'll set a bank of rue, sour herb of grace"—I rued every blow I had ever struck to Maura's self-esteem.

How fragile it had been all through her adolescence. So finely tuned was her falsity detector, she believed that to be true to oneself, one had to follow out any emotion to its full, exhausting resolution. Why am I angry? How do I truly feel? I could still see her taking a seat on the train to travel between her father's house and her mother's apartment, sinking into the ether of dislocation, accepting as her subjective home this impersonal in-between. Rather than read to take her mind off it, she would stare out the window, passively itemizing the unfamiliar people and strange cars, letting the inconsequential conversation of passengers in the surrounding seats stick to her brain cells: collecting the artifacts of anomie. If there was one dead tree in the flora and fauna that swept past the train window, she would fix on it . . . isn't that sad? a beautiful old tree, dead, isn't that just typical? . . . allowing her own mood to ooze out and color everything, and then concluding that was indeed the true, unvarnished, shabby condition of the world.

As for my own resurgent adolescence, it was passing. I was coming into a new country now, out of the valley of depression where I had spent much of the previous spring. After ten months with Mohm, the magnitude of her demons and her determination to overcome them so dwarfed the regrets and insecurities I had allowed to hobble my passage into mid-life, I could only laugh at myself. Being close to a survivor is the best tonic for the blues.

I was learning the power of suppression. If it's not bugging you so badly that you are nonfunctional, forget it. Sooner or later the messy emotions underneath will sort themselves out. In the meantime, find a reason to laugh so you can get on with the day.

Despite the latest rupture with Maura, I felt optimistic. The fact was, Maura had felt displaced from the moment Mohm came. Her arrival had coincided with Maura's yielding of her own childhood and the inevitably painful tearing of ties. Everyone gives the entering college freshman a big buildup—"These will be the best years of your life," "I remember when I was in college"—but what no adult remembers is the coma one enters along about the first Thanksgiving when there are four days to pack, reconnect with family, see your old friends, write three papers, study for exams, disconnect from family, travel back, unpack, and realize what a singularly miserable failure you are because this is *not* the best year of your life by a long shot.

For nine months Maura had put her needs second, refusing to admit any envy for all the attention Mohm was receiving. Why? One answer was, that was Maura, a person constitutionally incapable of holding back when someone else needed help. But in another light, giving to Mohm was also a way of healing some wounds in herself. A fully realized relationship with her half brothers had been always just out of reach. And her yearning for love as a child of divorce had been consuming, insatiable. When she gave to Mohm, she was lavishing on a surrogate the intensity of love she had wished for herself.

She bore Mohm no grudge at all. She sincerely adored having a sister. But she felt as if she had lost a mother.

Trying to look at Maura's situation dispassionately, I knew that a young person in a hard passage to independence must make the separation with physical distance. Some youngsters don't need that to achieve the autonomy everyone seeks at that stage; and some, bless them, can even maintain an unbroken positive relationship with their parents. But for Maura and me, it was like trying to pull bittersweet vine off an apple tree. Their bond is stronger than the strongest clipper, outlasts the meanest acids; always some tenacious roots remain underground, requiring cutting back season after season. More than the usual emotional distancing would be necessary for Maura to get beyond the obstacle of her mother. It would be important to her to stay alone in the New York apartment, to support herself, for the summer anyway, then to find a place of her own up at school.

It would be important for me, too, to stay alone, without circling over the same ground with Clay or Maura, and without the buoyancy of Mohm. It was time to take stock: What were the most important things when one came to the middle of the journey of one's life?

*

At the end of her first week at camp, after a series of brief, pleasant, but unrevealing calls to Mohm, I telephoned her for the final decision. The faint, soft voice came on. "I'm think about you a lot," she began, "every time I'm eat or sleep. I been thinking you really nice mother in the whole world that I never see before, you like my real mother, and I'm sorry about everything that I say."

Tears came to my eyes. "Thank you, sweetheart. But how's the camp?"

"Mmmm, I *think* I'm having a good time here. Maybe I'm going to learn tennis." Then her voice raced off, "Sorry, Mom, got to go. I'm table girl tonight, bye!"

*

Back to planting where "daisies pied and violets blue" now painted my weedy old bank with delight, wondering if the garden weren't some fey little scheme allowing me to indulge my Celtic penchant for fancies. But the more I concentrated on the Shakespeare garden, the more effortlessly clarity seemed to come to the matter-of-fact problems. For one, it was time to put aside playwrighting. I had taken a year out to try it and consumed the year completely, at least in the Zen sense, having concentrated on that effort and burned down like a good bonfire. There should be no remains, but that did not mean I would forget all about it. The time spent studying the play form would always be part of my writing, and now I was ready to go on to something else. For another thing, I needed to make some money. But I'd be damned if I'd do the next book for any reason other than that it was the only thing I could think about. In the meantime, I'd take free-lance magazine assignments. And for the next year—resolved, I would practice concentrating on my everyday routine: What could I do to make it more natural, more elastic, so that time would be made without pressure for the people I loved? I would reseed my garden.

I understood now why the wildflower garden had not come up the previous year: because I had gone at it slapdash. All my life I'd tried to do too much, with the result that I was habitually late, made unnecessary mistakes, and put unfair pressure on those around me—or blamed them when I couldn't finish. It was time to change. I had seen enough of Mohm's survivor concentration to know at least where to begin. This time, I would make it a garden of perennials.

If the seeding was done slowly, attentively, perhaps by the following summer I could begin cultivating the garden of my middle life.

First Reconciliation

In August I gave up my house to renters. With a portable word processor in my shoulder bag and several intriguing assignments, I decided to stay with various friends along the seaboard and see what happened. Luckily, the one night I spent in New York was the night Clay chose to stop by with wonderful news. He wanted to transform a bankrupt city tabloid into an Upper East Side version of *The Village Voice*, and he had a financial backer. He fairly wriggled with pride and pleasure as he told me about it. And I, well, that night I fell in love with the same man all over again. How many times had it been now? ten? fifteen? once a year for as long as we had known each other?

We sat, that hot August night, with our legs propped on the terrace railing as we talked, but I wasn't in Manhattan at all. . . .

*

I am with Clay in a hotel with high ceilings and tall glass doors opening onto a stone terrace over the Tyrrhenian Sea. The view is sharply down over the red-tiled roofs and crumbling towers of medieval stone churches. Violins of a traveling opera company are climbing octaves across the street. We are on the terrace, mesmerized by the incandescence of shimmering light on a sea with blue sky pouring into it. Later in the afternoon, purplish tones will come into the blue and the sun will set off random fires in the low pines. By morning, the fire will have burned off and streaks of smoke will wrap the coastline in a pale violet vapor. We will go out for a walk.

In the village square we join a celebrated American writer who has a house nearby. Gore Vidal and Clay are of the same vintage, mutually respectful and knowing; New York has been a fickle mistress to both of them. Vidal had left it at the top of his game. I had always wondered why. He was the hot playwright on Broadway for the five-year interregnum between the waning of Tennessee Williams and the advent of Edward Albee, coining money on his prolific screenwriting career, involved with the Kennedy clan, and didn't he even run for Congress?

"In 1960, I doubled the Democratic vote," he says, leaning back in his café chair and recalling it all with a contented smile, "and in my district I ran twenty thousand votes ahead of John Kennedy. But I was boxed in by becoming a personage. I split in '62 because I had to get away from politics and the New York game"—he paused, smirked, and pulled out one of his favorite quips—"which is celebrity as practiced between consenting adults on the island of Manhattan. I wanted to go back to the novel."

Vidal can now well afford to lavish indifference on those who play the game in New York. He has found himself in living between Italy and Los Angeles, producing an uninterrupted flow of estimable novels, beginning with *Julian* in 1964, that also weigh in on top of best-seller lists. Unsapped by the celebrity bloodletting so popular in the lit-crit circles of Manhattan—except when he chooses to sneak into town for a guerrilla attack—he makes a case for getting out of that fishbowl. It is tempting. But a best-selling author and screenwriter over the course of forty years should be well provided for, as opposed to an editor-publisher with no independent means who must, alas, depend on the kindness of others.

Vidal walks us along a mountain footpath to the gates of his villa, flung out over terraces of vine and vetch and an incomparable drop to the sea. We dine on fresh gnocchi and cold zucchini soup and a fine lemon soufflé.

"I wouldn't know how to start the work of the day without a walk through an allée of cypress," the writer jokes as he gives us a tour of his gardens after dinner, luxuriating in the irony of being a leftist who lives like a noble. Yet being inescapably American, the writer confesses that he is unable fully to enjoy suspension in the stage of having made it.

He is hardly a bitter failure, we observe.

"No, I'm a bitter success—a rare category," and he laughs.

Vidal proceeds to outline the campaign he is planning to run for United States senator in California. "The voters one has to get are the faggots, Jews, and Chicanos," he says, enjoying the perversity of his own conversation. Deeply tanned, still handsome, he adds, "The only thing that scares me to death, is suppose I *get* it. Imagine having to leave all this for *Wash*ington."

Clay is also contemplating a new course for his future. He is between publications. And like the writer, he has had years of living by his wits and riding strange new horses, sometimes being bucked off. New York can fulfill a person or destroy him, depending a good deal on luck. As E. B. White used to say: No one should come to New York to live unless he is willing to be lucky. It is hard to tell the difference between the sincere self-promoters and the charismatic liars, Manhattan being a place where small men like to sit around and discuss big ideas.

Before we leave, Gore has brotherly advice for Clay. "We're both patriots, and we can't bear to see assholes mess around with the Republic." But anyone who plays the New York game, he warns, anyone who has to depend on rich people, must know how to load the dice, because *they* own the bank.

Understand that Rupert Murdoch is not your friend, I used to tell Clay. He will court you, promise you, pick your brainpan clean, but he is a cannibal—the kind of guest you invite to dinner and he eats the host. As it happened, we were out of town when the Australian publisher launched his hostile takeover. Clay lost his brainchildren, *New York* magazine and *New West,* and a purchased stepchild, *The Village Voice.* After joining in a spirited battle by the staff, more than fifty of whom walked out on the new owner, Clay was left peculiarly bland, for months exhibiting none of the pain. It was like watching a recent stroke victim smiling vacantly as he stands in the movie matinee line. He had bounced back and started again, of course, but he had never stopped looking for a new horse to ride, not for seven years.

Now he had found it. I felt optimistic. Clay was at his best in action; performing under high pressure he felt most alive. He was, in his fashion, another survivor.

*

"I wonder if we'll always find each other exciting," I mused.

"I know we will," he said.

"Then we're going to have to stop making up like this. One day we'll drop from exhaustion."

There was only one thing to do. Since we couldn't live without each other, we would have to teach ourselves how to live with each other.

The Hard Part

When I arrived at Aloha Camp, the word passed swiftly up the mountain to where Mohm was on a cookout with her group. Moments later, hair swinging and socks bunching, she came running down the sun-dappled path. She threw herself at me.

"Oh, Mom, I teach everybody how to make fire!"

Judging by the crowd of girls who gathered around Mohm to exchange addresses, insisting she promise to return the next summer, she had charmed them.

On the drive home, I suggested she might earn some money by babysitting for friends who had adopted a baby. Mohm had already met and fallen in love with the child. But her face screwed up into a fierce scowl whenever I mentioned "babysitting." Why?

"Because I not a slave!" she blurted at last. "I really hate"—and she was off reliving one more pocket of pain about which I knew nothing—"I mean, they wanted me to be like a slave, and I really hated it."

"Who wanted you to be a slave, sweetheart?"

"I don't want to tell you before," she said, suddenly contrite. "It's really long, my story. . . ."

"You can tell me more now, if you like."

"I mean, what I say before is right, not wrong, but some of it I just don't say, okay?"

"Okay."

"They test you again and again, and maybe you can't come to America. That's why. I told myself I got to be thinking all the time. I just don't want to put in the hard part."

"I understand. They probably tried to poke holes in your story in the interviews."

"Yes! They keep asking me, 'How do you know so much about the Khmer Rouge?' I said, 'I just hear,' but they can't believe me."

"Do you want to tell me about the hard part?"

She said yes, and began, speaking quickly in her now characteristically mongrelized verb tenses. "A woman in Kompote speak up for me. It's when I was so weak, I think I can't work anymore. She wanted to keep me in the town; I stay home and carry the water and take care for her child."

I asked if the woman was part of the Khmer Rouge.

"She's a Pol Pot woman but from a higher family than most of them. She say she knew my parents from before. Her husband is sort of head man for that town. I always say hello to her baby whenever I came back from work, so one day she said, 'I want you to live with me.'"

"You couldn't say no?" I probed.

"Why can I? Have to live."

I asked naïvely if living with a Khmer Rouge family was less difficult than being with children on the mobile team.

"You have food to survive. And it's more protection than you living alone." Her tone of voice became sharp and defensive. "Maybe you don't want to look at survivors like this, you would kill to survive."

"Of course I do, Mohm. Go on." She hesitated. I asked her if it had been harder to work inside than out on the irrigation terraces.

"Mom, you feel worse, because it's like being a family slave." Her voice changed again, the shading now was guiltily tender. "They sort of like me . . . they don't tell the truth to the Pol Pot that I'm complaining, they only say good things about me."

Retreating into the cool of the journalist, I asked, "Did you feel, you know, warm toward the woman?"

She stammered. "I don't—I mean—she has black teeth all rotty from chewing the betel leaf, but she has a sweet voice though . . . she always wake up singing."

"And she protected you."

She paused. "I think the wife was really nice."

"Did the husband actually kill people?"

"No, well, it's a Pol Pot family, okay? They can save by saying 'I know that person, she's a good worker, loyal to *Angka.*' But if they hate somebody, they can lie about them. They don't kill by the gun, but their words can kill." She stared out the car window for a while. "I think if I act like her daughter, I won't die."

She wasn't ready to examine her feelings about becoming part of an enemy family. Much later she struggled with the subject: "Am I supposed to be happy, because she picks me as her favorite?" She described her shock at seeing how well the supposedly spartan Khmer Rouge leaders lived. They moved into the best houses of the enslaved New People. "It's just like I read in *Animal Farm*," and she quoted, " 'Everybody is equal but some are more equal than others.' The Khmer Rouge always lecture everybody else how to be equal, how to make property sacrifice for *Angka*, bla bla, but they the ones have all the special privileges." She remembered in detail her first meal with the Khmer Rouge family: It was the first real meal she had tasted in three years.

The sweet, thick smell of roasting animal flesh caught her like a hook in the stomach as she returned from the communal dining hall; she ran to the back of the house; yes, it was true, the rogue crackle of meat cooking on sticks over an open fire! The family had gone to the communal dining hall along with everyone else, but they had a cook living with them. She had nests of rice and vegetables and a basket of fresh fruit waiting for them later. Mohm felt faint. The cook let her taste the meat, but as the first spurt of juice slipped down her throat, a sour swill came up in her mouth and she had to turn away.

After some weeks, she was allowed to eat a second meal with the cook. She marveled at being allowed to pick fruit from the mango and coconut and papaya trees around the house; it was like a secret heaven in the backyard of hell. And there was the day she stole the woman's hairbrush.

But the woman didn't report her. Instead, she took the brush and pulled it gently through Mohm's scabby hair, stroking, stroking. After that, the woman always woke her up with a playful remark. Mohm knew she was being treated as a daughter.

"It's very confusing to feel affection coming from someone who's on the wrong side," I suggested, hoping to open up her feelings on the subject.

"Uh-huh."

"Did you ever feel a little ashamed, I mean about wanting her to act like your mother?"

"I guess so," Mohm said quietly. "That's pretty desperate." She sat lost in her thoughts for a few moments. "But I find out a Pol Pot family can love, too," she told me with equanimity. "Parents love, children love. It gave me hope that one day Cambodia can change again."

Mohm's instinct not to tell "the hard part" of her story had been a good one. By now I could understand how a child living through that long nightmare would respond indiscriminately to the first offer of affection. But if she had told me nine months before, when I was her newest surrogate mother, told me she had warm feelings for any member of what I saw then as a uniformly barbaric Khmer Rouge, she was correct, I would have been shaken.

Again, the moment the conversation threatened to undermine her defenses, Mohm found something to delight in. We had a trip planned with Maura to a dude ranch in Montana.

"I can't wait, this year, do everything a second time," she said, rolling her eyes in delicious anticipation. "This time I know to ski, sled, go subway, tennis, dance—now I can learn to ride backhorse—so fun!"

I swelled with pride for her victory. "It's about time for you—" but we were so attuned by now that Mohm could finish my sentence for me.

"—to be happy."

*

The first day of our holiday started out badly. I was hoping it would bring the two girls together, although Maura had come reluctantly, and Mohm, when she saw the rough wood cabin, turned sour.

But almost immediately Maura came to life, levitating on Hemingwayesque visions of a true writer's hideaway. And with some nudging, we got Mohm on a horse. From then on nature took its course.

Maura, who knew her way around horses, took charge of Mohm on the rides every morning. With her long black hair switching from side to side, Mohm on her mount looked like an Indian squaw. She was in her element again. The two girls trotted and loped and stopped in the green, drippy woods to study a frog pond or a moose antler or to watch chicken hawks soar. On the way back from the tack room, Maura would ride Mohm high on her shoulders and then dump her in the grass where they'd roll and laugh. For Maura, it was a delicious reprise of being in a child's world. "She's like having a pile of comic books!" she told me.

We worked up to an all-day ride to Tinker's Creek Rim, where the wind teethed on the tall pine and the pink grass waved and sighed, and you were in another world.

That evening we read together from a fantasy by C. S. Lewis, and after dinner we gathered around the campfire where one of the cowboys sang. Mohm inhaled the lore of wranglers and rodeo bums, and late into the night practiced letting her high soft voice break into a reedy whine.

One morning we were awakened before dawn by the wild percussion of hooves hammering the hills behind our cabin.

"Who is it mean, this one?" Mohm ran into my room to ask excitedly.

"It's the one night the horses are turned loose and the wranglers have to round them up at four in the morning," I explained. I imagined the open ride, the cowboys pasted with sweat to their horses, and as they came closer we could hear them let out their loopy call . . . *hai yao eee.* The horses' legs flared on all sides as they danced down through the grass and past our windows, one heaving a flank into our porch.

"Let's round Mom up!" Mohm shouted. Maura heard her call and the two of them dragged my bed into the middle of the room and jumped on me, whooping and tickling.

Impulsively, Mohm reached for Maura. "My *bong srei.*"

Maura wrapped her arms around the little girl. "You don't know how long I've wished for a sister."

*

That night at dinner I could hear evidence in Maura's conversation with the other guests of the new state of mind she was cultivating. A few hours before she had been weepy, feeling her own childhood ebb in the shadow of Mohm's childlike exuberance. But tonight she was witty and charming, telling a story about the dude lady from the East who had asked one of the cowboys, "Are you gilded?" She had stopped viewing her fits of depression and anomie as moods that had to be followed to their exquisitely bitter conclusion; rather, she saw them as the enemy, to be cut short with a cookie and a cup of tea. With that new attitude, she was discovering that she could actually have one good day after another.

I could see Maura wriggling, as if out of an old snakeskin, to be free of her childhood conflicts. She was sloughing off the chubbiness that had kept her company and was beginning to show a strong sense of personal style. Her speech, too, was beginning to shed the soft outer skin of pleasingness in order to permit sharp observations. Maura was coming into focus. And what I saw emerging was a strong, engaged, fearlessly honest young woman.

She broke into my thoughts to tell me about the fiction-writing course she intended to take the next semester.

"I'm so excited that I'm really starting to write," she said. "I've considered it and stuff, I've kept journals, you know, but I've never started to *do* it."

A flush of pride spread through me. "I think it's right for you, Maura."

Suddenly I had a brainstorm. If I could get into Cambodia over Christmas vacation, I would try to take Maura with me. It would be an irresistable adventure to get her started writing.

"Oh, Mom, I'd love to go. I think. But I'm still a little scared of you. . . ."

"Don't worry, over there you'd have guerrillas to be scared of. The real thing."

Before Maura left to return to college, she reminded Mohm to bother me, just on general principles, at least once a day. "Oh, Mom," she bubbled as we hugged good-bye, "I'm happier than I've ever been in my whole life. I think it's because we're getting along better, don't you think we're getting along better?"

Demons

"I kill you."

She had me down on the bed, her forefinger pressed hard against the carotid artery in my neck. I tried to laugh.

"I have to kill you because you laugh."

I couldn't move. She was straddled across my abdomen, her feet bent inward to clamp my thighs, one hand clenching my wrists in an astonishingly powerful lock. "We're alone in the apartment," I thought, "anything could happen," and I felt the damp, sour patches of nervousness spread under my arms. I saw a part of Mohm I had glimpsed before and would again, a flirtation in her between all that was playful with something sinister. If it had been a true life-and-death struggle I could have lurched free, but instead I found myself going limp, as one might in fending off a rapist, offering no resistance that might stimulate the passion for combat.

She released the pressure of her finger and snickered.

"I see this too many time," she said quietly, "so easy, two minute, three minute, you have to die." She was in a dialogue with her self, playing with that tattered line between executioner and victim and taunting her own shadow-self—death.

Working an arm free, I began to tickle her ribs. She whooped with delight and rolled to one side and let me devastate her with spasms of pleasure. Then she sprang at me, her head butting mine. I let out a little cry.

"Hey," I said, "that hurt a little bit."

"Oh, I don't want to *hurt* you."

Mohm was instantly back to her daylight self, back to clearing the table and moving with graceful, contained, self-effacing gestures. Our wrestling bouts offered a breaking of those restraints, and out of them came a burst of spontaneous, pent-up feeling every bit as intense as the outbursts of laughter. Raw anger.

We had roughhoused almost every night since the previous spring, but as Mohm passed her first anniversary in America, the play had begun to border on the violent. It was essential to her to establish her potential to overcome me physically, to know she could be the stronger one, that she need not be victimized again. She also had to establish the limits of my ownership of her. But the anger was showing up at school as well.

*

"I hate boys," she seethed. "Thirteen-year boys so dumb, Mom," and she searched for a verbal weapon to combat their taunts. A new word entered her vocabulary when a *Time* magazine cover turned up with two men hugging each other, and for all the pains I took to put a compassionate face on homosexuality, Mohm must have intuited that the word could be used to embarrass. The next time the boys shouted names at her, she demanded, "What's the matter with you—you *gay?*"

She stopped as soon as I explained to her the cruel unfairness of her taunt, but the tactic had already served to warn the boys not to take Mohm Pat for some speechless shrinking violet. Yet at the same time she was not sure enough of herself even to speak up in the snack shop where all the kids congregated. Standing before the racks of unintelligible junk food, unable yet to read many English words, she would point, trembling, to her choice. In the usual din the countermen ignored her. She registered the observation that in America, if you do not speak the language well, no one bothers with you.

One afternoon Mohm came home with a shocked report. She had seen the flags of all nations, and the flag for Cambodia was all red. "Pol Pot's flag!" She had to know, was Pol Pot still alive? Still in Cambodia? "Everybody say things, I don't know if really."

The answer had to be a doubly brutal blow. Yes, Pol Pot and thirty thousand of his soldiers were still alive, fighting the Vietnamese, and being supplied by the Chinese. But the worst of it was that the United States and most of the world community were now supporting a coalition that included the former butchers of her country.

Mohm was shaken as I had not seen her before.

"When did you first learn about Pol Pot?" I asked her later.

"Mom, I didn't even know Pol Pot was a human being."

"So you had nobody to blame for the cruelty," I suggested.

"Yes, you see? All is *Angka*. Who is *Angka?* You can't even see what it look like."

"It's pretty hard to direct your anger at an 'it,' " I commiserated.

"When people keep telling you you're wrong, you believe you *are* wrong, and you're mad at yourself," she explained. "It's not *them* punishing you; they're only doing what *Angka* said. And *Angka* is as big as God."

She had a dream the next night about Pol Pot coming to the United States. The Americans wanted to ask him questions, as she told it, and of course he lied, and the Americans gave him a nice house in California. "Then he start throwing balls of fire, just like he did in Cambodia. But it's too late to stop him."

Another dream was becoming persistent. A headless ghoul would appear, wielding a knife, and fly around her face threatening to scoop out her eyes or cut off her head. The terrifying aspect of this apparition was its hidden identity—it wasn't like the spirit of a dead parent that haunted the dreams of many other Cambodian children. Yet it was unspeakably familiar.

The anachronism of anger grew and spread inside her like some rampant amoeba; she became incensed when she heard about the years of French colonial rule, furious at what she learned about Lon Nol's weakness, contemptuous of the passivity her people had shown during the Khmer Rouge regime. And whenever the name "Pol Pot" was mentioned now, her mood spiked as if with fever.

"Why do people let him be commander still?" she demanded. "Why doesn't somebody take a gun and shoot him in the head?" Receiving no satisfactory answer, she would mutter darkly, "That's what I'm going to do."

We had discussions about revenge, and I tried to point out how it usually initiates a cycle of violence that prolongs and spreads the bloodshed. She saw the point. There had to be a different, constructive way to channel her anger into justice, or at least to raise the level of debate. The world had to be alerted if the next Pol Pot was to be stopped.

"But how *could* a man be so bad?" she implored me. "He's Cambodian, why did he kill Cambodians?"

They were the kind of questions that stain the mind like blood. Nothing satisfactorily washes them out.

*

An innocent question . . . it was put to Mohm by a sensitive man friend who visited one evening.

"And what happened to your grandmother, dear?"

"They kill her. I knew they're going to kill her." Her tone was that used for a casual announcement.

"Did you call out?"

She didn't answer at first.

"You told us you called out once before when something terrible was about to happen."

Mohm lifted her eyes with painful indifference.

"How *did* you know when to cry out and when to keep still?"

"No one knows," she said. "I don't know now either."

She didn't want to go over the incident again, I knew that, but neither did she want to be conspicuous by her silence. She knew that my friends were aware of her story, and she knew that when the talk turned to the subject of survivors or surviving that we were talking about her, her kind, and that if she so much as twitched or moved the muscles of her mouth oddly, people might take it the wrong way.

"Mohm has never cried," she must have heard me say. And when others searched her face for signs of what went on in her heart, and found few obvious clues, she must have felt worse; she knew what they thought. They thought she couldn't cry because she couldn't care. They thought she had a stone heart.

By trying to understand Mohm's experience with the Khmer Rouge, I had thought it might be possible to make a stab at understanding the nature of evil, its seductiveness and its weaknesses. After all, she wasn't one of those who had survived merely by chance. Mohm had secrets to unlock. She also had the power of insight with which to appease the shocks of self-discovery. One haunting question surpassed all others. How could human beings be so bestial to their own people?

But the closer we came to locating keys to such secrets, the more Mohm retreated from facing the door to her past directly. And I wasn't as ready as I thought I was.

It was easier for me to intellectualize. Let us look at the history of the Khmer (clear throat, get out the pointer): The Khmer appear to be a gentle people. They love poetry, dance, music, and nature. Had they not welcomed the aesthetic contributions of India and later France? On the other hand, a sudden arbitrary violence against people defined as enemies was a pattern in rural Cambodia even into the nineteenth century . . . public executions, torture, village burnings.[1] One finds the same pattern in studying ancient temple carvings or consulting contemporary scholars.

"Beneath a carefree surface there slumber savage forces and disconcerting cruelties which may blaze up in outbreaks of passionate brutality," as the French scholar Bernard Groslier expresses it.[2] Another Frenchman, analyzing the Khmer smile, points to "the abandonment of all prudence and patience, without warning, the revealing of a capability for total excess."[3]

Nevertheless, the notion that killing can have a positive value is the antithesis of Buddhist teaching. How, then, could a society steeped in pacific beliefs fall under the thrall of extreme violence? I discussed the question with a professor of Southeast Asian studies from Berkeley, Charles Keyes, chairman of the department of anthropology at the University of Washington, at dinner one night. Professor Keyes pushed his chair back from the table.

"It's a question that all of us who have worked on this area puzzle over. I'm not sure I wish there were an easy answer."

"You mean if there were . . ."

"It would be very disturbing to all of us. It would suggest that we're all like that in some basic sense."

Professor Keyes suggested alternatively that the chaos into which Cambodia was plunged in the early 1970s might explain it. Moral constraints were removed, faith in government shattered, and in the outlying provinces a collapse occurred in the teaching of ethics to young men. Instead of shaving their heads and learning to contain their passions at the feet of the monks, sons had to join in the war. Preadolescent boys enticed or kidnapped into joining the Khmer Rouge were too young to have been exposed to any formal education in the monkhood. And in the secret society of Pol Pot's forces, their most aggressive instincts were rewarded.

Buddhism had in the parable of Pol Pot no better, and no more bitter, proof of its basic assumption: that unless people are trained and morally tempered, by nature they will express aggressive passions.

"Do you believe that in the absence of an ethical or religious code that preaches nonviolence," I asked Professor Keyes, "passion will inevitably give way to violence?"

"If you take the constraints off, that's the way people are naturally" was his opinion.

But that familiar Lorenzian explanation seemed too pat.

"Anger is as much psychological as biological" was how Jerome Kagan began our stimulating discussion of the same subject. Kagan is a developmental psychologist at Harvard and one of the more original thinkers on the subject of his latest book, *The Nature of the Child.*[4]

"Even though biology plays a role in our bouts of anger, it is not inevitable that we will become angry," Kagan insisted. He pointed out that in Eskimo society (before the white man entered it), anger was an infrequent emotion. However, he agreed, every human being is capable of intense anger if one of two psychological incentives is present: Either the person becomes frustrated and thinks he knows the cause, and that there is malevolent intent behind it; or the person suspects another or others believe he is inferior or flawed in some way—less smart, less attractive, less worthy in any of the aspects the society values.

"Anger is on the increase in our society," Kagan theorized, "because Americans keep externalizing the source of their frustrations—'somebody is out to get me.' [If not an individual, some force of society, racism, sexism, elitism.] But it is also possible to live a life in which those thoughts are never made conscious, either because you are deeply religious, or because you truly see the world as a crap shoot and you don't take personally the frustrations that each day brings."

Cambodian society would fall into the first category, where the Buddhist proscription against aggression of any kind taught people to repress anger. As a result, people had no experience in understanding or modulating the emotion of anger. That is probably why, traditionally, when anger did break through, it flashed from smoldering frustration into passionate brutality without a moment's warning—a man would suddenly beat his wife in a jealous rage, or two people would have an argument and hold the grudge, never speaking, for the next twenty years. Forgiveness did not come easily to Cambodians.

Enter the Khmer Rouge, who not only tore up the proscription against anger, they drew out whatever frustrations they found among the peasantry and diabolically enflamed them by offering easy targets to hate: *The city people and the monks are out to bleed you economically, and the Americans are the cause of all the bloodshed associated with war, and all of these bloodsuckers see peasants as inferior, right?* Both of Kagan's conditions for fomenting anger were well met. The Khmer Rouge went on to give the license to destroy these enemies in the name of a new higher power. And once the strange and uncontrollable emotion of anger was released, those strong young Cambodians who showed themselves most readily violent were rewarded and honored as the new model of ultimate merit. Anger became an emotion not to be avoided but to be emulated.

That is different from saying it is biologically necessary for human beings to express anger. It is not in the *nature* of man to express anger, it is the personal or cultural *interpretation* of events that incites the emotion of anger. What does seem to be in the nature of human beings is a susceptibility to the charismatic leader who rises to power by magnifying to phantasmagorical proportions an unfamiliar enemy, until that target becomes the repository for everyone's petty personal frustrations. Think of Hitler and the Jews, Mao and the intellectuals, Joseph McCarthy and American leftists, Khomeini and the Great Satan he made of an American president. Pol Pot was hardly an original.

The anger of those victimized by such tyrants is something else. It was like a flu of the spirit, and I didn't know quite what to do to help Mohm shake it.

*

Early that October, Clay launched the *East Side Express.* The staff he recruited was young but sophisticated, talented, and hungry to learn. Clay loved nurturing new writers almost more than anything, and to draw out the individual voices from this bunch, mostly women under thirty, was a particular challenge. It wasn't all that bad walking into an office full of lusty single women either, all of whom complained there were simply No More Men. It was, he told me, rather like walking into estrogen shock.

In my delight for Clay (and not a little jealousy), I was soon taking assignments. "It's about time a woman was put on a national ticket," he called one day to say. "The Republicans already have Reagan and Bush. That means the Democrats are very likely to choose a woman."

"Who's your pick?" I asked him.

"Geraldine Ferraro," he said.

"Who?"

"She's a congresswoman from Queens."

"Why her?"

"She's a conservative woman—an ethnic Italian, law and order, a Queens housewife—she's the only one who fits." He always dazzled me with his analyses. "You see, whenever you take a radical step in politics, you want it to be as small a step as possible. Can you do the story on her?" he asked. "I need it in a week."

"You've got it."

The story, when it appeared on October 27, 1983, with the headline WILL THIS QUEENS HOUSEWIFE BE THE NEXT VICE-PRESIDENT?, was the first to explore the possibility of Geraldine Ferraro's historic candidacy. I worked hard on it, but this time I didn't let the work spill over into my private life.

Meanwhile, however, Mohm was learning only too well how to cut people off to meet the demands of scheduled time. After all, that was the value system of the new culture to which she was determined to adapt. She had come out of a culture where one's well-being was indistinguishable from the well-being of the group. Now she had to function in an individualistic society. Here, waiting for the group to catch up only slowed one down, and the winners in American life clearly did not wait for anyone. In Pol Pot time, the whole children's group was summoned to work collectively by a bell. Now she set her own alarm and decided unilaterally whether or not to roll over for another snooze, making herself too late to fulfill her commitment to meet her subway-mate. Rather, my commitment.

Trying to prod her into making an American friend, I had found a new girl in her class who rode the same train. Having arranged a time for them to meet on the corner each morning, my hurrying her to meet Justine became a source of daily irritation. At last she blurted, "I don't *want* Justine." She could not afford to give priority to casual social friendships.

Much later I found out that Mohm resented efforts to encourage her to make American friends. She was not ready to extend herself in friendship. With all the rest of the demands on her—self-imposed as well as the subtle expectations—she looked forward to weekends in the country as time alone. She needed that time to replenish the inner life that had been her refuge for so long: time to process, time for reverie, time to dream.

Like any recent survivor, Mohm's own needs were still her first priority. Child survivors who were separated from or who lost their own families did not take quickly to sharing, even after they were safe. They had to learn selfishness in order to endure. And because no one could be counted on to tell the truth or to live through the next ordeal, forming any close relationship had been dangerous or painful.

When she had the words for it, she was able to tell me, "You can't tell a thing to anyone. You can't be a friend to a child because they turn right around and stab you in the back. It happened to me many times, Mom, I know it." To a survivor, those were the predictable perils of friendship until proved otherwise.

Having been stripped of all cherished human attachments, Mohm seemed to feel that any but essential connections only got in the way of her practical goals. Yet a longing for love must have been raging inside her. I had a premonition that we were headed for a showdown.

*

When Clay and I wanted to go away for a few days together, Mohm did everything she could to block my efforts to set up amusements for her. She *wanted* me to feel guilty. When I returned, Mohm had written an allegory that alerted me all over again to her continuing struggle.

Her new tutor, Gail Seidon, had explained what an allegory was. "You take something from life, only instead of telling it as it is, you make it happen to something else." Mohm hesitated; what could she write about? Why not her life, the tutor suggested.

"Bird in the forest," she said immediately.

Once there was a beautiful forest. Many animals lived there peacefully. There was always a lot of room and a lot to eat. One bird lived happily in a nest with her parents, brother and sister.

One day lions came and took over the forest. They ate the smart animals, and all animals had to work for the lions. The bird had to leave her nest to go to a different place. One day she came home and her mother was gone. She had been eaten by the lion. The bird waited for her father to come home. She heard that the lion had eaten him too. She flew back to her nest and decided to run away from the work. She found her little sister and brother sick. After three days they were dead. And then the lion sent her older brother away and she never saw him again.

The elephants came and fought with the lions. The elephants took over. The bird took a chance to fly away to the jungle. She

was looking for a way out. She end up in the forest all alone.
After that she made friends and she was happy.

One day a deer came into the forest and saw the young bird.
The deer wanted to take the bird to another beautiful forest. The
bird was sad because she had to leave her friends and she
didn't speak deer language. After a year she learned deer
language and she was safe

It trailed off without an ending, without so much as a period. The
tutor had tried to steer Mohm into saying how wonderful life was for
her now. She adamantly refused to add another word.

"Nobody knows about the problems I have every day, living in the
United States," she had said with finality.

*

On Halloween weekend we drove out to the country. A greasy sky
developed into dense fog. With Clay at the wheel, and me fussing, and
Mohm keeping watch for the exit sign, tension was high, and we nearly
had a head-on collision.

Company was expected for lunch not long after we arrived ourselves.
Mohm and her "friend," Justine, were vying to make the best dessert.
Mohm asked for real pumpkin to produce a Cambodian specialty.
When Clay and I returned from the store without it, a spat flared up
and before we knew it, Mohm had pulled off her apron and stomped
out the door, vowing as she passed Justine, "I'm going to run away."

While Justine searched in vain for Mohm, we went on with the
lunch for our guests. Several hours passed.

*

I come so close to crying, my nose bleeds. It drops down brown on my
shirt but I'll find the water, wash it off with seawater—I can't let them
see. I'm never going to ask them for anything again. I'll just sit quiet
like a clamshell so they won't even notice me.

I walk on the beach a long time. I think about the nice things Mom
does every day that I remember. Mom understands so much and I want

to keep it that way, but when the person you love is mean for no reason, it makes your heart hurt. I think it might happen to anybody who loves another person so much.

*

She came back at dusk. Clay tried to tease her out of her mood. Picking up on Mohm's newfound feminist philosophy, he insisted she would have to do the dishes, that was "woman's work." She looked from Clay to me with a lid-fluttering, "Where'd you find this turkey?" kind of look. But beneath the pout she could barely contain her appetite for teasing back—"Woman's work is karate chop!" and she made a rigid rake of her knuckles and plunged them into his stomach.

"Hey, that hurts!"

She added a few remarks of undisguised hostility. "Why American men have stomach like ice cream? Why American men have no hair?"

"Notice how she goes immediately to the weak spot?" I tried unsuccessfully to remove the sting.

Children spot vulnerability very quickly, especially deprived children who have so often felt helpless themselves. They attack weakness in order to make themselves feel more powerful. Mohm was at war with Clay.

She changed into her nightgown and withdrew silently into Maura's room and lay in bed, stony face to the wall, for the rest of the weekend. Sunday brought a downpour and Clay tried repeatedly to pry her loose from her sulk. "C'mon, we're driving to the ocean for lobsters!"

Nothing seemed to work. She looked like a different person. When she was happy, her face was a fountain of smiles, animated as a small child's, sometimes radiating such gaiety it appeared lit by bright lights. But when she was angry, her face was foul.

"Now look, Mohm, you can't just sulk." He raised his voice only slightly, but I knew that to her ear it must have been a roar. "C'mon now, get dressed!" He walked out on the gust of that command.

Dutifully, she dressed and accompanied us to dinner, never saying a word, not one. I knew that as an Asian she had been offended by Clay's raised voice, but it must also have revived the old sense of helplessness and shame when she had had to submit to the loud authority of self-important Khmer Rouge. It was becoming evident that what had filled her mind in those first months in the refugee camp, when she found it impossible to concentrate, was not fear. It was anger. It must have been everywhere, in the lice in her hair and the limpness of her limbs, in the gunshots at night and the guards and the aloneness. She couldn't express the anger then, just as she had been unable to express it through the years of Pol Pot. But now she could feel again and express what she was feeling, and she was naturally progressing through the stages of mourning.

*

I knew that any loss required some mourning, as a preparation for new emotional attachments and new investments in the future. And although we usually associate the mourning process with death, it is evoked by almost any life accident. All life accidents (being fired, becoming redundant, sudden illness, severe financial loss, unexpectedly losing someone you love) represent a loss of the familiar and predictable. But the unwilling émigrés to that unknown territory beyond fear sometimes emerge annealed by the crisis and take control of their lives.

Suddenly I remembered something very useful I had learned in studying the behavior of the American hostages in Iran when they were returned home.[5] Apathy is the natural protective state for any hostage of war or terrorism. When one cannot afford to show emotion to one's captors, it becomes essential to suspend any feelings. But after the return to safety, the buried emotional self must work its way back to life. And this transition is usually made through anger.

After their ordeal, survivors take strength from telling stories of small acts of defiance. They may even unconsciously act them out. Those acts can then become emblematic of their endurance throughout the ordeal. By retelling or reliving such defiant moments, the individual can develop rationalizations to relieve the shame attached to his or her weaker moments.

But although the transition from apathy to hostility is essential to restoring mental health, it can create a strain on family life. I remember the struggle the hostage families experienced, which followed the same pattern as that of released prisoners of war in Vietnam. After a brief period of euphoria upon reunion with their families, the released captives were dependent on their wives for several months, whereupon a striking change often occurred. The former captive became increasingly irritable, even belligerent. He found fault with the decisions his wife had made in his absence and became critical of his children and colleagues. His abrupt reassertion of a dominant role in the family often left his wife feeling emotionally isolated: *Shouldn't he be proud of me?* The wives, having held the reins of family life through the long ordeal and often made independent decisions for the first time, were unprepared for a survivor husband who inevitably took out on them some of the frustration he had felt when his captors removed his autonomy.

Most foster parents who receive refugee children are caught by surprise when their good intentions are misinterpreted as bad; no one prepares them for the probability that the survivor child may project onto them the cruel authority of his former captors.

Peter Pond's son Arn had described to me the scene that took place during his first months in America whenever his foster father so much as reminded him to make his bed. Arn interpreted such commands as "He hates me, he wants to kill me," and furiously rebelled. Two years later Arn could laugh about it, but at the time it was no joke.

I began to understand that recent survivors of authoritarianism have no capacity to discriminate well-meant criticism and dictatorial control. So long as Mohm was operating under the Khmer Rouge code that forbade any defense against criticism, she interpreted my attempts to help her ("Why don't you finish your homework first?") or to prod her ("Chop-chop") as an intention to humiliate and totally control her. She could not respond in degrees. She had only two modes of response: attack or submit. Kill or be killed.

Eventually, I was able to alter her cultural interpretation of my suggestions: "It's because you mean so much to me and I want things to be good for you." Only then was she able to manage her resentments in a way that most Khmer find difficult, if not impossible: She began to forgive.

*

When I went in to talk to Mohm on that Sunday night in the country, she was openly defiant. She said she knew that Clay had never wanted her. "He only pretends to be nice. He hates me." No amount of talking would convince her otherwise. "If you go with him, you find another girl like me to be your daughter; my dream is over."

"No, angel. You are my only new daughter. You are chosen."

"Shosun?"

I had hit a nerve, but what did it signify for her? I thought for a long time. At last I said, "Like your jogging shoes were chosen."

"Ohhhh," and she gave a long, sweet exhale of relief.

*

Later that night I was staring at the ceiling.

"What?" Clay said.

"What say we make a baby?"

"A what?"

"You know, one of those things that drinks and wets and wakes you up in the middle of the night but there's no way it can psych you out."

"You're just suffering from adolescent shock," he said.

I laughed at his accuracy and then grew serious. "Do I really go around, the way Maura says, like some American Lady Bountiful who saved her Asian refugee?"

"A little."

"But she's already given me more than I can return. I mean, this is a mutual rescue. Mohm is more than a survivor. She's a life force. She can find delight in the midst of the worst circumstances. She makes me appreciate things. It's really amazing—"

"Do you think she'll ever, uh, well, like me?" he whispered.

I must have done a double take. Here was the hardboiled journalist with the triple-testicle voice reduced to the stammering bashfulness of a little boy. I seized the moment and pounced on him with a pillow.

"*If* you lose twenty pounds, *if* you do the dishes for the next year, *if* you let me do the driving . . ."

Cambodia Revisited . . . December 1983

It was something about the shadows. The center of Phnom Penh was bright enough in the evening, the fluorescence of shop lights casting a blue haze over the coal fires of families grilling supper just off the street. A foreigner like myself was free to walk alone, at least until the curfew at nine, free to browse at private stalls in the Central Market displaying pre-'75 music tapes, despite a ban, and brightly colored clothing smuggled from Thailand.

The main drag had noise and life, too; especially near the radio store where teenage boys congregated to listen to Russian rock on cassettes. Others stood on the site of a future Aeroflot Hotel, agape at the billboard just erected, showing images of strong young Soviets setting up a satellite dish and working in a space lab and other unimaginable and inapplicable pursuits.

Compared to Ho Chi Minh City, the old Saigon where I had just spent three days, Cambodia's capital was far more animated and even appeared marginally more prosperous. The girls in their floppy sunhats and high-heeled sandals pedaled home from work with smiles on their faces. The pharmaceutical factory just outside town was operating again, although what it did was sift antibiotic powders out of decade-old American capsules and put them in new jars.

A mysterious, superficial transformation of the city had started the day I arrived: state signs replacing family names on storefronts, spotlights around the victory monument, the first half-hour of TV programming in Khmer appearing on old screens. The work was being done under orders from the Vietnamese, so they could congratulate themselves on National Liberation Day, January 17, for the occupation of Cambodia five years before. By the end of the week the main hospital was overrun with street accidents. Bicycles, cyclos, motor scooters, trucks groaning full of government workers, Volgas purring along carrying Russian advisers, the whole hurtling human herd in a hurry to make up for lost life had been subjected, without warning, to the infuriating modernity of—traffic lights!

But under the cosmetics, Phnom Penh, the city of cosmopolitan reputation, the former Paris of Southeast Asia, had been reduced to a village squatting on a city's sidewalks. Immediately off the main boulevard, the side streets fell away to dirt byways roamed by pigs and chickens. And the residents, most of whom had never lived in a city, rocked on their heels beside baskets of fruit or cigarettes they had to sell in order to supplement their meager government salaries.

The heart of Cambodia was still hidden, but at least its stomach appeared full enough to allow the mind to function again, within limits.

The happiest scenes I saw were of the renewed possibilities for mere living—being able to enjoy a meal with one's family or to operate a shop, being strong enough to have babies and grow them fat and jolly —these were privileges still new enough to bring satisfaction. For those with any literacy or technical knowledge, provided they demonstrated their loyalty to the regime every day, there might be a job in one of the government ministries, free living quarters in Phnom Penh with a small salary, and perhaps one day enough money to buy a shiny red Honda motorbike and show it off by racing up and down the riverbank.

Yet the very coloring and smell of an American on those streets seemed to unsettle the air, to disturb thoughts put precipitously to sleep years before. So far as people on the street knew, I was just another pale-skinned, pointy-nosed, milky-smelling, blond Russian, being driven around like the Soviet officials in a shiny Volga with a guide from the Foreign Office. No one smiled at me—uncharacteristic for the Khmer—unless I made clear I was an American, and then the reaction was mixed. Sometimes a shiver of distaste showed on the face, followed by a smile. "Number One," said the hair-parlor girl when I occupied her chair, but it was only the blunt manipulation of the survivor; a few moments later I heard her greet the wife of a Soviet official the same way.

There were only two hotels. The Monoram, assigned to Western relief workers, was full. That left officials no choice but to quarter me in the White Hotel, which was chock-full of Reds, a joke I could enjoy only with myself.

When the lights went out, which was not infrequently, an urgent whisper would attach itself to me if I was passing in the corridor—"I like to talk with you about many things, but when I open my mouth my heart drops." Cambodians were forbidden to speak to a nonsocialist foreigner unless permission had been given and a translator provided to monitor the conversation. Almost every evening a soft knock on my door announced another furtive visit from a hotel employee. "Please, you help me to escape! I'll do anything!" And then, before the director came by, "Good night, sister!"

I had come to Cambodia to see what Mohm's fate might have been, if she had made the choice to stay. But I had gone to some lengths to obscure any personal connection to Cambodia. It had frankly baffled me to receive a Telex from Phnom Penh granting my visa. When I had presented the visa issued by Cambodian officials to the Vietnamese Embassy in Bangkok, the press officer scoffed, "Not legal, not sufficient," and I was detained for a week waiting for permission from Hanoi. It was embarrassingly obvious that the Cambodian officials were little more than flunkies.

Under strict orders not to mix with the Khmer people, Vietnamese soldiers and technicians and low-ranking diplomats called no attention to themselves on the street and never showed their faces at the National Theatre performances. They were like owls in the dark, however; sooner or later one knew they were there.

Their methods of political indoctrination by manipulating indigenous art forms were quite ingenious. At a riverside restaurant one could hear a new love song . . . *"Bong,"* "my dear," the girl sang softly to her unemployed sweetheart, accompanied by the layering of sounds familiar to Khmer music, and then the lyrics pounded home one of the approved post-liberation themes: She would not love him unless he joined the army or a solidarity rice production group.

It was the same thing with the Buddhist temples, where old people were allowed again to gather and enjoy the harmless anachronism of their chants, before the monk mounted a Marxist lecture. Religion must serve the interests of the State, I was told by officials. The Vietnamese were not so vulgar as to rape the Cambodians with their politics; they just slipped it in.

But judging by the protocol observed at the official functions I attended, the Vietnamese had been thoroughly vassalized by the Soviets. It was symbolic that whenever the diminutive President Heng Samrin stood to make one of his flowery speeches, paeans to solidarity between the three Indochinese countries and the socialist bloc, it was always hard to see him over the podium.

*

In the middle of a performance in the darkened National Theatre, a faceless voice whispered to me:

"Tell Mohm to come home."

I went stiff. "Tell who?"

"Your girl, Mohm."

It was as if a dragon's tongue had been loosed in the dark and found my ear and tickled it with fire.

"How do you know about her?" I whispered back into the blackness.

"We read your article."

The shape of a man rose from the seat from which I'd heard the voice, and left. A chill went through me. Was this why they had let me in? Would they try to coerce me to send Mohm back, or detain me, or —I couldn't think straight. It was the shadows and the uncertainty, the same psychological weapons used so cleverly by the Khmer Rouge.

Another voice leaned over from the seat behind to explain the shocking reenactment onstage of Pol Pot soldiers engaged in a massacre. "The people don't like to see these tortures," the voice whispered, "but it is necessary they remember the past." Male dancers in black trousers were leaping over the heads of wailing girls, who crouched with their hands bound behind their backs and their long hair sweeping the ground as they swayed in the agony of anticipated death. The shadowy stage and slow motion evoked a terrible drawn-out groan from the audience.

In the midst of the universal destruction, a young man sang out, "But no! The People's Liberation forces are coming!" Drums preceded the obligatory scene in which Heng Samrin's forces flooded onstage and killed the king and his guards and the victims awoke and joined the chorus. Fists shot up, all eyes turned to the massive People's Republic of Kampuchea flag suddenly projected at the back of the stage, and hands stretched religiously toward it. The lead clown, now unmasked as the political spokesman of the theater group, explained to the audience that they should not allow the enemy, who seemed to have disappeared, to keep manipulating and haunting them.

I couldn't wait to get out of there.

*

"So, one of our orphans lives with you?"

"Yes, you already know that."

"Her family name?"

"We don't know the real name."

The foreign minister, Hun Sen, sat on the brocade couch of a former palace with knees projected akimbo, like the King of Siam, questioning me. I was seated on a lower chair. He chain-smoked from a dish of imported filter cigarettes.

"We have twenty thousand orphans here," he said. "The government has to feed and look after them. We have to spend as much money as if we were training an army of ten divisions. The party has decided to put the most resources into these orphans—millions of riels each year are committed to their food, clothing, schooling, their own pocket money. They consider the government and the party their parents." He concluded triumphantly, "Because they have suffered much, they will be the most loyal."

He sat back puffing smugly as he listened to his words repeated by an interpreter and leaned over often to be certain they were being immortalized by my tape recorder. Hun Sen proudly described why Mohm's counterparts would be better off than anyone else in Cambodia. Some were being trained in orphanages, others in solidarity groups in the countryside. Adolescents over the age of fifteen were looked after in apartments and communes. The brightest would be sent to socialist countries to study. "None are beggars," he bragged.

"It sounds as if the foreign minister is banking on the orphans as the future."

He beamed like the proud division commander he once was for Pol Pot's forces. "They are the *vanguard*."

Hun Sen was very much still the arrogant young warrior. He did not like it at all when I brought up his past record. He insisted that he had recognized the "wrongness" of Pol Pot and escaped into Vietnam taking one of his battalions with him. He had not realized the "wrongness" until 1977, however, which coincidentally dovetailed with the paranoid purges of Pol Pot's forces when commanders stationed near the border with Vietnam, like Hun Sen, were being sent for R&R to Tuol Sleng torture center.

I asked to visit an orphanage and follow a clever child through a typical day and evening to see for myself what Mohm's existence would be if she lived in Cambodia today. Hun Sen gladly agreed.

*

"Aw kun! Aw kun!"

The children's shouts rang through the clear air of Orphanage Number One on the outskirts of Phnom Penh. *"Aw kun!"* "Thank you!"

A female drill instructor moved up and down the columns of barefoot children, levering their arms higher when it came time to punch their fists in salute.

"Long Live the People's Republic of Kampuchea!"

In this display orphanage were housed about four hundred of Hun Sen's vanguard of twenty thousand children, some as young as age six, although most were concentrated in their early teens. All of them, like Mohm, had been orphaned by the war or the Khmer Rouge, but these were the children who "stayed quiet," as the director put it. They had not tried to escape.

A girl answering my specifications was brought to the reception room. Dary was her name; she was eleven and smiled delightfully. I saw Mohm's face pass like a ghost over hers.

Dary's father had been a high-school teacher in Takeo Province. She remembered the takeover well, remembered a rocket falling onto the neighbors' house, and she was very definite about the date on which Pol Pot took power (she would have been four at the time). "My father was forced to pick up animal dung." She wanted his embrace, and he gave it, but night after night she almost swooned from revulsion.

Dary looked down at the floor. "I wasn't there when they took my father away." But she was very clear about being liberated by the National Front in cooperation with the Vietnamese forces who drove out the Pol Pot soldiers. All the people from her village had run behind the Vietnamese.

Had her mother considered escaping to Thailand?

At that time, she replied, her mother did not speak of another way. Shortly after their journey on foot back to Phnom Penh, her mother had died of exhaustion.

The orphanage director explained the children's daily program. They rose at five A.M.; before classes they did gymnastics and chores and sang the new national hymn. All the children belonged to the Young Pioneers (a Soviet bloc children's political organization) and worked outside the camp for several hours a week directing traffic or helping to harvest rice. Two evenings a week were devoted to political meetings and self-criticism. "We teach them to compare the Pol Pot regime with our present regime. We remind them, 'Who killed your mother and father? Who made orphans of you?'"

My translator this time was an elegantly boned woman who wore a striped French T-shirt. "These children only hear about socialist countries, never about the USA or France or Canada," she mentioned privately to me with an expression of disapproval. "So they stay quiet and don't try to be refugees, only wait to see if they can be sent to socialist countries."

*

Dary has a math class. The fourth-grade math teacher criticizes his students for not executing correctly the exercise he gave them the day before. Out of his mouth comes a fusilade of rules, which the children echo in unison as he moves up and down the aisles smacking his wooden pointer on their desks. Rote learning has always been a hallmark of Khmer education. What is new are the posters of Lenin and Stalin hanging on the back wall; what is different are the wrappers around the children's books, now printed with Soviet cartoons, and the fact that half the students seated in the front row, reserved for the brightest, are girls.

Dary's feet twist around the chair legs as she writes, every bit as fiercely concentrated as Mohm. The teacher stands over Dary and taps the top of her head with his stick as he shouts commands to correct her mistakes. What a contrast to Friends Seminary.

In geography class there are no maps. The teacher refers to "the new Indochina," an all-red, water-winged shape drawn on the book covers that blurs any national borderlines between Vietnam, Laos, and Cambodia.

For reading class the children go to the small library. Dary moves listlessly around the book shelves. The choices are tomes on the *USSR in World Politics*, Leninist theory, PLO tactics, and faded reports on such compelling subjects as "Theses of the First Communist Party of Bulgaria." For lighter reading the children are offered picture magazines about Soviet cultural life, and several of their faces disappear behind *Soviet Woman*. The nearest thing to a storybook Dary can find —the sole nonpolitical book in Khmer—is a second-grade reading-exercise book. I think of Mohm reading *Animal Farm*.

Much is made at the orphanage of working toward the award of a scholarship to study abroad at the university level, which is preceded by a year of preparation at the new Language Institute in Phnom Penh to learn Russian, Spanish (for study in Cuba), Czech, Hungarian, or Bulgarian. "No," I am told frostily, "they will not be sent to Vietnam; their level of learning is no higher than ours." On further investigation, I found that no orphan had yet attended the Language Institute. Most of those youngsters who have finished their studies at Orphanage Number One have been sent directly into state tailor or mechanics shops.

Dary takes me to her dormitory. Tacked to one wall at the foot of her cot, on which her few pieces of leftover clothes from UNICEF and Oxfam are rolled up, hangs a page of copied Vietnamese words. The language of occupation is not compulsory until the children reach fifteen, but Dary is determined to get a head start.

Would she like to learn English? I ask through the translator.

"No." Simple as that. The study of English is prohibited (although I found some adults who were working with illegal tutors). Dary has never met an American before, so I ask if she knows anything about the United States.

"Oh, yes, she reads about all countries," the administrator interjects.

I press; the girl looks down uncomfortably. Finally, her natural politeness struggling against her wish to please the authorities, she says softly, "The USA is a superpower that wants to infiltrate socialist countries."

"And do the political books in the library teach you how to deal with this?" I try to convey.

Her response pops out like bubble gum from a machine: "Be vigilant. Do not permit the enemy to infiltrate our society."

And what did Dary think about, in the dark, before she went to sleep?

Sometimes a nightmare of Pol Pot time (just like Mohm), but usually her lessons are on her mind, she says. Not Buddha, she makes sure to say; she does not pray. Sometimes, she runs a few overheard Russian words through her mind. Clever survivor that she is, she wants more than anything to learn Russian. That is the ticket in Cambodia today.

The bell rings, summoning the children to stand in line, single file, with their tin spoons. During meals the children must be silent. Staff members patrol the plank tables. "The children are taught not to speak while eating," the administrator explains; "it is contrary to digestion." They are served fish soup and rice by their peers and a few beans with ginger. Boys and girls are seated at separate plank tables. I think of Mohm in her anarchic lunchroom, piling catsup on a hamburger or cream cheese on a bagel, the boy on one side of her likely to be scalped in high punk style while another is seriously pre-preppie, and after lunch kids bash one another and blow Coke through straws.

After lunch, the children are drilled to march, which they do at all of the frequent liberation celebrations. They seem to derive confidence from the strong new national identity in formation.

While Dary is being completely Vietnamized, Mohm is being thoroughly Americanized. Back home, we have resettled hundreds of thousands of refugees from Southeast Asia, the great majority of them Vietnamese and from 15 to 20 percent Cambodians. In 1983, the last year for which the INS reports figures, 18,120 Cambodians came to the United States. In the New York metropolitan area alone, about 6,000 Cambodians are learning what it means to be American. Nearly 100 of them are orphans like Mohm, many of whom will be eligible for scholarships to college. In all of Cambodia, according to their own officials, there aren't more than 100 college-educated people left.

Another 250,000 Cambodians are still caught in the limbo of camps up and down the Thai border, their children growing up with the most rudimentary education and no present hope of resettling in their homeland or any other country. They are symbolic of the deadlock of superpowers that dragged Cambodia into the Indochina war in the first place and that continues to play its people off as mere pawns.

I wonder how many years it will take before the deadlock will make it all but impossible for the Darys and the Mohms to communicate.

Before leaving, I am asked to sign the guest book. My translator looks in amazement over my shoulder at the sentiment. I express the hope that the children will have the chance to learn all languages . . . "so they can decide for themselves what words really mean, and never again be fooled by bad leaders."

"Me too," the translator whispers. "Me too!"

First Cry

It was the Christmas holidays for us, attack season for Cambodians, when Maura and I joined up to visit refugee camps and rebel camps along the Thai border. Mohm was engaged in a perilous journey of discovery of her own.

Tucked away in the snow-muffled mountains of New Hampshire with the Pond family, enjoying a house devoted to Cambodian ways, with the reassuring din of many voices and the snap of ginger in the kitchen, Mohm was beginning to feel sorry for herself as an only child placed in that largest of outdoor mental hospitals, Manhattan. Peter Pond's advocacy of foster care for Khmer unaccompanied minors began at home—he now had eight of them.

It was 1980 when he had met Arn Chorn, then a fourteen-year-old pile of bones who lay on a mat in the camp hospital, yellow with malaria, feet still a mesh of thorns from months of wandering through the jungle to escape the Vietnamese. The next two problem cases Peter had brought over were Soneat, a bright boy who immediately scored high marks at school but who assumed as his defense an offputting air of superiority, and Lakhana, a frail boy with an old man's face who sought a retreat from the past in poetry. After the boys came the elegant young girl whom Mohm by now considered her "heart sister," Jintana Lee.

"Fireballs academically," the principal of the White Mountains Regional High School had pronounced them. "Our American kids just don't see education as the ticket, they take it for granted. These kids are up finishing their homework by flashlight under their bedcovers." All four Pond children had made the honor roll and been elected to National Honor Society; three had received scholarships to New England prep schools. They were also models of good behavior. When several Cambodian children were summer students at Gould Academy in Bethel, Maine, the director commented, "American adolescents will buck against adult experience and be irrational, but these kids bring real moral weight to discussions."

Among the Pond children's secret weapons was Shirley Wilson, Peter's earthy fiancée, who offered to get up at 4:30 every morning and come over to work with any youngster wanting help with homework. Lakhana had taken the fullest advantage. The hundred-pound boy would curl up in Shirley's lap and ask to be fed words. Shirley understood from the start that the selfishness the Cambodian children had adopted to survive did not equip them easily to become members of a family, but it wasn't until Lakhana wrote a series of dark and powerful poems for her that she began to comprehend the children's appalling lack of self-regard.

> I know I am a human being.
> But sometimes I feel like animal,
> Which has been made inscrutable,
> And now everything has become stink.
> Sometimes I find myself never learn,
>   never thought, never change.
> Which makes one have a presumption—
>   that I'm in the darkness of pain.
> It's hurt, and hurt so much I
>   couldn't describe
> Couldn't show, couldn't talk,
> Worse than a handicap who
>   uses a crutch but I don't
>   have a scar or a mark.
> Am I a victim? A deserver?
> Or it's just a sin.

Mohm looked up to Arn. He had been close to a *tabula rasa* in the hands of the Khmer Rouge. He had never known his father, who died before his mother gave him away to an aunt. Seven of her twelve children had died before the takeover in 1975, from disease or Khmer Rouge rockets or American B-52s; it was hard to keep track. After the takeover, Arn had been quartered in Wat Ayk, a former Buddhist temple, which was next to a killing ground.

"I don't think anybody saw more killing than me," he had told Mohm and me. "The blood was in my eyes all the time." He had been given the job of overseeing other children at work in the fields. When they came to him fainting from sickness and unable to work, or begging to search for roots, leeches, rats, anything, he was in a position to cover for them. He was twelve when the Vietnamese invaded in 1979, and like most boys his age was issued a rifle by the Khmer Rouge and pushed to the front lines, to die first. Only when his unit was chased into the woods did he finally see his chance to escape; he lost himself in the jungle.

When Mohm looked at him, I sensed, she saw her older brother and felt the yearning and frustration that swirled around the memory of their last meeting. *Why hadn't he come with her, his own sister?*

But for all Arn had been through, he had a gregarious nature and a smile that splurged easily. As a result he won people's affection almost without effort. For Arn, the reek of shame had not begun to surface.

*

One afternoon Arn and Soneat were at the kitchen table while Mohm and Jintana were doing the dishes. Fresh from his social successes at prep school, Arn could not resist rubbing it in; he began needling Soneat about his sour disposition. Soneat snickered at first. A brushoff was apparently not what Arn expected, and he grew a little huffy, but nothing that remotely foreshadowed Soneat's explosion.

"I know what you are," Soneat accused Arn, his lips whitening with rage, "you're—"

As if to silence the unknowable words before they were spoken, Arn emitted a high, thin cry, "Nooo."

But Soneat screamed out for everyone to hear—"You're KHMER ROUGE!"

Arn sprang across the table. He threw the astonished Soneat down to the floor in a grunting, clawing struggle. Mohm and Jintana pasted themselves, slack-mouthed, against the sink. It was their faces Shirley first saw as she appeared in the doorway. From the rabid sounds under the table she knew what was going on but not the identity of the writhing combatants.

"I will not have it!" she shouted with fully clipped schoolmarm scorn. "We are *not* wild animals."

When one face emerged, dazed as he stumbled awkwardly to his feet and looked down at his bloody shirt, Shirley must have registered her profound disappointment . . . not *Arn!*

He dropped his head, strode through the kitchen and out the front door and fled.

Mohm brooded. She would not speak to Soneat. Arn did not return that night. Knowing he was barefoot somewhere in the cold white hills, sick with self-contempt, running, Mohm slept fitfully.

"It's my fault," he murmured when the state trooper brought him home the next morning. "Everything's my fault." He begged Shirley's forgiveness, but she wanted to know what had produced the outburst. Mohm and Jintana sat with him until the story came out.

"My sister," he mumbled brokenly, "the Khmer Rouge killed my sister. I was carrying the gun for them so I was in the same position." He repeated the self-accusation over and over, "I was in the same position as the Khmer Rouge!"

It seemed the Khmer Rouge had used his sister to carry heavy bags of rice on her head deep into their jungle redoubt. Arn would some-times meet her on the way, wearing his gun, able to exchange only a furtive message of concern or hope, if that. He remembered how she tried to cheer him, whispering, "Wait and see, one day we'll escape and go to find our mother." He remembered how she depended on him. One day Arn abandoned his feigned indifference in front of his superi-ors, demanding to know why he hadn't seen his sister in several days. The next day they carried her out of the jungle and laid her in front of him. The girl looked up at her brother, recognizing him but unable to speak. Her broken body was smeared all over with dirt, as if people had been stepping on her like fallen fruit. Arn stood over her shaking, his hand twitching on his gun. Was he responsible in some way for her death by asking about her? He would never know.

"I didn't want to see her suffer," he told the girls. "I'd seen too much suffering, it's all my fault . . . so I go a little crazy, I almost shoot everybody. I even want to shoot my sister, yes! I was shouting, 'Go ahead, die! *I want you to die!*' "

At a family meeting called by Peter Pond that evening, the boys asked if Arn would have to be sent away. Peter explained that none of them should take personal blame for the horrors that occurred in Cambodia. Given the choices—cooperate or die—they had done what was necessary to survive. He set out his philosophy. "You are my chil-dren. I am Number Two parent—forever." The more the children tested that commitment, he let them know, the more vehement he would be about sticking to it.

Mohm said nothing at all during the meeting. Tensions in the household subsided and preparations for Christmas Day seemed to absorb any unspoken grudges—until Christmas morning, one of those occasions that generates a surge of emotions leading to blowups and, with luck, breakthroughs. When I first heard about it, what happened that morning seemed to me unimaginably horrible. That was before I heard the story told by Mohm.

The living room had been a picture of family warmth: a brightly lit fir tree cut from their own woods, a carpet lapped over with handmade gifts. There had been a lavish Christmas dinner and toasts with wine. Through all of the jollity Lakhana's face had remained stony. Peter commented on it. When Shirley criticized the boy for not clearing the table, he went into the kitchen and she heard the shattering of glass, one of the crystal wineglasses, two of them. It wasn't an accident. Blood flashed scarlet in Shirley's face, as she recalled it, and the woman who had worked for two years to break through the boy's stone face all at once lost control.

"You wear a mask, I don't know who you are, you don't let anyone in on you!" she heard herself shouting.

The boy turned away from her, toward the dishwasher, and picked up a handful of utensils. "Don't you ever do one single thing because you love somebody?" she demanded. The boy dumped the utensils loudly into their pockets. Shirley was no longer simply raising her voice now, she was screaming as she shoved the boy toward the stairs, "I'm sick of hurting because of you," jabbing his shoulder, pushing him up the steps. "You're not worth it, Lakhana, you're too hard to love!"

Lakhana, a young man in whom self-contempt had become suddenly a rampaging animal, reared and bit down on Shirley's finger.

Peter entered a few seconds later and began bellowing. The whole delicately woven skein of civility seemed to have snapped. Arn was the first to go upstairs to comfort Lakhana. Soneat followed. Then Mohm and Jintana. Presently, they were all on the floor taking turns holding the boy, whose sobs seemed bottomless, not the cries of a young man weeping, but of a child who is frightened of the dark yet afraid to scream. They rocked and rocked him, for hours. And when his confession poured from him at last, it was their confession, all of theirs. He too had "let" a sibling die.

*

"I cried with him," Mohm told me triumphantly, "the first time, Mom!"

"You cried? Real tears?" It was the first thing she told me when I came home from Cambodia.

"Only once I really cried since Pol Pot time began, remember? With Maura, when we looked at the book together? But I never cried for the suffering."

"That's good, sweetheart, that's fine."

"From that day on, I begin to be able to do it more and more, even a little tiny memory and my tears kept coming out. It was a crying time. It's not even hard!" She might have been describing the slow conquest of a fear of heights, or of boys or public speaking. But for a survivor, to be able at last to break through the wall of repression and reconnect emotion to memory, this was an occasion for great celebration. So many times before she had endured pounding headaches or nosebleeds as the consequence of holding back. But now she seemed determined to unearth another hidden part of her story.

I had brought home for her a small bronze statue of the Buddha and several sarongs. Thrilled, she had quickly fashioned an altar and kept it supplied with fresh flowers. Wrapping herself in a sarong, she sat before the Buddha and searched her spirit.

"I wish I remembered . . ." she said, coming out of her room. "My aunt, she came to the house where I was babysitting for the Khmer Rouge woman. She probably knew them from somewhere, I have no idea how. My aunt tried to get me to go with her. She told me that my older brother was staying in the same village where she lived. That was a lie I found out later. She wasn't nice. She didn't care about me that much, I remember feeling that."

"Did you want to go with her?"

"I wanted to do right. I didn't know what to do. The Khmer Rouge woman told me, 'Don't go, you're going to have a very hard time.' I'd lived with them and eaten with them, but I knew I had to go away because they were different from me. No matter what happened, I never wanted to be part of Pol Pot people."

"Was this an aunt you were fond of?"

Her eyes narrowed and a look of stale resentment came over her face. This was an aunt by marriage, whom Mohm remembered for the stingy funeral she had given Mohm's uncle. "We were never close," Mohm said, adding darkly, "I never trusted her."

I asked if this was the rich aunt she had turned to when her sister was dying, the one who refused to give her medicine?

Mohm nodded miserably. "She looked at me like a stranger. It made me realize we were helpless." This memory, this burden of shame on her own family, came to the surface slowly.

"Did you leave the Khmer Rouge woman and go with your aunt?" I prompted her.

"I told her, 'I'm not going to stay anymore.' But I never really had any choice." The Khmer Rouge woman ordered her to stay. Mohm felt ashamed of her acquiescence. "I did a lot of things wrong," she mumbled. "People told me what to do and I did it."

"But," I soothed her, "you had no choice."

It wasn't until the Vietnamese bombing began that Mohm had the chance to run away. But after a month alone in the jungle, she knew she wouldn't make it if she didn't find some older people. That was when she came upon a fleeing group that included her aunt. Mohm could appreciate they were smart people; she attached herself to them.

"It got really bad during that time," she continued. "We had to survive three or four months, just walking, running under bombs, crossing Pol Pot soldiers' camps." She described then in chilling detail escaping her own grave. With her aunt's group she had been recaptured by soldiers from one of the remaining Khmer Rouge camps near the border of Thailand.

"The leader was a dummy, but he was desperate. One day they told us to dig a hole, about fifty feet wide and sixty or seventy feet long. So many people had gone with the Vietnamese, they wanted to finish us off before we might try it."

For the first time, Mohm was certain she was going to die.

A secret plan took shape. A bogus order was drawn up under the name of a former Khmer Rouge leader who supposedly wanted them back. In the deepening gloom of the burial pit, Mohm watched for signals about what to do next.

"Who told you about the plan?" I asked.

"Mom, in Cambodia then, nobody told anybody what they planned to do."

"Then how did you—"

"You hear things, you just know. The people who came with us can go with us. Fifteen people, that's it."

The trick worked. The leader released them, and no sooner had they reached the anonymity of scrub forest and started to run than they heard a sickening round of gunfire that marked the filling of the mass grave.

I shuddered. "Every time you had those narrow escapes, did you feel stronger, Mohm?"

"Yes! The more I feel—special. I began to think that life was not over, if I just kept going, someday luck will come to me. I will be important and help other people to better thinking. You know, Mom? Someday, I thought, I can talk about this."

"Just as you are doing now."

"Yes. I always wanted to survive but"—she hesitated—"I never knew. Some days I thought 'I will!' Some days, not."

She talked about the trek to the town of Mong and the next secret decision, to make a run for the border. It wasn't more than a hundred kilometers away, but the terrain was treacherous and their feet were bare. Little children cried out in pain, and old people bleached out like ancient trees until they seemed to take root in the ground, petrifying there.

"Now and then I remember something of that time," Mohm said in a whispery voice, "fire spitting out of the ground, a face floating by . . ."

"Oh, Mohm."

"You can't describe it in detail, but you know it's true, that's what happened. Sometimes it comes up and sometimes it won't."

All at once her voice became matter-of-fact, as if it were necessary to ostracize the nonsurvivors. "No one had water. A lot of people drank from bad streams, they got sick and died, and many people stepped on mines—I wasn't one of those people."

She described tossing sleeplessly as she thought about how to find safe water. The next day she came upon a trickle of water springing out of the ground. As she stood there, the spring grew stronger. She tasted it. The water was fresh. Euphoric, she searched everywhere for a container one of the fleeing soldiers might have discarded, and she found one. This incident she took as a sign.

"I kept thinking, 'Maybe God has a plan for me.' If I didn't think that way, I would have given up so many times. I kept thinking, God has done so many things to keep me going. Everybody else in my family is dead, so I have to come through."

"You began actively collaborating with God on your survival," I suggested.

"Exactly."

"But what about your aunt? She did help you escape from the Khmer Rouge and cross the minefields."

Mohm tried to convey the isolation she had felt, attached to a grasping woman and her two older daughters who were neither smart nor attractive. Once they reached the border, the same aunt set up a food stall; Mohm was passed off as her pretty daughter and expected to serve and charm the soldiers and smugglers and warlords. I imagined her, this young-old Mother Courage, scouring pots and putting on a smile and cooking for her homely non-sisters. She fell silent, as if by giving up her tongue she could turn away from this false identity and return to infancy; it was a silence that would stretch into months of muteness.

When finally they were able to cross into Thailand and found Camp 007, Mohm drank water indiscriminately until she contracted dysentery, lost her hair, and for the first time, amid the shock of brightly colored clothes and family reunions and flashing gold and greed, lost her zest for life. In the end, she ran away.

"Even though my aunt was part of my family, I wasn't welcome anyplace," she told me. "That's why I had to forget about family and love and caring, and just be, you know, how I was in the beginning last year. Remember?" She was talking now about a stranger. "I could never wish. I could not have a dream. I had so much angry inside of me, remember, Mom?"

"Yes, I remember."

"I got mad at little things, so mad I could not control it. But I could not cry. Never really cry the whole first year. Could not."

"I know."

"But now I can cry." She looked up at me and the roundness of her cheeks shone full with light. "I think it is good."

"You are good, Mohm."

"I can talk about the past with you," she said. "So many things I lost, so many mistakes I made . . ." The tears spilled down her cheeks. "I still get sad but now I can cry, because now I believe I have a new life."

"Do you think you can dare now to wish again?"

She was able now to explain what she had meant by the outburst *"No wish, never wish!"* "I meant if you want wishes to come true, you can't just sit there and wait. I have a strong feeling from my experiences that I'm the one who has to do it for myself. Nobody else can do it for me. They can help in different ways, but I have to live my future."

We made cocoa and curled up on the floor and played with wishes. She twirled them like the marshmallows melting in her cup . . . should she wish to be a writer? an actress? a model? an astronaut? . . . but these were dreams too soon and too delicate to carry much weight. And then she told me of a dream she had had several times in recent months.

"I'm in a quiet pond filled with lotus flowers and water lilies, big and pink and opening up. There's a temple nearby. I'm in a canoe with somebody, a friend, a boy I think, but nobody I can tell. He picks a beautiful lily and gives it to me. I think I know what it means."

I asked her what it meant.

"It's my new life, opening up, in America. Where I can do whatever I believe is the best to do. The pond is calm and safe and the temple is near, so I think that means God is close to me."

"You're coming out of the dark night of the past," I said. "You're coming into the sun now, Mohm. Whatever you can do, or dream you can, you are ready to begin it!"

"But I know the flower must be grown well," she added solemnly. "You can't snap it off the stem and put it on your dress just to be pretty, and not water it or care for it. No, then it will die and people will throw it out."

*

It was natural for Mohm to think that dream marked the end of her mourning. But it wasn't the end, of course. Confessions and revelations continued to spill from her over the next months, but not from the Mohm I knew, rather from a small child locked inside, a child who after her first six years had never felt happy or good.

"Always Something to Laugh"

"**E**eeyouuu—did you really eat cricket, Mom?"

The pictures from my trip to Cambodia had come back.

"The only thing that bothered me," I teased, "was the way the wings stuck out from the body."

"Hmmphh, that must be Vietnamese food," she dismissed it. I told her about the evening I dined on a riverside barge with a press officer who had worked for the Americans in Phnom Penh in the early seventies. When the waiter brought a platter of hors d'oeuvres—sautéed crab, leeches and fried crickets, my companion had urged, "Eat all, good sources of protein in Pol Pot time." Over the loudspeaker blared a lament about the recent past. . . . *If I can stay alive this one night, I can live one more day.*

Mohm wanted to know if that was the only kind of music Cambodia had now. No, there were also the new "love songs." I played her one I had taped, the one about the girl who told her unemployed sweetheart to join a solidarity rice production group.

"That's a *love* song?" Mohm rolled her eyes.

"They seem to know how to pull the strings of Cambodian people's feelings," I said.

"Whatever Vietnam knows," she said darkly, "all the Cambodian people tell. That's the problem."

I passed along an insight from the press officer. Comrade Sarsamboth, as he was now called, had studied English in Texas and was drawn toward Christianity, amazed to see how members of a church took responsibility for one another's travails.

"Buddhism taught us to pray to Buddha to lift ourselves toward individual enlightenment," he had told me. "But the Khmer people were never given any idea of how to support one another cooperatively or charitably."

"See, that's how Pol Pot got all the information!" Sarsamboth's comment had struck a chord in Mohm. "Everybody reported on everybody. . . ."

She noticed my puzzled look. "Mom, even my relatives didn't know me after my parents were taken. Maybe it's because they were afraid, who knows?"

"Since everyone was stripped of possessions and differences in status," I suggested, "they had only one thing to trade—information."

But Mohm was not ready to be forgiving. It was, after all, the central point—"People not holding together at all, not at all. I think it's a shame on people," she vowed. "It's *not* nobody's fault. If every family kept a gun and held together, we would have won that war. There weren't that many Pol Pots! If our soldiers hadn't given up we would live in peace today—" Suddenly the diatribe broke off, and her voice fell to a hush under the enormity of the indictment she had delivered. "It's a shame on all of us."

*

Shame. This is the most secret, the most painful burden of the survivor. It is a handicap greater even than guilt and quite different. Shame was, after all, the emotion that accompanied the original sin, and it is the emotion used as a weapon by many parents to inculcate toilet and social habits. Guilt is responsibility for committing some offense or failing in one's duty. Shame is more intimate, a painful emotion caused by falling beneath one's minimum standards of human behavior or status. For survivors, the memories associated with shame represent degradation, dehumanization, and the total forfeit of autonomy.

I thought of the many times Mohm had described herself as feeling like a little bug or an insect or a slave. Lakhana's poem had referred to feeling like an animal and "stinking."

Dr. Peter Neubauer, an eminent Freudian analyst who specializes in treating children and adolescents, finds it striking that patients confess their guilt with more ease than they can reveal their shame. They will explore almost anything—how they hate their parents or dream of killing those who oppose them or entertain sadomasochistic sexual wishes—but they hide as long as possible that they may have stolen a few dollars as a child. That is shame.

Those who have studied concentration camp survivors are also keenly aware of this dramatic difference in the willingness to expose guilt as opposed to shame. Such survivors have experienced a state in which every value of being human was stripped from them, destroying their self-image: "I cannot tell anybody how I was an animal, how I had no dignity, how I was nothing." It is not their guilt that makes them silent, observes Dr. Neubauer. It is their shame over what they allowed to happen. Children of victims of the Holocaust know about this silence of their parents.

Often, their parents' silent shame transmutes, in children of the Holocaust, into a numbing rage. As described by a veteran who went to fight in Vietnam expressly to prove that he too could be a survivor:

> They [his parents] don't have to tell you they're angry. You *feel* it. It's in the air. But at the age of ten, what are you going to do with that? When they talked about the family I got enraged that they were all *dead.* The fact that they were all dead, and I couldn't do *anything* about it.[1]

Surviving genocide for Cambodians—like surviving the Holocaust for Jews or their children—confers an identity but provides no continuity around which to shape a life.

*

Mohm and I sat quietly for a while. I told her that when she was older she would help her people to understand these things. It wasn't going to be easy, of course, because children like Dary were being trained so differently.

"Can I write to Dary?" Mohm wanted to know.

"Unfortunately, no. That's the problem. And she can't get outside of her country to look back at it with a broader view, as you can, and see the good and the bad."

I told Mohm how surprised I had been, after all they had lost, to see how easily people in Cambodia seemed to be able to laugh among themselves. She faced me and said something I found astonishing.

"Mom, there's *always* something to laugh."

"Well, maybe now. But certainly not in Pol Pot time, right?"

"Always. You have to laugh or you'd go crazy. So you find something to laugh, every day, every day. Especially children, they can always find something to laugh."

I asked her if she could recall a specific instance. She thought for only a moment and remembered a scene during the darkest period, when she had been sent with her group to a wilderness area where they were quartered without supervision and the children whimpered all night in fear of ghosts and wild animals. One day during their midday rest, the girls and boys were all sitting together when one young woman walked by carrying a basket on her head. She wore the black sarong with an elastic-gathered waist that all the girls had to sew for themselves.

"Suddenly a big wind came and blew her skirt up." Mohm giggled telling the story. "You could see her undies, brown shorts, the ugly brown shorts both girls and boys had to wear alike in that time—so funny! Everybody laughed at once. But I was laughing so hard, I couldn't stop. When I walked away, I thought, 'That was horrible of you, to laugh at somebody like that.' But the laughing was something I needed to get out, and it felt so fine. The wind that blew her skirt, I began to think, must come from God. God knew we needed a breath of joy. So He put a breath of joy on the wind and blew it our way."

*

The work of healing progressed rapidly for Mohm throughout that spring and summer of her second year. Summer school in Maine and especially the annual Khmer Institute gave her a welcome chance to identify with other children, both negatively and positively, and to sort out her own value system. Her ready laughter was a source of joy for everyone who met her. And of course it was reciprocal: The more she liked herself the more easily she was liked.

"When I go anywhere I learn something from other people," she expressed it. "I see all my mistakes in them, and I see what they're doing that might be good for me too; I pick out from them. I can look back and say, gee, I went through that period but I passed out of it, I made a jump."

We were talking nonstop now. In her zeal to know and test her insights, she jumped into the middle of my sentences as if onto a surfboard in mid-wave, and off she sailed onto her own next thought. And as we became partners in this daring sport of discovering Mohm, more and more freely she would throw her arms around my neck or flop down in my lap, reveling in the ease of physical affection.

That fall, driving across the Queensboro Bridge almost two years after the evening I had taken Mohm and Sarouen to the first party for foster children and their parents, Mohm let out a whoop of joy. "I can't wait for school to start!"

"Great! What's the big rush?"

"This year I feel I can belong," she said. "My English is good, I did well in summer school. I just feel right in the middle of things, not outside anymore."

"Not everybody's asked to write for the school newspaper and be on the debating team."

"You've been a mirror for me, Mom," she said, squeezing my hand. "But you know what? Now when I look in the mirror I feel I am myself, not anybody else."

*

In November, we joined for a day a Children of War tour sponsored by a task force of sixty religious groups. Twenty-six teenagers whose families had suffered deaths or disintegration by war came together to tell their stories. As they gathered in an Episcopal retreat house in New Jersey, their dreadful pasts disguised under the spiffy parkas and ubiquitous jogging shoes, they were addressed first by Peter Pond's nineteen-year-old son, Arn.

"The special thing about children may be that we are less sure we are absolutely right," he began. "Adults who are certain they are absolutely right make war over their absolute rightness."

The adults in the room, myself included, shifted uncomfortably as if a flaw in our genetic code, replicated many thousands of times, had been detected.

"Maybe children know more about our imperfections and like the chance to laugh at ourselves," Arn continued. "We don't take ourselves, our religion, our position, so seriously. And children have an ability to forgive and forget."

One by one, the young refugees related their stories, simply, without self-pity.

A sixteen-year-old refugee from Guatemala, Marvyn Perez, told about writing a letter with his friends to "officials" in Guatemala City asking for a better education. Several days later he was kidnapped.

"They take me into bathroom and ask me, 'What you want to do when you grow up?' I said, 'I want to be a doctor.' They bring my friend into the bathroom and shot him in the head and they say, 'You want to be a doctor? Take care of him.' He died."

Mohm was struck by Donal Daly, a twelve-year-old from Northern Ireland, who recited for the TV interviewer what he knew of the political "troubles" in his country. Dropped into the middle of a sentence with no particular emotional coloring was "and then they shot me Mum dead."

Touched deeply by the day, Mohm stayed up that night to write an article for her school newspaper. "Everybody in the room suffered with pain, but they knew it was worth it. These children understand about war more than anybody else. They've lost everything. Now they're strong and willing to go around the country and tell their painful stories to American teenagers, hoping that they will understand and help to make peace for the world."

The next evening, Mohm unburdened herself of many thoughts.

"I'd do anything to get out of that camp and get to a free country. Two years ago when I came to live here with you, I wasn't really ready to give any love or care for anybody yet. Especially, I wasn't really planning to have a mother or father. One side of my heart said, 'No way. I don't want to open up my heart. I'm going to lose them and get hurt again. I don't want any parents—I just want to live here and have an easy life.'

"I found out there is no way I will have an easy life without working hard. That's the first step. If you want to be the best, you have to take the hardest part first and then the easy part comes much later. But then, when I tried to open my heart and get all the anger out of it, and try to bring out the love and caring that I do have inside, I started to blame myself. For many years in my Cambodian life I didn't show any love or care to my family to make other people happy—I'm sure I didn't, but maybe I was just too young to feel anything.

"Then last night I heard all those speeches and I remembered . . . I just dreamt it over again . . . I dreamt the war was over in Cambodia and peace was coming. I felt like I could fly around—my body got so light! Then I met someone who said, 'Your mother's coming!' and I ran so fast to find her, my eyes all over everywhere. Except I have to cross the river, back from where I came. I saw her and I tried to call to her but she didn't hear me. I tried to swim to her but the river carried me back and then—" She broke off.

Feature by feature, her face ruptured into angles of anguish. She lowered her head to the table. This time, instead of rubbing her back, I covered her with my arms and coaxed her to hang on to the pain and cross to the other side. This time, she let herself sob. "I wish," she faltered, "I wish I had a last time to show my mother and father how much I loved them."

Later, incense wafted from under her door and I knew she was sitting before her Buddha in a meditation of love. But she was not finished talking. When she asked me to come in and sit on her bed, her face was as tranquil as I had ever seen it.

"It's just a dream make believing that my father is still here, that my old mother is with me. They are gone forever." Having said it, she looked relieved.

"You have come so far, angel. I'm very proud of you. When you're ready, if you go just a little farther, you can come home."

"That's been the hardest thing to decide. It took me very long to be able to feel close to you and be part of your life. But now I think I can open my heart."

For the first time, the very first occasion in two years of sharing our lives, her arms bloomed up into the night and she pulled me down to embrace me.

"I love you, Mom," she said.

The Victorious
Personality

$\mathbf{M}$y whole attitude about children and risk was changing. Whenever I put on my theorist's hat, I found myself now routinely expressing some unconventional notions:

The premise that disturbing early childhood experiences inevitably lead to a neurotic adulthood is dangerously uninformed. Children of trauma are far more resilient than has been assumed. The unique characteristic of the human brain, after all, is its plasticity—the ability to learn and change, based on new experience, altered perceptions, and flashes of insight. By exposing children to risks rather than overprotecting them, parents actually can help a child to develop that most precious of attributes—the victorious personality.

I had stumbled into the territory of survival as an outgrowth of my work in *Passages* on the predictable crises of adult life. For the book that followed, *Pathfinders*, I explored the *un*predictable crises, the life accidents we are powerless to predict or prevent, and the people who not only survive but benefit from them. In the histories of the most satisfied and successful adults I studied, I was struck by one common denominator. Most of them had endured a traumatic period during childhood or adolescence. Faced with the life accident of being born into poverty, or the loss of a parent through abandonment, divorce, or sudden death, or with an alcoholic or mentally ill parent or sibling, the children who were to become the most resilient adults leapt over childish limitations and found themselves performing—temporarily—on a level of maturity well beyond their years. Despite being dealt an inadequate parent or parents, they were able to reach out into their environment and connect with someone who became a transformative figure for them—a polestar. In some cases it was a grandparent or a teacher, in others a coach or social activist, any adult who did have purpose and direction and endorsed the young person as worthy, who offered a goal that was healing, and who helped seed the future with the hope that somehow things would get better.

Fascinated on an intellectual level, I had wanted to explore the phenomenon in greater detail. But the truest work cannot be predetermined, as in "my next project." Something has to happen, an accident, that hooks you in the gut and excites and obsesses you until you write your way out of it. That was what happened when Mohm entered my life.

Every nerve ending was alerted to the central question about life accidents. Why do they break some people, and make others into pathfinders? What is the difference between the temperament of one who succumbs to trauma and one who emerges victorious? Are the skills and defenses of the survivor learnable? Unlearnable, once the crisis has passed? Would childhood trauma be Mohm's lifelong affliction, or might it be the foundation of her rebirth as a more knowing, able, and joyful human being?

Western psychiatrists and psychologists since the 1940s have been trained to believe that childhood trauma will be echoed in an anxious or troubled adulthood. Such thinking has accumulated all the weight of superstition, even Homeric myth, so that many disgruntled adults are encouraged to look for excuses in their childhood saga for failures of will or defeats of circumstance in adulthood. We are also bombarded by popular literature reporting that alcoholism, child abuse, or teenage pregnancy are cyclical, i.e., people with those problems usually had parents who exhibited the same behavior. But because we study the small proportion whose adult lives do become blighted, we forget to acknowledge the much larger numbers of their sisters and brothers who break the cycle.

What about all the children of alcoholics who do not become alcoholics when they grow up? How shall we explain the legions of children of divorce who emerge as purposeful, stable young adults, observably better equipped to survive normal crises or life accidents *because* they have learned so much about mastering stress?[1] If the sudden death or desertion by a parent were universally devastating to a young child, how do we then explain the fact that many highly accomplished people have this experience in common?

It is my premise that a person's temperament—or characteristic frame of mind—is not fixed by the age of two or six or twenty-six, but is plastic. The introduction of sudden and disorienting change into the family or social, or political environment of a child up through early adolescence does not necessarily leave permanent scars on temperament, leading to impaired or neurotic behavior in adulthood. Quite the contrary. Stress is part of life. And learning mastery of stress is one of the basic ways by which people gain a sense of self-confidence and self-esteem. Disorders of behavior that may develop while a child or adolescent is in the midst of crisis or upheaval later commonly subside or disappear once a consistency of environment and relationships is reestablished. And the very experience of *knowing one has survived* what seemed insurmountable offers a shield of perceived invulnerability against future disasters in adult life.

*

The Cambodian children now resettled in the United States offer a fascinating study in the resilience of the human personality. All were coerced into cooperating with the forces of evil in order to survive. Either sole survivors or fugitives from families marked for death, they were raised for four years in a climate of terror and emotional apathy.

Here were children separated from all normal sources of love and guidance and exposed to the most malevolent in men and women. Most were at a stage—latency—when moral development is not yet proactive, only reactive to reward and punishment, and the overriding wish at that stage is to please figures of authority. The children of Pol Pot were rewarded if they could live with horror and show no pain or compassion.

The question they bring with them is compelling: Given a recovery period in a society that offers them safety and caring and choices, might they even surpass in achievement many American children cushioned by privilege? These young survivors have much to teach us about the victorious personality.

What happened to children under the Khmer Rouge is a textbook case in behavior control. All children, not only peasants but city children, were taken over by the government militia. Nayon Chenda, an author who escaped from Cambodia during the Khmer Rouge period and who is now a correspondent for *Far East Economic Review*, told me, "They gave the children better food. It was just like training animals. The children would do almost anything to get an egg or a whole fish." All moral standards were acquired through careful titration of reward and punishment.

Mohm herself had provided the keenest insights into how the Khmer Rouge used children as informers. "In the criticism sessions for children," I asked her once, "did they teach you not to think about your own good or privileges?"

Mohm said dryly, "You didn't have that thing."

"But they must have explained—"

"Mom, I told you a million times, communists don't explain," Mohm broke in. "You gotta do it, whatever they tell you to do. You don't say that's wrong, that's right. You don't ask questions."

"Did you begin to believe what they said?" I asked her. "That it's better for everyone to work with their hands and be the equal of a peasant? Did you believe you were becoming a better person?"

"Well, not a better person, but they want you to care about everybody, not just for people who are related to you," Mohm replied. "They think they got that feeling almost all out of our system, but I don't think people change much underneath. Even the Pol Pot children. The way they behaved was the same old way everybody always behaves, plus they didn't see what they were doing wrong."

I suggested, "You mean they thought about themselves and their families first?"

"It's not that simple, Mother." That response was one I heard more and more often now, a good sign: Mohm herself was beyond seeing things in black and white and took pains to convey the shades of gray. "They say everybody's supposed to be equal, the work time and the hair and the clothes are equal," she continued, "but of course your leader always has some favorite. It's not doing any favor to the child, the leader is only using you."

We talked about the kind of things for which the Khmer Rouge used children. The physically robust ones over twelve were sent away to do hard labor, but, being stronger, they also got more food and therefore often survived. Children between the ages of six and twelve were used for spying. Those are the ages of the latency period, developmentally speaking, when, as I have noted, children want only to please their authority figures and to be thought of as good. I asked Mohm if the Khmer Rouge told children to spy on their own families.

"The counselors don't really say straight you have to spy on others, they don't even have to ask. A lot of people did that in Pol Pot time.

That's why you can't trust anybody. Any secrets that people have they know might pop out any time."

Mohm elaborated: "When people want to use you, they can find a way into you really easily, right?" I agreed and ventured that the leader must have taken the place of parents who were either separated from their children or dead. Mohm said, "Mom, listen. I don't know how to explain to you. You have to *live* in it. It's not that they tell you, 'Okay, you have to spy on your parents.' The leader sort of does you a little favor, always talks a little nicer to you than the other children, just puts a hand on your shoulder, asks how you're doing. All they do is listen to you, let you make a little joke and fun with them. They do things that everybody needs. After a while, the children begin to feel warm and protected and happy and important."

Soun Schwartz, an adult survivor now married to an American, shed some more light on the process. She saw first cousins, even older sons and daughters, inform on their own family for the reward of a little food or medicine. But the young children were mostly unaware. Soun reiterated what other witnesses told me: "If the Khmer Rouge wanted to find out about a person, they'd take the children out and give them a treat and ask questions that appeared friendly and trivial. 'What kind of house did you live in?' 'Did your father have a gun?' Or they'd show the child a picture: 'Did your parents have a car like this?' Children naturally want to please anyone who is being nice to them." Some children were taught by their parents to resist such tricks, but for many the warnings came too late.

Can any of us say for certain that we, as children under conditions of severe deprivation, would be resistant to such manipulation and trickery?

*

Why did the Khmer Rouge focus the highest status and rewards on children? I put the question to a former Cambodian teacher from Phnom Penh who lived through the Pol Pot years and now, having renamed himself Windsong, lives in Brooklyn, New York.

"Because it is easier to make children act like communists," he replied. "We adults could never forget capitalism, no matter how hard they try to wash our brains. Therefore, adults had to be destroyed." The moral code was flipped upside down. Windsong maintained that every child who survived learned how to steal and lie; those who didn't died, a simple principle quickly grasped by those lucky enough to be over the age of six or so.

We discussed the behavior that was rewarded in children and adolescents. "The child must not talk much, unless reporting information, and always use communist vocabulary. They had to keep moving all the time, and never be sick. It should appear the child does not care about his own life. And there must be no emotion—this was an absolute principle. The child cannot cry." He continued, "But I don't think most of the children believed in the communists—I think the children just wanted food."

That recalled the revelation from Arn, when I had asked him, "Why, when you would wake up in the jungle feeling sore and sick and fevered all over and totally alone, why did you keep going?" He had said, "Eat. Had to eat. Think about eat. Walk and eat. Walk to eat."

Children coaxed to give information about adults were given no idea of the consequences, I was assured by all my interviewees. But the uncertainty and moral ambiguity made certain that every moment maintained the listless terror.

I asked the perceptive Cambodian teacher if he believed these children would be able to adapt to normal life again.

"No difficulty," said Windsong. "Not with the mind. The only problem is the heart."

*

The heart is truly a lonely hunter during trauma. Deprived of all normal sources of affection and support, what girds the victorious personality to persevere?

At the height of distress, when Mohm was running under Vietnamese bombs by day and covering herself with soil and leaves at night, she stopped once next to an old woman too weak to go on. The woman told her that God would help her, not to give up, and that if she kept going perhaps she could reach a place where she could go to school and be a normal girl. This encounter must have been an astonishing beacon. For anyone in extremity, the shattering of time collapses any literal sense of growth and purpose in life and leaves the haunting question: What good can come from merely staying alive?

"I don't know how I dared to do it all," Mohm would say later in

America, distanced and already mystified. "I don't know if I could do it now."

Of course she could if she had to again. Precisely because the survivor does not die or give up, the self with its wanton appetite for life comes upon the true innocence of itself. Mohm had registered the old woman's words as a sign of hope and run to the top of the mountain as fast as she could. By then, Mohm's resourcefulness was second nature. She found fresh springwater and a container to hold it, but these practical triumphs were accompanied by an illumination. With the transcendent clarity of vision possessed by victims at the point of committing to their own survival, Mohm awoke the next morning with a thought clear as springwater, as she had told me in one of her early revelations. " 'Stop blaming yourself. If your sister is still alive, you cannot survive. She cannot make the mountain, her feet would get blistered. You'd have to stop, you must not leave her. You'd give up.' I don't want to give up. I want to live!" By changing the perception of her situation from *I am all alone, my family is gone, what's the point of going on?* to *If I weren't alone, I might not be able to go on,* she could see some benefit in her bleak circumstances. And thus she arrived at a new idea of herself in the world: Perhaps it was her destiny to be a survivor.

Destiny or fortune is known in the Buddhist belief system as *veseana*. Good *veseana* is the consequence of one's noble actions in a previous life,* but *veseana* also refers to a person's life force. Although a person may be born with good *veseana*, it, like the grace of God, might be perpetuated only by the performance of good actions.

"Of course I have good *veseana!*" Mohm looked at me almost incredulously when I first asked about it. "Why was I not killed and all my family died? How did I come to America?"

She said that with such conviction, I suddenly grasped that survivors with her belief system have a rationale with which to answer that awful spiritual question: "Why me?" Given our Judeo-Christian ethic, survivor guilt can be a crushing burden. "Why me?" is interpreted as "How did I deserve to be spared? Why me and not my mother, my father, my sisters? Why not the rabbis, the priests? Why not the innocent children?"

* *Veseana* has a positive connotation—the Thais even combine it with the word for merit. By contrast, *karma* has a negative connotation, referring especially to the consequences of ill actions in past lives.

Finding no answer, a survivor may lose all faith in a just divinity or a just world and limp through the rest of his life as if through the minefield of pure chance. But the survivor who believes in destiny views the process quite differently. Each narrow escape, each instance of being in the right place at the right time, avoiding detection, seeing the bomb drop just behind or the mine explode just in front, eluding poisonous food or throwing off infection, increases the belief that one is endowed with a concentration of luck. As Mohm had expressed it, "The more that happened to me, the more special I felt."

The result I call *survival merit.* Like many others, Mohm had started out as a shy and passive child. Tested again and again, she developed strength, resilience, and the self-directedness to fix her sights and chart her course without dependence on outside forces, indeed, often in spite of them. As she became virtually invulnerable, she perceived herself as invulnerable. She described how "I used a lot of my power," eventually warning the Pol Pot children that if they gave her trouble she could summon God to punish them.

Once safe, Mohm was able gradually to cast off survival guilt by seeing the miracle of her survival as indicating merit.

"For a period of time you feel very guilty," Mohm elaborated, "but then I realized that if I stay unhappy and feeling guilty it won't do any good for anyone. I begin to see the other side. If I'm the only one in the family alive, probably God had some purpose I was saved for." She added, "It's really helped me to see things that way, Mom."

Now I understood what Mohm meant when she had told me driving home from camp the previous summer, "I know I must learn for myself first, then I can do good acts for others." Mohm believed she had been spared for a reason. How else to explain the grotesque unfairness and stunning luck of it, if not by some divine intervention that concentrates a supernatural life force in certain individuals? But in order to continue to be blessed with good luck, she had to give back; it was rather like a savings account—to maintain the good fortune she had to make regular deposits through acts of merit.

Survivor merit is obviously a more healing concept than survivor guilt. In a discussion with me, Erik Erikson, the authoritative and creative theorist of the life cycle, agreed that culture determines which interpretation will predominate.[2] "In India, guilt is a less important concept," Erikson said. "What is important is to fulfill your *dharma,* or the existential identity set for you in this life, so you can move higher in the next life." The notion of survival merit, he reminded me, is not exclusive to Asians.

Reflections by twenty-eight French-Jewish men and women, hidden as children with Christian families, were collected by Claudine Vegh in her excellent book, *I Didn't Say Goodbye.*[3] In her introduction Miss Vegh expresses a common theme:

> Having escaped persecution by the Nazis, I have always had the impression that life has been "granted" to me a second time. And so I had to show that I deserved that life, that I was worthy to live it. It was no longer even mine: I was living, in a way, by proxy.

A number of therapists agree that the concept of survivor merit can be powerfully healing. Cecily Stranahan, a pastoral psychotherapist on eastern Long Island, said of her patients who perceive themselves proudly as survivors: "The crux of it is they act as though 'I have a secret'—something they know about the world that shields them. It's often linked with the conviction that they have some work to do in the world, a purpose they must discern."

*

The sense of oneself as special, as capable of triumphing over major adversity, has been a generating force for some of the finest minds in Western history.

Freud, whose mother idolized him as "my golden Siggy," was convinced as a boy that despite the handicap of being Jewish in the anti-Semitic Viennese society, it was his destiny to follow Darwin into history. Isaac Newton was a drastically premature baby, at a time in history when seven out of every ten premature infants died. But he was born on Christmas day, and some offer the hypothesis that his parents must have said to him, "Isaac, having been born on the Lord's day and having lived, when no one thought you would, you are very special."

The term "victorious child" originated with Erikson in his work on Albert Einstein. "My parents were worried because I started to talk comparatively late . . . certainly not younger than three," wrote Einstein. His teachers and family servants called him stupid and lazy, reports Erikson in his insightful paper.[4] Even at the age of nine, Einstein often chose not to speak or communicate, and he later failed his entrance examination to university. But he resisted being "broken" by enforced instruction or giving up because according to social norms he was a failure. Like many who are victorious despite disconfirming experiences, Einstein looked around the dim world by his own match. His parents eventually supported his differentness, and he was "fed" in early adolescence by a medical student (a figure I would call a polestar) who recognized the young Einstein's "exceptional intelligence" and affirmed it. He also maintained sense of wonder and playfulness, and an outgoing attitude that gave others the impression of an entertaining and vital person.

*

The foundation of all adult development is said by Erikson to be basic trust, first established through the relationship of child with mother and later transferred to the world at large.[5] But for children betrayed by virtually all they have been taught to trust, what can be the root of hope?

Child survivors are confronted early with the paradoxical nature of human beings: the fact, as Ernest Becker elucidates it in *The Denial of Death*, that man is split between an animal and a symbolic nature.[6] He is aware of his own splendid uniqueness and the brain that allows him to tower over the natural world, yet he also knows he is part animal. Many humans try to deny it. Survivors of extremity, however, must return to their creature nature and rely on it, acting and moving much of the time by instinct. As a result, they may develop an extraordinary self-trust.

The awareness of their peculiar majesty as human beings naturally suffers in the process. I think of Mohm when she at last found her way into a refugee camp and was issued her first possession: a plastic mirror. Her sense of disintegration was so nearly complete, she would not look at herself; she had for so long moved collectively as one among many worker drones, unidentified by sex, she could not remember whether she was a boy or a girl.

But if and when benevolent circumstances are restored, the extraordinary self-trust developed while in danger can be affirmed at every stage as one builds a new life. For Mohm, that self-knowledge, together with the sense of herself as victorious, becomes more evident every day in her commitment to excellence in work and compassion and service to others. Ultimately, to merit your own survival means being ready to allow the spirit of love to work through you.

*

A natural question—is the victorious personality inborn, or can one develop it? The answer is, both.

One quality of temperament any parent can observe in an infant's first year is the susceptibility to arousal or anxiety under stress. Children differ markedly in this regard.

About 10 percent of children, maintains Jerome Kagan, the Harvard developmental psychologist who has conducted research into the study of temperament, are born with the tendency to be shy, vigilant, fearful, easily upset by the face of a stranger or a change in feeding or sleeping routines.[7] At the other end of the spectrum, 10 percent are born with a sociable, effervescent, spontaneous temperament and are usually intrigued by a change in routine or a new face. As they grow, these "easy children" continue to show less vulnerability to stress, and in the first days of nursery school or when there is a change in caretakers, "they keep on laughing."

But all inborn temperaments—particularly those of the 80 percent who fall between the naturally anxious and the naturally resilient—can be influenced strongly during times of stress by the way their parents perceive, and react to, such events. In a group of two- to six-year-olds Kagan has been studying in the Boston area, one third of those born with an anxious temperament are becoming less so, largely because their parents are encouraging them to be less afraid.

Except for that 10 percent born with a biological susceptibility to arousal or anxiety under stress, children who are taught to "tough it out," Kagan agreed, may learn to profit by trauma. "What then does trauma *do* for you? It causes you to reflect and try to understand—and that facilitates growth." I would go further, from my research with pathfinders and survivors, and predict that it will enable the person to handle later life accidents more calmly and effectively.

Recently published birth-to-maturity studies offer a stunning contradiction to the old premise that emotionally traumatized children are doomed and parents' early mistakes are irrevocable.

In a group of 133 middle- and upper-middle-class children born in New York the same year, whose childhood struggles were with parental conflict, death, divorce, or dangerously rigid demands, almost half did develop significant emotional problems in adjustment at some point in their early years. But by their mid-twenties, only six of that subgroup were in worse shape, while the others with early adjustment problems had developed some psychological immunity and were functioning as healthily and happily as those who had experienced no trauma in child-hood.[8]

Among the youngsters in the New York Longitudinal Study conducted by the husband-and-wife team of Alexander Thomas and Stella Chess, the death of a parent did not exert a negative effect over the long run (a finding with profound meaning for the many Americans who today postpone childbearing or begin second families in middle or late life). Nor was divorce predictive of continuing emotional adjustment problems; on the contrary, many of the children in divorced families developed mature coping mechanisms early. The more tenacious problems were caused by constant parental quarreling, which presented the child with double messages about how to be good, or a mismatch between a parent's demands and a child's temperament or abilities.

One young man, evaluated at the age of twenty-five, was self-assured, happily married, and launched on a brilliant scientific career. His father had been so hypercritical of him throughout his childhood and adolescence that Dr. Thomas had thought the youngster didn't have a chance.

"How did you do it?" Dr. Thomas asked.

The young man said he began to get better when he went away to college, but when he was home on vacation, his father had started attacking him unmercifully again. By then, the young man knew that if he didn't get away from his father, he was lost. He gave his father a reasonable choice: either stop criticizing and they could be good friends, or they would be merely casual friends. The father could not stop. So the young man kept a distance that enabled him to function healthily.

The reader might well ask at this point, are we talking only about middle-class and white children? (Dr. Kagan's research is limited to white children.) The conventional wisdom is that below a certain level on the socioeconomic ladder, particularly for black Americans, barriers to escape are almost insuperable. Evidence is accumulating to the contrary: that even among these groups, trauma, although it doesn't help, does not inevitably destroy.

Another longitudinal study followed the lives of inner-city children, both black and white, whose impoverished and chaotic childhoods would call forth the standard label "underclass," and compared them with children in "stable" working-class families.[9] From a total sample of 456 junior high school students in Boston, the two groups were followed from the age of fourteen to forty-seven. Individuals were compared by social class and income level attained, physical health maintained, and by the number of adult years employed, sociopathic symptoms, and months in jail. By middle life, the children of the chronically poor and multiproblem families were almost indistinguishable from those without such initial disadvantages. The only significant difference was that the men from impoverished backgrounds had spent more time in jail.

Chronic poverty and unfavorable family conditions "do not necessarily prevent the *majority* [emphasis mine] of the next generation from attaining by midlife the same levels of occupational success and psychological well-being achieved by the children of the more stable and steadily employed working class," conclude the authors, Dr. George Vaillant, Raymond Sobel Professor of Psychiatry at Dartmouth Medical School, and his colleague Jancis V. F. Long, Ph.D.

Twenty-six black men and women who "beat the odds" are the subject of an important study by Dr. Edmund W. Gordon, a professor of psychology and Afro-American studies at Yale University, and Dr. Ronald L. Braithwaite. These subjects were at high risk of failure, starting into adulthood from the lowest income status, yet they defied the negative predictions. Perhaps they belong to that 10 percent who are, by nature, more resilient. Managing to acquire good educations, they turned their competence into career success, and as adults live and work enthusiastically and effectively with all those around them. What did they have in common? Dr. Gordon kindly summarized for me the conclusions of his book *Success Against the Odds*, to be published by Howard University Press in autumn, 1986:[10]

Defiers of negative prediction are highly self-directed. They have the capacity to set goals without depending on, or sometimes in spite of, the push and pull of others. But autonomous effort alone is not enough. To overcome the odds, a strong relationship with another person who acts as a model, a provider, or a mentor is essential. For these subjects the role was filled by parents, teachers, guidance counselors, ministers, or peers. The capacity to defy negative prediction also depended on the individual's outlook: If he or she believed that change was not only possible but also rewarding, that became the source of a sense of power. (This is another variation on the self-fulfilling prophecy I have called "survivor merit.") Anger, rather than acting as a depressant on their development, buoyed their resistance. Some of the subjects spoke of "showing them that they are wrong" or "proving that I am as good as they are." As important as it was to believe in oneself, it was also sustaining to believe in a religious ideal that goes beyond self. More than half of those who beat the odds held to their faith, despite disconfirming experiences.

After decades of studying pathology in children, one of the nation's most esteemed child psychiatrists, Dr. Robert Coles, has also come around to a new emphasis on how children from the least promising of backgrounds often emerge as brave, thoughtful, and compassionate people. In his most recent book, *The Moral Life of Children*, he presents a portrait of Ruby, a six-year-old black girl pitted against the fearsome odds of desegregating the schools in New Orleans.[11] Day after day for months this child, the daughter of sharecroppers, walked through murderously heckling mobs to attend a school boycotted by white parents, all by herself. Yet she showed no signs of psychological wear and tear. Dr. Coles cast about for explanations within the canons of classical (white, European) psychoanalytic theory: Was it denial? Reaction formation? Or some other neurotic defense mechanism? Then he uncovered some new information about Ruby:

A woman spat at Ruby but missed; Ruby smiled at her. A man shook his fist at her; Ruby smiled at him. Then she walked up the stairs, and she stopped and turned and smiled one more time! You know what she told one of the marshals? She told him she prays for those people, the ones in that mob, every night before she goes to sleep!

Presumably Ruby, like Mohm, as she perceived herself to be unassailable, became unassailable. At the age of six she so impressed a teenage white redneck heckler with her implacable courage, he joined her side.

In attempting to explain the courage under fire of so many black Americans who had so few prospects, Dr. Coles began to see a strength accorded far too little significance by many white observers, one pointed out by Dr. Gordon in his study—the religious tradition of black people. Dr. Coles reports on the literal identification with Christ he found in many homes, where young children were taught to regard themselves as "anointed ones, of sorts: those who will lead their people to a better fate."

*

As interest gathers around the study of individuals who function optimally in the face of adversity, they are often referred to as "invulnerables." Dealt disadvantageous beginnings and/or confronted as children with stressful life events, invulnerables become galvanized to turn rags and bones of opportunity into the silk of achievement and equanimity.

The term "invulnerable child" was coined in 1971 by Norman Garmazy, a professor of psychology at the University of Minnesota who holds a lifetime research award from the National Institute of Mental Health.[12] Garmazy has focused on abysmally poor or neglected children who have prospered emotionally. His work has been extended by Dr. E. James Anthony, a British-born psychiatrist who worked with Jean Piaget and who is professor of child psychiatry and director of the Edison Child Development Research Center at Washington University Medical School in St. Louis.[13]

Between 8 and 10 percent of the hundreds of children born to schizophrenic parents and studied by Dr. Anthony for over a decade appear to be invulnerables. They probably correspond to the 10 percent Professor Kagan cites as born temperamentally resistant to stress. Between Anthony and Garmazy, a number of qualities emerge as characterizing invulnerable children. The same qualities are usually apparent in what I call "the victorious personality" and in what Dr. Gordon refers to as "defiers of negative prediction."

*

Resourcefulness: They seem to know how to make something out of nothing. A girl of eight, for example, whose father had died and whose mother was so severely depressed she could not make her daughter lunch, invented the name "bread sandwiches" to dignify the meager fare she made for herself to take to school.

Social ease and savvy: They are adept at attracting and using adult support, and as a result, invulnerable children gain early a sense of their own power. They know how to make others feel comfortable. That recalls the observation of social workers, noted earlier, who visit a chaotic home but know, when one child comes forward to offer the visitor lemonade, that he or she is a natural survivor.

Curiosity: Whether it means learning about their parent's alcoholism or mental illness, or the tricks of their enemies, invulnerable children become knowledgeable about the nature of the crisis around them. Knowledge increases their sense of mastery.

Compassion—but with detachment: One boy with a psychotic father and an irrational mother retreated into the basement with his stereo and books and set up a refuge. Asked by Dr. Anthony why he went there, the boy was direct and clinical in his answer. He understood why his parents screamed and he didn't complain, but he also knew he had to get away from them. A child who identifies too closely with a sick or neurotic parent is not an invulnerable, according to Anthony. Detachment allows the child to build up a psychological immunity to long-term distress.

Ability to conceptualize: The invulnerable child eventually comprehends the experience not only as a personal travail but also as a phenomenon. This is the crucial mental leap—"I'm not the only one!"—that releases him from feeling like a loser, allows for intellectual distance and possibly creative interpretation, and may spur him to be a guide for others similarly burdened.

Some of the invulnerable children studied by Dr. Anthony became exceptionally creative and original, expressing symbolically in sculpture, painting, essays, or short stories the turmoil they had witnessed.

"Vulnerability and invulnerability are states of mind induced in the child by exposure to risks," asserts Dr. Anthony.[14] Mastery of one such experience usually leads the child to test himself again, asserting himself against ever greater odds.

If there is such a thing as an invulnerable child, every parent would like to know how to produce one. The work of Garmazy and Anthony offers some clues and echoes the work of Kagan.

Parents of invulnerable children are not less protective but *less anxious* than average parents. They are more likely to leave the charting of his course to the child himself, even if it means taxing his maturity. Such parents are not less loving, but they are less possessive, than the average. They are more willing to allow the youngster his own territory within which he can operate with a degree of autonomy. And such parents do not demand conformity.

*

In summary, development is far more fluid than was previously thought. It does not even have to be sequential. Although all children pass through the same behavioral stages, learning one ability does not depend on having learned another ability first.[15] "All children crawl before they stand, but a child would stand at about one year of age, even though he was prevented from crawling," writes Professor Kagan. By the same token, if a life accident prevented a child from learning to read until he or she was, say, ten years old, as in Mohm's case, there is no interference in the development of reasoning ability. The new ability requires only maturation of the central nervous system and the experience of living.

Research data is accumulating to confirm that many children who suffer deep pain or emotional trauma grow toward stability in adulthood. The work of Thomas and Chess in the New York Longitudinal Study, the findings of Long and Vaillant in birth-to-maturity studies among the underclass, and Braithwaite and Gordon's "defiers of negative prediction," together with the recovery experiences of Cambodian survivors recorded in this book, suggest that the Freudian and Piagetian models of development are too narrow and deterministic.

In fact, Freudian child-development specialists too are changing their emphasis. The greatest weight in determining mental health used to be placed on the severity of external events experienced by a young child. "Today," says psychoanalyst Dr. Peter Neubauer, "one adds the internal component, which is the degree of vulnerability due to one's congenital makeup." More broadly, psychological development could be said to be constantly dynamic, depending on the interplay of a person's temperament, accumulated external experiences, and on the nature of society in that particular historical period.

It is even becoming respectable to suggest that children may need challenges and high-risk conditions in order to develop the self-generated immunity to trauma that characterizes survivors. To be tested is good. The challenged life may be the best therapist.

The new studies also affirm my observations on the importance of a "polestar." Resilient children are usually said to have a knack for turning to friends, teachers, or religious guides for the help they cannot find in their own families.[16]

*

A survivor must of course develop specialized defenses in order to be victorious against seemingly overwhelming odds. Plasticity—the ability to bend into the shape or form demanded by circumstance but without forfeiting an inner conviction of a reason for being—appears to be the paramount defense. Intuition is vital because moments of choice come seldom and abruptly, and the survivor must rely on intuition to make immediate character judgments and decisions. A private or family myth that allows one to feel superior to one's tormentors is a useful psychological defense. And the ability to fantasize offers great solace. (Belief in her past life as a member of nobility, and her flights of fantasy back to that life, provided Mohm with an incalculably powerful shield against the shame of being degraded to a slave.) Mind control, or the ability to suppress emotions, is an important skill for any survivor. But for a long-term survivor it is vital to maintain some secret inner life. Humor and a sense of the ridiculous allow for that startling, sometimes comic force that renews the zest for life even in the darkest times. These are the most potent weapons I have noted among young refugees exposed to prolonged trauma. Many of the same defenses have been cited in the psychological evaluations of American prisoners of war and hostages who endured their ordeals most effectively.[17]

*

The fact that survivor defenses must be surrendered or moderated once benign circumstances are restored is far more easily said than done. The sarongs I brought to Mohm from Cambodia carried her back to an idealized time in her early childhood. But the need to make gods of her parents gave some evidence of subsiding, and that seemed to me healthy. A discrete but decisive part of the work of healing was now underway.

Mohm had already removed many of the masks of the survivor she had worn. But she had never, literally or psychologically, faced her father. That moment, if it ever came, would raise all the questions.

Was the father "good" or "bad"? Was the collective father, or her country, good or bad? Was the divinity entrusted with her ultimate faith one whose benevolence still could be believed?

These were the tests that lay ahead for Mohm. As we drew closer to her, and she gathered the courage to face those tests and to feel again, way led on to way until we all were able to return home—but a return with a difference.

Coming Home

Clay tried to say it in his toast at our wedding that winter: "I feel in a sense that we have given birth to this child, together. In some mystical way, Mohm has been a joy to Gail and me, and to Maura. She's brought us love and wonder and . . ." but there was no ready phrase to describe the calm that had settled over our stormy relationship, no demonstrable proof that Mohm had been the catalyst. Yet we both knew, knew it every time we were tickled by picking out a museum or a movie we could all enjoy together, every time we didn't argue because it would be upsetting to her. The need to listen to Mohm with every sense attuned had taught us both to take the time to listen to each other, and accept our differentness. With Maura gone, we might both have withdrawn into habits of ambition and self-absorption. With the coming of Mohm something much larger had been falling into place, something both compelling and centering that all four of us had needed far more than we had let on—the commitment of family.

I had a hunch something was up when we'd walked into Clay's apartment at the end of Labor Day weekend and the place was an excavation pit. He mumbled, as he had been doing for several months, about creating a new room, closets, a family dining area . . . *family?* Shortly thereafter, Clay made a business trip to London. Mutual friends telephoned me to say, "Clay's over here talking about linens. Is there something you want to tell us?"

What I knew nothing about was the daughter-housekeeper cabal that had set it all in motion. Maura had stayed up half the night with Iris, Clay's devoted housekeeper, the two of them dissecting our relationship and coming to the unassailable conclusion that we would both be better off—and a lot less bother—married. They mapped out a campaign. Maura, who was working as an intern at Clay's publication, took him out to lunch for long soulful talks, and in the mornings before he was fully awake, Iris would blow smoke in his ears . . . "Mr. Felker, it's time you get married to Miss Gail."

I told Mohm in an unplanned almost casual way that Clay had asked me to marry him.

"Oh." She sounded surprised. "Do we have to move, then?"

"Yes, but Clay is making more room in his apartment. And you'll have a wonderful room of your own."

"Sounds like fun." A beat. "Can the dogs come, too?"

That was all she said. The momentous announcement was accepted with such a light touch and look of delight, and so soon and effusively did she enter into the selection of wallpapers and planning of her bridesmaid's dress, I thought it was just further evidence of Mohm's equanimity. But in the last weeks of preparations her hair began to fall out. The nosebleeds returned. Maura urged me to calm her down by explaining to Mohm in detail what our new day-to-day routine would be like, which I did one night at a Thai restaurant.

Maura choked up. Her best friend mooned, "Wow, I'd love to move in."

But for Mohm, my talk was about as enthralling as a lecture from her old *Me-krum*. She couldn't know how she would feel until it happened.

*

We were married at home in a candlelight ceremony, the mantel laden with lilies, lighted wreaths at the windows. Surrounded by old friends whose presence sealed our vows, while they renewed their own, Clay and I could scarcely keep our eyes off the two girls who stood to one side of the fireplace altar. They were two graces, one from the West with her delicate pearl skin and demure lowered eyes, one from the East serene and glossily golden as a sandalwood candle: our daughters.

After the ceremony, the living room was transformed into a banquet hall and the string quartet was whisked away to be replaced with a dance band. Maura made an eloquent speech, Clay celebrated the joys of family life, but it was Mohm who brought everyone to the emotional edge. People choked up when she spoke, not with sentimental tears, not with state-occasion tears of the sort summoned by hortatory statements about genocide or holocausts or the six million, but with tears of recognition for the struggle we all share to continue believing, despite all the abandoned and annihilated children of the earth, that the child who survives is one more angel sent as a sign of hope. Light leapt in the mirrors that night. Laughter was as quick to pour as the tears. It was, simply, magic.

*

Not long after we had settled into our new home, Clay and I came in late one night and apologized to Mohm for not being there sooner to tuck her in. She was ensconced in a fancifully carved wood fourposter that Clay and I had once bought in Bath, England, having no idea what for; Mohm had claimed it as her favorite bed in the world. She pretended to be asleep until I bent to kiss her. Then she tossed a lace pillow at my head.

"Hey, you don't act like a neglected child."

"I don't mind being home alone anymore," she said with a simple shrug. "I'm not even afraid of ghosts now."

"Not afraid of ghosts, Mohm!"

"Well, maybe of a certain witch . . . with red hair," she said playfully. I tossed the pillow back at her.

"Know what, Mom?" The revelation that came out then, had I fished for it, might have sounded like a homily offered because she thought I wanted to hear it. But the way she strung together the words, they were as simple and true as waking up on a fine morning. "I've begun to see it's not a ghost I was afraid of before—" Mohm said, "the real thing was, I was terrified of not having somebody else close to me, somebody to hold on to and know that they are there."

Unmasking the Face
of Survival

Floating along a California freeway toward Long Beach four months later in a rented car:

"What's unique about your mother," Clay was saying, "is she went to Thailand and she found you."

Mohm then asked me an uncharacteristically direct question: "When you interviewed me, did you know your goal was to find a daughter?"

"In my heart, yes," I admitted, "but not in my head."

"Gail interviewed many children," Clay said. "But she fell in love with you."

"Somehow," Mohm said softly, "I think it was meant to be that we get together."

*

It was a milestone in many ways, this trip into the heart of the largest Cambodian community in America to celebrate Khmer New Year. The centerpiece of festivities that year was continuous showings of the film *The Killing Fields*. I was struck by the relief the movie engendered in the Cambodian audience. Seeing their personal hells rendered gigantic on the screen and their suffering as ubiquitous seemed to remove some of the personal horror and shame. They were also hopeful that the film might alert Americans who knew next to nothing about Cambodia. Most Cambodians, I discovered, having lived through genocide, had a real missionary feeling about alerting others to how easily it could happen again. They were eager to share their most personal experiences with Mohm and me.

At a picnic celebration in El Dorado park, we were welcomed into the California-ized Cambodian community. It was wonderful to see healthy teenagers playing tag, the girls with their short permed hair bouncing, the boys with neat white shirts and braces on their teeth. It delighted us to be looked at directly, unshyly, by grinning toddlers who wanted to show off blue and white sailor suits or chew on footballs or plastic pocketbooks—the new generation of unscathed Cambodian-Americans. Mohm proudly introduced us around. We shared a picnic of cellophane noodles and egg rolls with a group of animated Cambodian women and their American husbands.

Eugene Schwartz, a carpenter, leaned over to indicate that the beautiful woman sitting on our picnic blanket, so demure in her white dress and high heels, had lost all her family, escaped from a Vietnamese prison, and was now his wife. She had written a diary of her saga, he said, and would like to show it to me.

That night, we visited the Schwartz family in their home in North Long Beach. It was a mixed neighborhood of blacks and whites, Hispanics and Cambodians, living close together in small stucco and wood houses. Soun seated us in her tiny kitchenette and brought out the precious diary. Although she knew five languages, Soun's English was not facile enough to convey the full intensity of emotion locked in the beautiful Khmer script.

"Can you translate Soun's diary for me, Mohm?" I asked her.

"I'll try." It was the first of several intense collaborations between Mohm and me on interviews, which I'm certain unlocked and shed light on many of her own memories.

Soun had fled across the border near O Chrau where Mohm had crossed. After several hours of interpreting the diary, Mohm attempted to translate a poem of Soun's, "The Adventure." One verse struck us both.

> I am woman
> but my soul and my
> strength is a man's.
> Many people look down on me.
> I am disappointed
> by all I have lost,
> my husband, my child.
> In my lifetime I pray
> not to be afraid,

and that in future
I will meet only
people of good heart.

I observed that, like Mohm, Soun seemed to have gained through her experiences a remarkable self-trust and self-respect.

Mohm translated Soun's response. "She says that in normal times, if nobody had invaded the country, she would have been shy and fearful, just somebody's housewife. She wouldn't have known her own strength, that she could be as tough as a man."

Soun's husband set a bowl of strawberries in front of his wife and said tenderly, "She's going to have our child in another four months."

Afterward, on the freeway, Mohm expressed the view that because Cambodian survivors who had made it to this country had learned so much about life, it was important they use their experience to benefit others.

"It's only in the past year and half that I feel confident and proud and I want to make something useful of my life—to alter myself from what I've learned. Before that," she added, "I was sort of denying what I am."

"What?" It startled me to hear the psychiatric terminology.

"I was denying what I am because of the pain. Instead of accepting the truth, I was trying to pretend that my past was all happy time and my parents died because of some other reason. It's not facing reality. But if I wrote in my diary now, it would be so clear."

"Well, honey, don't criticize yourself for not doing it sooner."

But Mohm was adamant. "I want to find out the truth and accept it for what it is. It's not the happy times, but the lessons of life that I should remember."

"It's possible to put together a shiny new outer life," I said, "but it's probably not possible to feel comfortable in your own skin—*sok sabai* —until you accept the reality of what has gone before."

"Exactly," Mohn said. She began to talk about dreams. "Dreams helped me a lot last year," she said softly, "thinking about what I've been through. I thought for a long time I couldn't live with my dreams, but I couldn't live without them."

I had introduced the concept of "fantasy." She was intensely interested that there was a word for the imagination that allowed one to invent another world, another set of parents, and to put some distance between oneself and the literal reality. The fragments of memory that would not fit together for Mohm over the last year, that she had not wanted to fit together for fear they might form a pattern that would bind her to the shame of Cambodia's past, I'd thought perhaps could find expression indirectly, through the imagination. It was as though she had read my mind.

"I think I want to write a story," she said. And having set that task as a way of mastering her past, she snapped back to the microcosmic world of our little family in a rented car and the reality of maps.

"Mom, you missed the exit to Westwood!"

*

I had not yet looked the survivor full in the face. Not even after two and a half years with Mohm—why? I must have been relying still on the protective filter of humanistic philosophy. We humanists insist upon seeing some good in our enemies or dismissing their behavior as psychopathic. I did not want that comforting belief stripped away, but there was no means to enter Mohm's deepest experiences without setting it aside. Mohm had accepted that one's enemies can be freely evil and not mad.

One day Mohm and I were looking through a portfolio of paintings by Leon Golub, an artist who paints North and South American revolutionaries and mercenaries and interrogators engaged in casual violence. One print showed adolescent boys torturing a naked man tied to a chair. I explained to Mohm that the artist's intention was to show the nervous intoxication that overtakes some young men when they see others go even beyond killing.

"The dominant feeling of having control over someone is a great feeling to have," she commented with utter equanimity.

"You're saying that any one of us might run along with the pack if—"

"If we believe in the excuse they use," she finished.

"That's the sense I get when I see pictures of the Khmer Rouge guards," I said. "They look completely comfortable with themselves."

"Of course they were." Mohm shrugged. "They didn't think they were doing anything terrible. They don't see it that way." She reminded me of Pol Pot's incessant smile.

No matter how many torturers and despots we read about who go home to kiss their wives and caress the cheeks of their children and who are described by their intimates as kindly family men, not pathological sadists, we cannot—or we don't want to—accept this as the rule and not the rare exception.

"The Khmer Rouge man you lived with," I heard myself ask, "was he affectionate at home with his family?"

"Yes. He was." She went on speaking in a nonjudgmental tone. "I don't think they see themselves as being cruel. They think of themselves as being very tough and absolutely right. They believe just like" —she wasn't sure if she should say this, but went ahead—"just like President Reagan speaks as the father of the country; he thinks he's doing only great things for America. They believed they were making a better society for everyone."

"But the actual torturing and killing of their own people . . ."

"Mom, when you torture your enemy, that just means you're getting back. That's why Pol Pot used young people, teenagers, to control all those older people. Because young people like to put the whole world in their own pocket. And when children believe something, it becomes totally their goal. To be able to walk around and have everybody terrified of you—Mom, doesn't everybody like to feel dominant?"

As Mohm led me toward a synthesis of my naïve ideas on the subject of violence, I tried to find more creative outlets for her anger. Conversations like that one allowed her the grateful detachment of the researcher. But her natural gifts were as a storyteller. She had tried poetry, essays, short stories; she was ready now to attempt a novella. To write about Cambodia was too direct. Searching for another country and a different period of history, Mohm interviewed Clay and me for several hours about Russia and World War II. The result was a stunningly revealing piece of work, excerpts from which are reprinted here with Mohm's permission.

A sweet smile in front of my face, what did he think he was to put a million people to death? Was I supposed to be happy, when he picked me as his favorite? That smile! Made me sick; I knew what was behind that smile: hate and slavery.

Yes, he spoke the truth! The truth, which not many can see deep down in his mysterious mind, that changes the good to bad, the empire to slavery.

I could taste the pain in everyone's eyes; if I could bring back the ones they've lost, I would!

I could feel the pain in each child, the pain that cried out for help. Did he care? Could he feel?

I was just a little girl then, and I could feel it, those millions of children could feel it.

Why couldn't he see, or feel? He had a human body, that could eat, sleep and cry like any other.

When I was a little girl, I used to think that anybody who could take another human life was not human, it must be some kind of creature that had come to earth and taken human form, but deep down in its heart was still animal.

I found myself standing there, waiting for him to change to another form. For the first time in my life I realized that a human being could be as evil as any other animal.

"Dreams and fantasies we all have, but some dreams and fantasies lead you out of this world, until you cannot find your way back."

Signed, Your secret admirer. P.S. Look to your right.

I turned to my right and there was the same sweet guy who had been writing notes and leaving them in my door for the last few months. I put the letter in my pocket and ignored him.

The meeting was over, and I was sent to Moscow. The job was a lot better, I didn't have to work fifteen hours a day, and I was able to have good food and a place to stay. But could I face him? What would I say to him? It was he whom I despised more than anything else in this world.

I remember one day, when I sat down near a red river full of innocent blood, with his name drawn in it. Every step, it was death, death had turned the country upside down. But it was death that made me strong; it was the love of those who died that gave me strength.

I was one of the innocent, now I'm part of the people whom I despise. I'm the one who put death on those innocent people, who I knew only by their names, but not their physical appearance, nor what crime they had committed. Every day, in the Moscow office where I work, new names are added to the blacklist. And I pick the names.

So many times I look in the mirror and see myself as one of them, cold-blooded murderer.

Three days later I was asked to see Comrade Vassilov, leader of the country. When I got there my legs were shaking like little trees when the wind blows hard; I didn't dare to look at his face. Then he asked me to sit down. My legs shook even harder; I was about to get down on my knees and beg him for forgiveness, but I didn't know what I had done wrong, so I tried to stay calm as I could.

I expected his big voice to scream at me, but instead there was only a soft and sweet voice.

"Don't be afraid, I just wanted to know a little bit about your background," he said.

I wasn't sure what was going on but I knew that something must be wrong. So I tried to convince him that I didn't remember anything about my family background, which I didn't really know much about anyway.

This time my legs stopped shaking, but I felt hot, my face burned almost like fire. I felt suddenly a pull toward him, this man I so despised. I wanted to ask him if I could go. When I was about to open my mouth, he said, with that sweet smile on his face, as though something extraordinary had happened, "It's all right, you can go now, but if you remember anything come here and tell me."

As I reached the door and was about to open it, a voice behind me said, "Would you turn around one more time?"

I turned around; he looked straight at my face and again he gave me a big smile. I could feel the excitement inside him bursting out.

I didn't know what made him so happy, but I'm glad that it was nothing I did wrong.

Two years later I was sent to see the head of the working field. He showed me around and told me the rules. I was glad to be with people again, even though I had to work like everybody else.

The whole group was about two hundred people, working together without a word or any reaction toward each other. The first thought I had was that they probably had been brainwashed.

Later, I found out that you can force humans to do anything, but you cannot wash away their feelings for one another.

The place was full of soft whispering from ear to ear, people leaning over like baby birds stumbling on each other as they try to get under their mothers to be warm and safe once again. There were activities after work, but I wasn't included in them.

Some thought that I was dangerous, some that I was a spy. No one dared say anything to me. It was the first time I feel people afraid of me.

There was nothing but hate. Brother against brother, husband against wife, friends against friends.

What was the glory of life? When there is no love or trust?

Some saw my way of life as glorious; I ate anything I wanted, I could go anywhere I wanted.

People wanted to live in fantasy and dreams that would take them away from reality. We lived in the dark and the coldness of winter, but in their fantasies it was the beginning of spring, where everything is white, yellow tulips, and forsythia opening to collect the morning dew.

I remember very little of my grandfather, but his last words I can never forget. "Reality could be a dream, but dreams can never be reality. Dreams are inconstant as the wind; if you aren't careful, they will carry you away further and further, then no one can help you, not even yourself."

In the next chapter of Mohm's story, Natasha falls in love with her secret admirer, Sergei, who turns out to be a revolutionary planning to overthrow the Vassilov regime.

I agreed to help Sergei. Later that night we had a meeting, and I realized what I was getting into: the whole town was involved in it, plus another two or three towns. Sergei introduced me and I told them that I had an idea to get more men to fight. . . .

Three months later, everything was ready as planned. We had enough weapons and men to take over Moscow. Mr. Kloshnikov (the head of the town), Sergei and I went to lunch to celebrate our first movement.

"Here's to us and the armies," Sergei toasted.

As I picked up my glass, a car stopped in front of the restaurant and a man walked toward our table.

"You must be Miss Natasha."

"Yes, I am, is anything wrong?"

"I don't know, Miss."

Sergei didn't say a word to me, and I didn't blame him. The fact that Comrade Vassilov had sent a car to pick me up made it obvious enough that I was probably very important in some way.

The driver took me, not to the office where I used to work for Comrade Vassilov, but straight to his house. It was beautiful, different from any other place I'd ever seen.

A man opened the door and took me to the garden. There were flowers with every color you could want. In the middle of the garden sat a little table with three elegant chairs; one was taken by Comrade Vassilov, one was prepared for me, and another was covered with a dark sheet.

Mr. Vassilov gave me a big hug and showed me around.

"Isn't it beautiful? Your mother would have loved it. Pink was her favorite color." He pointed to the rose garden.

My words stuck under my tongue, nothing came out. He went on.

Vassilov then describes how he met and married Natasha's mother, was sent to the army while she was carrying their first child, and never saw her again.

"What happened to Mother?" I tried to stay calm. But I felt dizzy with the questions I had lived with for all these years. *Does he love me? Was I wanted? Who is my father?*

I'd never felt so close to my father as that day. I wanted to spend all my life showing him how much I wanted a father.

But he knew his life was short.

"In 1940, there was a big war that killed over twenty million of our people," he told me. His face turned red; he was silent for awhile and then went on.

"When I came back to look for both of you, you were gone. I didn't know if you both were killed or what. I looked through all the dead bodies that were still in one place, but there was no sign of you or your mother. After I came to power, I sent men to look for you. They found you long ago, but I couldn't tell you that your father is a comrade, whom you hated so much! Don't hate me, dear Natasha."

His tears came down like rain. I noticed that he didn't even try to stop them.

"Our country had been corrupted and more than half the people were too weak to work. It would have taken us a million years to build our society to the way it is now. I brought back the country, but no one thanks me. Do you think it's easy to do what I have done?"

"Father, you have killed your own people. Why?"

"I do not expect you to understand it. I don't even understand myself why I have gone this far," he said.

"You're damn right I don't understand! Millions of innocent people have been killed because of you. Don't think you don't have enough food for them to eat. They can make their own food if you'd let them."

I found myself standing there, screaming at my own father as though he was my child. My anger from all those years had come to the surface, as if about to explode.

My love for him was there too, but I couldn't express it.

He said I could stay there as long as I liked, but I told him I would have to leave in a week. Everything was fine until the third night.

The first gunshot sounded far away. I thought it was the guard shouting at a dog or something. Then I heard a second gunshot in the house. I ran toward my father's room. The door opened itself and a young man stood in the doorway, pointing a gun at me.

I put my hands up and said, "What is going on?"

He took off his mask and said, "It's me, Sergei."

I pushed him away. There was my father lying on the floor, one bullet in his forehead and one below his belt.

I was in shock until Sergei touched me. I took his hands off me and ran to where my father was lying. I put my head on his chest, hoping he would say something. He didn't move. I lifted his head and saw the bullet had gone through the back of his neck. Sobs broke in my throat and my tears burst out.

"No!"

Admiration and dismay swept over me when I read the story. Natasha, a character loosely based on herself, certainly was not the bland Buddhaface of Mohm I knew. And this was a far cry from the perfect little garniture of family Mohm had presented to me in the past, glazed and proud and appropriate for setting on a mantel. This was anything but the cherished father, loyal defender of the realm. It was fiction, of course. But the narrative line of her previous poems—the calm lagoon with its lotus flowers standing tall and silent in the murderous sun, personifying her purity—Mohm had permitted to collapse. She had dared to re-create herself out of mud.

"Maybe you don't want to look at someone who could be a pathetic crawling little animal, do anything they tell her," she said to me out of the blue one Sunday afternoon. Her chin was down, but she fastened her eyes on me with an almost defiant desire to be revealed.

"You must have felt helpless. I'm sure most people did, Mohm."

"Especially when I began living with the Old People," she muttered.

I was led to the question she wanted asked. "Did you begin to worry that they were taking your mind, that you were becoming one of them?"

"I did for a while," she said, "when I was with that Khmer Rouge family. Her son was a spy. I think maybe . . ." She faltered but would not give up. "Who knows? He's probably the one who found out about my father." She finished with the wan rattle of a laugh.

The pieces of the jigsaw puzzle began to fit. The Khmer Rouge woman had told Mohm she knew her family from before the takeover. The son was in his mid-twenties, unmarried, a member of the elite spy network known as *kawng chhlop*. Perhaps he had been the one who heard Mohm bragging about her past life in a temple mountain with a father who must have been a king. As Mohm had described to me long before, "When my mother hear me tell the story, she say, 'Forget! Don't talk about it! Do you want to get us killed?'"

We talked about the spying son.

"He was the character I used in my novella, except I changed him to be the father."

So that was the source of her inspiration. The son of the woman who had chosen Mohm as her favorite might have pointed the finger at Mohm's parents.

"The son did that spying for a living," Mohm seethed.

"If he wasn't responsible for the execution of your father—"

"—he did it to hundreds of others," she completed the thought.

I asked if when she looked at him, she'd had the kind of thoughts described by Natasha in the novella. "Some of them," Mohm looked down modestly. "My story is a little exaggerated."

"Of course. But the feeling that you'd gone over to the wrong side and couldn't help yourself because you needed protection . . ."

"Hating myself for being part of what they are"—she let out a ragged sigh—"does that put blood on my hands?" Mohm paused for a few moments and shut her eyes, digging a knuckle into her forehead the way she always did to concentrate her energy on transcending pain. "At least I didn't do the blacklist," she said finally, "thank God."

I had a freakish inspiration. "Luckily, you couldn't write yet!"

She dissolved in giggles, like the little girl of her dreams who wanted another chance to be happy and good.

*

Several months later, I was trying to clarify with Mohm some facts about her life for the book I seemed compelled to write. We began by talking about her father. A surviving member of the Lon Nol government had told me the name sounded like the former chief of military police.

"I don't know," Mohm said uncertainly. "My father drove a motorcycle and usually came to sleep at home, so I think he had some extra privileges more than a regular soldier."

I said that would fit with an MP because his post would be in Phnom Penh.

"But what doesn't fit is, the last year before the Khmer Rouge took over, he was away almost the whole time. He took his gun with him." She flopped back in the living-room chair, exasperated by the glaring blanks in her past. "I thought my father would never come back home," she added solemnly.

"What did your home look like?" I thought it might help to begin with concrete objects.

"It was two stories, I think, with a high fence all around. I remember locking the gate every day, except one time—wait, I remember something." It was the reason their dog had been stolen to be eaten; Mohm's mother had forgotten to lock the gate. Despite the wincing memory, her face smoothed and her eyes glittered. She was actually seeing something of her childhood at last. She asked for a piece of paper and eagerly began drawing her first home.

"Let's see, it's white stone, what kind?" She was drawing a stairway. "I remember walking up one flight of stairs to our apartment so there were neighbors on the first floor. It was a two-family house, that's it! Oh, and the young couple had no children, the ones downstairs, they liked me, sort of like a daughter. They always rode me on back of their motorcycle to the market to have a treat for breakfast." She stopped short. So it hadn't been her father she rode behind through the streets of the city, hair flying, as she had idealized him in one of her favorite fantasies. Intrigued now by the truth, she stalked on after her remembrances.

"The wood fence all around was high, how tall is that window, ten feet? Ten feet then, and all covered with, what did you call it, we saw it in California? yes, bougainvillaea. And behind the house was water and we could see other families on their second-floor verandas." She finished her drawing with a smack of satisfaction. "That's it, the house! Now it makes sense."

All through our detective work that day she wore a half smile. If some of the recollections smarted, the pain appeared to be dissolved in the relief of recovering substance from the void. It was as if she were digging up ancestral bones.

"People all around our district respected my father," she said at once. "But I didn't believe he would ever come back for us. That's why I wrote in my story that I didn't love my father until just before he died."

"But he did come back for you, didn't he?"

"I was so surprised and happy." Mohm looked off into a clear distance, now prepared to stroke in each tiny detail. "My father was different all of a sudden. When we walked in the street with all the frightened people, he held my hand. When we stopped beside the road to eat, he put the food on my plate and passed things to me. He'd never done those things before. Something important had changed. I couldn't believe this was the man I knew as my father. Before the downfall of the country, we had no relationship."

As she spoke, I recalled the knotted emotions of the young woman in the novella.

"I wanted his love, his warmth, but it seemed truth over a lie, because my earlier picture of my father was just like I described it in my story—a tough, outgoing man with no feeling for his family."

She had, of course, heightened the drama of the father in the story, casting him as a communist leader capable of both mass brutality and private tenderness. But it was suddenly clear to me that to a child's mind (and Mohm had been only six at the time) the cause and degree of violence a parent is capable of is not the point; it is that he or she is capable of violence at all.

"There was something frightening about my father," she was saying. "I can hear his motorcycle coming up the street, my mother running out to greet him, the big gate would open, and he would be there—" She hesitated only for instants, then hurtled on toward the inevitable collision with the father: face to face. "He's coming through the gate very tall—now, I can see him!—with the big gun hanging over his back, always he has the gun, and another small gun buttoned on his belt. My older brother runs out to unbutton his gun and play. My father shouts at him in a harsh voice. He's in a bad mood from his work. He walks just like a cop. He's demanding. He comes in the house and takes off his big gun." She shuddered. "I had the feeling that if he didn't like someone, he'd just shoot them. My father terrified me."

She sat very still, letting the truth sink in.

It could not have been easy, surrendering the cameos of paternal solicitude she had earlier painted for me, convincing herself that her father always tossed her up in the air when he came home. "But after Pol Pot time, he changed. He seemed to see me for the first time. He built the new house with my mother—it was just a hut, but I didn't see it that way. He even picked me up and threw me into the air, a couple of times, he did. He became a father. Maybe"—her voice broke off, and she looked into the distance as if her soul were stretching toward him—"maybe all he had left then was family."

The moment opened up, deep and sad. I had a feeling there was something Mohm could be proud of: Her father must have given her some potent final messages. If there was one influence that appeared to guide surviving children profoundly, it was the last wishes and warnings —a condensed ethical framework—communicated by parents just before they died.

"My father told me it's not good to be too shy to present yourself, or too shy to state things that mean a lot to you. It's all right to cry, he told me, but you also have to *do* something about it."

There it was, counteracting thousands of years of cultural instructions to Asian girls: her father's parting permission, once he was gone, for Mohm to think and speak out and act. In the moment of choice— when Mohm and her older brother had met on the run with only moments to decide their fates—it was she who had taken the risk of escape. Today, although she mourned his absence sorely, it was she and not her brother who was alive and flourishing in a free country.

Suddenly her mood shifted to melancholy. "It took me a long time to get the message that my father had changed into a loving, caring man. I guess I never really got it before his death." She sat motionless, as if not to disturb the full lakes of recovered memory nor the connectedness between them. "Everything else fades away so fast, the way your parents looked, all the physical details," she mused quietly. "Their last words become enormous in your mind. That's all you have left. Those last words *are* your parents."

She had brought out the agonizing regret that had surfaced in her novella and tapped the universal longing to be reunited in love, across whatever crimes of the heart or history, with the father.

Bringing up these memories, giving them specific faces, signifying moments, feeling the stab of pain or sweet private delight as if it were happening now, right here, had released her. The aftermath was calm. Mohm indulged in a natural washing of tears.

Later, Clay came into the room and listened. I was showing Mohm a restaurant place mat with the years of the Chinese calendar on it.

"I don't know the exact year I was born," Mohm said. "I feel like I'm fourteen. I know how to act sixteen, but I don't do it with my friends because"—all at once she bit her lip—"because I don't want to grow up."

She lifted and dropped her shoulders, a gesture that said: It's as simple as that.

"All my friends at school tell stories about their childhoods," she went on in a whisper. "And I don't have a childhood." Her upper lip trembled and she clamped her lower lip over it as a barricade against self-pity. But a tear broke loose. She let it.

Clay wrapped his arms around her. "You can have your childhood with us."

*

Now we could appreciate the full weight of the words Mohm had said in her speech at our wedding.

"I want to say this in English," she had begun, "but if I get too nervous I might have to speak Cambodian, and if you want to, you can come and ask me later what I said." Her trill of laughter was infectious.

"What I want to say is how much I want a family—the people that I love and care about, being together.

"Two years ago, when I came into Mom's life, I always thought that I could have her as my family. But, you know, there was something missing in it.

"When Mom told me that Clay asked her to marry him, I was"—she stopped and let out a gust of relief—"so happy that I"—another gust—"couldn't say anything. But right after, I began to be really scared. I didn't know what it was going to be like. But now . . . I can say that I love Clay to be part of my life."

Mohm stood, straight and strong as a lotus with a firmly rooted stem, to deliver her last words to all of us.

"And now I feel like I have everything I ever needed."

Source
Notes
and
Index

Foreword

1. T. S. Eliot, "Little Gidding," in *Four Quartets* (Harcourt, Brace & World, Inc., 1943).

PART I

Bangkok, 1981

1. William Shawcross, *The Quality of Mercy* (New York: Simon & Schuster, 1984), pp. 228–29.
2. Press Department, Ministry of Foreign Affairs, People's Republic of Kampuchea (Phnom Penh, September 1982).

Stopped Time

1. *The Selected Poems of Shuntaro Takikawa* (San Francisco: North Point Press, 1983).

Rainy Season

1. Gerald Diffloth, chairman of the Department of Linguistics, University of Chicago, assisted the author in transliterations from Khmer to English throughout the book.

Before the Fall

1. Bernard Groslier and Jacques Arthand, *The Arts and Civilization of Angkor* (New York: Frederick A. Praeger, 1957), p. 10; and author's interview with Bernard Groslier, Washington, D.C., April 27, 1985.
2. Michael Vickery, *Cambodia: 1975–1982* (Boston: Southend Press, 1984), pp. 18–22.
3. Ben Kiernan and Chanthou Boua, eds., *Peasants and Politics in Kampuchea, 1942–80* (London: Zed Press/Sharpe Inc., 1982), p. 15.
4. Ibid., p. 230.
5. William Shawcross, *Sideshow: Kissinger, Nixon and the Destruction of Cambodia* (New York: Simon & Schuster, 1981), p. 224.
6. Author's interview with Stanley Karnow.
7. Shawcross, *Sideshow,* p. 211.
8. Sidney H. Shanberg, "The Enigma of Khmer Rouge Purpose," *The New Republic,* August 23, 1975, pp. 30–31; and Shawcross, *Sideshow,* p. 73.
9. Robert Sam Anson, dispatch to *Time,* Phnom Penh, June 6, 1970.
10. Shawcross, *Sideshow,* p. 211.
11. Ben Kiernan, *How Pol Pot Came to Power* (New York: Schocken Books, 1985), p. 413.

12. Lon Nol government sources placed the number of the population in 1972 at between seven and eight million; and Shawcross, *Sideshow*, p. 318.
13. Tuol Sleng Museum of Genocidal Crimes, Phnom Penh.
14. Author's interview with Chan Dara Lot, assistant director of Tuol Sleng Museum, Phnom Penh, 1981.
15. Kiernan, op. cit., p. 416.

The Prince of Darkness—
Pol Pot

1. *CBS Evening News*, April 20 and 21, 1978.
2. François Ponchaud, *Cambodia: Year Zero* (New York: Holt, Rinehart and Winston, 1977), pp. 153–54; and Kiernan and Boua, p. 22.
3. Ponchaud, op. cit., p. 152.
4. Ibid., pp. 153–55.
5. Charles Krauthammer, "The Escape from Liberation," *The Washington Post*, April 19, 1985, Op-Ed page.
6. David P. Chandler, *A History of Cambodia* (Boulder, Colo.: Westview Press, 1983).
7. Author's interview with Dr. May Ebihara, New York, N.Y., June 12, 1985.
8. Vickery, op. cit., p. 16.
9. Chandler, op. cit., p. 6.
10. Vickery, op. cit., p. 4.
11. Author's interview with Dr. May Ebihara.
12. Vickery, op. cit., p. 2.
13. Author's interview with Dr. May Ebihara.
14. Kiernan, op. cit., p. 260.
15. Kiernan and Boua, op. cit., p. 251.
16. Ibid., pp. 270–71.
17. Author's interview with Chan Dara Lot.
18. Kiernan and Boua, op. cit., pp. 248–49.
19. Author's interview with Chan Dara Lot.
20. "Vietnam: The Cambodia Quagmire," *The New York Times*, April 25, 1985.
21. Kiernan, op. cit., p. 415.
22. Shawcross, *Sideshow*, p. 224.
23. Oriana Fallaci interview, *The New York Times Magazine*, August 12, 1973.

24. Document of a working session with Comrade Deng Xiaping, January 13, 1979. Published by the Press Department of the Foreign Ministry of the People's Republic of Kampuchea.

25. Kiernan and Boua, op. cit., p. 321.

26. Ibid., pp. 321–23.

27. Ibid., p. 242.

28. Chandler, op. cit.

29. George Cedes, *Angkor* (London: Oxford University Press, 1963).

30. National anthem of Democratic Kampuchea.

31. Kiernan and Boua, op. cit., p. 232.

32. Ibid., p. 230.

33. Joan Lebold Cohen, *Angkor: The Monuments of the God-Kings* (New York: Harry N. Abrams, 1975).

34. Author's interview with Dr. Suphot, United Nations High Commission for Refugees, Education Department, Bangkok, Thailand, January 1983.

35. Author's interview with Jintana Lee, Jefferson, N.H.

36. Kiernan and Boua, op. cit., p. 326.

37. Ibid., p. 327.

38. Author's interview with Chan Dara Lot.

Myth, Mores, and Madness

1. Charles Meyer, *Derrièr le Sourire Khmer* (Paris: Plon Press, 1972).

2. Ibid.

3. Robert J. Casey, *Four Faces of Siva* (Indianapolis: Bobbs-Merrill, 1929), pp. 88–99; and Jewell Reinhart Coburn, *Khmers, Tigers, and Talismans* (Thousand Oaks, Calif.: Burn, Hart and Company, 1981), pp. 11–26.

4. Frank Lebar, Gerald C. Hickey, and John Musgrave, eds., *Ethnic Groups of Mainland Southeast Asia* (New Haven: Human Relations Area Files, 1964), p. 94.

5. Chandler, op. cit., p. 9.

6. Groslier and Arthand, op. cit., pp. 15–16.

7. Chandler, op. cit., p. 12.

8. Author's interview with Bernard Groslier.

9. Chandler, op. cit., p. 10.

10. Author's interview with Dr. May Ebihara.

11. Sam Yang, "Khmer Buddhism," presented at the Scholars Conference on Cambodia, April 24–25, 1985, Washington, D.C.

12. Meyer, op. cit.

13. Author's interview with Kheiu Khanarit, publisher of Kampuchea's only newspaper, Phnom Penh, December 1984.
14. Kiernan and Boua, op. cit., p. 234.

A Separate Planet of Death

1. Kiernan and Boua, op. cit., p. 245.
2. CBS News, *60 Minutes,* spring 1985.
3. Justin Ackerman, director, *Beneath the Angka.*
4. Author's interview with Soun Schwartz, Long Beach, Calif., April 1985.
5. Kiernan and Boua, op. cit., pp. 238, 241.
6. From the film *Year Zero: The Silent Death of Cambodia,* directed by David Munroe, released by Central Television, London, England.
7. Kiernan and Boua, op. cit., p. 284.
8. Ibid., p. 232.
9. Ibid., p. vi.
10. Gail Sheehy, "A Home for Cambodia's Children," *The New York Times Magazine,* September 23, 1984.
11. Precise figures given by Bernard Hamel, who for ten years was a correspondent in Phnom Penh for Reuters in London. He collaborated on three books about Cambodia, the first of these with Soth Polin.
12. Author's interview with Khieu Khanarit.
13. Hamel interview.

Moment of Choice

1. Gail Sheehy, "The People America Forgot," *The Washington Post,* June 27, 1982.
2. Ibid.
3. Author's interview with Mom-Mom, Phnom Penh, December 1983.
4. Sheehy, "The People America Forgot."
5. Shawcross, *Quality of Mercy.*
6. Gail Sheehy, "Report from Cambodian No-man's-land," *Boston Globe,* February 6, 1983.
7. Sheehy, "The People America Forgot."

PART II

Sakeo II Camp

1. Sudden death at night from heart failure became a well-documented syndrome among young Cambodians later resettled in the United States. Among the 80 to 150 autopsied, no cause of death could be determined. All were young men. One hypothesis was that they might have had night terrors that caused sudden heart failure. Baron et al., *Journal of the American Medical Association* 250:21 (December 2, 1983), p. 2947.
2. Author's interview with Dr. Jean-Pierre Higel, Khao-I-Dang Camp, Thailand, December 1983.

PART III

Sakeo . . . August 1982

1. Sheehy, "Report from Cambodian No-man's-land."
2. Ibid.

The Silent Period

1. Donatella Mazzeo and Chiara Silvi Antononini, *Monuments of Civilization: Ancient Cambodia* (New York: Grosset & Dunlap, 1978).
2. Author's interview with Bernard Groslier.
3. A. S. Carton, *The "Method of Inference" in Foreign Language Study: A Summary* (New York: The Research Foundation of the City University of New York, 1966); and P. Pilsleur and T. Quinn, eds., *The Psychology of Second Language Learning: Papers from the Second International Congress of Applied Linguistics* (Cambridge: Cambridge University Press, 1969).
4. H. H. Stern, "What Can We Learn from the Good Language Learner?," *Canadian Modern Language Review* 31:4 (March 1975), pp. 304–318.

Searching for Cambodia in Brooklyn

1. Author's interview with Dr. Chinary Ung, professor of music at the University of Pennsylvania.

The Reckless Period

1. Andrew H. Malcolm, "A New Generation of Poor Youths Emerges in the U.S.," *The New York Times*, October 20, 1985, p. 1.

Demons

1. Vickery, op. cit., pp. 6–7.
2. Groslier and Arthand, op. cit., p. 10.
3. Meyer, op cit.
4. Jerome Kagan, *The Nature of the Child* (New York: Basic Books, 1984).
5. Gail Sheehy, "The Private Passages of the Hostages and Their Wives," *Life*, March 1981.

"Always Something to Laugh"

1. Helen Epstein, *Children of the Holocaust* (New York: G.P. Putnam's Sons, 1979), p. 228.

The Victorious Personality

1. Alexander Thomas and Stella Chess, "The Longitudinal Study of Behavioral Disorders," *The American Journal of Psychiatry*, January 1984.
2. Author's interview with Erik Erikson, November 26, 1985.
3. Claudine Vegh, *I Didn't Say Goodbye; Interviews with Children of the Holocaust* (New York: E. P. Dutton, 1984), p. 20.
4. Erik H. Erikson, "Psychoanalytic Reflections on Einstein's Centenary," *Albert Einstein: Historical and Cultural Perspectives*, ed. Gerald Holton and Yehuda Elkana (Princeton, N.J.: Princeton University Press, 1958), pp. 151–173.
5. Erik Erikson (with Joan M. Erikson), "Growth and Crisis of the Healthy Personality," in *Symposium on the Healthy Personality*, ed. Milton J. E. Senn (New York: Joseph Macy, Jr., Foundation, 1950), pp. 91–146 (prepared for the White House Conference, 1950).
6. Ernest Becker, *The Denial of Death* (New York: The Free Press, 1973).
7. Kagan, op. cit.
8. Thomas and Chess, op. cit.; and author's interview with Alexander Thomas, June 1984.
9. Jancis V. F. Long, Ph.D., and George E. Vaillant, M.D., "Natural History of Male Psychological Health, XI: Escape from the Underclass," *American Journal of Psychiatry* 141:3 (March 1984).
10. Edmund W. Gordon and Ronald L. Braithwaite, *Success Against the Odds* (Washington: Howard University Press, 1986).
11. Robert Coles, *The Moral Life of Children* (Boston: Atlantic Monthly, 1986).

12. Norman Garmazy, "Vulnerable and Invulnerable Children: Theory, Research and Intervention," master lecture on developmental psychology, American Psychological Association, 1976.
13. E. James Anthony, "The Syndrome of the Psychologically Invulnerable Child," *The Child in His Family: Children at Psychiatric Risk*, eds. E. James Anthony, M.D., and Cyrille Koupernik, M.D. (New York: John Wiley & Sons, 1974), pp. 529–44.
14. Ibid.
15. Kagan, op. cit.
16. Daniel Goleman, "Traumatic Beginnings: Most Children Seem Able to Recover," *The New York Times*, March 13, 1984, pp. C1–2.
17. Sheehy, "The Private Lives of the Hostages and Their Wives."